CORPORATE ETHICS

CORPORATE ETHICS

PETER A. FRENCH

Lennox Distinguished Professor of Philosophy
Trinity University

Harcourt Brace College Publishers

Fort Worth Philadelphia San Diego New York Orlando Austin San Antonio
Toronto London Montreal Sydney Tokyo

Publisher	Ted Buchholz
Acquisitions Editor	David Tatom
Developmental Editor	J. Claire Brantley
Project Editor	Betsy Cummings
Production Manager	Jane Tyndall Ponceti
Art Director	Scott Baker

ISBN: 0-15-501124-3

Library of Congress Catalog Card Number: 94-77844

For Sandra
and Sean and Shannon

PREFACE

In this book I explore some of the most important ethical issues of our time, those that involve business corporations. Corporations rose to prominence in our social world during the past one hundred years. Now we are a thoroughly corporate society and it is crucial to our future that we fully understand the implications of that fact.

Corporations are the central focus of this textbook, and the book attempts to provide a persuasive theoretical superstructure for treating them as proper targets of ethical discourse. Many of the other books in the field of business ethics utterly ignore the corporation itself and treat the issues as if they involved only the decisions and actions of managers. Others briefly note that perhaps corporations are important parts of our society, but cannot think of the corporations themselves as proper subjects of ethics. Many of the anthologies on business ethics include a section on the theory of the corporation as a moral person, usually reprinting a paper I published in the *American Philosophical Quarterly* in 1979 and one or two responses from the group of philosophers that John Danley has called the "anthropocentric bigots." Little attempt, however, is made to examine the sociological facts or the metaphysical grounds on which this theory stands. The reluctance to see the corporation as a genuine subject of ethical judgment, when all is said and done, seems to bubble out of a single intoxicating bottle of old wine: the doctrine of liberal individualism that has dominated Western ethics since at least the seventeenth century, apparently the beverage of choice of most of those writing in business ethics.

Sociologists who have taken a serious look at corporations report matters to be radically different from the picture sketched by many business ethics books. This book is built on their work and on my own experiences with the various elements of the corporate world, with business as it is, not as a dated philosophical theory would prefer it to be. Perhaps it will shock some readers, especially those in dogmatic slumber, but it will not seem all that radical to those who cash paychecks from corporations.

The book is divided into six parts. Part One attempts three things: the role of corporations in our society is briefly discussed in terms of the radical change that corporations have caused in the status of humans. Then a theory of the corporation as a moral actor is offered and the types of ethics that could be relevant to a corporate entity are examined. Part One concludes not only with an affirmation of the view that corporations can be moral actors, but also that they may be better suited than human persons to being ethical. That argument is based on some rather elementary findings in game theory.

Part Two looks inside corporations, first at those at the top of the standard organizational charts and then at managers and other employees. Certain specific issues are examined in Part Two, including the reengineering of the corporation theory and related new organizational structures intended to flatten the traditional corporate power hierarchies. Also employee issues such as heroic whistle-blowing and various kinds of harassment are discussed. Sexual harassment cases are examined in some detail.

In Part Three, the role of corporations is explored with respect to environmental issues. A specific case (lumbering in the California redwoods) is used for two reasons: it not only highlights certain peculiarly corporate issues regarding the preservation of our natural environment, it also reveals the interwoven strands of business activities that initially seem unrelated to the environment, but turn out to have drastic impact on it. In the case in question, those are leveraged buyouts, takeovers, stock manipulations, and windfall profit-taking.

In Part Four, I am concerned with issues that involve the corporation with various constituencies outside of its decision structure. Spike Lee's film, *Do the Right Thing*, serves as a backdrop for the examination of civic duties and obligations to patrons and neighborhoods, while a scandal involving Honda dealerships focuses the discussion of bribery in a context seldom examined in business textbooks. Advertising and job alienation problems are raised. Part 4 also introduces a principle of moral accountability that will be tracked throughout the issues raised in Part Six.

Part Five takes on, if briefly, the differences between American and Japanese conceptions of business. An argument is made that the Japanese experience demonstrates that capitalism is not necessarily linked to individualism, despite the Western tradition that tends to identify them together. Perhaps most important, however, is the discussion of how the conception of corporate success as a matter of national security radically changes the very vocabulary in which business practices are described. The Japanese view business as war, Americans think of it as a kind of game. The difference is of no small consequence in the global marketplace.

Part Six offers and examines new ways to police corporations. It supports a modification of our judicial procedure for the efficient handling corporate offenses and it explores a number of innovative sentencing options for the punishment of convicted corporations.

Students not trained in philosophy, particularly in traditional Western ethics, might appreciate a bit of background on some of the philosophical figures and theories mentioned in this book. Boxes provided throughout the text offer brief sketches of the relevant theories of the major philosophical figures mentioned. I am confident that most of the book will not strike students as too difficult, although some may find sections of Part One tougher than the other parts. Be assured that I have tried to keep the technicalities to a minimum and that those sections are absolutely critical to understanding the discussion of more practical issues in the remainder of the book.

A comparison between this book and a number of others in the field of business ethics will reveal, as should be expected, a number of common topics. Some topics, however, are unique to this book, and in some cases I have gone into far more detail than other business ethics books (e.g. the topic of sexual harassment).

Also, seek out some of the film references, if unfamiliar with the movies that I occasionally bring into my discussion. The availability of cable channels featuring films and the ubiquity of the VCR and the movie rental store make access to the film literature easy. The movies included in this text are now important elements of our culture.

A number of people are responsible for the fact that I wrote this book and now suffer from a currently fashionable syndrome that makes the raising of my right arm painful. David Tatom of Harcourt Brace persuaded me to take on the project, and Claire Brantley kept me at the task. Thanks also to Harcourt Brace production staff members who worked on this book: Betsy Cummings, Scott Baker, and Jane Ponceti.

I owe a great deal to a number of people with whom I have discussed and learned about the issues that comprise this book. J. L. Mackie, Donald Davidson, H. D. Lewis, and David Pears were early influences. Robert Solomon, Brent Fisse, Larry May, John Martin Fischer, Roger Scruton, Michael Palmer, and Michael Kearl have been most helpful and stimulating. I have benefited a great deal from reading books by James Coleman, Robert Nozick, Peter Danielson, Robert Jackall, and Clyde Prestowitz. In my position as editor of the *Journal of Social Philosophy,* I have had the opportunity to read some outstanding work by relatively unknown young scholars, some of which has certainly influenced my thinking on matters raised in the book. I am especially grateful to Kathleen Eicher, my secretary, for putting the manuscript into final form.

I read sections of this book at Marquette University and the University of Colorado at Boulder. The discussions were useful in sharpening my arguments. My daughter Shannon, working on her Ph.D. in philosophy at Brown University, read segments of the typescript and offered extremely cogent comments and suggestions. I incorporated most of her recommendations. When she was born, I had no idea it would come to this! My wife, Sandra, took time from her art to listen to sections and then made suggestions that undoubtedly improved the style of the book.

Thanks are also due to the reviewers: Benjamin Abramowitz, The University of Central Florida; Patrice DiQuinzio, The University of Scranton; Carlo Filice, The State University of New York–Geneseo; and Michael Palmer, Evangel College.

Philosopher Boxes

If you've had little or not training in philosophy or ethics before tackling this book, you might feel more comfortable if you knew a bit more beyond what is provided in the main text about the theories of some of the philosophers to which I have occasionally referred. To help, I've included brief and basic sketches of the relevant work of those philosophers. The Sketches are thinly drawn and, therefore, do not convey the depth or the historical significance of the positions taken by the philosophers. After all, this is not a book on the history of ethics. These sketches cannot, nor do they pretend to, substitute for what you could, and probably should, learn about these philosophers and their accomplishments. You can do this by reading a history of philosophy or history of ethics or even by looking over the entries devoted to them in an encyclopedia of philosophy. Reading their works, of course, would be preferable.

The boxes appear in the book near the point in the text where the philosopher is first mentioned. A table of contents of these Philosopher Boxes is provided for quick reference.

TABLE OF CONTENTS

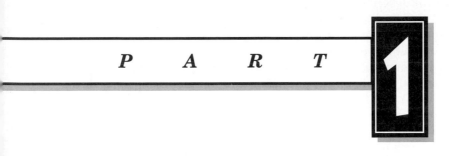

INVASION!

 ## 1. The Middle Ages, the Seventeenth Century, and Today

"Things today are not what they used to be!"

That sentence, of course, is true at almost every occasion of its use. Usually it is said by someone older than the intended audience and implies that things were somehow better in the past. Actually, most things were not better in the past, but at some point in aging we cross a threshold after which we spout such romantic drivel on a regular basis with virtually no provocation. Some do it at forty, others forty-five, but the majority, in my experience, hold off until they have passed fifty. In so far as I have passed fifty, I find the phrase almost irresistible. So I've decided to begin this book with it.

Things today are not what they used to be! Think of home appliances. When I was young, we had no televisions, VCRs, CD players. I lived in an apartment, and later in a house, that had no refrigerator. The coming of the iceman was a crucial weekly event. Surely that qualifies me to say "Things today. . . !" It is not often appreciated that three household improvements, the refrigerator, the air conditioner, and the television, made an enormous impact on our morality. These three items provoked and abetted a radical upheaval in our practical understanding of community and neighborhood, changing American social life from what it used to be to what it is (or isn't) today. But this is not a book about household improvements.

1

All forms of technological innovation, we are told by legal historians, force changes in the law, especially in tort (civil suits for injury compensation).[1] But they also must alter the way morality is conceived and the way moral description, evaluation, and judgment affect our social practices. Technological innovation causes sometimes great, sometimes minor, changes in social practices. A world with automobiles, for example, is not the same world, sociologically and, I think, morally, as the world with nothing but horse-drawn vehicles. Entirely different social relations become possible, become ordinary. When your mode of transport moves at 55 miles per hour and can travel for hours without resting,there are a lot more people and kinds of people you must deal with, that you may want to deal with, that can cause you problems, and that you can influence for good or ill by your actions. Likewise, your community radically changes when a television enters your experience and you witness live transmissions from Bosnia or Somalia. And your moral and ethical obligations may change as well. At the very least, what you know, or should know, vastly expands, and therefore, what you ought to take into consideration when you decide on courses of action is greater than it had been in the past. Technological developments have made living in the contemporary world morally more taxing than our ancestors could ever have imagined.

In a sense, this book is about a world that changed because of innovation and invention, but this change is even more fundamental than those brought about by new gadgets like telephones, jet airplanes, and computers. The change with which I am going to deal is more than an invention that forced us to adjust our worldview or community perspective. For rather than the introduction of another wonderful contraption into our daily lives, it was an invasion that not only disrupted the community and the existing notion of persons or moral actors, it redefined both. It makes the Norman Conquest of England look like no more than an exercise in modest cultural assimilation. This invasion not only brought about a change in the basic institutions of society to accommodate the invaders, it changed the very idea of what counts as fundamental parts of the society in the first place.

Most of us are at least vaguely familiar with the H. G. Wells novel, *The War of the Worlds*. Or we know of the Orson Welles radio version or have seen the 1953 movie. The story is one of panic when the human populace of Earth discovers that creatures from Mars have landed and that they don't play by human rules. The plot has been rewritten dozens of times with the alien invaders either being benign conveyers of cosmic wisdom or bent on the destruction of the Earth's stock of humans. (Sometimes they're even just victims of their own bureaucratic fumbling, destroying the Earth to make way for a hyperspace bypass before the purpose for which they had created the Earth is realized.[2]) In any event, the world in which we discover that there are nonhuman entities that are rational, intentional agents must be a world of moral ambiguities and confusions, a world where one's duties are not as clear as before, where what's right and wrong may need to be revised,

How are we to treat invaders who reveal that they are purposeful, intelligent, have interests and goals, act intentionally? Should it matter if they find it impossible to view us as anything other than inferior beings, comparable to the way we view water buffalo? What if they really **are** in most ways superior to us?

These questions may not seem that pressing because, of course, alien invasions from Mars or some other planet have not occurred. (Well, I don't think they have.) Even if it would be entertaining and perhaps instructive to work out what the morality should be like in a community in which aliens have been assimilated or in which aliens have assimilated humans [the film *Alien Nation* (1988), in a minor way, attempts to do that], the invasion I have in mind actually *has* happened. The world has been radically changed but the requisite morality to deal with these changes has not been worked out.

The invaders were and are business corporations and their appearance *en masse* in what used to be an exclusively human domain has made things today not what they used to be. The "used to be," then, is that precorporate society that was dead or dying before I was born. A number of philosophers and economists, then and now, seem not to have noticed the corpse and blithely go on as if things today are fundamentally unchanged from those happy days of yesterday: the seventeenth-century.

The reason I mention the seventeenth century (when any century before the twentieth would do as well) is because seventeenth-century political thought stirs the hearts of those who see human society as an aggregate of individual humans contracting together for personal benefit. The great political theorists of what may be called atomistic individualist liberalism, Thomas Hobbes and especially John Locke, saw the individual natural person, the mature human, as the cornerstone of society. In fact, as they understood society, individual human persons are its elemental parts. The civil state is, for them, built on and composed of consenting individual human contractors out to try to protect and preserve their natural rights to life, liberty, and property. Thinking in terms of social institutions and organizations is just another way to think about individual humans who happened to be involved in certain kinds of group enterprises. Those enterprises were thought to be, by and large, goal-directed activities in which the individual humans freely engaged and disengaged, usually for prudential (self-interested) reasons. Hobbes and Locke may have overlooked the Catholic Church and its corporate history, but, after all, they were Protestant Englishmen. It is noteworthy that the frontispiece engraving of Thomas

THOMAS HOBBES (1588-1679)   Hobbes was the first of the great English political theorists. He lived more than ninety years in some of the most turbulent times in English political history. The story goes that he was born prematurely when his mother was frightened by news of the Spanish Armada. He lived through the reign of Elizabeth I, the divine-right Stuart kings, the English Civil War, and the Protectorate of Cromwell, and the restoration of the monarchy. His political theory is based on his conception of human beings and human nature. Hobbes believed that in the world only bodies in motion exist and that they are motivated by attractions and repulsions. His was a mechanistic view. Though he allowed that humans have thoughts, he explained thoughts away as mere epiphenomena of brain activity, not as independent entities in the mind with the capacity to cause activity. Freedom, for Hobbes, was nothing more than unimpeded motion. Something is free only insofar as it is not restrained. He maintained that there are only two basic human motivations: self-interest and power. Whatever people do, Hobbes believed, they do in some sense to either make themselves better off or to garner more personal power. We are all egoists. Simply, our actions are always governed by the drive to do the best we can for ourselves. Hobbes reasoned that if humans were not controlled or restrained from doing whatever they thought would improve their personal situations in a world that never provides enough power or goods to satisfy everyone, they would live in a perpetual state of war against each other. "Every man is enemy to every man." This state of nature would be fraught with conflict and, in Hobbes' famous description, human life in it would be

Hobbes' *Leviathan* shows a gigantic monarch that on closer inspection is revealed to be composed of the figures of hundreds of his subjects, or rather, in the fashionable language of that time, consenting citizens. In fact, the primary aim of the atomistic individualist liberal was to work two conversions: (1) medieval subject to Enlightenment citizen and (2) social relations from matters of status to matters of contract. Charles Taylor writes:

> We inherit atomism from the seventeenth century. Not that we still espouse social contract theories (although various transposed versions are still popular.) . . . [E]ven though we no longer understand the origins of society as reposing in agreement, we nevertheless both understand and evaluate its workings as an instrument to attain ends we impute to individuals or constituent groups.[3]

This seventeenth-century conception of society was not born in full glory out of the heads of either Hobbes or Locke. It culminates an individualist movement in Western thought that emerged in the twelfth "solitary, poor, nasty, brutish, and short." What is missing from the state of nature are the constraints we associate with law and morality. Also missing is the right to property. That is so because Hobbes, recognized only two "natural rights": the right to life and, following from that right, the right to everything, or at least everything one believes necessary to protect one's life. If everyone has those rights, no one can have a property right in anything, at least not in the sense that we understand property rights. Such a state is, of course, intolerable because people living in it will soon determine that it is irrational to grow crops or engage in any long-term productive enterprises. At any moment they are likely to be smashed over the head by a neighbor who will make off with the fruits of their labors, and they will have no more legitimate claim against that thieving neighbor than he or she has against them. They will never be able to turn their backs on one another. Fear will dominate their lives. (Hobbes is said to have remarked that he and fear were born twins.)

Well, it is certainly irrational to continue to live in such a state. But what are the options? Hobbes says that people in the state of nature will come to a rational decision to cooperate with each other. But, unfortunately, they will not be able to trust each other to keep that agreement to cooperate, knowing full well that if the occasion arises, they would themselves break it in order to enhance their own interests. Human nature is our fatal flaw. The only solution to this mess is to create an absolute power in the community that will ensure that the people will keep their cooperative agreements, their contracts. People in a state of nature, Hobbes maintained, will rationally choose to establish a civil state and invest in it, in the form of a sovereign, absolute power. They will trade in their natural rights for the protection, the security, that enforced contracts, including the basic contract, the social contract, brings them.

(See Thomas Hobbes, *Leviathan* [1651].)

century and that, in the sixteenth century, also fostered the Protestant Reformation with its rallying cry of the "priesthood of all believers." In the Middle Ages, however, the abstract theory that incorporated the conception that the individual was the sole and essential unit of social relationships was significantly different from the contractual one for which Locke provided the rhetoric and to which the political revolutions of the eighteenth and nineteenth centuries gave substance.

In the Middle Ages, society was understood to be but an arrangement of humans, but it was also seen as a fixed organic whole. Every individual human had a specified place or station in the community, a rank set by birth and therefore by God. Elemental to the law of the Anglo-Saxons, for example, was that persons in each social rank were each assigned a specified monetary value, or *wergeld*. A *thegn*, or knight, was worth more than a *ceorl*, or freeman farmer, and a *ceorl* more than a *laet*, or serf, etc. If one injured or killed a *thegn*, the legal

JOHN LOCKE (1632-1704)   Locke, an English-man with considerable influence in the power circles of his day, is one of the more important philosophers in the Western tradition. He is regarded as the founder of British empiricism, the general position that knowledge is not innate in us nor can it be derived from rational contemplation alone. For Locke and the empiri-cists, knowledge is derived from experience. Locke's theory of knowledge and his meta-physics were extremely influential. Indeed, many of the problems he raised and the puzzles he examined play central roles in philosophical discourse today. Of special interest to the issues discussed in this book are Locke's theory of personal identity and his political theory. Locke distinguished between the identity of a human and the identity of a person. He claimed that a human was the same human that we saw yesterday if a continuous history of that human body links the two occasions. X, seen yesterday, is the same human as Y, seen today, if a continuous history of a human body links X to Y. To be the same person, however, is to have a continuing stream of conscious-ness. For Locke that means is that X is the same person as Y if they share the same specific first-person memories. Because Locke distinguished between the identity of humans and persons, he could make some other-wise utterly fantastic stories seem plausible, though still perplexing. For example, he could ask us to imagine that someone we know wakes up tomorrow morning with all of the memories of Michael Jackson and none

compensation was therefore significantly greater than if one injured a *ceorl*. The Code of Aethelbert, King of the Kentings (England, AD 600), fixed a price on those of every level of society in relation to each other. A *thegn* was worth six *ceorls*, and a King's *thegn* double that.

This odd bit of social arithmetic was preserved in British law for some time after the legal system of the Anglo-Saxons, indeed the Anglo-Saxons themselves, had left the stage of British history. In the later Middle Ages testimony by an oath (compurgation) sworn by a higher ranking member of the society was worth more than the oaths of a number of lower- ranking persons. In a court case in which the par-ties could only defend their positions by amassing the sworn oaths of others, the victory went to the party that secured the oaths of the higher-ranking social members. The oaths of two thegns would beat those of nine ceorls any day![4]

In Anglo-Saxon law each part of the body of members of each class was also priced, a practice that, with some modifications, survives to this day in cost/benefit analysis and personal injury claims. Imagine, for example, that mutilating a thegn by putting out his eye went for of his or her own. Would that person then be Michael Jackson even though he or she doesn't look any different than he or she did yesterday? These Lockean-type puzzles set off a tidal wave of philosophical activity on the problem of personal identity that continues today. Are we the persons we are because of our memories? Doesn't bodily identity count? Does the memory criterion beg the question because it already entails having a sense of the self doing the remembering? "I remember I did such and such yesterday." Who remembers?

Locke also is well known for his political theory, which has been hugely influential in political, social, and economic thought. Locke, like Hobbes, begins with a conception of the state of nature, but his idea of nature is radically different from that of Hobbes. For Locke, the state of nature is one in which humans have rights: life, health, liberty, and property. It is a moral state and one of abundance. Its only problems are some humans might take advantage of others and by their actions disrupt the idyllic character of the place. These are inconveniences in the state of nature, but they are sufficient to lead people to form a government with limited powers to protect their rights and punish offenders. Locke also provides a theory of property acquisition. He restricts one's right to accumulate property to that which will not spoil when accumulated. But neither can property be acquired if there is not enough and as good left for others, or if one's acquisition will be harmful to others. The original acquisition of property, for Locke, was accomplished by the human using his or her labor to alter a place or a thing from the way it was in nature.

(See John Locke, *An Essay Concerning Human Understanding* [1690] and *Two Treatises of Government* [1690].)

50 shillings. A laet's eye would then be worth considerably less. The cry might be "ten shillings for an eye," but not "an eye for an eye. "As no market probably existed for mutilated bodily parts, it is unlikely those of the lower classes could offer self mutilation as a way to recompense their higher-class victims. Aethelbert's Code is, however, silent on the matter of whether a ceorl who had killed a laet, whether or not intentionally, could pay the penalty (apparently to the kin of the victim) with some of his own body parts.

Ullmann has noted that the following principle of vocation dominated the social thinking of the Middle Ages:

> [E]ach member of society should fulfill the functions which were allotted to him, because this was . . . the effluence of the divine ordering of things.[5]

The root of this notion of the importance of *vocatus*, or one's calling, is found in Christian theology. Saint Paul, in I Corinthians 12:4ff, wrote:

> There are different kinds of gifts, but the same spirit. There are different kinds of service, but the same Lord. There are different kinds of working. . .

James Coleman argues that in the structure of society in the Middle Ages "the central and overriding fact was that all social organization was organization of persons."[6] "That is, all of the relationships that comprised a community were associations of humans, (which included) "rigid differentiation[s] of persons in fixed positions."[7]

The point of all this is that though we may rightly think of the society of the Middle Ages as dominated by rigid structures that bound people to stations and tasks for life, the only functional elemental units of society were individual human beings. The medieval manor was not a prototype for the twentieth century business corporation. The manor was not an active player on the social scene. It was only a way of organizing the players. A chessboard, for example, does not play the game of chess, but provides the "grounds" on which play occurs. Business corporations are viewed wrongly if they are seen as nothing more than playing fields for managers, stockholders, employees, etc. Corporations are active social interactors. Manors were not.

In the Middle Ages, and indeed in seventeenth-century political theories, individual humans bore the responsibility for sustaining the social system. They had little or no freedom to move within it. Bakers would not become butchers, nor would weavers become knights. And bakers, butchers, weavers, serfs, and lords would ensure the continued occupation of their vital roles either by apprenticeship, primogeniture, indenture, or familial tenure. Ullmann writes:

> What mattered was. . . the office which that individual occupied. The office itself is capable of precise measurement, capable of a purely objective assessment: it is to be measured by its own contents. . . [T]he office and the power it contained were not of human origin or making but of allegedly divine provenance.[8]

Ullmann goes on to cite the art of the period, especially the illuminations in medieval manuscripts, as supporting the view that people were not viewed as individuals, but as types.[9] This is certainly true, and Ullmann might have also cited the preperspective church paintings that size humans not as they actually looked but according to their social, and therefore religious, rank. Bishops and cardinals were huge, the serfs tiny, etc.[10] What is clear, however, is not that the medieval conception of society did not see the individual human as its primary, even sole, foundational unit, but that the individualism identified with Enlightenment thought had yet to blossom. The society of the Middle Ages was indeed a society of fixed status, yet it was a society comprised only, or almost only, of natural persons.

The seventeenth-century political theorists also saw individual humans as the only elemental functional units, but theirs was a society of contract, a society of individuals, using the term as we are prone to today, making deals with each other. Status, for them, was magically transformed into citizenship through contract. (See Philosopher boxes for more information.)[11]

It is perhaps ironic that the individualistic contractual world of the seventeenth-century theorists gave birth to the corporate invaders that utterly transformed society in the twentieth century by rendering individuals less relevant to the structure of society. The irony is furthered by the fact that by individuals contracting for rational self-interested reasons the new type of social creatures were created.

 ## 2. Human Persons and Corporate Actors: Freedom Without Relevance

The very notion that artificial entities, which corporations certainly are, might be members of the moral community upsets a number of people, especially philosophers who work within the liberal individualist tradition explained in the last chapter. They may be willing to admit that corporations are important and powerful and even play essential roles in our social world, but they balk at the notion that corporate invaders are proper subjects of ethical criticism.[12] Of course, if their view turns out to be the correct one, the study of corporate ethics would have to be dissolved into an ethics of human persons who just happen to work for corporations. There are hundreds of books on ethics and moral theory, though I have noticed blessed little improvement in the behavior of humans. Might that be a sign that humans are not proper subjects of ethics, or is it just that most humans don't read ethics books? In any event, the anticorporate-ethics crowd insists that the fact that the majority of humans in the Western world and now much of the Orient spend most of their lives in corporate jobs is only an incidental matter, one of ultimately no real ethical significance. Their ethics are little changed from those of the medieval manor. They turn a blind eye to the actual elements and structures of our society that have been identified by sociologists for decades.

If sociologists such as Coleman and I are right about the radical changes society has undergone, but ethics, as many philosophers and economists would have it, just cannot be applied to corporations,[13] then much of the social picture will never come into ethical focus. It will always be an ethical blur. Rather than admitting to flaws in their ethical vision, some of those economists and philosophers have simply trumpeted their reductionistic anticorporate theories so loudly and frequently that the sheer force of repetition has persuaded many business people that ethical considerations are out of place in the corporate world, that they only apply to the private lives of humans. Business is business. Business ethics is an oxymoron.

I have written at length, over almost twenty years, in defense of the idea that business corporations should, in and of themselves, be treated as moral persons, members of the moral community. However, it has become clear to me from many of the questions and concerns prompted by my past use of the term "person" in reference to corporations, that calling corporations moral persons creates more confusion and misunderstanding than clarity. I propose, therefore, to take another tack that begins by borrowing a certain conceptual strategy from Coleman's rather commonsensical way of talking about humans and corporations.[14] Suppose we say that actors and not persons are the primary units of the moral community. To be a member of the moral community, to be a proper subject of ethics, something must be, at least, an actor. Human persons are a variety of actors. Human persons may have a number of traits, over and above being actors, that are not shared by other things that are actors. Whether or not something resembles a human being is irrelevant to whether or not it qualifies as an actor. And analogy to characteristics will play no role in determining whether or not something is an actor.

But what is an actor? Actors are those entities that display a certain set of functional capacities as they perform on the social stage. There are at least three crucial capacities, starting with the ability to act intentionally. If something has to be a human person to act intentionally, then corporations, and any other nonhumans, will be disqualified from ethical consideration. There could be no corporate ethics. Fortunately, intentionality does not require human personhood. Therefore corporate ethics may be possible.

To say that something acts intentionally is to say that it has purposes, plans, goals, and interests that motivate some of its behavior. Essentially, to intend to do something is to plan to do it. If I intend to go to Hawaii in February, then I plan to go to Hawaii in February. Or at least I have made some plans to do so. It isn't that I just want to go to Hawaii in February. I may intend to go even though I don't want to, even if I have no desire to go there. I'd rather go to Colorado, but I agreed to attend that conference in Hawaii. I'm committed to doing it. I intend to do it.

I may, however, do little to indicate that I have such a commitment. I'll put off buying the tickets, and I won't start packing my tropical-weight clothes. You might not be able to tell from any of my current intentional actions that I am now intending to go to Hawaii in February. The reason for this is that any number of things that I might now be doing are compatible with my intention to go to Hawaii in February, though they have nothing to do with a Hawaiian trip. On the other hand, it couldn't be the case that I intend to go to Hawaii in February if I book up that month with trips to places on quite the other side of the world. So some things are excluded from my possible current activities, if I intend to go to Hawaii in February. That is what it means to be committed to doing it. But my intention seems to have little to do with my current desires and beliefs. In fact, desires and beliefs seem, at most, to be only tangentially involved. My plans and my commitment to them are at the heart of the matter.

A number of philosophers, including Alvin Goldman,[15] Elizabeth Anscombe,[16] Donald Davidson,[17] and Robert Audi,[18] in their analyses of intentionality and intending, focus exclusively on intention as it seems to appear in actions rather than, in Michael Bratman's terms, "the state of intending to act."[19] Because they do that, they seem compelled to believe that "what makes it true that an action was performed intentionally, or with a certain intention, are just facts about the relation of that action to what the agent desires and what the agent believes."[20] For some, like Davidson in his early papers on the subject, that relation is made out to be a causal one. Desires, coupled with beliefs, cause intentional actions. If I have the desire to go to Hawaii and I believe that I have the means to do so, then I intend to make the trip. Others, such as Audi, argue that there is no state of intending, because intentions with respect to future activities always reduce to appropriate sets of desires and beliefs. In other words, if I say, "I intend to go to Hawaii," I am saying no more than that I desire to make the trip and believe that I can make it.

It should be expected that those who interpret intention on the popular desire belief model would think that any talk of corporate intentions (and so corporate actors) must be metaphorical or reducible to the intentions of humans who have the requisite desires and beliefs. Obviously, corporations cannot, in any normal sense, desire and believe. If intentional action must reduce to desires and beliefs, then corporations will fail to make it as intentional actors. But I agree with Bratman that the desire-belief theory should be rejected. As it happens, the desire-belief model does a better job of explaining the behavior of my Shetland sheepdogs than it does my own or most human future-directed intentions. The dogs evidence the desire for food or to go outside, and it seems reasonable to attribute to them the belief that if they bark at me long enough, they will get me to bring about the things they want. What is lacking, or at least seems to be lacking, in the dogs is that they do not plan.

Bratman writes:

> Our understanding of intention is in large part a matter of our understanding of future-directed intention . . . Plans are not merely executed. They are formed, retained, combined, constrained by other plans, filled in, modified, reconsidered, and so on. Such processes . . . are central to our understanding of . . . intention. [21]

This explains why it is senseless to ask someone whether he or she intentionally sat in a chair, if when he or she entered the room, he or she just sat down in the chair. To raise the question of intention suggests that they are up to something besides sitting down. Was their sitting an act of protest?

Austin, with his usual insight, notes:

> "I intend to" is, as it were, a sort of "future tense" of the verb, "to X." It has a vector, committal effect like "I promise to X," and again like "I promise to X," it is one of the possible formulas for making explicit, on occasion, the force of "I shall X" (namely, that it was a declaration and not, for example, a forecast or an undertaking).[22]

I do not say that intention never involves desires and beliefs. They may enter into the various planning stages. (Austin, in fact, talks of the machinery of action involving such stages or departments as intelligence, planning, decision, appreciation, and resolve.)[23] I am saying that it is not reducible to desires and beliefs. Intention is a quite distinct state from a desire-belief complex, and I think the operative element of that state, planning, is typically found in corporate decision making.

The other two functional capacities we may expect actors to display are (1) the ability to make rational decisions and to consider rational arguments regarding their intentions, in particular arguments about the ways to realize their long- and short-term interests. And (2) actors must have the facility to respond to events and ethical criticism by altering intentions and patterns of behavior that are harmful (or offensive) to others or detrimental to their own interests. Human persons typically show these capacities, but so do many corporations. It, therefore, will be appropriate to refer to corporations as actors.

Today I received a letter signed by Kim S. The letter was on the stationary of Mazda, The Mazda American Credit Division, in Buffalo, New York. The letter informed me that, according to Mazda's records, I was delinquent in payment of a portion of a previous year's property tax bill on my leased Mazda. It asked me to remit the amount or contact the writer, Kim S. I telephoned Ms. S. and tried to explain, nearly to the point of exasperation, that this could not be true, because I had proof of having paid the tax bills, and that she must have made some error. She calmly rejoined each of my protestations with remarks to the effect that she had the bill and my records before her and that yes I had an excellent payment record, but there was no record of a remittance in this case. She must have repeated various versions of that line a dozen times without a perceptible elevation of emotion. At last we agreed on a satisfactory way to resolve the problem.

This little episode reveals a number of important points about the composition of the contemporary social world. I did not really get a letter from Kim S. , or rather Kim S. and I did not correspond. She and I did not really have a telephone conversation. The actors in this social transaction were not both human persons. (Though I am fairly certain that Ms. S. is a flesh and blood human and not an android or some virtual-reality entity with an expert systems voice-response mechanism.) The letter was from the Mazda American Credit Division of the Mazda Corporation, or more specifically from the Property Tax Collections unit of that division. The communication (letter and phone call) was between me and Mazda or between me and that unit of that Mazda division. Ms. S.'s only role was as an employee or an agent of Mazda. Whatever she personally felt about me or my charming manner or my situation or about the payment of property taxes on leased vehicles or anything else for that matter was immaterial to the interaction between me and the corporation. I have absolutely no idea how she views on any of those subjects, or anything at all.

She was relatively polite, if somewhat officious. She exchanged no pleasantries with me. Then again, I suspect I would have been more upset had she inquired about the weather in Texas or asked me about the playoff woes of the San Antonio Spurs. Kim S. simply was not a party in this social transaction. But if she wasn't, who was? A corporation and a human were communicating. I was the human. As it happened, I was dealing with Mazda about whether or not I had reimbursed it for the payment of taxes it had made to another corporate-like entity: a county tax board.

Perhaps someday I will be in Buffalo, New York, and I will meet Kim S. and we will get along and agree to write, and months later I will receive a letter from her. That will then be our first correspondence. In the meantime, Mazda and I will probably have amassed quite a collection of transactions, many of them signed by Kim S. That is the way our world is. There are Mazdas and Exxons and Harcourt Braces and Coca Colas and IBMs and Johns and Bills and Marys and Kims and me. Millions of natural human persons and thousands of corporate actors, and the important point is that the corporate actors are not just human persons wearing funny masks and lapel pins with logos on them. They are full-fledged participants in the social system. Actually, they are rather more than that. They are now the dominant members of the system, the ones on which its stability rests. Kim S. and I don't really matter much. We are rather less relevant to the social system than some illiterate baker or shoemaker was in a medieval village.

Both natural human persons and corporate actors have interests, goals, power, plans, and purposes. Coleman distinguishes them in the following way:

> A natural person encompasses two selves, object self and acting self, or principal and agent, in one physical corpus. A minimal corporate actor is created when principal and agent are two different persons.[24]

Historically, corporate actors were formed when humans (principals) came together, each with (usually) rational expectations of advancing or protecting personal interests, to form a corporate unit.

ROBERT NOZICK (1938–) Nozick teaches philosophy at Harvard University. Though he has written extensively on philosophical issues ranging from decision theory to metaphysics, his work on political theory is most relevant to this book. In *Anarchy, State, and Utopia*, Nozick defends a minimal state theory in which the responsibilities of the state are restricted to defense and judicial matters. He argues for a side-constraint interpretation of the role of moral/ethical considerations. The general idea is that our moral principles should serve to constrain or set the boundaries on our activities, not dictate what the goals of those activities must be. Nozick puts forth the maxim, "Utilitarianism for animals, Kantianism for people." The point is that there are absolute prohibitions about what we can do to other people, and they apply regardless of what good outcomes might occur if we were to violate them. Whereas animals may be used to benefit people, Nozick also adopts a version of Locke's property theory. He defends an historical account of justice in the acquisition of goods, and he attacks what he calls end-state theories like the one identified with such theorists as Karl Marx and John Rawls. According to Nozick, one's acquisition of property is just if one historically came to possess it in a proper and just manner. Considerations of end-state systems of justice, that is, theories about how things ought to be distributed ("from each according to . . . ., to each according to . . . .") are irrelevant to justice in distribution on Nozick's theory. Nothing is wrong with a situation in which a few people have most of the wealth, if they came by it without violating the side constraints and the principles of justice in acquisition.

(See Robert Nozick, *Anarchy, State, and Utopia* [1974].)

Whether, as Robert Nozick imagines,[25] the purpose of forming these corporate units was to create simple protection agencies or, as Hobbes thought, to create a full-blown civil state, the principals hired agents to do whatever was necessary to achieve their collective goals.

It is worth mentioning, as Coleman notes, that there are two distinct organizational problems for corporations. The first involves "collecting the resources and interests of the multiple principals to create a coherent set."[26] All relevant desires and intentions of the individuals who have agreed to form the corporation must be taken into consideration, and any conflicts that arise must be reconciled to everyone's satisfaction. To some extent that problem is solved in the charter of the corporation, which provides the "constitution for the principals."[27] But the incorporation act, though it does present some interesting ethical concerns, is less pressing than the other problem, the one corporate charters do not address: dealing with the acting "self" of the corporation. That problem has to do with "deploying the resources *via* the configuration of agents in a way that realizes the interests"[28] of the principals. I have called the framework in which solutions to this problem are attempted the Corporate Internal Decision Structure or CID structure.[29] It is the corporation's CID structure that allows it to be an independent rational actor on the social scene, and that converts various human behaviors and actions into corporate intentional action.

Before examining the elements of CID structures in detail, however, more must be said about the implications of the twentieth-century invasion of the social system by corporate actors. As I mentioned above, society is now organized around corporations. They provide the structural continuity previously supplied by humans in rigidly defined roles. Human persons, Coleman maintains,[30] now freed from the "fixed estates" of the social orders of the past, can and do roam over the stations created and maintained by corporations and, in fact, a single human can simultaneously occupy several positions. Positions may be freely changed and exchanged. Therefore, the invasion of the corporations, by Coleman's account, is responsible for the significant increase in human personal and vocational freedom that marks the contemporary world. The village baker's daughter need not learn her father's trade or marry someone who will become an apprentice to the old man. She can become a stockbroker, an accountant, a banker, a production manager, a philosopher. By and large the choice is hers. Corporations have made that possible.

Such individual freedom, however, may not, on closer inspection, be the blessing that the Enlightenment liberal might, on first reading, suppose. The invasion of the business corporations may have succeeded in bringing about the end of a status-oriented society in favor of a contract oriented one for human persons. But, as Hobbes had to admit and many modern-day liberal individualists try to ignore, contractual relations require a stable social structure. As corporate actors now provide the requisite fixed elements of the edifice, human persons are no longer the relevant structural parts of the social system they used to be. [31] We are occupants of the places, or stations created and sustained by the way corporations are organized and operated, just as Kim S., in most of the things she does from day to day, is but an agent of Mazda. On my view, the system in which we have come to understand our worth, our identity, our duties is now in the control of corporate actors. The invaders have radically changed the social, and so the moral, game. We're not in (rural) Kansas anymore. We're in the gleaming towers of corporate Oz, probably stuck away in a tiny office without a view.

If there is any doubt about these matters of personal worth and identity, they should be dispelled by the fact that studies show that most Americans over the last fifty years gauge their worth as persons in terms of the positions they have obtained in the corporate world. Generally, humans think of themselves as successes or failures because they have achieved, or failed to achieve, certain levels of authority in a corporation or corporate-like enterprise (such as churches, academic institutions, and government bureaucracies). Perhaps more importantly, we identify ourselves with the positions we occupy at work and with the companies for whom we work. Our self-estimations rise or fall with the fortunes of those corporations.

A few years ago, in the midst of the banking and savings and loan scandals in Texas, I was asked to address a meeting of the Robert Morris Society, a group of bankers. After virtually haranguing the audience for playing fast and loose with other people's money, caring more about real estate investments in Belize than investments in American research and development, violating the public trust in their industry by engaging in business practices that even a college philosophy freshman could identify as risky, self-serving, and unethical, and stuff like that, I was approached by a number of the bankers from recently failed institutions. My first reaction was to look for the nearest exit, wary about the Texas practice of carrying concealed handguns. I was certain that if I were lucky, I would be at least in for a tongue-lashing. Once again I had put my foot in my mouth. It was probably all right to say such things on college campuses, protected by the shield of academic freedom, but downright stupid to say them to real-world folks who had just experienced the collapse of the cushy lives they had built for themselves on their uncontrolled speculation with funds entrusted to them by unsuspecting dolts like myself. Many of their golden parachutes hadn't opened and they were emotionally and financially squashed. Parachute packing is an art, as I seem to remember from some John Wayne war movies. Golden parachute packing became a high art indeed in the takeover-frenzied days of the 1980s.

Rather than being shot, lynched, or even verbally harassed, my audience came forward to thank me for talking straight with them. The former executives of three failed banks not only agreed with me that things had been unethically, as well as illegally, done, they stressed that though they, most assuredly, had not been personally responsible for any of the misdeeds, they felt as though they had lost the sense of who they were when their banks' misdeeds were splashed across the front pages of the newspapers. "I was always known in my neighborhood, with my friends, the guys at the club, as the trust officer at Such and Such Bank". They were saying, "that's who I was. That's who I was to myself. That was me, my life. Then this happened. It took away my identity. I couldn't face the members of the club. . . ."

We are freer than any previous humans because our places in institutions and corporations are negotiable matters of contract and our whole lives are not inexorably linked to specific roles. Devastated as the members of my audience may have been, they could, and most probably did, find other jobs, some perhaps even in the banking industry. The market for humans and their talents is open. The postcorporate-invasion social structure exists independent of particular humans who have the choice to contract for their services, though they might not always find the job they desire.

What this means is that humans now have more economic and social freedom than ever before in history. But we have also become "irrelevant in a fundamental sense."[32] Anyone can be replaced at any time. I may get a letter from Louise Q. in a month or two telling me that she has the job formally held by Kim S. and inquiring about how this matter of a portion of the previous year's property taxes on my leased Mazda is going to be settled. People come and go. The positions endure.

John Ciardi wrote:

> Someone must make out the cards
> for the funeral of the filing clerk.
> Poor bony rack with her buzzard's
> jowled eyes bare as a dirk
> and as sharp for dead fact, she
> could have done it better than anyone
> will do it for her. It will be,
> to be sure, done.
> And the flowers sent. And the office closed
> for the half day it takes
> for whatever we are supposed
> to make of the difference it makes
> to the filing clerk
> where we can forget her.
> Someone will do the work
> she used to do better.[33]

So now we are free but generally interchangeable parts of society. How did we come to such a pass? Robert Nozick distinguished between "invisible-hand explanations" and "hidden-hand explanations" of this social phenomena. An invisible-hand explanation shows

> . . . how some overall pattern or design, which one would have thought had to be produced by an individual's or group's successful attempt to real ize the pattern instead was produced and maintained by a process that in no way had the overall pattern or design "in mind."[34]

While a hidden-hand explanation

> . . . explains what looks to be merely a disconnected set of facts that (certainly) is not the product of intentional design, as the product of an individual's or group's intentional design(s).[35]

Hidden-hand explanations are conspiracy theories. If the explanation of the corporate invasion is to be of the hidden-hand type, then we should look to the incorporators, the original principals that formed business corporations, as responsible for deliberately and purposefully altering the position of human persons in the social system, of giving them more freedom at the cost of relevancy. But no such explanation seems to fit the facts. Instead, the facts are more suited to an invisible-hand explanation. The principals who formed the early business corporations in America and Western Europe did so for their own rational reasons, that is, for personal gain. They certainly did not have "in mind," it was not their plan, their intention, to radically transform society. I wonder, however, if they might not now see themselves as in something of the dilemma of Dr. Frankenstein. After all, Frankenstein did not set about to make a monster to terrorize the world. His plan in manufacturing the monster was, depending on the version of the story (that is, which movie account), to further the ends of science, to prove he was the greatest scientist of his time, to gain personal glory. But he did create a monster that was soon out of his control. He could take a certain amount of pride in his accomplishment, but also be overwhelmed with shame and self-blame at the way it turned out.

I do not want to suggest that I think that the corporate structured world is monstrous. Quite the contrary. I think it is more likely to be susceptible to the influence of ethics than its predecessor. But, in large measure, it is no longer a world in the control of human persons, and I think there is very little likelihood that humans will ever again regain the status they once held in society. Perhaps that is not something to mourn.

 ### 3. Corporate Identity and Responsibility: Mob Behavior and Corporate Decision Making. The Role of Structure and Function.

The Exxon Corporation was responsible for the worst oil spill in American history when the *Exxon Valdez* ran aground on Bligh's Reef dumping 11 million gallons of crude oil into the waters of Prince William Sound, Alaska. Let us suppose that statement is true. It and its variants have been written and spoken untold times since that fateful day, March 24, 1989. And, at least to some degree, Exxon, the corporation, acknowledged its responsibility, took blame for the accident, and volunteered to clean up the mess. But many ethical theorists will tell us that the responsibility ascription targeting Exxon and Exxon's own acceptance of blame are really just ways of holding the captain of the *Exxon*

Valdez responsible for the terrible pollution of Prince William Sound and its effects on the animals and humans living there. Or they might maintain that all of those corporate responsibility claims really reduce to nothing more than the ascription of responsibility for the spill to some managerial team at Exxon, that is, its transportation division, or to the chairman of Exxon or to its president (both of whom were criminally indicted).[36]

Who would deny, except him, his lawyer, (and perhaps his mother), that the captain of the *Exxon Valdez* bears moral responsibility, in some measure, for the disaster? After all, he was, by his own admission, not on the bridge and was either drunk or hungover or sleeping in his cabin while his ship, in the hands of a junior officer, was traversing through the passage in Prince William Sound. A blood alcohol test, administered more than ten hours after the spill, still showed the captain to be legally drunk. But is there no one with whom the captain should share responsibility for the spill? What of those folks in Exxon's transportation division? Suppose that each of them conscientiously acted on corporate policies, especially those concerned with profitability, and none had any personal reasons to vary from that course, that is, they weren't being bribed to do so, they didn't harbor deep-seated hatreds for the Prince William Sound area, nor did they despise sea otters ever since traumatic childhood encounters with the creatures while on an outing to the zoo. They were just doing the jobs they were hired to do. Would it make sense to say that the transportation division's management team or its individual employees were responsible for the Alaskan oil spill?

If certain conditions can be shown to have existed, it might make sense to say that some of the managers, perhaps all in that division, were responsible. For example, suppose the transportation division had received reports that the single-hulled tankers Exxon uses are dangerous in Alaskan waters, that the Japanese fleet used multi-hulled vessels because of the high risk of puncture, and that certain officers of Exxon tankers were often drunk when they left port. Suppose they had records indicating that the captain assigned to the *Exxon Valdez* had a record of drunken-driving arrests and was known to frequent the bars in the port just before his ship was scheduled to depart. Suppose that they chose to ignore such reports and let the operations go on as in the past on the *Exxon Valdez*. After all, they hadn't had a disaster in the Prince William Sound area, and the captain's record at sea was spotless. It would cost a great deal of money and time to redesign the tankers, and recent directives from the top management at Exxon had mandated the implementation of as many cost-cutting measures as possible. A spill such as the one that occurred was thought to be likely to happen only once in 241 years. Perhaps they decided that Exxon's interest in getting its crude oil to its refineries as expediently and cheaply as possible should override all other issues.

Sorting out corporate and individual responsibility quickly becomes complicated in cases of this sort. The simplest thing to do, if your ethics comes from the seventeenth century, is to pin all of the responsibility, at least the moral variety on individual human beings; if not on the captain of the tanker, then on the senior executives of Exxon. But that solution is grossly unfair and flies in the face of the standard principles of responsibility that have marked Western ethics since Aristotle. Exxon's chairman may not even have known of the specific issues in the transportation division reports or the dangers of single-hulled tankers in the Alaskan waters out of Valdez. He might not have known of the captain's drinking habits. To hold him morally to account in this case is to regard as irrelevant the fact that he did not act with intention or with knowledge concerning the events of March 24, 1989, in Prince William Sound. It is difficult to say what he specifically *did,* let alone what he intentionally did, that resulted in the disaster. To hold him responsible would amount to making moral responsibility in corporate cases a strict liability ethical offense for such senior executives. That seems hardly just, though it is exactly the sort of approach that would be taken by someone who had abandoned the attempt to understand the corporate actor and the human person in our social world in order to preserve some antiquated theory.

As noted above, it has been relatively standard, since at least the time of Aristotle, to say that for something to be responsible for what it does it must have acted intentionally. It must be an actor. If, as I would have it, corporations, in and of themselves, are going to be susceptible to ethics (like holding Exxon morally responsible for the pollution of Prince William Sound), they must be intentional actors in a way that cannot be eliminated by merely and systematically reducing what they do to the actions of individual human beings, like the captain, the members of a certain managerial team, or the chief executive officer of the corporation.

The condition that requires that corporate actions cannot be simply reduced to individual human actions allows us to distinguish between corporate actors and other kinds of collectivities. It may be said, for example, that a rioting mob was responsible for destroying the stores on Crenshaw Boulevard in Los Angeles. Such an ascription of responsibility can usually be distributed to those who comprised the mob. That is another way of saying that the mob is not a moral entity. The mob is, for moral purposes, only an aggregate of human persons, each of whom may or may not be held individually responsible for the damage, or some of it, on Crenshaw Boulevard.[37]

An important reason for not holding the mob itself responsible is that a mob has no established way of making rational decisions, of planning or partial planning with respect to its goals, of setting goals in the first place, of assigning tasks, and so on.[38] The people in the mob could each have been on Crenshaw Boulevard for purely personal reasons. Some may have been shopping, some out for a walk, some doing business, some just hanging out. Something happened and, bang, the destruction ensued. There was no organization, it was just a mob. If you were a member of it, then you were probably responsible for some of the damage. So you may need a good excuse or an alibi if someone challenges your behavior. (You were just there looking for a good deal on a VCR. The store window broke. You have no idea how. And this four head, stereo VCR just fell into your hands. Well, if you left it there someone would have stolen it, so you took it to your house to protect it from theft and with the intention of returning it. You decided to hook it up to see if it really worked, as there would be little point in returning it if it were broken.)

Morally, you, as a member of the mob, might be thought to share in the responsibility for all of the damage on Crenshaw Boulevard. The mob itself, however, cannot bear moral blame. It goes out of existence when its members cease behaving in a riotous fashion and disperse.

Corporations are not like mobs in a variety of fairly obvious ways. In the first place, corporations will usually remain the same entity even though the group of principals and agents associated with them changes. The list of a corporation's stockholders, executives, board members, and employees is typically in a state of flux. Stock, for example, is bought and sold, employees die, resign, are fired, hired, and so on. Yet the corporation goes on, and it makes sense to talk of it as the same corporation regardless of such changes in principals and agents.

Imagine that we have two lists. One is the list of all principals and agents for IBM as of noon on Monday, May 17, 1993. The other is the list of principals and agents of IBM as of 4:00 p.m. on that same day. Let's say, though it would be highly improbable in the constantly changing world of the corporation, that the names on both lists are identical except that "Rebecca Martinez" appears on the first list as a stockholder and not on the second. Ms. Martinez sold her shares in IBM that afternoon in order to make another investment. Would it be right to say that the name "IBM Corporation" does not at 4:00 p.m. denote the same corporate actor it did at noon on May 17, 1993? Do we have two different corporations? Surely not. "IBM" refers to the same corporation whether or not Rebecca Martinez is one of its principals. And that would be true even if at 3:45 p.m. on that day the entire senior management of IBM resigned their positions and took up similar ones at Coca Cola. Coca Cola would not have become IBM. The identity of a corporation is not dependent on particular humans being in specific positions in the corporation.

Being a discrete and persisting entity, however, is not enough to make IBM or Coca Cola or any other corporation a member of the moral community, a proper target of ethical scrutiny. A corporation will, in and for itself, have to evidence the functional capacities of an actor. The primary one of those is that it must be able to act intentionally.

If a corporation, Mazda for example, is an intentional actor, then some events must be describable in a way that will support the truth of sentences that say that what Mazda did was intended by it and not just by its agents. Let's see how a case might be made. Start with events and the descriptions of events. A certain event may be described in a number of ways, all of which are there. In some descriptions it may not be an intentional action; in others, it is. In *Hamlet*, it is true that the prince intentionally stabs the man hiding in his mother's room. But it is not true that he intentionally stabs his girlfriend's father. As it turns out, however, that is exactly who was hiding. It wasn't the king, Hamlet's intended victim, the person he planned to kill. So although Hamlet intentionally killed the man who was hiding, and by doing so killed his girlfriend's father, it is not true that he intentionally killed her father. As I already noted, to say that something intended to act in a certain way is to describe its movements as upshots of plans it had for their occurring. Killing Ophelia's father was not a part of Hamlet's plan.

Now suppose we witness someone moving a pen across a piece of paper. We might be able to describe that event as just the physical movement of a human hand or as nothing more than certain muscular contractions. It can also be described as someone, Kim S., signing the letter to me about the property taxes on my leased car. The event will be an intentional action only if those physical movements can truthfully be described as done to bring about some state of affairs or done to realize certain plans or goals, to achieve certain interests, and so on.

Simply, if there is at least one true description of an event that says it was intended by someone, that event, no matter how it is described, is an action of that person. There is a true description of Hamlet's stabbing his girlfriend's father that says he did it intentionally; "Hamlet intentionally stabbed the man hiding in his mother's room." So, stabbing his girlfriend's father was an action of Hamlet's. It wasn't just a happenstance. Consider another example. If you dump out a glass of iced tea, believing it to contain coffee, while planning to dump out the coffee so that you can use the glass for iced tea, then it is true that you intentionally dumped out the contents of the glass—that is one of your actions. Because it is also true that dumping out the contents of the glass was dumping out the iced tea, that is also one of your actions, though it was not one of your *intentional* actions. It was not your intention, you never intended, to dump out iced tea.

So, you perform *intentional* actions and plain actions. Something you do is one of your actions only if it can be truthfully described in some way as one of your intentional actions. The same event described one way may be an intentional action, but when described in another way may only be an action. Pouring out the contents of the glass is one of your intentional actions; pouring out the iced tea, just one of your actions. In the absence of any true description of your pouring out the contents of the glass as an intentional action, however, it was just something that happened.[39] Perhaps it was an accident, but then it couldn't have been a mistake. Mistakes are actions. To make a mistake you must be intending to do something that you fail to do. J. L. Austin tells the story of a girl, Miss Plimsoll, who buys a book in which to keep daily accounts of her life and then carefully letters across its cover in permanent ink "DAIRY." She made a mistake. It wasn't accidental.[40] Accidents just happen to you.

When Kim S. signed the letter to me, she probably intended to affix her signature to that document, but we could imagine a situation in which she signed the letter mistakenly thinking she was signing something else, possibly a personal letter to her friend Rachel R. Though she intended to sign the letter to Ms. R., still, she intentionally wrote her signature, and signing that paper was signing the letter to me, so signing the letter to me was one of her actions, though not one of her intentional actions. In this case, however, much more is involved than in the example of your dumping out the iced tea. There are more levels of descriptions to be considered. Kim S.'s signing the letter to me was Mazda dunning me for a property tax payment. That is, the sentence, "Mazda dunned me for the property tax payment on the leased car," is a true description of the event that could otherwise be described as "Kim S. signing the letter to me." Her signing is Mazda dunning. But Mazda duns me whether Kim signed the letter to me intentionally or mistakenly thought she was signing another letter, one to Rachel R., that was also on her desk. Mazda acted when Kim S. signed the letter, even if signing that particular letter was not what she thought she was doing when she did it. In effect, by her signing the letter, Mazda opened a conversation with me, and a not very pleasant one, at that. For all intents and purposes, Kim S. then was irrelevant to this encounter between a human person and a corporate actor.

As we have seen, the same event can be described in a number of different and nonequivalent ways. Though a number of different descriptions may be true of the same event, some may not be substituted without a significant change in meaning. At various levels of description the same event also may be identified as an intentional action, and at each such level there must be an intentional actor performing it. So we can ask whether, when, and how the physical movement of Kim S.'s hand that was her signing a letter to me reveals the existence of a corporate actor acting intentionally and not just a human person acting, whether or not intentionally. Is there a level of descriptions of that event at which we can truthfully say that Mazda acted with the intention of dunning me for the unpaid tax? I think there is, but it will have to be a level at which the event is described as Mazda being committed to charging me for the property tax payment. That is what Mazda intends, what it plans.

A corporation's doing something usually involves or includes human persons doing things and those humans usually can be described as having reasons and plans with respect to their behavior in their corporate positions. I realize that you've likely had enough of my encounter with Mazda and Kim S., but there is just a bit more to the matter that is revealing. At the bottom of the letter she invited me to call her on a toll-free number if I had any questions. I had questions, the first of which was, "What's this about another property tax bill on the leased car? I promptly paid three of these already this year and I can prove it." Her first response was, as you would expect, "Sir, I'll bring it up on the computer, but I doubt we've made a mistake." "I'm sure you have. In fact, last year I only got two bills for such taxes. You hit me for three this year and now want a fourth. What are you trying to do?" "I'm just doing my job, sir. Oh, here it is. Yes, you did not pay the assessment from the county school district." "There is no county school district in this county. You've obviously screwed up. What are you going to do, pocket the money?" "Sir, we at Mazda have this bill here from your county school district. We've paid it, and according to your lease agreement, you are to reimburse us." "But this is wrong. I'm telling you, we have independent school districts here, not a county district, and if you will kindly check your records for the past years, you'll see that I have never been billed for such a tax before. Besides which, I have no record of ever having received a bill from you for this tax before or I would have complained months ago." We went on to talk about the dependability of the U.S. mails and actually drifted into some rather congenial conversation, though she staunchly stuck to her guns about the tax payment being overdue.

During this telephone call I had conversations with two different types of entities, a corporation and a human person. The conversation with the human took the least amount of time and accomplished little or nothing because Kim S. is a consummate corporate agent. From her perspective, however, there might have been an interesting moral conflict. At some point during our exchange, she might have been tempted to tell me that she would see that the whole matter was canceled and that all records of that tax bill were deleted from Mazda's computer system. Somehow she braced herself against that temptation and carried out her corporate duties. Though she had it in her control or power to manipulate the situation to my benefit, she acted to further Mazda's interests.

Suppose the call had not been from me but from Rachel R., her lifelong friend, and the conversation, in substance if not demeanor, went along the same lines. The temptation to use her control over the corporation's interests in the case to benefit her friend might have weighed more heavily on Kim S. than it did in my case. Would she have acted in the same manner? Should she have? The difference between human persons and corporate agents is especially clear in such circumstances. "Come on, do it for a friend."

Coleman rather nicely captures the situation when he writes:

> Analytically it is clear that any person in such a situation has two sets of resources: his own, that is, his as a personal actor; and those of the corporate actor for whom he is an agent. Any employee of a firm traveling on the firm's business at its expense has two kinds of money, which he could, if he desired, physically separate into two pockets. In one pocket would be his own money, which he could spend however he desires. In the other pocket would be the firm's money, which he may use only for expenses that are incurred in pursuit of the firm's business. Because the agent has physical control of expenditures, a common occurrence is the use of the corporate actor's resources by the agent in his own interests. Numerous devices have been employed in social organizations to prevent this appropriation from occurring.[41]

At first, at least, I suspect that Kim S. was personally indifferent to me and the communication with me which she had initiated. Admittedly, I may have given her some personal reasons to pursue the matter with more than usual vigor during our phone conversation.

How do we determine when actions performed by a human being, such as Kim S., are also the intentional actions of a corporate actor, such as Mazda? The answer has to do with the way corporations are run. Every corporation has an established way by which it makes decisions and converts them into corporate intentional actions. As mentioned earlier, I have called this the Corporation's Internal Decision Structure or CID structure. CID structures have two elements crucial to our understanding of how acting corporations emerge at certain levels of the description of events: (1) an organizational flow chart that delineates stations and levels within the corporation; and (2) rules that reveal how to recognize decisions that are corporate ones and not simply personal decisions of the humans who occupy the positions identified on the flow chart. These rules are typically embedded, whether explicitly or implicitly, in statements of corporate policy. Its CID structure is an organization of personnel (agents) for the exercise of the corporation's power with respect to its ventures and interests and, as such, its primary function is to draw various levels and positions within the corporation into rational decision making, ratification, and action processes.

When operative, a CID structure subordinates and synthesizes the intentions and actions of various human persons (and even the behavior of machines) into a corporate action. Because the workings and elements of CID structures are relatively easy to detect, they can be called epistemically transparent. Anyone with access to these structures can discover everything about how they work, so CID structures can be confidently used as the basis from which to transform the description of certain events. Described in one way, an event may be the actions or the mere behavior of humans (those who occupy various stations on the organizational chart). But seen "through" the CID structure, it is a corporate act. The corporate character of the event is exposed. The corporate invaders on the social scene appear in their full form at the level of description that CID structures make available to us.

To see how this works think of the CID structure of a corporation as containing two sorts of rules: organizational rules and policy and procedure rules. These rules make descriptions of events possible that would not be possible if those rules did not exist. These rules play a role similar to the role rules play in our descriptions of sporting events. A person may toss a round ball into a hoop on a gymnasium wall, but without the rules of basketball the activity is not describable as sinking a jump shot and scoring two points. In basketball, there are also two types of rules: those that define positions— the dimensions of the court, the number of players per side, and so forth—and those that allow certain activities of the players and forbid others. These include rules that permit attempting to shoot the ball into the basket in some ways and not others, that forbid certain ways of stopping an opponent from scoring, and such.

The organizational chart of a corporation distinguishes players and clarifies their rank and maps out the interwoven lines of responsibility within the corporation. The organizational chart could tell us, for example, that anyone holding the title executive vice president for finance administration, stands in a superior position to anyone holding the title, director of the property tax collections department, and to anyone holding the title treasurer. These "players" report to the executive vice president. He ratifies their actions, and so on. The organizational chart maps the interdependent and dependent relationships, line and staff, that produce corporate decisions and actions. The organizational chart provides what might be called the grammar of corporate decision making. The policy and procedure rules provide its logic.

Policy and procedure rules are, in effect, recognition rules.[42] That is, they are rules that yield conclusive and affirmative grounds for describing a decision or an act as having been made or performed for corporate reasons. Recognition rules in a CID structure may address either procedural or policy matters. Some of the procedural rules are already embedded in the organizational chart. For example, by looking at the chart, we should be able to see that certain kinds of decisions are to be reached collectively at certain levels, but that they must be ratified at higher levels.

A corporate decision, and subsequently an action, is recognized, however, not only by how it is made, but by the policy that is reflected in it. Every corporation creates a general set of policies (as well as an image) that are easily accessible to both its agents and those with whom it interacts. When an action performed by someone in the employ of a corporation is an implementation of its corporate policy, then it is proper to describe the act as done for corporate reasons or for corporate purposes to advance corporate plans, and so as an intentional action of the corporation.

Corporate plans and purposes might differ from those that motivate the human persons who occupy corporate positions and whose bodily movements are necessary for the corporation to act. Using its CID structure, we can, however, describe the behavior of those humans as corporate actions done with a corporate intention, to execute a corporate plan or as part of such a plan. That should expose to the light of ethics the corporate intentional actor that otherwise lurks in the shadows controlling much of what has become contemporary society.

4. Corporate Internal Decision Structures

It has long been a basic principle of moral fairness, one to which we should subscribe, that a person ought not to be held responsible and punished for untoward events that were merely incidental to his or her intentional actions, unless the person was negligent. In many of the recent, even widely publicized, cases in which corporations have been held responsible for untoward events, it is difficult to demonstrate that individual employees or executives intended or acted in ways that would normally be regarded as morally relevant with respect to those events. In other words, they didn't intend them, nor were they personally negligent with respect to them. Nonetheless, through a complex, though surveyable, process of corporate decision making, a collection of plans, goals, policies, and such, formed into a corporate intention or corporate negligence regarding the matter. Treating corporations as morally responsible actors in their own right, then, is consistent with the social facts and does not violate our standard principles of moral fairness.

Consider the well known pollution case of Love Canal involving Hooker Chemical. In 1905, Hooker Electrochemical Company built a chemical plant in the Love Canal area of Niagara Falls, New York. In 1942, Hooker secured permission to dump its chemical wastes in the ditch that was the since-abandoned canal. In 1953, the land was sold, but in the eleven years prior to the sale, it is estimated that more than twenty thousand tons of chemical wastes had been deposited there.

The chemicals were in drums, and the site was considered ideal for chemical dumping. It was an undeveloped, largely unpopulated area and had highly impermeable clay walls that retained liquid chemical materials with virtually no penetration.[43]

When the dump was closed, it was covered with what was thought to be leak-proof clay. The land purchaser was the Niagara Falls School Board. Hooker warned the board that they had previously dumped possibly toxic wastes there, but the board built an elementary school on the land anyway, and a neighborhood grew up around it. Construction of the school and housing development involved the removal of a great deal of the clay top over the dump. That, coupled with the effects of snow and rain, destroyed the seal, and moisture entered the dump and eventually caused the chemicals to surface and seep into basements and yards. Several of the residents reported severe illnesses, including liver diseases and epilepsy, pregnant women had a higher than normal rate of miscarriage, and birth defects were common. The health commissioner recommended closing the school, the state purchased the 235 houses closest to the dump, and in 1978 President Carter declared it a disaster area. What is the responsibility of Hooker Chemical in all of this?

Rather than examining the defenses put forth by Hooker to try to shift the blame for the situation to other parties, many of which seem to me to be persuasive, suppose we ask what we mean by the responsibility question in the first place. There is, no doubt, a temptation to transfer whatever responsibility may be assigned to Hooker Chemical for the Love Canal situation to the executives of the corporation. But why? And which executives? It is certainly true that few, if any, of the managers of Hooker during the dumping period had any personal interests or intentions with regard to the business for which the corporation now is held accountable. In fact,they most probably had little idea between 1942 and 1953 that there would be a problem or even that the chemical wastes they were dumping were as dangerous as they appear to be. Still, Hooker Chemical did dump the toxic waste. The courts rejected the "third-party defense" that Niagara Falls was solely responsible because it had ignored Hooker'swarnings about the site, and found Hooker fully responsible. But managers and employees of Hooker were not personally responsible for the disaster. As far as can be determined, none acted other than as corporate agents with respect to the dumping.

Holding Hooker Chemical responsible for the dumping of toxic waste, however, should not shield those who worked for Hooker from individual responsibility if they personally acted improperly with respect to the matter. For example, suppose investigation reveals that some of the senior executives at Hooker took bribes from the landowner to choose the site for the dump back in the 1940s. Those individuals should be morally condemned even though it was Hooker Chemical that brought the toxic wastes to the area. The fact that their illicit behavior occurred within the context of corporate actions explains, in part, how the bribetakers were able to work the bribes, but the fact that a corporate action was involved or necessary for them to do what they did does not alleviate their personal moral responsibility for bribery.

Imagine the senior executives of Hooker Chemical in 1942 engaged in the decision process with regard to using the Love Canal site as a chemical waste dump. They have before them a mountain of reports and studies prepared by lower-echelon managers and team leaders. There are factual reports, contingency plans, position papers from various departments, financial analyses, legal opinions, and such , (but probably no studies or reports on the effects the chemical wastes might have on humans should they build homes and schools over the dump site a decade after the dumping)—all having been processed through Hooker Chemical's CID structure. Whatever personal reasons any individual executive or management team member may have had for writing a report or making a recommendation were diluted by superior review and reformation well before it reached the senior executives who decided to authorize the use of the Love Canal site.

Hooker Chemical's CID structure allows redescribing those actions of its agents (and many more besides) as Hooker's using the Love Canal area for chemical waste dumping, but that doesn't say that Hooker acted intentionally in bringing the toxic waste to the Love Canal site. But Hooker's CID structure, as already noted, also provides grounds, in its corporate policy elements, for an attribution of corporate intentionality in this case. If using the Love Canal site as a dump for its waste implemented corporate policy, if it was an execution of corporate future directed plans, then Hooker Chemical's pollution of Love Canal was a corporate intentional action. Perhaps it was to increase productivity, cut expenses, enhance profits, and so on, all or any of which were rational reasons for Hooker to act as it did. Hence, the actions of the executives of Hooker meeting in 1942 and deciding to dump the company's chemical wastes in Love Canal can be redescribed as Hooker Chemical intentionally bringing chemical wastes to Love Canal for rational corporate reasons. Those reasons, which we could summarize in terms of maximizing the achievement of corporate interests, exist in Hooker's CID structure, whether or not some or all of the executives took bribes from the landowner to choose the Love Canal site for the dump. The action, therefore, was a corporate one.

The way a corporation typically has of achieving its goals is, of course, through the actions of its personnel. However, that does not change the fact that corporate goals, plans, and interests, may be radically different from those of the humans in such roles. Corporate intentional actions can even be accomplished without direct actions by its human agents. Computers may perform a number of corporate actions while humans in the company are unaware of what is actually happening. In any event, corporations have rational reasons for actions, because they have interests in realizing their established corporate goals and plans regardless of the reasons, self-interested or otherwise, that directors, managers, and other agents may have.

5. How Corporate Policies Really Work

It is in a corporation's interests that its agents view the corporate purposes and plans as instrumental in the achievement of their own personal goals. Although financial reward is the most common way in which corporations seek to achieve this end, it is not always the most effective. The agent's internalization of the interests of the corporate actor will be discussed in the next part of the book. For now it need only be noted that rarely do a corporation's policies just reflect the current personal goals of its agents, no matter how highly placed those agents are in its CID structure.

In some small or relatively young companies, it will be difficult to separate the goals of the agents from those of the corporate actor. This is especially true when some of the higher-placed agents are also principals of the corporation. But such a convergence of interests and goals is certainly not necessary nor does it practically occur in most corporations. In fact, in larger corporations that have been in existence for some time, it is almost never the case.

Usually, of course, the original incorporators or principals will have organized to further their individual interests and to meet goals that they shared. Even in a corporation's infancy, however, the melding of disparate interests and purposes gives rise to corporate long-range and short-term planning that can be distinguished from the plans, purposes, and interests of the collection of incorporators viewed individually. Also, corporate basic purposes and policies, as already mentioned, tend to be relatively stable and transparent when compared to those of individuals and not couched in the kind of language that would be appropriate to individual purposes. Furthermore, as histories of corporations show, when policies are amended or altered, typically peripheral issues are involved. Radical policy changes, because they would alter its CID structure, could actually constitute the creation of a different corporation.

Corporate intent undeniably is dependent upon relatively transparent policies and plans derived from the socio-psychology of a group of human beings. Corporate intent may appear a tarnished, illegitimate offspring of human intent, but such an assumption reveals an anthropocentric bias. If we concentrate on the possible descriptions of events and acknowledge that corporate reasons can exist for corporations doing things, then we should not feel compelled to reduce statements about corporate actions to ones about the actions, reasons, plans, or interests of humans who happen to be agents of the corporate actor. Corporate policies provide sufficient grounds to redescribe certain events as corporate actions. Still, the corporate agent's actions also must be procedurally correct for them to be corporate. So let us examine more closely how the CID structure works.

In some corporations, procedural rules in the CID structure may be minimal. Among various managers there may exist an understanding that superiors are to be kept informed of decisions made at lower levels and that superiors can veto inferior-level decisions. The notions of "within one's authority" and "exceeding one's authority" then will be defined in daily operations. Importantly, the CID structure must do a normative job. That is, it is prescriptive and not just descriptive. It tells the agents of the corporation how they *ought* to act. Kim S.'s actions are not those of Mazda just because she or even the president of Mazda says that they are. No corporate president or CEO has that authority. Otherwise anything a president did to enrich himself from the corporate funds or in using corporate employees, for instance, to clean his swimming pool, by his merely saying so, would be a corporate action.

Even though some procedures may be the result of common practice rather than official sanction, the recognition of procedures is a bit easier than identifying policy in most corporations. This is because formal documents, such as charters, do not come close to exhausting the sources of corporate policy. Most charters are rather vague about the goals, interests, and purposes of the corporation. They may say only that the corporation is formed to engage in business for any lawful purpose. In law, the doctrine that corporations can only act within the strict boundaries set by their charters has been superseded by an implied powers doctrine, which recognizes that it is impossible to anticipate and spell out in the charter every power that corporate agents may need as they pursue diversified corporate projects. This has given rise to what is known as the "business judgment rule." It says that corporations may pursue any legitimate corporate ends through legitimate corporate enterprises. As long as corporate agents work within the limits of those pursuits, as established by procedurally appropriate corporate decisions and corporate history, their acts will be understood as corporate actions. But what is a legitimate end or endeavor?

The use of "legitimate" has more to do with being in accord with general expectations and standards and with being reasonable in the circumstances, than with actual legal constraints. Hence, for General

Motors, the policy of closing old, expensive-to-operate plants in the north central United States and opening new ones in foreign countries where labor is cheaper is a legitimate corporate endeavor. Whether or not General Motors, from the moral point of view, ought to close its Michigan plants has nothing to do with the legitimacy of its doing so. The business judgment rule depends for its sense on an understanding of what is rational within the standards of business for the particular corporate enterprise, given the history, type of venture, and policies of that corporation. In effect, then, recognizing corporate policy involves understanding the type of business in which the corporation is engaged. It is not just a matter of learning some rules or slogans or boilerplate claims that may be preserved in its charter.

The policies of a corporation seem to be inviolate: Certainly the basic ones are — indeed, they must be. In that respect they are unlike policies adopted by individual humans. You could adopt a policy of honesty, but you may occasionally violate that policy by lying. Yet, when you lie, it is still *you* lying. If employees act in ways that violate corporate policy, their acts are no longer corporate.

There are, however, some problems with my account of policies. Imagine that Kim S. at Mazda knows of a clearly written corporate policy with respect to the operations in her department against giving an extension to any lessee who has not promptly paid the property tax assessments. If the lessee balks, the account must be immediately turned over to the collection agency. Kim S., however, is convinced that I may be in the right in this tax matter, so she offers an indefinite extension while we both try to "get to the bottom of this thing." Is Kim's act an act of Mazda?

She seems to have "gone out on her own" in handling my case in this way, so we might be tempted to say that it is Kim S., and not the corporation acting, but that is too hasty. Before we can authoritatively exclude Kim's handling of my case from the acts of Mazda, we need to know the reaction among her superiors at Mazda that her report on my case prompts. Suppose that after reminding her that she did not strictly follow policy, her supervisor decides to endorse her handling of my case. By his or her doing so, Mazda identifies itself with a policy different from its written one. That reveals that the actual policy of Mazda on such matters is not really the written one.

But now imagine a different case. A few days after cutting my deal with Kim S., I get a call from her supervisor. She tells me that Ms. S. had no business extending the grace period and that if I don't pay up in ten days, the matter will be turned over to a collection bureau. She insists that Mazda will not try to settle this business about phony school districts until I have met that obligation and informs me that Kim S. got fired for overstepping her authority. In this scenario, it could not be clearer that Kim's actions, despite appearances to me at the time of our phone conversation, were not Mazda corporate actions. The written policy would still be governing at Mazda. (Whether or not the corporation has at least a moral obligation to do what an employee acting outside of the realm of corporate agency seems to have committed it to do, will be discussed later.)

The point is that whether or not a policy is actually in place in a corporation is dependent not on just what is on the written record, but on how those empowered to act for the corporation respond to apparent violations of stated policy. So, in practice, corporate policies are rather more flexible than my earlier comments may have suggested. Often they are no more than partial plans that will be revised, modified, extended, and reconsidered as the corporation confronts unanticipated situations and opportunities.

In any event, every corporation has a set of policies, and some are more central or fixed than others. Discovering which policies are central and which are more peripheral at a corporation like Mazda would require careful sociological research on the way Mazda actually acts over time in many different circumstances. Its published documents might turn out to be little more than window dressing, but if they are, then there must be a tried and true way for both those inside and outside the corporation to ascertain whether a piece of behavior on the part of a corporate agent is corporate or not. One of the identifying characteristics of a corporate actor is that the elements of its decision structure are relatively easy to detect, even from outside the corporation. We will, in Section 14, see how this is crucial to the prospects for corporate ethics.

6. Rational Nonprogrammed Decisions

Another aspect of CID structures is crucial to treating corporations as actors and so as proper subjects of ethics. This is that corporations are capable of making rational nonprogrammed decisions directed to the satisfaction of their interests. Corporations are more than merely mechanical in the way they interact with various constituencies and respond to various issues. The most obvious cases in which corporations evidence rational nonprogrammed decision making are in new product and service development. Although adherence to established procedure is usually required, the development process cannot really be routinized. There are usually too many variables. So, for example, to make major product-development decisions, corporations must provide within their CID structures for nonprogrammable elements: reactive, responsive, and discriminatory elements. It is certainly a truism of business that a corporation that is incapable of innovation is unlikely to achieve its vital economic interests.

To be a proper target of ethical evaluation, as noted earlier, the subject must be capable of responding to what it learns about those with whom it interacts, as well as to ethical criticism. It must be able to responsively adjust its patterns of behavior and its policies and procedures to handle unforeseen problems and prevent reoccurrences of bad situations. Ethics requires of its subjects the capacity to respond. Of course, it is especially concerned with the entity's capability for effective response to moral criticism, as well as the ability to alter offensive behavior, and react to unanticipated outcomes. We have been taught to think of these functional capacities as peculiarly human, but insofar as the CID structures of most corporations are designed to encourage the development of new products, the initiation of mergers and other contractual matters, the relocation of plants, the selection of new board members, and the acquiring of properties, they demonstrate nonprogrammed responsive decision-making capacities.

Must a corporation have human agents to evidence this responsive characteristic? It might be supposed that nonprogrammed responsive decision-making capacities in corporations are merely derivative and dependent on the presence of the same capacities in their human agents. I can't offer an actual case for consideration, but the following scenario, adapted from a tale told by Meir Dan-Cohen[44] should prove suggestive.

Edward E., an entrepreneur, started and directed a manufacturing business. After a number of financially profitable years, a syndicate bought him out. The syndicate built up the company, and then it issued shares for public purchase. As the number of shareholders increased and shares were traded on the market, a professional management team took charge of the corporation. Throughout these periods the company was active politically and culturally in its community. After some time, the company decided to buy up its own shares. Finally it bought up all of the outstanding stock in the company. As its capital was mostly self-generated and its management self-perpetuating, this move produced no significant change in the regular operations at the company. The management team then decided to completely automate all of the company's operations. In effect, the corporation became both ownerless and fully automated. It continued to manufacture its product, its legal status didn't change, and it continued to act in the community as it had in the past.

The top management team then decided that because the operations were already computer-run, and efficiently and profitably at that, computers could also handle all of the management decision making as well. Of course, with the computers taking over the decision making, the human managers were redundant.

By following a policy of not filling positions when a human manager reached retirement, the company gradually became totally computerized.

Management functions and all decision-making processes were assigned to computers. The company went on manufacturing and reinvesting its profits. It continued to support community causes and cultural events and backed political candidates committed to increasing the constitutional rights of corporations. Hardly anyone who interacted with the corporation realized it had converted to computerization on so grand a scale. This totally computerized corporation was still capable of litigating its grievances and defending its rights.

Would the removal of its human agents cause the corporation to lose its status as a corporate actor? Its CID structure was not appreciably altered, despite the absence of humans in decision making positions. Nevertheless, the crucial factor that decides whether it is really a corporate actor or simply an artifact is whether it continued to have the functional capacity to rationally choose actions that serve its interests and whether it could adjust its procedures and policies to appropriately respond to those with whom it interacts. Could it recognize and discriminate between other types of entities with which it interacted, and did it have the capability of performing nonprogrammed adjustments in response to new developments? I don't know whether computers can or will be able to do so. I have friends in the field who are convinced that they can and that near-future generations of computers will display all of the requisite functional capacities. Peter Danielson maintains that, within certain limits, with respect to certain games, he has already designed prototypes.[45] If computers can perform the requisite functions, then corporate actors will not need human agents to qualify as members of the moral community.

Would traditional moral theorists find it more or less difficult to cope with invaders of that sort? Would they be tempted to reduce the actions of computerized corporations to the actions of computers and so hold the computers responsible for what the corporations do? Or would they finally give up the seventeenth-century conceit and admit that the social world in which ethics must be relevant has more than humans in it? In fact, corporations may be better suited to being ethical than we are, an issue I will discuss in Section 14. We are not alone. Neither was Frankenstein.

We now have something of a working description of a corporate actor, so that we can pick them out and explore their role in the moral community. Its CID structure accounts for the personality of the corporation because it contains the organizational relationships and lines of internal authority and responsibility as well as the rules by which corporate procedure and policy is recognized and implemented. Its CID structure not only forms the personality of the corporation, it determines its identity as well. It is constitutive of the corporation in every major respect. A corporation simply is that particular one because it has that particular CID structure. Hence, within the CID structure,

DAVID HUME (1711-1776) One of the most important of the British Empiricists, Hume carried the empiricist's program of demanding that all knowledge be founded in experience to its logical conclusions. He maintained that every statement is either analytic or synthetic or nonsense. If it is analytic, then it is necessarily true. It is true by definition. As an example, think of "All bachelors are unmarried men." But, according to Hume, it is therefore only a verbal truth, redundant or tautological. It gives us no new knowledge of the world. It just defines words. If it is synthetic, then its negation does not produce a self-contradiction. It is not true by definition nor is it necessarily true. Whether or not it is true is a matter for investigation and experience. As an example, think of "That man over there is a bachelor." But if the statement is not analytic, and if it is synthetic but there is no way to trace its concepts or ideas back

most of the puzzles of identity that plague our thinking about human persons[46] never arise. The issue of identity over time will remain, but David Hume's discussion of the identity of a ship provides clues as to the way a solution may be managed for that problem in the case of corporate actors.

> A ship, of which a considerable part has been chang'd by frequent reparations, is still consider'd as the same; nor does the difference of the materials hinder us from ascribing an identity to it. The common end, in which the parts conspire, is the same under all their variations, and affords an easy transition of the imagination from one situation of the body to another.[47]

Its CID structure provides both a corporation's "common end" and the organizational edifice in which its agents and principals "conspire." The bottom line is this: the idea that corporations are social actors worthy of ethical as well as sociological scrutiny should not be cast in doubt just because corporate actors do not mirror human persons and so are not prone to the same perplexities of identity as are humans.

It should be clear that corporations are not just macrocosmic versions of humans.[48] They are quite otherwise. But they evidence the sorts of functional capabilities we require of entities we count as subjects of ethics. We think that most humans possess those capabilities, but various classes of humans, for example, infants, those with extreme mental deficiencies, or those in vegetative states, are not regarded as having the appropriate capacities. So ethics is directed not at all creatures that are genetically human, but at only those humans who belong to a certain class, identified by its functional capacities. The corporate to sense experiences, then it is nonsense and should be discarded. When Hume applied this test to many of the theories of philosophy and the beliefs of ordinary people he determined that they should be discarded as nonsense. He eliminated beliefs in the existence of God, causality, and the self by this method. The identity of the self over time is a standard philosophical problem. Hume asks us to locate the sense datum that corresponds to our conception of the self. Has anyone ever seen a self? Hardly. We are only immediately aware of sensations or perceptions of being warm, cold, in the dark, in the light, feeling angry, happy, in love, and so forth. And these, as Hume says, "succeed each other with inconceivable rapidity." But we never experience the self. Must not the idea of the self then be nonsense? Yes and no. Our idea of self is a product of our imagination, a construct we use to bundle our perceptions together to make a whole. That construct allows us to think of ourselves as ongoing entities over time, when what we really know is only that there is a continual succession of perceptions from birth until death.

(See David Hume, *A Treatise of Human Nature* [1739].)

invaders, or at least most of them, because of their abilities and capacities, fall into that class.

It is not at all obvious that what has been thought for centuries to be ethically appropriate in interactions between human persons, however, would be permissible if it were done by corporate actors to humans or if it were done by corporate actors to each other. Although I have shown that corporations are appropriate targets of ethics, the question remains, "What ethics?" It might be a mistake to think that the ethics that have been designed to apply to human interactions will simply translate over to the corporate invaders. It may be that traditional philosophical ethics have been so human-oriented that it is inadequate to deal with the actions of all members of the expanded target class. Inadequate ethics are better than no ethics at all, I suppose. But we ought not resign ourselves to half a loaf before we have explored the possibility of getting the whole thing.

7. Rawlsian Individualism and the Power and Control Factors in Types of Social Interactions

Contemporary social interactions fall into three categories:

Type One: individual humans dealing with each other (Kim S. and I meeting on a blizzard-swept street in Buffalo);

Type Two: corporations interacting with humans (Mazda billing me for a property tax bill and responding to my objections);

Type Three: corporations dealing with each other (Mazda agreeing to handle the banking on its lease accounts at Marine Midland Bank in Buffalo).[49]

Type One interactions have been the focus of the history of Western ethics. Obviously, the ethics of human person interactions will be relevant to corporate actors only if its principles, rules, and judgments, are demonstrably appropriate to interactions in which corporate actors are a party. To claim that they are relevant would be to claim that from the moral point of view, no significant differences exist between human persons and corporate actors. Such a claim was suggested by John Rawls in his early work when he included corporate actors among the participants in the "Original Position," though he then asserted "a certain logical priority to the case of human individuals."[50]

Rawls derives his theory of justice from a thought experiment he calls the Original Position. Parties in the Original Position select the principles of justice that will order and regulate society from behind a veil of ignorance that deprives them of knowledge of any of the differences between and among them. They cannot know their ages, health, wealth, skills, race, sex, or other attributes. They cannot know whether they are acting as humans or corporate agents, though they do have certain concerns about recent pasts and near future familial relations. All they have is rationality and the desire to form a society consistent with the promotion of their self-interests and their interests as heads of families. Rawls argues that in such a state they will choose two principles of justice:

> First: each person is to have an equal right to the most extensive basic liberty compatible with a similar liberty for others.

> Second: social and economic inequalities are to be arranged so that they are both (a) reasonably expected to be to everyone's advantage, and (b) attached to positions and offices open to all.[51]

These principles are to apply to the basic structure of society and govern the distribution of the goods of society.

Robert Paul Wolff summarizes the Rawlsian program:

> The two principles of justice are the solution, in the strict sense of a bargaining game, the terms of which embody a minimal notion of practical reason together with the so-called conditions of justice, plus the single additional premise that the players are prepared to make a once-for-all commitment to a set of principles for the evaluation of practices, the principles to be chosen unanimously on the basis of self interest . . . By virtue of the characteristics of the bargaining game, the solution is guaranteed to be just, so that the actual play of the game is an instance of pure procedural justice.[52]

The idea is that we will have a ready answer for anyone who questions why our social institutions should be organized according to the

JOHN RAWLS (1921–) Rawls is a professor of philosophy at Harvard University where he has spent most of his career. His most famous book is *A Theory of Justice*. Its influence on social theorists, political philosophers, economists, and philosophers throughout the world has been enormous. It has been translated into all of the major European languages and most of the Asian ones as well. Rawls' basic position may be described as the philosophical liberal's defense of the modern welfare state. He presents his theory by creating a thought experiment in which we are to imagine that people are placed in a bargaining position where they must arrive at the basic governing principles of justice for the institutions of their society. Before bargaining, however, they are all placed behind a "veil of ignorance" so that no one knows his or her age, sex, wealth, health, race, and so on. Rawls argues that, in that condition, which he refers to as the "Original Position," they will agree on two principles of justice. The first will be that each person is to have "an equal right to the most extensive liberty compatible with a similar liberty for others." The second will be that economic inequalities are to be set up so that they will benefit the least advantaged and be attached to positions open to all. The people in Rawls' Original Position will agree to abide by such principles and set up their social institutions to reflect them. In his newest book, *Political Liberalism*, Rawls revises positions he worked out in *A Theory of Justice*. He takes account of the fact that modern society is not as homogenous as the first book suggests, that it is composed of those who hold incompatible and often irreconcilable points of view, and that fairness in a democratic society requires tolerance. Moral agreement may not be possible, but Rawls argues that agreement can be reached on a political conception of justice that will at least champion toleration. It will, therefore, embody a principle of extensive individual liberty.

two principles Rawls has identified. It can be maintained that those principles were the result of a fair bargaining situation involving those, like ourselves, who will live under them or at least that those principles would be chosen by people like us, including us, if we were placed in the Original Position. There is a great deal more to Rawls' theory, but the above sketch is sufficient for present purposes. Not particularly relevant here is the analysis of Rawls' principles of justice or of the modifications he provides to bolster his theory with a model of rational choice and the concept of "reflective equilibrium."[53]

Rawls' theory of justice is, on two crucial counts, individualistic in the extreme, and therefore I think we should find it inadequate to address the moral and political issues of our contemporary corporately saturated society. In the first place, Rawls' theory is metaphysically individualistic. By that I mean that, for him, individual humans are the primary elements of social life. The essential characteristics of each human are independent of his or her relationships with others or the positions he or she occupies in the institutions and organizations of society.[54]

In effect, for Rawls, all human dependencies are contingent, not necessary to the human person's identity. Rawls might find the identity problems of the Texas bankers perplexing. On his account, they should not think of who they are as so completely and inexorably bound to their corporate roles. In this, Rawls, I think, evidences an academic's perspective. Faculty members seem to feel less of an identification with their institutions than with their disciplines. But in that respect they are rather different from most Americans who work in corporate settings. Academics tend to think of themselves as chemists or sociologists first and employees of this or that university or college second. Universities, for them, are seen to retain a cherished medievalness despite the corporatization of their administrations. Faculty members typically imagine themselves to be essential to the stability and preservation of the specific academic community in which they have secured jobs. It is not just that they are the Civil War historian, the nineteenth-century English poetry expert, and the geneticist. They are the unique historian, poetry expert, and geneticist in whose absence this school would not be what it is and would probably lose its academic reputation, students, everything. Administrators tend to take a less medieval view of the whole business of higher education. The better ones have come to grips with the fact that universities are businesses and faculties are comprised of interchangeable agents. In any event, the position Rawls defends stands squarely against that articulated by F. H. Bradley who wrote:

> What we call an individual man is what he is because of and by virtue of community . . . if you take him as something by himself, he is not what he is . . . [T]he child at birth . . . is born not into a desert, but a living world, a whole which has *a true individuality of its own,* and into a system and order. . . . [55]

The preceding discussions of the corporate invasions were intended, in part, to expose the failings of a metaphysical individualist's conception of society. However, they were not meant to endorse a Bradleyian conception. I am not suggesting that in the absence of the corporations we would not be something: individual human persons. We need only formulate our conception of society for the purposes of ethics to reflect its pluralistic character. By "pluralistic," I mean that society is not reducible to one type of component unit and, therefore, that any attempt to discuss the moral and ethical issues within society will be inadequate if it depends on a monistic, atomistic individualism as its metaphysical base.

F. H. BRADLEY (1846-1924) Bradley was one, perhaps the best known, of a number of late-Victorian British philosophers who were strongly influenced by the work of the German idealist G. W. F. Hegel (1770-1831). Bradley was also influenced by the theories of Charles Darwin. Although Bradley made contributions to the literature of most of the major fields of philosophy, in ethics he attacked both the Kantians and the Utilitarians and created a kind of self-realization theory whose centerpiece is the idea that everyone has a place or station in society. The community or society is an organic whole and individuals are merely parts of it. Outside of the community they have no real identity as individuals. Realization of self amounts to finding where one belongs, discovering one's place, and then fulfilling the duties of that station. Bradley maintained that once you had grasped the fact that you are but a "pulse beat of the system," found your role in the community, you would, by intuition, come to appreciate what you had a moral duty to do. As long as a person performs the duties of his or her station, he or she will be an ethically good person. Nothing more could or should be asked of a person. (See F. H. Bradley, *Ethical Studies* [1876].)

Rawls' other individualism is of the moral variety. By that I mean that, for Rawls, only human persons and their interests and welfare are to be given any moral (and political) value. No claims with real moral weight can be made by or for nonhuman actors. The governing consideration in Rawls' theory seems to be that "what makes any socio-political arrangement good is that it constitutes or brings about something . . . that is good *for* people,"[56] for humans.

Rawls' theory is so individualistic that the whole procedure from which it is supposed to emerge, the bargaining game of the Original Position, is ultimately reducible to the "standpoint of one person selected at random."[57] Such a reduction can be worked because Rawls insists that no significant differences exist between the parties of which any are informed while in the Original Position, each must be convinced by the same arguments, and all will arrive at the same conclusions about the principles of justice. "Therefore, we can view the choice in the original position from the standpoint of one person selected at random."[58] In effect, one human is as good as any other, and the conference of many can be reduced to the decision of one. That is extreme moral individualism.

I see there are many problems not only with Rawls' version of liberal individualism, but with other types of liberalism as well.[59] Liberal individualists attempt to formulate the moral and ethical principles by which the organizations of any social system are to be judged without paying attention to the actual elemental units of the societies in which those principles are to be applied. Not only do the liberals, like Rawls, arrive at abstract principles that are somehow to be applied to concrete social problems, they do so by deriving them from abstract social units that can represent only a portion of the membership of society.

Recent communitarian criticisms of Rawls' and other liberal theories generally hit the mark. A morality constructed from the abstractions of Rawls' Original Position, one that systematically ignores the common (in the sense of ordinary *and* the sense of shared) experience of social living, is unlikely to produce any standards or principles that will be applicable to actual communal life. On Michael Sandel's account, the persons in Rawls' theory are "radically disembodied subjects" when they need to be understood as "radically situated" in order to have the motivation and the capacity for deliberation required for rational choice.[60] The utter detachment of the parties in the Original Position renders their choice of principles merely arbitrary.[61]

Unfortunately, if we recognize that the social world has more than one kind of elemental unit, we lose the neat, clean, antiseptic approach to ethics that Rawlsian moral individualism provides. Things are messy, and philosophers have never much liked that. But then, from as far back as Plato, philosophers haven't much cared for treating society as it actually is.[62] Rawls himself noted that if he did not place the veil of ignorance limitations on the parties, "the bargaining problem of the Original Position would be hopelessly complicated."[63]

There really is no bargaining in Rawls' Original Position as conceived in *A Theory of Justice*, because there are not really two or more parties each bringing different interests to the table. Everything immediately reduces to a single person deciding on the principles of justice. A person doesn't bargain with him- or herself. Nonetheless, the fact is that society in the postcorporate invasion world is complicated, and if we are going to do a reasonable job of addressing real ethical problems, problems of justice and right and responsibility, we must confront those complications. An abstract ethics of metaphysical and moral individualism simply will not do.

Let's look more closely at Type Two interrelationships and interactions to see why ethics appropriate to Type One, individual human to individual human, interactions may be inadequate to Type Two. Type One ethics are typically based on the relative equality of the parties. That is, they tend to treat equality of the parties as a baseline and most of the rest of their ethical principles and rules as adjusters and reequalizers designed to keep things as close as possible to the baseline.

Hobbes famously anchors his account of the state of nature, and ultimately the social contract, in a proclamation of basic human equality:

Nature hath made men so equall, in the faculties of body and mind; as that though there bee found one man sometimes manifestly stronger in body, or of quicker mind then another; yet when all is reckoned together, the difference between man, and man, is not so considerable, as that one man can thereupon claim to himselfe any benefit, to which another may not pretend, as well as he.[64]

If anything is obvious in our world, however, it is that humans and corporate actors are not equal in morally important respects and pretending that they are is mere fantasy. A vast power asymmetry exists between humans and corporations that no ethical theory should whitewash. In fact, many of the powers humans do enjoy are dependent on corporate contexts. That should come as no surprise, because all power is social-context dependent.

Suppose we define power in terms of the capacity for control in any situation. To have power in a situation is to be able, if one wants, under certain conditions to cause an outcome or to prevent one from coming about. If some person or actor has power with respect to a particular occurrence or event, that person or actor can perform some intentional action or actions at a crucial time that will ensure that the event will occur, and that same person or actor can perform some intentional action or actions that will prevent that event from occurring. In effect, to have power in a situation is to have control with respect to it.

John Martin Fischer identifies two different kinds of control.[65] Typically, when we think of someone being in control of a situation, we mean that person actually has causal control of it. If I'm in control of my car, then I cause it to move in the way it does. If I lose control, the car moves without my causing it to do so. Other than actual causal control, a person will have what Fischer calls "regulative control" if that person has the ability both to ensure the occurrence of an event and to prevent its occurrence. Fischer's example is of an airline captain whose plane is flying on automatic pilot. The computer turns the plane to the west and the pilot doesn't intervene, but the pilot has the ability to ensure that the plane will turn west. For example, should the computer instruct the plane to turn south, the pilot can switch to manual control and bring it around to the west. By the same token the pilot can prevent its turning west by overriding the automatic pilot. Fischer's way of putting this is that "the outcome is here *responsive* to the pilot."[66]

It seems to me undeniable that by any measure of actual causal and regulative control, corporations are far more powerful than individual humans with respect to most things in our society. The range of events over which they have regulative control is enormous and humans, especially in the political arena, throughout this century, from Theodore Roosevelt's trust-busting to the post-Watergate restrictions on corporate political donations, have been trying to contain that power. Practically, however, there seems to be almost no way to level the playing field in most Type Two interactions. Corporate resources are significantly greater and can be marshaled to support corporate interests in ways that most humans could never hope to duplicate. As it happens, most human financial resources are tied up in corporate endeavors and are dependent upon corporate successes in achieving corporate ends, as depositors in failed banks and savings and loans have sadly discovered. Many humans found out that their money, or what they thought was their money, was under the actual causal and not just the regulative control of corporate actors.

Perhaps more importantly, as mentioned above, most of the power or control that humans have in both Type One and Type Two interactions depends upon a wider social context created and sustained by corporate actors. Many college professors of my acquaintance seem to think that they wield considerable power over their students because they grade them. Some have tried to take advantage of that situation in ways that can only be described as harassment. Thomas Wartenberg has pointed out that "the teacher-student relationship is extremely complex and is constituted by a multiplicity of overlapping and conflicting tendencies."[67] The professor's power, as Wartenberg notes, however, is not merely interventional, a result of the actions the professor performs. It is structural, a feature of a wider structure in which the relationship between professor and students is located. Wartenberg calls it situated.

> According to the situated conception of power, one needs to move beyond the classroom itself in order to gain an adequate understanding of the power of the grade, for the teacher's power over the student is constituted by the actions of social agents peripheral to the central dyad.[68]

The idea is that many institutions and corporate actors enable the professor's power of the grade over the student. Power, especially among humans, is seldom a simple one-to-one relationship. Suppose the professor decides to fail the student in the course. The social elements peripheral to the professor-student power relationship might then be revealed as including the university in which the course is offered and which will now not graduate the student, the student's parents who will not provide the lavish support previously expended on the student, the law schools to whom the student has made application that will now reject the student, the legal firms that now will not offer the student a job, and so on. The social corporate circles involved may be quite wide. In isolation from these mostly corporate actors, who may not play an obvious role in the professor-student relation, the failing grade has virtually no negative effect, and so in the absence of them the teacher has little or no power over the student. It is the alignment of those peripheral social elements of corporate, mostly, actors that really gives the professor power over the student through the instrument of grading.

The power of corporate agents, like Kim S., is more obviously situated, however. The power of Mazda itself is also situated. That is, it also depends on a peripheral network of mostly corporate actors in much the same way as does human power. Still, corporations have far more power and control than humans because they, by and large, structurally constitute the situations in which humans, whether personally or as corporate agents, exercise power.

Corporations, however, do pay a price for the power imbalance. For example, in Type Two interactions, they get little sympathy when they are shortchanged or cheated by humans. Coleman writes:

> There is evidence that individuals do not feel bound by the Golden Rule in their interactions with corporate actors (for instance, there are persons who will cheat the telephone company but not another person).[69]

Two points are worth making: corporations are not always the villains in Type Two interactions, and the little guys are not always in the right just because they start off with a significant disability. Cable television systems have been particularly hard hit by humans who believe that if they steal from a corporate actor it isn't counted against their moral record. Recently the cable TV company in San Antonio, Texas, uncovered thousands of illegal drops (people tapping into its lines). When offenders were interviewed, they expressed little or no remorse, generally insisting that it was a big company and wasn't really being damaged by their piracy of its programming. It was not surprising that the majority of those in the city who were polled about the situation thought that the cable thieves should not be penalized or prosecuted.

I spoke with a security officer for a major supermarket chain that was installing detection devices at every checkout stand and entrance to its stores to catch shoplifters. He told me that theft of foodstuffs had reached epidemic proportions and that the prevalent attitude of the shoplifters was that the stores were charging too much for the goods and wouldn't really suffer from the loss of a few things here and there. When asked if they would think the same about taking things from their neighbors, they responded that that would be a different matter altogether. Stealing from a corporation and stealing from a fellow human are not put on the same moral footing. Even the nicest people, I've been told, will pad insurance claims without giving it a second thought.

These types of human misbehavior aimed at corporate actors reveal another major difference between them. Humans respond differentially to each other, treating those among them that they regard as unsavory with suspicion and caution and those with whom they are closely associated with kindness and trust. Corporations are typically unable to make such discriminations and so tend to treat all humans the same. Hence, those of us who do not shoplift are still forced to go through the detectors, and we all have our insurance claims double-checked.

8.The Realization of Corporate Goals by the Exploitation of Human Weakness of Will: The Twisted Tale of the Advent of the Commercial Television Situation Comedy

It is interesting that in some things we expect more of corporate actors, honesty and accuracy, for instance, than we do of human persons. But in other things we expect less, for example, understanding and forgiveness. I want to argue that corporations so easily maintain so great an imbalance of power *vis-à-vis* humans largely because of a fundamental intrinsic difference between corporations and humans with respect to the springs of action. Because of that difference, corporations are both particularly well suited to becoming and remaining ethical and to exploiting natural human motivational weaknesses. The latter is especially true of all-too-human weakness of will.

The standard philosophical examples of weakness of will usually involve cases in which people break vows or resolutions, giving in to the temptation of immediate satisfaction.[70] In effect, weakness of will amounts to letting short-term interests and goals overwhelm those of the long term. The dieter cannot resist the double chocolate cake his wife has baked and so, despite his resolution to lose weight for long-term health reasons, he indulges, telling himself that he must not offend his wife and that he will cut back on his calorie intake even more tomorrow or tomorrow or tomorrow. Well, sometime in the future; and what's a guy to do?

There are many accounts in the philosophical literature of weakness of will, ranging from the view that it really doesn't occur at all to accounts of how it is a basic fact about humans. The latter seems to me to be nearer the truth. Let's face it, humans are self-indulgent creatures who really have to work to exercise willpower. They prefer to succumb to their short-term interests, gaining the full satisfaction and benefits they expected, and then feel badly about it in the morning. When one human interacts with another, both are prone to weakness of will or to attempting to achieve short-term benefits.

> Some may be able to withstand their impulses better than others, and thus may attain better outcomes in the long term. Some may even be able to exploit weakness of will in others and achieve more at their expense . . .Weakness of will is a part of the human condition . . . to which

all persons are subject. Precommitment, keeping in mind long-term consequences, and other mental efforts may reduce its effects, but it is a human characteristic.[71]

At a more concrete level, we have ample evidence, albeit anecdotal, that sustaining the long-term commitment over the short-term benefit is especially difficult for most of us humans. Mañana never comes! But, of course it does, and usually with a fury and a bill that is much bigger than we thought we'd agreed to pay. Whole industries now are flourishing that have the sole aim of keeping us on one right long-term track or another, despite our inclinations to immediate gratification. The diet industry, the health club industry, Alcoholics Anonymous, stop-smoking clinics: the list goes on and on. For every enjoyable indulgence there is somebody or some company trying to help us stop impulsively indulging. And their message is the same: recognize your long-term interests and work to realize those or you will have no long term in which to continue to gratify your short-term appetites.

The CID structures of corporate actors can be designed so that they are not prone to weakness of will. They can be specifically built to override human weakness of will. Perhaps that is one of the reasons humans view them with the same sort of suspicion the human characters in science fiction view androids that are not capable of being tempted by double chocolate cakes. What Coleman calls precommitment[72] is built into most CID structures. Long-term planning and interests, in the form of corporate policies, typically dominates decision making in CID structures. That does not mean that corporate actors cannot or do not act impulsively. Of course they can and do. And when they do, it is usually because they think that short-term interests need to be satisfied to further long-term ones. In this sense, they are quite different from human short-termers. Most dieters, for instance, have no doubt about the fact that those two pieces of cake are going to set back their long-term interests in weight reduction. This is not to say that many a corporation hasn't tried to take the short road to financial success. The corporate history of the 1980s is replete with examples. The leveraged buyout frenzy and junk-bond financing of that period provide abundant evidence that corporate actors and their agents can be blinded by quick bucks and short term windfalls. But even in those cases, the corporate actor was not evidencing weakness of will. Bad judgment, even outright stupidity, is not weakness of will. Long-term rational interest in profitability, by and large, still governed and was not overridden by, say, human personal lust for a new plant location because sunny Arizona is a great place to live.

Corporations, we should admit, have decision structures constructed, unlike human minds, to focus their actions on and to maintain a virtually unswerving commitment to specific long-term goals and plans. This distinct difference between corporate and human decision mechanisms, however, allows corporations to exploit human weakness of will without serious concern about reciprocation. The playing field is seriously tilted. Consequently, our moral reaction to their doing so is markedly different from the way we respond to humans who are able to capitalize on their fellows' susceptibility to seek short-run satisfactions. The corporation's near invulnerability to that to which we are so prone undoubtedly fuels our mistrust of corporate actors, and the fact that we don't regard their exploitation of our weaknesses as worthy of praise, in the way we do if the same debility is played to victory in a contest between humans, provides further evidence of our, at least vague, awareness of the power imbalance. When we discover how they have used their inherent advantages against our weaknesses, we typically express resentment and anger at corporations. The important moral question is whether we should be angry or we should give them credit and lay the blame at our own doorsteps.

Nowhere is the power of corporate actors to profit from their ability to sustain long-term interests and exploit the weakness of will of most human persons more evident than in marketing and advertising: from cars to perfumes, from beer to underwear, from frozen dinners to motion pictures, from motel chains to television sets, from virtually anything a human consumer might imaginably use to virtually anything else that a human wouldn't imagine using but can be persuaded to desire more than anything else. Beer is advertised with bikini-clad voluptuous women bouncing around on a beach; automobiles get a similar treatment. Ads urge us to buy now, use a credit card, and pay it off in the future. Actually, of course, paying it off seldom happens, and the finance fees and interest are more than twice, in fact closer to three times, as high as the rates offered for savings accounts.

A significant difference has often been pointed out between buying consumer goods using a credit card and using a layaway plan. Layaway goods are not received until the payments are completed. When one enters a layaway scheme, one is making a commitment in favor of one's long-term interests in the product, rather than immediate gratification and an inflated price that now includes monthly finance charges at 16-19 percent APR.

Turning Americans into credit-oriented consumers was the primary project of the corporate invaders following the Second World War. The story of the consumerization of America is indicative of the power of corporations in manipulating human weakness of will. Its unequivocal success spotlights some of the basic ethical issues in Type Two interactions that will be of concern in later parts of the book.

It is the story of the calculated use of commercial television in the 1950s to destroy a style of human life and create one in which the corporate actor's power in Type Two interactions was secured. The war had provided a temporary economic reprieve from the Depression, but at its end manufacturing corporations needed to develop new markets for new products. To do that, they had to rebuild the confidence of the people in capitalism and convert them into unrestrained consumers. That required discouraging habits of generations that were firmly entrenched in the ethnic backgrounds of the majority of the human population.

> The Depression years had helped generate fears about installment buying and excessive materialism, while the New Deal and wartime mobilization had provoked suspicions about individual acquisitiveness and upward mobility. Depression-era and wartime scarcities of consumer goods had led workers to internalize discipline and frugality while nurturing networks of mutual support through family, ethnic, and class associations.[73]

The future was looking rather gloomy for American corporations. If they were going to prosper, they had to reverse middle- and working-class patterns of behavior and unteach the hard lessons of the recent past. They had to break the hold of fiscal caution that had been fostered by the ethnic traditions of Europe and by the economic and political events of the 1930s and '40s. Television was the godsend of the American corporation.

At first the novelty of the "box" sold them to many households. The day the first family on the block got a TV is etched forever in many of our memories. On my block, it was a friend's family three houses down. The screen measured only nine inches and was octagonal. I tore into the room just as they were plugging it in and turning it on. The screen filled with nothing but black and white specks dancing about wildly. We all, young and old, sat there for a few minutes staring at it. What was going to happen? I don't know what we expected, but nothing changed. My friend's father grabbed the rabbit ears antenna and started jiggling it. Still snow. I suggested that maybe it was not set on the right station. Was there a dial to turn, like on a radio? There was, but they were channels, not stations, I was told by my friend. They clicked when you turned the knob. We tried another channel and another, until the granular specks were replaced by a test pattern. Although this was New York, the image on the screen was a head of an Indian surrounded by a bunch of numbers. Someone wondered aloud if that was all the box did. No one joked. There was something reverential in everyone's attitude. Self-doubts were expressed. It must be something we'd done. My friend, rather discouraged and embarrassed about having us all over to see his TV, turned the knob again and the miracle happened. On the screen appeared, in glorious black and white, a cowboy riding across the vistas of Texas (or Arizona or California, it didn't matter; it had cacti). Out of the speakers blared—no blasted—galloping hooves heading to the inevitable showdown with the bad guy, probably a banker. We'd been fiddling with the knobs and had paid no heed to which was which. His mother yelled that we would wake the dead. As there were no cemeteries in the near vicinity, you get some idea of how loudly those hoofbeats sounded to those gathered in my friend's living room. It was Sunset Carson. Sunset Carson! I'd seen the movie, *The Cherokee Flash*, about a year before at the corner theater's Saturday afternoon show. It was the second feature on the bill along with a serial, five cartoons, *Movietone News of the Week,* and three sing-alongs, all for fourteen cents. Oh, it was Sunset Carson all right, though he'd been shrunk from that impressive huge image on the movie screen to just about one and a half inches tall. Still, this was incredible. Next week, Allan "Rocky" Lane in *Rustlers of Devil's Canyon*, then Johnny Mack Brown in *Range Law*. Who could believe it? Sunset Carson was riding the range right in my friend's living room. Who would ever again pay fourteen cents to see him do it in the movie theater?

The Sagebrush Trail Theater and similar old movie formats could hold the attention of the neighborhood for a while and sell TV sets, but they weren't selling much else. Network programming was created to do that. The manufacturing corporations had to turn wary humans into eager consumers, that is, they had to first create short-term desires and then exploit human weakness of will, luring them to forego their long-term interests and go in debt to buy the latest model of this or that appliance or gadget. The way they accomplished the feat was masterful. They funded the creation of situation comedies that ostensibly extolled the virtues of the old, ethnic-based values, while they subtly—well, sometimes not very subtly—converted the role models they had molded into full-fledged avaricious consumers. The message came through loud and clear.

From about 1949 until 1958 the television screens of America were filled with urban, ethnic, working-class-family situation comedies. The Italians had *Life With Luigi* (set in Chicago); the African-Americans were given *Amos 'n Andy* (set in Harlem); *Mama* provided the Scandinavians with a focus (set in San Francisco); *The Honeymooners* and *Hey, Jeannie* were for the Irish (set in Brooklyn); *Life of Riley* was aimed at the working-class migrants out to find the end of the rainbow in sunny southern California; and *The Goldbergs* (later *Molly*) featured working-class Jews living in an overcrowded Bronx tenement. At first blush, it might appear that setting its prime time shows in ethnic, economically depressed, working-class households would not likely advance the goal of promoting corporate sponsors' products. Why were they showing worn-out kitchens and people riding buses and subways, if they were advertising Westinghouse refrigerators and Chevrolet cars during the commercial breaks? The idea was to sell those commodities, wasn't it? Lipsitz comments:

[T]he mass audience required to repay the expense of network programming encourages the depiction of a homogenized mass society, rather than the particularities of working-class communities.[74]

So why give the people evocations of their ethnic origins and the difficulties of working-class urban life? You want them to move to the suburbs, become homogenized, start buying the new Fords, new and improved General Electric washing machines, this year's model this or that. You want to destroy ethnic identity and its link to the notion that one should sacrifice in order to realize long-term interests. The situation comedies of that period

> . . . displayed value conflicts about family identity, consumer spending, ethnicity, class, and gender roles that would appear to be disruptive and dysfunctional within a communications medium primarily devoted to stimulating commodity purchases.[75]

That's how it may have seemed on the surface, but what was actually happening was the carefully orchestrated legitimizing of the change in American society that the corporate invaders required for their sustenance. And it was happening to us, the humans sitting in front of the magic box.

The ethnic sitcoms drew huge audiences. Their story lines contained a basic structure: the ethnic traditions were not to be insulted, but they were to be slyly revealed to be outmoded, and to work against both individual and general social interests. A new ideology of consumer spending rather than saving for a rainy day, though it might occasion conflicts in the sitcom families, would always prevail. The workplaces of the fathers are not to be seen, and workplace problems are to be treated only as they intrude on domestic tranquillity.

Almost all of the tensions on the shows involved what Lipsitz calls "dilemmas of consumption"[76] within and among the sitcom families themselves. The near violent domestic fights in *The Honeymooners* usually end with Alice being appeased when Ralph buys her a household appliance or a new dress. Chester, in the *Life of Riley*, seemed able to restore himself to his wife's good graces—she who was always complaining that he never took her anywhere or bought her anything— only by lavishing some luxury or other on her. In *Mama*, the daughter, after learning that a friend's father has been promoted and so was able to pay for wallpapering his house, complains to Mama that Papa never gets promoted, and they never get new things. Perhaps he should give up carpentry and become a banker. Papa overhears the conversation and accepts a promotion to foreman that he was inclined to turn down because it was likely to destroy his friendships with coworkers. Fathers must not disappoint their children when it comes to providing the funds for new and better stuff. Children become the masters of the new family lifestyle, the first converts, then the teachers of consumerism to parents whose memories, habits, accents, fears, and commitments to long-term interests might have starved out many American corporations at that critical time in their existence.[77]

Perhaps the best examples of how the subtle shift was worked through television were on *The Goldbergs*. Originally set in a Tremont Avenue Jewish tenement in the Bronx, neighbors regularly participating in the family's squabbles *via* shouted conversations from window to window or down dumbwaiter shafts, the Goldbergs, and especially Molly, the mother, were systematically indoctrinated into the "American way," that is into the consumerism required for the flourishing of the corporate actors.

> In one episode . . . Molly expresses disapproval of her future daughter-in-law's plan to buy a washing machine on the installment plan. "I know Papa and me never bought anything unless we had the money for it," she intones with logic familiar to a generation with memories of the Great Depression. Her son, Sammy, confronts this "deviance" by saying "Listen, Ma, almost everybody in this country lives above their means—and everybody enjoys it." Doubtful at first, Molly eventually learns from her children and announces her conversion to the legitimacy of installment buying, proposing that the family buy two cars in order to "live above our means—the American way."[78]

Then the real conversion occurs. The Goldbergs decide to leave the ethnic urban neighborhood and move to the suburbs, to Haverville, the community of the "haves." While preparing for the move, Molly's daughter Rosalie persuades her to sell off all of the family's old furniture to help pay the downpayment on the new house, which is to be filled with new furniture bought on the installment plan.

By 1958, the conversion of America to a life-style of consumerism, the triumph of the weakness of will, was secured and the ethnic situation comedies, by and large, disappeared to be replaced by ones featuring homogenized families living in Havervilles or rather anywhere suburbia: *Father Knows Best, The Donna Reed Show, Leave it to Beaver, The Adventures of Ozzie and Harriet*, and so on.

Suppose we ask whether we *can* ask if the corporations that controlled the network programming in the 1950s did something morally wrong by exploiting human weaknesses, creating and nurturing the growth of the suburbs and turning America into a nation of consumers living in excessive debt. How that question should be answered is not at all self evident. What principles of ethics are appropriately applied to Type Two interactions? Are the same sets of rules and principles to be applied to both the human and the corporate parties to such interactions? Suppose we try that option first.

Exploiting the weakness of another for your own benefit would usually not be thought of as an ethical or moral thing to do. Immanuel Kant's famous ethical theory[79] surely decries such behavior. One way to formulate the basic tenet of Kant's conception of morality is that one should treat persons always as ends and never as means only. Kant meant that in our dealings with other people we are to regard them as having intrinsic worth and therefore never use them solely as ways to

IMMANUEL KANT (1724-1804) Kant is generally regarded as one of the giants of Western philosophy. He lived in the town of Konigsberg in what was then a part of Prussia. He was renowned for his methodical habits, especially his regular afternoon walks. A rather undistinguished professor, it was a reading of Hume's works that provoked in him the philosophical fervor that gave rise to his major contributions to Western thought. His metaphysics and epistemology have been most influential in both European and Anglo-American philosophy, but it is Kant's ethics that are relevant to the issues in this book. Kantian ethics are most often confused with the Christian Golden Rule, "Do unto others as you would have them do unto you." But that is far from Kant's position. Though he was clearly influenced by his Christianity, he founds his ethics in reason, not religion. The central feature of Kant's ethical theory is his conception of the unconditional moral command or what he calls the "categorical imperative." He formulates the categorical imperative in three ways, though he claims that all the formulations are ultimately equivalent and will never produce conflicting results. The first formulation is that a person should always act so that the maxim of his or her actions could be rationally willed as a universal law. Kant, in effect, is claiming that ethical principles as action-guiding rules must be able to be universalized without committing a logical contradiction, without offending rationality. A person morally must not lie because if lying were to become a universal rule—if everyone always lied—lying would have no sense. For lying to ever have any sense, people must usually tell the

continued on following page

bring about our personal goals. It might seem obvious that exploiting for your own benefit the knowledge that someone is likely to give in to the temptation to place short-term satisfactions over long-term interests violates Kant's principle. It would seem to if, for example, the parties in the interaction were both human persons.

If Ann, an excellent poker player, knows that Luis, a lousy poker player, has not the willpower to resist gambling away his hard-earned paycheck to her, she would be using him as a means to her aggrandizement should she entice him into a game. She might be doing something morally reprehensible, but I am not sure whether we should be confident in saying so. Perhaps there is more that we should want to know before we would pronounce her exploitation of Luis's weakness morally wrong, as using him only as a means to her ends. How did he come by the weakness? Is he aware of it? Is it something he can help? Can he overcome it with willpower? Does he have it because she has cleverly cultivated it in him? All of these seem like relevant questions from the moral point of view.

Immanuel Kant cont'd

truth. The very statement of the principle of always lying would break itself, for it would not be the case that one should always lie. Kant's second formulation of the categorical imperative is the one on which I have based the side constraints. It tells us that we are always to act in such a way that we treat humans as ends and never as means only. This formulation implies that humans have absolute worth, that they have dignity and integrity that must not be compromised, and that using them for one's own purposes without their consent would do just that. The third formulation requires ethical persons to act always as both subject and sovereign in a kingdom of ends. That means that ethical persons are autonomous. They both make and follow their moral rules, and they recognize that others do so as well. Kant's ethics are duty-focused, hence, using the Greek term for duty, they are deontological. In fact, Kant rather goes to extremes in his denial of the ethical value of any other motivation than duty. He does not think that actions that are motivated by our emotions or inclinations deserve moral credit. The consequences of what one does are not as ethically important as the motive or the reasons why one did it in the first place. Kant does capture some of our intuitions in this regard. Suppose, for example, that a man rushes out of his house and rescues a woman who is being viciously attacked. The rescuer wrestles the attacker to the ground and beats him unconscious. The police finally arrive and take the attacker into custody. The media lionizes the rescuer, but after basking in the limelight for awhile, the rescuer admits that the reason he risked life and limb was not because he saw it as his duty to protect the woman, but that he really gets a kick out of beating up people. The outcome of his actions, of course, was highly desirable, but his reasons for acting were hardly morally admirable. We should, on Kant's theory, give him no moral credit for rescuing the woman. A person's intentions are crucial to moral value, not just the consequences of what that person does.

(See Immanuel Kant, *Groundwork of the Metaphysics of Morals* [1785].)

If Luis has the weakness because of his own past actions, is aware of it, and has done nothing to overcome it, and Ann just happened to learn about it, we might think her somewhat less reprehensible than if she had been the one who corrupted him so that she could exploit his resources. It is probably worse to exploit those one has corrupted, because two moral principles are being violated: one prohibiting exploiting the weaknesses of others and another prohibiting corrupting them in the first place. The former is clearly a violation of the Kantian prohibition against using people as mere means. The latter seems, to me, to be an even more basic moral notion: corruption of anyone, including self-corruption, is bad.

In any event, the Kantian principle against treating humans as mere means has intuitive appeal, but perhaps primarily because of what we perceive to be the basic similarities of the parties. Both are human persons, and we generally believe that even though some of us have certain foibles that others do not, we all have, or are prone to, weaknesses that could be exploited to our disadvantage. We are all vulnerable to each other, some more so than others.

The weaker among us, we seem to believe, should be protected from being turned into slaves of the stronger. That is a central doctrine of Christianity, one against which Friedrich Nietzsche railed. Another of Kant's formulations of his basic ethical principle, the categorical imperative, tells us that we should act always so that we can will the maxims of our actions as universal laws for all humans. That has the ring of the Golden Rule to it, though on Kant's account they are not at all equivalent. Nonetheless, the Kantian universalization principle conveys the idea that one must consider that one could be the target of the actions one is contemplating and that should constrain one from choosing to do those things that one could not rationally will on oneself.

This raises a sticky problem for the application of such Type One interaction ethics to Type Two interactions. It might scuttle the attempt to make sense of the business of not using humans as mere means in corporate cases as well. Kant maintains that all of his formulations of the categorical imperative are basically equivalent. If, however, it is impossible for an entity to conceive itself as ever being the target of a contemplated action because it is not susceptible to the conditions presupposed by the action, then the rational element of the universalization formulation would not kick in and kick out the contemplated action. If the entity cannot be killed, for example, then how is it to universalize the maxim of its intent to kill someone in a way that includes itself? It cannot. The universalization of the maxim of its action might be "kill all entities of this type." Will it reject that maxim as irrational, as Kant would have it? No. It would only be irrational if there were some contradiction in the universalization, if to will it would be to will a contradiction. But there isn't any. Unless, that is, "type" is taken to refer to some category that includes all rational entities. It would not be rational to will the end of all rational beings, as that would amount to willing the end of rationality, making the action being willed irrational, and, of course, it would include willing the end of oneself.

But would it be irrational for a rational being that cannot be killed to will the destruction of all rational beings that can be killed? Maybe not, and if the simplistic Golden Rule is applied, the issues become both clearer and cloudier: Do unto others as you would have them do unto you. But they cannot, even if they were to try. Bertrand Russell is purported to have said, "The problem with Golden Rule ethics is that there is no accounting for taste." He might have added that there is no accounting for disproportionate degrees of power and control in them either, yet that is exactly how things stand in Type Two interactions. In short, a universalization ethics based in Type One interactions that assume basic equality of the parties could prove rather impoverished with respect to Type Two interactions. But there are other, perhaps more fruitful, possibilities regarding the Kantian principles.

9. Moral Side Constraints: Kant, Nozick, and Corporate-Human Interactions

Nozick characterized the Kantian principles, or more specifically the principle about not using people as means only, as side constraints on action.[80] A side constraint is a prohibition against doing certain types of things as one pursues one's personal goals. The idea is that you are not morally forbidden from, for example, amassing a great fortune, but you are prohibited from doing so by using other people as mere means to that end, for example, by stealing from them.

A side-constraint conception of moral principles can be contrasted with a goal-oriented theory. In a goal-oriented theory, the idea is to produce a society in which violations of the principle are kept to a minimum. But that does not rule out occasionally violating the principle in order to keep violations of it to a minimum in the society at large.

A goal-oriented conception of principles is incorporated in utilitarian ethics, whose lack of absolute prohibitions has left it prone to attack from those who imagine scapegoating-type scenarios to test its intuitive appeal. For instance: if cruise-ship passengers being held captive and tortured by a terrorist group would be freed providing they would sacrifice an innocent person from their ranks to be killed by the terrorists, would they be morally justified in doing so?

Utilitarians, it is widely—but I think wrongly—believed, support, as the basic tenet of ethics, a principle that says that an act is right in the circumstances if its consequences produce the greatest good for the greatest number of people. Their primary concern, it is said, is to ensure that the good be maximized over the population. Doing so could occasionally lead to sanctioning the use of people as mere means to that end, giving up the innocent passenger to the terrorists. That is a price that may have to be paid.

Utilitarians might agree to a constraint on scapegoating to the effect that using people as mere means to maximizing the benefits of the larger group are kept to the barest minimum, that they are allowed only as absolutely last resorts. Still, such a modified side constraint hardly does the work for which the Kantian prohibition was intended.

Nozick writes:

> Side constraints [of the Kantian prohibition variety] express the inviolability of other persons. But why may not one violate persons for the greater social good? . . . Why not . . . hold that some persons have to bear

THE UTILITARIANS: JEREMY BENTHAM (1748-1832) and JOHN STUART MILL (1808-1873)   Mill was a student of Bentham, the founder of utilitarian ethics. Both were British and concerned about the social and legal issues of British society, which was in the throes of the Industrial Revolution. Utilitarianism attempts to ground ethical judgments in empirical conditions. Bentham argued that an act is one that ought to be performed in the circumstances if doing it will maximize happiness for those people affected. Utilitarians emphasize the consequences of actions rather than the reasons acts are performed. What matters is the way things turn out with respect to the people affected by our actions, not why we did them. For Bentham, the happiness that an action is supposed to maximize was defined as pleasure, and he provided a calculus to both characterize the pleasures and evaluate them. The idea was that when deciding to do anything, one should apply the calculus to it and thereby determine whether or not it will likely increase pleasure. If it does so better than the alternatives in the circumstances, it is the right thing to do. Bentham's calculus included such questions as: How intense is the pleasure? What is its duration? How certain is it to happen? How free from pain is the pleasure likely to be? How many people will experience the pleasure? One of Mill's modifications of Bentham's version of utilitarianism was to take the ranking of pleasures out of the hands of every person and put it in the hands of competent judges. Where Bentham seemed more interested in quantifying pleasures and maximizing them, Mill was concerned about the quality of the pleasures as a crucial factor in determining what one ought to do. Mill argued that some pleasures are more valuable than others and so are to take precedence when we try to determine what is the right thing to do in the circumstances in which we find ourselves.

(See Jeremy Bentham, *The Principles of Morals and Legislation* [1789], and John Stuart Mill, *Utilitarianism* [1861].)

some costs that benefit other persons more, for the sake of the overall social good? But there is no *social entity* with a good that undergoes some sacrifice for its own good. There are only individual people, different individual people, with their own individual lives. Using one of these people for the benefit of others, uses him and benefits the others. Nothing more. What happens is that something is done to him for the sake of the others. Talk of an overall social good covers this up. (Intentionally?) To use a person in this way does not sufficiently respect and take account of the fact that he is a separate person, that his is the only life he has. *He* does not get some overbalancing good from his sacrifice, and no one is entitled to force this upon him . . . [81]

Nozick, not surprisingly given his radical individualism, ignores the possibility that the stability of the social system itself might require that entities other than individual humans thrive at the occasional cost of a disproportionate sacrifice of humans.[82] If, as I have argued following Coleman, corporate actors now sustain the society, then it may not be self-evident that the exploitation of human persons in ways that seem to serve the ends of those corporate actors, even if it occurs on a regular basis, is morally unjustifiable.

Can an ethics of Type One interactions of the Kantian side-constraint variety be made applicable to Type Two interactions as well? Should corporate actors be forbidden to treat humans as mere means? And vice versa? To try to answer that we should first get clearer about how the side-constraints conception is to be understood when applied in Type One interactions. Might it mean that I'm not to use you in any way toward the achievement of my ends unless you choose to be so used? If that were the case it would create an utterly unworkable precondition blocking most contractual dealings between us.

We aren't using those with whom we contract (for example, employees) as mere means just because those people haven't approved, and maybe wouldn't approve, of all of the things we intend to do through their agency. People get hired to do certain jobs and are paid on contracted wage scales or salaries. As long as they agreed to the wage, understand what they are employed to do, and consent to doing that, they're not being used as mere means, even if they don't or wouldn't approve of all of the ends to which those hiring them plan to put the results of their labor.

But we can tell the story a different way that may alter the intuitions to which it gives rise. Suppose that you would most definitely choose not to interact with me if I were to tell you the ends to which I intend to use your actions, your labor. I do not reveal them to you, though you, taking me to be a fine, upstanding fellow, never ask. You assume I am about some purpose you would endorse or, at least, not find objectionable. After our interaction is completed, you discover my purposes. Have I used you in a way that violates the Kantian side constraint? I paid you the agreed sum for your labor. Should the matter turn on your likes and dislikes, your tastes?

How much ought the fact that I had or should have had reason to think you would not approve of my plans count? Suppose you're a bricklayer, and I am secretly a Nazi official, and you have just built a sturdy building for me that, unbeknownst to you, I intend to use to warehouse Jews before gassing them. Suppose you are Jewish or have Jewish friends. Ignorant of my plans and the way your labor is to be instrumental in bringing them to fruition, most of us would agree, you have been used as a means and not treated as an end. In a similar kind of case, suppose you are vehemently opposed to abortion and I, a doctor, hire you, a carpenter, to remodel my clinic, never telling you that I intend to reopen it as an abortion facility. Suppose I have seen you on the TV evening news protesting outside of other abortion clinics. You are a member of Operation Rescue. I find the irony most amusing, my private joke. Were you used as a means and not an end?

I confess that my intuitions in the abortion clinic case are less clear than they are in the concentration camp case. Perhaps that is because I have not resolved the moral status of abortion in my own mind. That is my failing and should not affect our understanding of the way to deal with the cases, for what is relevant is not that I am certain about how I feel about the holocaust and vacillate on abortion, but how you feel, your beliefs, your commitments, what you stand for, detest, and so forth. If your views in the first case govern, then they should in the second. We should conclude that you were used as a means in both cases.

So, does that entail on me a moral obligation to explain my plans to you when I have reason to think that you would not interact with me if you were apprised of them? Would I be breaking the Kantian prohibition if I keep you in the dark? I am inclined to say that I would. It would seem then that the Kantian side constraints permit human persons certain rights vis-à-vis each other: in particular, the right not to be used in a way they would not have approved of were they fully informed of the goals of the person interacting with them. This sort of "right" is codified in informed consent laws regarding medical procedures and has especially come into play in cases where doctors doing research on alternative therapies are disinclined to apprise patients of the fact that they are being administered experimental drugs because that knowledge, in and of itself, may have an effect on the outcome. Courts and medical ethicists in hospitals have been in wide agreement that patients must be fully informed or their rights have been violated.

Another issue regarding the application of the side constraints is suggested by Nozick. At first, instances of it seemed to me to be obviously restricted to Type One interactions, but I now think that may not, after all, be the case. Nozick wonders:

> In getting pleasure from seeing an attractive person go by, does one use the other solely as a means? Does someone so use an object of sexual fantasies?[83]

The interaction between the parties in these cases is minimal. In fact, there may be no meeting at all. Across a crowded room. A crowded office. Yet, there does seem to be a sense in which the attractive person is being used as a means, and without his or her consent. Insofar as the interaction, such as it is, occurs in the mind of the viewer and the fantasy leads to no further actual interactions, the whole business may be harmless, though to be discouraged on moral grounds. The Kantian side constraints seem to have been overstepped. Of course, there is plenty of evidence to suggest that such fantasy encounters sometimes lead to unwelcome actual attempts. Some corporations, aware of the disruptive risks being run, insist on dress codes and nonfraternization to lessen the likelihood that fantasy may be turned into reality.

Spokespersons for the feminist movement (among others) regularly criticize corporate actors, who, though they may discourage sexual fantasy in their workplaces, wallow in it to sell their products. Are the attractive persons who are bounced around the television screens or draped over and about products being used as mere means and not treated as ends? It seems to me that if we use the gauge that they are well aware of the purpose for which their services have been contracted, if they know that they are jiggling about in skimpy spandex to entice an audience to buy Coors Light Beer or Chrysler convertibles or Orange Crush soda and contracted (consented) to do so, then they are not being used as mere means to the ends of the corporations. It has, however, been noted by many writers that the acquiescence of attractive people in commercials, and in such grand entertainments as beauty pageants, is a product of a male-dominated, fantasy-driven, immoral culture, and that the individuals in the skimpy clothes are the victims of many generations of the propaganda of that sort of culture. They are, on this account, being used as mere means, even though they have consented. Their consent is not really informed. This matter will be taken up in more detail in Part 2.

This seems to me to be an important argument and one that may be appropriate to those Type Two interactions of the 1950s in which corporations transformed the human public into the consumer nation required for the future well-being of the corporations. What might be superficially understood as acts of consent, because they were not fully informed, and especially if that lack of information was due to the actions of the party that stood to benefit the most, may be violations of the Kantian side constraints. In effect, such deliberate shielding of information makes the person benefiting more morally culpable.

If the ignorance is due to general cultural attitudes and conceptions that have grown and prospered for centuries, then the one benefiting may be morally culpable for taking advantage of them, for not trying to change them. But at least that person or corporate actor is not specifically causing the ignorance. In both types of cases the Kantian side constraints against using people are being violated, but the deliberate attempt to keep those used in the dark about one's motives seems to be the more unethical type of behavior. The companies that today, for example, advertise cigarettes on billboards with sophisticated people lounging around in beautiful surroundings might not be violating the side constraints at all, at least not with respect to their intended audiences, because those audiences generally are not ignorant of the health dangers of smoking. The tobacco companies today are not then as morally culpable as the rather large group of manufacturing corporations that produced the ethnic sitcoms of the 50s. Of course, for many years the tobacco industry deliberately did everything it could to keep consumers in the dark about the hazards of its product. Clearly, the

Kantian side constraints were then overstepped; assuming, of course, that the Kantian side constraints are applicable to Type Two interactions, and that is far from clear.

Let's explore that issue by reversing things a bit. Given that I have dwelled at some length on the way a number of corporations manipulated humans through television in the 1950s, suppose we look at the other side: is it morally permissible for humans to use corporate actors as means only? On many theories of the corporation based in the liberal individualism of the seventeenth century, that is all that corporations were created for, pure and simple. They are to be used as engines of profit for humans. Milton Friedman has written:

> There is one and only one social responsibility of business—to use its resources and engage in activities designed to increase it profits . . . in open and free competition . . .[84]

Well, okay for now (and more of Friedman later), but if we adopt such an account, as Friedman makes clear, the only way to understand any apparent corporate violations of the Kantian side constraints would be to translate them into Type One interactions. They are unethical actions of human persons who happen to be corporate executives or managers interacting with other humans, and that, in the majority of cases, as I have been arguing throughout, would be to utterly fail to appreciate the complexity of the contemporary social world. Remember that Kim S. is not personally interacting with me in my correspondence with Mazda American Credit. Despite the fact that ignoring reality and accepting the reductionistic individualism will help some economists defend their theories, fantasy is still fantasy. So it seems at least fair to ask: When humans use corporate actors solely as means to their personal ends, and surely many of us do, are they doing something immoral, something they ought not to do?

We probably could make a convincing case that, in so far as many corporate actors put company shares up for sale to humans (and other corporate actors) fully aware that most purchasers plan to use the shares to achieve personal financial gain, that the corporate actors are consenting to such a use, and so the Kantian side constraints are not violated in those cases. But in other cases humans use their corporate positions to treat their corporations only as means and not as ends. For example, a senior manager of a highly respected company might use that position to vault himself into the public spotlight for personal political or social gain.

Friedman cites types of cases in which executives use their corporate positions to perform acts of charity in the name of the "social responsibility of business" despite the fact that such acts are not consistent with corporate policies. To use two of Friedman's examples: Should a corporate executive "refrain from increasing the price of the

product in order to contribute to the social objective of preventing inflation, even though a price increase would be in the best interests of the
corporation"?[85] Should an executive "make expenditures on reducing
pollution beyond the amount that is in the best interests of the corporation or that is required by law in order to contribute to the social
objective of improving the environment"?[86] It should, of course, be
remembered, as quoted above, that Friedman is committed to a very
narrow definition of the interests of a corporation: increasing its profits. It might well be argued that both of the Friedman examples could
easily fall within the policies of many corporations, that trying to control rampant inflation and improve the environment could well be legitimate corporate policies with long-term profitability bases. But that
will be a matter for factual research, not mere theoretical speculation.
Within the CID structures of such corporations, in their policy statements or in their histories of actual corporate behavior, will be found
(or not found) the evidence.

Perhaps we should explore another alternative with respect to the
ethical differences between Type One and Type Two interactions. Let
us try the proposal that the Kantian side constraints are applicable to
Type One interactions and to Type Two interactions only when humans
are the object but not the subject of the actions. In other words, if what
is being done is being done to humans (whether by other humans or
corporate actors), then the prohibition against using others only as
means applies. But if corporate persons are the object of what is being
done, then the prohibition does not apply. This would support moral
condemnation of the corporations that conspired to turn the American
public into credit-dependent consumers, but it would not morally
reproach humans who use corporate offices for their personal or for
social benefit.

Still, not everything we do to or with corporations is likely to pass
moral muster. Unrestricted use of corporations for human personal
profit is probably going to offend our moral intuitions. That might be
because we can endorse an underlying element of Friedman's thinking:
that to use corporations for certain personal or social benefits would
actually be to use some other humans without their consent, particularly in cases where it will effect the corporation's profitability and so
the return it pays to its shareholders. For the moment let us grant this
point to Friedman. It is not as important as he seems to think. In some
rather notorious cases, someone achieved personal gain using the corporation as a means and not only did not harm profitability and stockholders' interests, but benefited them. They made windfall profits,
though perhaps at the ultimate cost of the corporation's long-term
plans or even its existence.

Also, it is not clear how this proposal is to deal with cases in which
corporate actors and human persons contract for mutual benefit.

Should the Kantian side constraints regulate the way the corporation deals with the human, but leave the human to do whatever he or she wants to the corporate actor?

10. The Moral Ranking System vs. Classical Utilitarianism

It might be useful to see if something comparable to the view Nozick defends with respect to the use of animals would satisfy our ethical intuitions if applied to the human use of corporate actors in Type Two interactions.

Nozick asks:

> Are there any limits to what we may do to animals? Have animals the moral status of mere *objects*? . . What entitles us to use them at all?[87]

I must admit that, with a majority of Americans, I relish a good steak cooked over a mesquite fire. I eat hamburgers more often than is probably good for my cardiovascular system, and I even enjoy an occasional veal or lamb chop. Some of my friends have tried to convince me that my diet is immoral, not because it is unhealthy for me (that seems of little interest to them), but because it's wrong to kill animals for the gustatory pleasure of humans.

I side with my animal protectionist friends on a number of fronts, if not on my diet. For example, I am repulsed by the hunting of wild animals purely for human pleasure. My revulsion is somewhat tempered, however, by the argument that, with respect to some game animals, there is a periodic need to thin the herds, to maintain a reasonable balance between the number of animals of a certain species and their food sources in a particular locale. I am prepared to grant that such a managed environment argument is persuasive, but still wonder if it justifies sanctioning humans hunting for pleasure. Maybe.

If culling the herds is justified, why should it matter that the humans doing it are getting a personal kick out of killing? Wouldn't that be a desirable second effect? Does it matter morally how the herds are culled? Suppose a number of aggressively violent humans with strong preferences for iron pipes and tire chains are rounded up from America's urban areas. Would there be anything morally wrong with corralling the wild animals targeted for destruction and letting the sociopaths batter them with pipes and chains, thereby working off their aggression and sheer meanness? It would surely be unpleasant to witness, but so is a slaughterhouse. There may be positive gains for society if the aggressions of antisocial humans are taken out on animals and not on us.

Would there be something morally wrong with culling the wild herds by lobbing hand grenades at them? Of course there would. But why? And lest we forget, domestic animals are also raised to satisfy the dietary tastes of people like me. Do we have a right to breed and kill them just for that purpose? If we do, can we kill them in whatever way might please us?

All of these are interesting and important questions, but they don't need to be tackled here. I raise them only because they provide a framework in which to draw attention to Nozick's handling of these sorts of issues.

Nozick provides us with the following dictum:

Utilitarianism for animals, Kantianism for people.[88]

Sentient animals are to be placed in the same category as humans for the purposes of working out the utilitarian calculus, so Nozick's dictum requires that the total happiness (or utility) of sentient beings be maximized, while stringent Kantian side constraints against using humans as mere means are also in effect.

Animals can be sacrificed or used for the benefit of others, but only if those benefits are greater than the losses suffered by the animals. As it seems fair to assume that animals have certain interests in staying alive and that they express pain and suffering in ways that we can appreciate, benefits and losses for them can be factored into the maximization of total happiness. Animals can be justifiably sacrificed or used in ways that would run against their interests, only if a greater benefit to all sentient beings will be realized. We can use animals to better the lives of humans and other animals. So the use of animals in scientific research is justified, as long as it is intended to produce, for example, medical breakthroughs that will enhance human life, cure diseases, and so forth. It probably will not justify sacrificing animals to make cosmetics or to provide fur coats for socialites. Raising and killing animals for food for humans remains something of a puzzler with regard to the use of the utilitarian calculus.

Humans, protected by the Kantian side constraints, cannot be used against their wills for the gain of animals or other people. The application of Nozick's dictum, "Utilitarianism for animals, Kantianism for people," suggests—though he ultimately, and I think too hastily, rejects the idea—that entities are arrangeable on a moral scale such that those lower on the scale may be used against their wills as means "to achieve a greater total benefit for those not lower on the scale."[89]

Imagine three ranks or levels on the scale:

Rank A: Entities that under no circumstances may be used as means only;

Rank B: Entities that may be used as means only to benefit those in Rank A, but not for the benefit of those of this rank or lower;

Rank C: Entities that may be used as means to benefit any or all in Ranks A, B, and C.

In which rank do humans and corporate persons belong?

Classical individualists and economists like Friedman will put humans in Rank A and corporations in Rank B or lower. That would formalize the dictum "Kantianism for humans, utilitarianism for corporations." Human interests and goals, then, should not be sacrificed to better the situation of corporations. But why should humans be put in Rank A? Suppose there are beings in the universe that stand to us as we think we do to animals. For most people that is not difficult to imagine. One only has to read passages from a number of ancient sacred texts for examples of divinities that rank above humans and that are permitted (or permit themselves) to use humans as means to their divine ends regardless of whether or not humans have consented to be so used. Interesting, but I'm not at all about to pursue the issue of whether God has a place in the moral ranks. The morality of the stance taken by God in the Book of Job and in the story of Gideon in the Book of Judges has disturbed me since my college days, but I will resist the urge to say anything more about it here.

Rank B, as well as Rank A, might appear to capture the intuitions of an absolute Kantian side-constraint theory protecting humans from being used as mere means, so it shouldn't matter if humans are in A or B. But I do not think that is true. Admittedly, there will be no difference between the way humans are to be treated if they are moved from A to B, so long as there are no entities in Rank A or if humans do not know of the existence of any Rank A entities. Therefore, two questions are important: (1) Is this hierarchical structuring of entities the best way to conceptualize the post-corporate invasion social world for the purposes of ethics? and (2) if it is, what qualifies something to be in Rank A rather than in either of the other two ranks?

What are the alternatives to adopting the ranking system? The only alternative that leaps readily to mind is some version of our old friend, utilitarianism, as applied to all entities in the social mix. There are many ways to formulate the basic tenets of a utilitarian ethics. They all share the position that the consequences or outcomes of actions are their morally relevant features, that the reasons actions were undertaken are not ethically important.

The classical version of utilitarianism maintains that the way consequences are distinguished is in terms of the pleasure and pain to which the actions give rise. John Stuart Mill wrote:

> [A]ctions are right in proportion as they tend to promote happiness, wrong as they tend to produce the reverse of happiness. By "happiness" is

intended pleasure, and the absence of pain; by "unhappiness" pain, and the privation of pleasure.[90]

To hold the classical utilitarian theory of ethics, one must believe that pleasure, and so pain, can be quantified. Fred Feldman has explained this notion in a useful way. He writes:

> [L]et us suppose that every episode of pleasure can be given a score, or rating. We can pretend that there is a standard unit of pleasure, which we will call the "hedon." The pleasure resulting from eating a tasty meal might be rated as being worth 10 hedons . . Our second assumption is that episodes of pain can be evaluated in a similar fashion. We can call our standard unit of pain a "dolor.". . . The third assumption is the most difficult. We must assume that hedons and dolors are *commensurate*. This means, roughly, that you can add and subtract hedons and dolors.[91]

Using Feldman's version of the utilitarian calculus, if my hitting you in the face with a lemon custard pie gives me ten hedons of pleasure, but gives you eight dolors of pain, then the action has a pleasure/pain value of two hedons. This may be called its utility value. Another act I could perform in the same circumstances: giving you a magazine I had just sat down to read, we will suppose gives you three hedons of pleasure, but gives me one dolor of pain. Its utility value is also two hedons. It would seem that, for a utilitarian, there is no way to decide which of these two things is the right thing for me to do. Both have the same utility consequences. Both increase the pleasure of those in the world by two hedons. Isn't there something wrong with such a result?

One way that classical utilitarianism has been formulated is to say that an act is right, the thing one ought to do, if and only if its consequences have a higher utility than any other act the person could have done. If in those circumstances the only two things I could have done were to hit you with the pie or give you the magazine, then it would seem that, on the theory, there is just no way for me to do anything right. Neither has a higher utility than the other.

The proper formulation of the utilitarian's position, however, as Feldman clarifies it, is:

> An act is right if and only if there is no other act the agent [person] could have done instead that has higher utility than it has.[92]

Following that formulation, we would have to conclude, not that I can do nothing right in the circumstances, but that if my options are restricted to just those two actions, either would be morally permissible in the circumstances. There would be nothing morally wrong with my doing either.

It should be noted that this formulation of the classical utilitarian position differs from the way that theory is typically presented.

As I mentioned above, we are often told that the utilitarians maintain that an action is morally right only if it produces the greatest good for the greatest number of people. The problem here is "the greatest number." The Feldman formulation, one that I think does capture what John Stuart Mill was addressing, simply calculates in terms of pleasure and pain values in the particular circumstances. Therefore, if ten people are made ecstatically happy by an action and a million are pained to only a minimal degree, the action may pass moral muster. Broad distribution of pleasure is not necessary to maximize utility across a population.

In fact, the "greatest good for the greatest number" version of utilitarianism would require the maximization of two independent variables, the pleasure variable and the population variable. Trying to do that can produce not only extraordinary headaches, therefore skewing the calculus by increasing the dolors, but it can lead to utterly ambiguous results in which the highest pleasure to be realized does not have the widest distribution, a wider distribution of the pleasure would have a lower utility, and vice versa.

Suppose that Kim S. has two actions available to her in dealing with me on the property tax matter. In one case she can cancel the whole business, giving me ten hedons of pleasure, Mazda three dolors of pain. No one else, including herself, gets any pleasure or pain from this resolution of my problem with Mazda. I assume that Mazda has paid the bill (though it probably should not have) and that it cannot recover the sum. However, the money involved is small, extremely small, to Mazda. It is petty, petty cash. Hence, the three dolors may be generous. So Kim S.'s action would have a utility of seven hedons or a plus seven. Her other option is to refuse to cancel the charge, giving me five dolors of pain, Mazda three hedons of pleasure, and herself, because she is fed up with my carping about this, three hedons of pleasure. If she does that, this corporate action would have a utility of one hedon, but it would positively affect more parties than the action with the greater utility.

If utilitarianism requires Kim, that is Mazda, of which she is but the agent, to act so as to produce the greatest happiness for the greatest number of people, then Mazda, and Kim S., receive no moral direction from it in this case. Mazda, through Kim S., can either produce the greatest amount of happiness or give some happiness to a greater number of people in the circumstances. Both cannot be done. Should Kim S., acting for Mazda, choose to make a bunch of folks a little bit happier than they were, or make one person very much happier than he was? Of course, I know what I think should be done, and the Feldman formulation of utilitarianism supports my preference. It is the utility that should be maximized, even at the cost of distribution across a population.

An obvious objection to the purely hedonic interpretation of the utilitarian calculus will surely occur to you. It did to Mill. The theory seems to reduce all of what is valuable in life to undifferentiated amounts of pleasure. Are there no higher ends, noble pursuits, that outweigh the mere obtaining of moments of even intense pleasure? Shouldn't quality count as well as quantity?

Think of the following situation:

A wealthy man decides to give away $1 million to someone. He narrows his choice to two possible recipients. One, a medical researcher, says that he will use the money to further his search for a cure for an extremely rare disease that afflicts only the dozen or so males per generation of a small, remote tribe in the Amazon jungle, causing a loss of eye-hand coordination, making it impossible for them to successfully hunt an endangered species whose skins are used in ceremonial dances intended to ward off the disease. (No part of the animal is included in the tribal diet. They are vegetarians.) The other candidate wants to throw a drunken bash for two thousand people. He will rent a large hall, hire a famous rock band, provide all the beer his guests can guzzle, and lay out all the food they can eat. What would be the right thing for the wealthy man to do?

Clearly, the partygiver will produce the greater pleasure and he will do so over a greater population. A double maximization! But could it possibly be morally right to give the money to him rather than to the researcher, albeit there are serious moral ambiguities in the researcher's proposal? Isn't there something morally undesirable about encouraging feckless behavior? There must be more to ethics than merely increasing the amount of pleasure in the world. Shouldn't quality count as well as quantity? The researcher's pleasure in trying to find the cure, and, indeed, his ecstasy should he do so, are going to be factored, but shouldn't the relative value of medical research over partygiving be a part of the equation as well? Mill thought so. Feldman comments:

> We must assume that for each episode of pleasure there is a number that represents its quality. Perhaps a "low" pleasure, such as one of the pleasures allegedly enjoyed by those who engage in lascivious behavior, would rate a 1 or a 2. A "higher" pleasure, such as the pleasure one receives from exercising his intellect, would be scored a 20 or a 25. An even "higher" pleasure, such as the pleasure we experience when we behave nobly, would rate a 50 or a 60. In each case, the numbers represent the quality of the pleasure being felt.[93]

As Feldman points out, there are major problems with this way of factoring quality into the calculus. Most importantly, how do we know how to assign the numbers? Is the pleasure of exercising one's

intellect really ten or twenty times higher in quality than the pleasure of sitting around on a beach with some friends on a starlight night
with a campfire blazing, drinking one beer after another, singing lewd
songs?

Another concern ought to bother us. We are proposing to use classical utilitarianism as an alternative to the hierarchical ranking system approach. Do all entities, natural and artificial, count the same in
the calculus? Is one hedon of Mazda pleasure equivalent to one hedon
of my pleasure? It could be argued that Mazda's pleasure is either
greater or less than mine. Greater, in that when Mazda is pleasured,
presumably, a number of human persons, some Mazda agents, are also
pleasured as well. Less, because it is very difficult to imagine what
the pleasure of such a nonsentient being could be if not the pleasure of
its agents and their pleasure is already factored into the equation. Still,
Kim S.'s pleasure in all of this just wasn't corporate. Did she experience
some other corporate pleasure over and above her personal pleasure?
Does that double her pleasure? And do the pleasures of all nonhuman
sentient animals get counted in as well? Peter Singer argues rather
persuasively that all sentient creatures should be placed in the "sphere
of equal consideration of interests."[94]

I think the matter of corporate pleasures, indeed the whole business
of pleasure calculation in the contemporary social world, is hopelessly
tangled. Kim S., on my account, gets some personal pleasure out of one
of the options, but her personal pleasure is surely not corporate pleasure
writ small, nor is her personal pleasure derived from or a reduction of
whatever pleasure Mazda may be thought to have gained from dunning me. Her little satisfaction is hers, all hers, and she has it because
she was the Mazda agent that dealt with me, that endured my vituper-
ative remarks. Mazda can take no pleasure in that. But can a corporation take pleasure in anything? Well, they often say that they do.

As it happens, the day after I got that fateful letter from Mazda, I
received a package from the Lincoln-Mercury Division of the Ford
Motor Company. In the package, which included a beautiful poster of
a red Lincoln Mark VIII in a private parking place that had my name
stenciled on it, was a letter telling me that it was Lincoln's great pleasure to reserve a new Mark VIII for me. Lincoln had learned that I
was leasing a 929 Mazda and thought its product would be better
suited to my life-style. Parked next to the Lincoln was a Lear jet! Lincoln was apparently in the dark on two counts: my life-style and my
hassle with Mazda over property taxes.

The letter was signed by Robert C., a vice president at Lincoln. It
seems to me pretty obvious that whatever pleasure was involved on the
side of Lincoln, it wasn't Robert C.'s personal pleasure. None of this
was making him one iota happier. I doubt that anyone at Lincoln was

getting any pleasure out of this correspondence at all. But I also doubt that the Lincoln-Mercury Division of the Ford Motor Company was receiving anything comparable to what the classical utilitarian calls pleasure. After all, it's a corporation.

Whatever pleasure and happiness are, it is pretty clear that they must be felt states of sentient creatures. They are something experienced, states of consciousness or at least states of conscious beings. I don't know whether animals, such as my Shetland sheepdogs, can feel pleasure or experience happiness, but I certainly think that they can. They are conscious sentient beings. I'm not sure whether they are self-conscious, but if you knew my Shelties you would suspect that they are that as well. They would be taken into ethical consideration in a thoroughgoing utilitarianism of pleasure, the classical variety, but corporations are not sentient entities and so the sense of their feeling pleasure or undergoing pain must be either metaphorical or just a shorthand way of referring to the pleasure or pain of (some of) their agents. So adopting the classical utilitarian alternative to the ranking system approach seems to have the undesirable outcome that corporations will disappear completely from our ethical calculations.

If that happens, however, then the morally right thing for corporate agents, like Kim S., to do on most occasions would seem to be to act to favor the interests of people like me who stand to get a considerable amount of pleasure out of having their debts to corporations forgiven. Of course, if she adopted such a practice as her regular way of dealing with matters such as mine, Mazda would undoubtedly fire her. Her loss in dolors (and dollars!) would then probably outweigh my gain in hedons. Therefore, classical utilitarianism would recommend that she ought to act in roughly the way she did. But that will only be the case if she adopted a rule about favoring human debts over corporate actors and usually followed it. She doesn't have to do that to give me a break. So, just doing it in my case will be morally right, provided Mazda doesn't fire her or severely punish her for this one deviation from corporate policy. But, of course, the same argument will hold for every other similar case when each is considered in isolation. So each time she should favor the human over the corporation. But that would lead to her acting in accord with the rule that will surely result in her getting fired.

Furthermore, as noted above, if we adopt the classical utilitarian position across the spectrum of entities that can feel pleasure and pain, nonhuman animals, such as sea otters, will have moral weight (as argued by Singer), while corporate interests, such as those of Exxon, will not or will be taken into moral consideration only in a derivative way. The hedonic arithmetic would be exasperatingly complex, and the social world will be no better represented than it is in the atomistic individualist theories. Suppose we explore an alternative account of utilitarianism to see whether it can be profitably substituted for the ranking-system approach.

11. The Preference Utilitarian's Alternative

Singer describes preference utilitarianism as judging actions,

> . . . not by their tendency to maximize pleasure and minimize pain, but by the extent to which they accord with the preferences of any being affected by the action or its consequences . . . According to preference utilitarianism, an action contrary to the preference of any being is, unless this preference is outweighed by contrary preferences, wrong.[95]

Perhaps the best way to think of preferences is in terms of interests. A being's interests are, in effect, what that being prefers, or would prefer if it reflected on the relevant facts in a situation, assuming it has the capacity to reflect. Beings that are future oriented will have many more preferences than those that are incapable of conceiving of themselves as existing into the future. So they will count for more in the preference utilitarian's calculus. Still, a being may be said to have certain interests and therefore preferences even though we do not regard it as being self-conscious and so capable to conceiving of itself in a future time. It seems to me obvious that my Shelties have an interest in a number of things, including continuing to exist.

Singer notes that fish when hooked exhibit the sort of behavior that may be described as a preference for the cessation of the pain being inflicted on them, though we would not say that fish can conceive of their existence in the future and so prefer their own future existence to nonexistence.[96] Using the preference utilitarian's calculus that might justify a moral prohibition against killing fish by hooking them, but, if there are nonpainful ways to kill them (and assuming that their deaths are required to satisfy the preferences of humans) not against killing them. Fish are hardly my concern, but preference utilitarianism looks promising because it seems to provide some room for corporations in the utilitarian's moral world.

As I have noted throughout, corporations certainly have interests, and those interests are conceived of in terms of their future existences. Planning and development are central to corporate operations, regardless of the type of enterprise. Current expenditures are typically gauged against projected future earnings. It seems self evident that corporations can be described as evidencing preferences on all manner of matters, from politics to corporate image, from profitability to community cultural opportunities. A wrong is therefore done when a corporate preference is obstructed, when a corporate interest is blocked, unless that interest or preference is outweighed by contrary preferences of others affected by the action or its consequences.

To determine whether a corporate action is morally permissible is to work out a calculus that is not much different from the one used by the classical utilitarians. The difference lies in the substitution of interests or preferences for pleasures and pains. However, although such a substitution should allow corporations to have full moral consideration, the process is prone to the same problems that plague the classical utilitarian. Consider the use of television in the 1950s as a prime example.

Suppose we want to know whether the corporate advertisers should have used their power to control the content of the early sitcoms to forge an unsuspecting and ill-informed public into a market for its products. Corporate interests definitely required the creation of new markets to prevent the post war years from drifting into a Depression-era economic bust. The primary interests of many humans who worked for or were in some way dependent on the public's consumption of the products, salespeople, repairpeople, installers, and such would have aligned with those of the corporations.

But then there are the interests of all of those people who were being manipulated, whose hard-learned virtuous habits of frugality and patience were being assaulted, trampled, slyly maneuvered. Surely their preferences would have been, at least early in the process, to stay out of debt.

This gets even more complicated because after the programming and the advertising took effect, the preferences of a significant portion of those people probably shifted. Did what was in their interests shift as well? Then again, what was in their interests? The vitality of the economy on which they depended for most aspects of their lives and for the prospects of success of even their modest preferences was at stake.

It seems to me that preference utilitarianism will either have to sacrifice some people's preferences, and so interests, to the maximization of preferences or redefine preferences in terms of what is really in their interests even if they do not know it and so lack the preferences that they would have if they did. In any event, preference utilitarianism does not seem to escape the debilitating problems that beset classical utilitarianism, and it has a few whoppers of its own, albeit corporations can be, at least to some extent, accommodated within it.

12. The Return of the Ranking System and the Moral Side Constraints

I find myself drawn back to the hierarchical ranking system conception for dealing with the problems of ethics in our postcorporate invasion world. The utilitarian alternatives are not attractive because they are either unrealistic, failing to include major elemental units of society, or they are prone to such complexity due to interlocking and dependent interests that the corporate actors can be expected to prevail in any weighing of preferences. In many cases, that will likely offend our moral intuitions.

In the hierarchical ranking system, clearly, the best place to be is in Rank A. Those in all other ranks may be used to further the interests of those in Rank A. Rank A members are the only entities to which Kantian side constraints apply in an unqualified way, for although a Rank B-er may not use another Rank B-er to benefit him or herself, he or she may use the same Rank B-er to benefit a Rank A-er. As already amply noted, if power and control in the social world were the defining characteristics for entry into Rank A, corporations would be in, and humans would be out.

Power and control directly relate to the assessment of moral responsibility, but the possession of power and control does not relate to our notions of moral worth. Just the opposite seems to prevail in our ethical intuitions. Bullies are powerful, but clearly not thereby owed a higher moral status and more respect than those they bully. Chief executive officers of corporations, senior managers, presidents of various institutions, universities for example, usually have enormously more power than laborers, other employees, professors, and students, but their interests are owed no more moral respect or consideration just because they wield such power. In fact, one of the primary aims of most Western moral systems has been to defeat the notion that power translates into moral status, that "might makes right."

We might admire people who have attained the lofty positions of power in our society, but such admiration is not due them because they have achieved a higher moral ranking than we have. Many who have ascended to the power heights conveniently forget this. In some culture, seventeenth-century Japan, for example, power alone constitutes absolute worth. All other beings in the social system who do not have supreme power are treated as having only instrumental worth or value. Simply, their value is dependent on what they can do for those in power. An historical look at Rank A shows that in many cultures and often in our own, it has been reserved as the dominion of the gods. Many of those gods were bullies, and all had considerably more power and control than humans. It's not surprising that we are sometimes inclined to think of our current political and business Olympians as Rank A-ers. They, of course, have a tendency to encourage us to think of them in that way. I suppose that's natural.

We are often told that power corrupts. Those with power indeed evidence a tendency toward self-elevation, to basking in a self-created glow of absolute worth and irreplaceability in their special place in the social system. The glow, of course, is from artificial light, probably the lamp on their large mahogany desks. We are all replaceable in the positions we occupy. If social power is, by and large, tied to position, usually corporate position, as it surely is, then though the positions may endure, occupants are quite transient and so is their power. Moral worth, as anyone holding a Kantian side-constraint view would insist, should be more permanent than that!

The Greek (and the Nordic) gods were not elevated for moral reasons, a point made on a number of occasions by the Greek philosophers. The Judeo-Christian God, on the other hand, is generally presented as having a moral claim to the top rank. The point is that merely being strongest, smartest, most rational, most resourceful, freer, and the creator, whether god or human, has no particular moral force in securing one's place in this sort of ranking system.

Being in the top rank is solely a matter of right determined or identified by whether or not one can be used as a mere means to further some other entity's interests without one's consent without having one's rights violated, or which I think comes to the same thing, without having one's integrity compromised. Other abilities and capacities are not apparently relevant. Nozick points out:

> That a being can agree with others to mutual rule-governed limitations on conduct shows that it can observe limits. But it does not show which limits should be observed toward it ("no abstaining from murdering it"?), or why any limits should be observed at all.[97]

So, the crucial question is: What characteristics must an entity exhibit to gain Rank A status? Some are obvious and have been the primary consideration for centuries of philosophers interested in the membership criteria of the moral community. They include being an intentional, rational actor with independent interests and preferences linked to its long-term life planning, being capable of regulating and guiding actions by rational principles and of responding to moral evaluation. Most human beings, and, as I have argued, corporate actors as well, are said to possess those capacities. Perhaps both humans and corporate actors belong in Rank A: Kantianism for humans and corporations, utilitarianism for animals.

Not so quick. I think the list of characteristics required to be deserving of a place in Rank A is incomplete if it does not contain another qualification. We must remember that any actor or person in Rank A has a special privilege (or right) in the moral system: its ends cannot be overridden by its being used to further the ends of any other actor or person or entity of any rank. To use it as a mere means will always be wrong. Its integrity cannot be compromised without doing moral wrong. And further, others at lower ranks may be used as mere means to achieve its ends, to further its interests. The possession of what sort of characteristic or property would morally justify receiving such preferential treatment?

I realize that at this point matters are going to get a bit swampy for me. I could simply plea that I cannot come up with the requisite characteristic and slink back into something like a preference type of utilitarianism for all entities capable of preferences and interests. But I have rejected all versions of utilitarianism as inadequate to the situation. I could slip humans into Rank A on the grounds that they are natural actors, and assert coming by the functional capacities naturally is the requisite additional characteristic. But why should the mere accident of being biological rather than artificial count for so much?

"Actor," as I am using it, is not a natural-kind term. That something is natural, an animal, or "a sort of animal,"[98] is not especially relevant to whether it is an actor. Evidence that it has certain rational intentional capacities is what is crucial.

Remember the film *2001: A Space Odyssey*? We surely ought to root for the astronaut against HAL, the computer, but not because the one is an actor and the other is not. Both are portrayed as planning, purposive, self-motivating, project-makers that can, in David Wiggins' terms, "conceive of themselves as having a past accessible in experience-memory and a future accessible in intention."[99] The class of entities to be included in the moral world is formed around such a series of functional descriptions of actors. We should root for the human astronaut, Dave, against HAL because HAL is an intentional killer. It has killed a number of humans and has evidenced the intention to kill Dave. This is not an actor vs. non-actor issue. HAL has turned into a psychopathic killer.

On the other side of matters, I can imagine a day when, though I am still a human, I will not be a person, an actor, that I will no longer be a functioning member of the moral community. I may now have a number of desires about what should be done to me should that day arrive. Right now I hope someone will end my human life when I am no longer a person. At other times, I just as strongly hope that my biological functions will be maintained, even by extraordinary means, as long as possible, in case I should regain those crucial functional capacities. My euthanasia hopes vs. my cryogenic hopes.

In my case, as far as we know, I cannot be an actor, that is a member of the moral community, and not a human person. My functional capacities seem to require the human apparatus on which to perform. But that seems only a peculiarity of human persons. Anything that is a member of the moral community must have some way of evidencing that it possesses the requisite capacities or we should not be able to recognize it as such and so extend it the moral treatment it deserves. HAL has the structural elements of virtually the whole spaceship, Exxon has both human and machine components.

So what is left for Rank A? I could say, with a nod to the religious tradition, that the additional qualifying characteristic is divinity. But I won't. The characteristic we are looking for must be more morally significant than merely being a deity, even the Christian God of love and forgiveness. It seems to me that there is only one property or quality the possession of which justifies elevation to the status in question. It is not just a capacity for, but an unswervable commitment in all of one's actions to ensuring the maintenance of the basic social conditions necessary for all sentient beings to lead worthwhile lives.

Such a commitment is not purely altruistic, as Rank A-ers would know that they will benefit, as well as those in the other ranks, from the social stability they are ensuring. In effect, Rank A-ers cannot achieve their own ends without maintaining the conditions necessary for Rank B-ers to have the opportunity to lead what Rank B-ers would regard as worthwhile lives.

I am not equating being in Rank A with actually providing the functional structural stability of the social system. It may be one thing to do that and quite another to act so as to ensure that is done. Humans once were the "intrinsic part of the structure," but their interests and ends were clearly not essential to its stability and "the reorganization of society around corporate bodies made possible a radically different kind of social structure than before.[100]" Corporations may give way in the future to altogether different entities. Then they may become incidental to the majority of society's productive activity. For the present, however, ours is a corporate social world.

What is important with respect to Rank A membership is not being the dominant organizational component of society, but being an entity all of whose actions are charged with the commitment to ensure that a social structure consistent with the pursuit of worthwhile lives in all of the ranks is sustained.[101]

I am certain that no actual entities, neither human persons nor corporate actors, qualify for Rank A. Its population is entirely mythic. It therefore doesn't matter whether there are many Rank A-ers or only one. In that regard and others, Rank A membership might mirror Rawls' person(s) in the Original Position.

In Rank B are those humans and corporations that are intentional, rational actors with independent interests and preferences linked to their short- and long-term plans, and partial plans, capable of regulating and guiding their actions by moral principles and responding to moral evaluation. Nonhuman animals and humans and corporations who fail to qualify as Rank B-ers populate Rank C.

This means that corporate actors and human persons ought not use each other as mere means to their own ends. But it does allow them to use each other for the ends of those in Rank A. But Rank A is vacant, so it would seem that corporate persons and humans can never use any Rank B-ers as mere means. But that does not have to be the case. Although, as far as we know, no actual entity occupies Rank A, we know what an entity would have to be like to qualify. We know that among its traits would have to be that its ends are essential to ensuring the maintenance of the social conditions necessary for worthwhile lives. Rank B-ers are then justified in using each other as nonconsenting means only if in doing so they would be serving the interests of a mythical Rank A-er in the only way we can be sure would do so: by ensuring the preservation of the conditions necessary for Rank B-ers to try to lead what they would regard as worthwhile lives.

The Kantian principle forbidding the use of others as mere means is not a hard and fast side constraint on the actions of Rank B-ers. It is dominated or restricted by another side constraint: Other Rank B-ers can be used without their consent if doing so is necessary for the maintenance of the basic conditions for any Rank B-er to attempt to lead a worthwhile life.

13. A Defense of the Consumerization of America

It will, no doubt, be suggested that the dominant side constraint on Rank B-ers is just a disguised version of the utilitarian's principle. It isn't. The dominant side-constraint appeals to no calculus, hedonic or preferential. Instead, its content is determined by sociological and environmental facts. To render it meaningful in its application to any particular circumstances requires an understanding of the economic-environmental-sociological conditions in which the constituent members of society have the best chance of realizing their ends. In the post-corporate-invasion world, that requires taking into account the conditions necessary for the flourishing of corporate enterprises as well as human endeavors, as long as those enterprises and endeavors do not use other corporations or humans as nonconsenting means to their own ends.

I think that rarely will the content of those conditions come under discussion, but on those rare occasions the outcome of those discussions will be crucial to the well being of the society at large. Such a time was in the 1950s when the future of many manufacturing corporations was apparently at risk unless the human public could be converted into consumers financing their purchases by debt.

There was at the time, of course, no general discussion of whether the corporate actors were justified in using human persons in the way they did. But, could the corporations have successfully defended their exploitation of the humans by appeal to the limitation on the Kantian side constraints on the treatment of other Rank B-ers? I think they could. Doing so is not to provide a philosophical argument, but to offer something I would, with some reluctance, call a sociological-historical argument. In short, the argument would need to defend the following propositions:

1. The social world of the United States in the twentieth century is dependent for its stability on the flourishing of corporations. Until the 1980s, those corporations were primarily in manufacturing and not service industries.
2. Without that stability, as the Depression Era painfully demonstrated, the conditions necessary for the basic units of society, both human persons and corporate actors, to flourish are not met.
3. With the end of the Second World War, manufacturing corporations that were no longer filling military orders with assured government contracts were desperately in need of dependable markets for nonmilitary products.
4. The American public was the most viable option to provide those markets because most of the rest of the world had been economically crushed by the war.
5. Concessions won by labor unions on working conditions and wage hikes following the war required expansion of the consumer economy or those costs would deplete corporate profits.
6. The American public, in large measure a collection of ethnic groups with frugal habits, relatively little discretionary money, and a deep distrust of debt financing after the '29 crash, needed to be converted to consumers.
7. That radical transformation of values could not be worked if the humans were informed of what was happening and required to give their consent to have their life-styles altered. (Few people in those days would have volunteered to be turned from modest life-styles that were relatively free of the worry of debt, refinancing, foreclosure, and bankruptcy, into "shop-until-you-drop" consumers, bent on the accumulation of stuff that would probably irreparably break down or become obsolete before it is paid for.)
8. The creation of the desire for products and the exploitation of the weakness of will characteristic of most humans were justified, although the corporate actors were clearly using other Rank B-ers as means. But in the first instance—and this is overriding—doing so served Rank A interests: the preservation of the conditions necessary for any Rank B-er to lead a worthwhile life. Had the manufacturing corporations collapsed in the '50s, they would have brought the entire country back down to its already scarred knees.

Hence, the actions of the corporations were within the dominant side constraints.

The United States government seemed to have put its stamp of approval on the consumerization of America by the corporations. Advertising costs for manufacturing corporations were excluded from taxable corporate income and the Federal Communications Commission allocated television stations only on the twelve channel VHF band, granted the three networks "ownership and operation rights over stations in prime markets," and froze the licensing of new stations from 1948–1952.[102] These actions worked "to guarantee that advertising-oriented programming based on the model of radio would triumph over theater TV, educational TV, or any other form."[103] It is fair to say, with Lipsitz, that American government policy—certainly influenced and probably formulated at least in part by the business corporations and not the market—created commercial television dominance in America. Much as I hate TV commercials, it was probably the right thing to do.

14. Why Corporations May Be Better Suited to Being Ethical than Human Persons

It will be helpful to summarize where we now stand. I have defended the view that there are three ranks on the moral scale. I put animals in the lowest rank and both human persons and corporate actors in the middle rank. The highest rank, I think, is currently vacant, or rather it is or would be populated with a constitutionally benevolent mythic entity or entities whose interests always include preserving the conditions necessary for the flourishing of those at the lower ranks. It needn't be of concern that Rank A-ers are imaginary. They are constructs that help us understand the purposes of ethics. There should be no need to talk about Rank A-ers in the remainder of the book. Discussion of Rank C-ers can be restricted to those cases where their interests are involved in the interactions of Rank B-ers. These sorts of cases will be discussed in Part Three.

Rank B-ers interact in three different ways: human person to human person, corporate actor to human person, and corporate actor to corporate actor. The ethics of the Type One interaction will be relatively unimportant throughout the rest of the book, though an occasional look at them will prove useful for comparative purposes. In the class of Type Two interactions are two varieties: those in which the human is the subject and those in which the human is the object of the interaction. In the first variety the human person is doing something to the corporation; in the second, the corporate actor is doing something to the human. It is important to realize that often, though not always, corporate actors interact with humans through their agents who are also humans. Still, in those cases, the interaction is Type Two, not Type One.

If they are to be ethical, all three types of interactions should be governed by two side constraints: one that forbids the use of any Rank B-ers without their consent to further the ends of any other Rank B-er, and the other that overrides that constraint only if the interests of Rank A-ers are served. Both of these constraints would seem to counsel cooperative rather than noncooperative strategies for all types of interactions.

I want now to argue that among the Rank B-ers, not only are corporations more important to the stability of the contemporary social system than human beings, they are also better suited than humans to an ethics of side constraints on rational decision making. That is, they will probably prove more capable of consistent and dependable ethical behavior than humans.

The side-constraint conception of ethics I have adopted amounts to the view that to be ethical (or moral) a human or corporate actor must constrain its actions for the sake of the mutual benefit of others in its rank. It must not exploit others without their consent in order to maximize its own interests. The game, Prisoner's Dilemma, is used by a number of theorists to characterize the sort of social interaction problems in which constraint on individual maximizing tendencies is essential to achieving optimal mutual benefits. The game is often used to show that acting on rational self-interest or straightforward maximization principles can produce the mutually worst outcomes in those interactions for all involved. (See accompanying box for a representation of the game of Prisoner's Dilemma on a game matrix that shows the outcomes of various plays.)

Prisoner's Dilemma pits two actors against each other over a problem; if they cooperate, they will both benefit to some extent. If one cooperates and one does not, the noncooperator realizes a major gain, while the cooperator suffers a corresponding major loss. If they both fail to cooperate, however, they both suffer a loss that is not as great as in the second case, but is nonetheless substantial. Rationally looking out for one's self-interest would seem to recommend not cooperating, because by doing so one stands to gain a great deal or lose less than if one cooperated and the other person didn't. The problem is that if both players reason that way, they will produce a situation in which they both suffer serious losses. They cannot achieve the only mutually beneficial outcome in the game, the one that requires them to both cooperate.

It has been pointed out by me and a number of other writers, following the work of Robert Axelrod[104], that if the game is played over and over by the same players, called Iterated Prisoner's Dilemma, another strategy will recommend itself. That strategy is tit for tat. A tit-for-tatter in Iterated Prisoner's Dilemma cooperates on the first move and then plays whatever the other player has played on the previous move. So, if the tit-for-tatter's opponent does not cooperate in response to a cooperative move, on the next move the tit-for-tatter will not cooperate and will continue not to cooperate until the other player responds with a cooperative move.

Peter Danielson has written that tit for tat is a basic moral principle.[105] It certainly induces widespread cooperation in game-theory tournaments and seems to be a principle that is impartial, and mutually beneficial to the players. It may have that effect, but as Danielson, in his latest book, now concedes, "TFT [Tit For Tat] is not a moral principle,

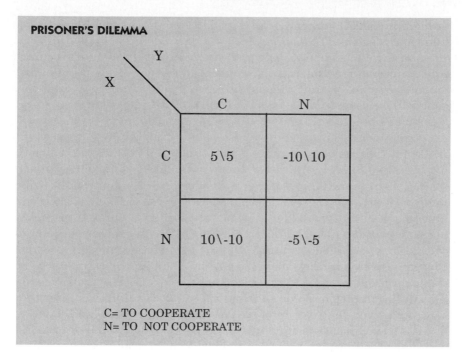

PRISONER'S DILEMMA

C= TO COOPERATE
N= TO NOT COOPERATE

because in Iterated Prisoner's Dilemma it is straightforwardly in the agent's interests."[106] A player will choose tit for tat because it has proven to be the most likely strategy to maximize the player's gain. With David Gauthier,[107] we should agree that tit for tat does not therefore really constrain the person who plays it. Instead, it is adopted because it is beneficial to the player.

However, as Danielson rightly maintains, in Iterated Prisoner Dilemma, tit for tat certainly is the rational strategy. That proves that we don't need ethics to produce cooperative outcomes in social interactions that mirror Iterated Prisoner's Dilemma. Straightforward maximizing by the persons involved in those situations will produce the optimal results for all, because it will drive them to adopting tit for tat and that strategy stabilizes into a cooperative relationship. I think this is an important point because it may explain why people like Friedman wax on so glowingly about the virtues of the market. If the market encounters they have in mind are really Iterated Prisoner's Dilemmas, then rational marketeers will adopt tit for tat strategies and cooperation will occur without the importation of moral constraints. That outcome, however, does not make either the market or the strategy that gets adopted for straightforward maximizing reasons ethical. It only shows that in some interactions ethical constraints would be redundant. That variety of interactions, however, probably accounts for a relatively small percentage of market interactions and few interactions of Types One, Two, or Three.

As I have maintained, being ethical essentially involves accepting constraints on maximizing one's own interests in social interactions when such maximizing will not produce the optimal outcomes that benefit the interests of the Rank A-ers. It means not using other Rank B-ers as mere means to one's gains even when that appears to be what rationality counsels.

What if Prisoner's Dilemma is not iterated, if it is played just once between two Rank B-ers? What then is the rational move for both to make? What is the ethical move? The answer to the former question, we are usually told, is not to cooperate, while the answer to the latter question is to cooperate. So there seems to be a chasm between what is rational and what is ethical. After all, it hardly seems rational to commit oneself to cooperating when that just sets oneself up to be preyed upon by the other player. You'd be a sucker. Or, what seems to come to the same thing, a saint. (I do not wish to be construed as denying any differences between suckers and saints. After all, P. T. Barnum said, with some degree of authority, that a sucker is born every minute. That is surely not true of saints. They're few and far between.) Can cooperation in a single-play Prisoner's Dilemma-type interactive situation ever be the rational choice?

Gauthier could argue that his principle of constrained maximization preserves both the rational and the moral element in such interactions.[108] By following it, one cooperates in the single-play Prisoner's Dilemma with those one believes are most likely to cooperate in return. But Danielson argues that Gauthier's principle, which we can call "conditional cooperation," does not fare as well rationally as the principle Danielson calls "reciprocal cooperation." The principle of reciprocal cooperation tells us to "cooperate when and only when cooperation is necessary and sufficient for the other's cooperation."[109]

The difference between the two principles is that Gauthier's principle is used to induce others to cooperate, while Danielson's principle would have players constraining themselves when they must to get cooperation from others in social interactions. Again, tournament results of playing these two strategies against each other and against those who always cooperate (unconditional cooperators, saints) and those who never cooperate (unconditional noncooperators) seem to support Danielson's claim. Reciprocal cooperators do better over all.[110]

But a moral problem arises with Danielson's principle: his reciprocal cooperators do very well and seem to satisfy most of the demands of morality because they constrain any inclinations they may have to just straightforwardly maximize their interests at the cost of others. There is just one glitch. They will exploit the saints, the unconditional cooperators, by not cooperating with them, because they need not cooperate to get them to do so. They will use them to their own ends. Perhaps that doesn't sound very moral, at least not at first. But it may not be much of a practical problem, because saintliness is difficult to rationally sustain in a population where there are predators and reciprocal cooperators. Still, some saints may persevere; that is what makes them saints. They will be exploited by reciprocal cooperators, but they will not be exploited by Gauthier's conditional cooperators. It looks as if conditional cooperation is more ethical than reciprocal cooperation, though reciprocal cooperation is ethical to some degree because it is constrained by moral considerations.

Conditional cooperators, however, are not so morally righteous. They will cooperate with reciprocal cooperators, so they will not protect the saints from the reciprocal cooperators. They will stand by when the saints are exploited.

Perhaps the most ethical strategy to adopt in single-play Prisoner's Dilemma interactions would be one that will cooperate only with those who do not exploit the saints. Such a strategy, however, is irrational, or at least not as rational as reciprocal cooperation or conditional cooperation. To see this, we only need to understand that the protectors of saints must refuse to cooperate with the reciprocal cooperators. They must sanction them. But, as Danielson notes, "I cannot sanction you without hurting myself. Sanctioning is costly."[111]

The protectors cannot enter or sustain themselves in a population that contains reciprocal cooperators. Those with strategies that do not sanction the reciprocal cooperators, such as the Gauthier conditional cooperators, will do better than the protectors in maximizing their own interests. The saints, on the other hand, attract reciprocal cooperators (and noncooperators), like honey attracts flies, even if there are protectors of the saints in the population. Again, if the players are rational, they will adopt reciprocal cooperation rather than the more moral saint-protector strategy or the conditional-cooperator position. In other words, adopting the reciprocal-cooperator strategy is the most rational yet moral, though not the most moral strategy that one seems to be able to take in single play Prisoner Dilemma interactions.

Consider the game of Chicken (or Hawks and Doves). [See accompanying box for a game matrix for Chicken.] The game of Chicken was played where I was a teenager by two guys driving cars on a narrow road directly at each other. The loser of the game was the one who first veered off the straight course. If neither veered, the two cars crashed. I admit to engaging in this entertainment on only one occasion. I still remember the surge of excitement and anxiety it produced. The whole business was made worse, or better, by the crowd that gathered to cheer the winner and scorn the loser. In my case, the event was declared a tie. My opponent was someone from a crosstown Polish gang who must have made some deprecating remarks about something or

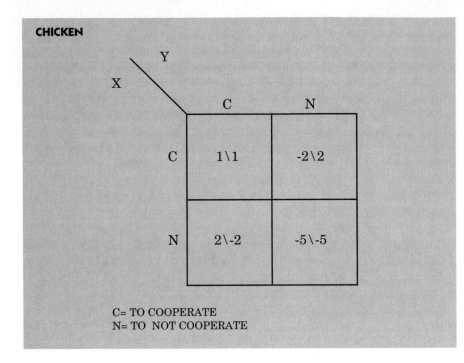

CHICKEN

	C	N
C	1\1	-2\2
N	2\-2	-5\-5

C= TO COOPERATE
N= TO NOT COOPERATE

other that seemed extremely important at the time and required the risking of our lives, but is now not even a remnant of the memory. We simultaneously decided to veer off on our respective sides about twelve feet from a collision. Each of us and our friends proclaimed for weeks that the other had chickened out first, but both of us knew we'd been overcome with sanity at the same time.

The possible payoffs in Chicken-type interactions are different than those in Prisoner's Dilemma. The major variation is that if neither player cooperates in Chicken, if both continue on the collision course, they both achieve the worst possible outcome in the game. Yet, if you do not veer and the other person does, you get the best outcome. But the loss you take for veering is nowhere near as great as the one you suffer if neither of you veer. Of course, in the bellicose moments that precede the game both participants threaten not veering and proclaim with loud assurance that the other will chicken out as the fateful moment approaches.

In social interactions involving threats, such as those modeled by the game of Chicken, Danielson maintains that a less broad cooperation strategy than reciprocal cooperation will be more rational.[112] The less broad cooperator will concede only to unconditional noncooperators in Chicken-type interactions, while refusing to go along with the threats of any other morally constrained players. My opponent and I both must have believed each other's hype. Each of us was convinced that the other was an unconditional noncooperator.

So a rational-ethical strategist or, perhaps better put, a moralized rational interactor will adopt a combination of reciprocal cooperation and less broad cooperation to deal with social interactions of both the Prisoner's Dilemma and Chicken varieties. From these game theoretic results, Danielson concludes:

> [I]nstrumental rational agents must be capable of morality in the sense of a capacity to constrain their actions for the sake of benefits shared with others . . . [T]heir morality must be responsive; they must limit the class of agents [persons] with which they share cooperative benefits . . . Responsiveness requires players who can discriminate; depending on the context, they must be able at least to identify other cooperators, or similarly constrained players or, in Chicken, unreasoning threateners . . . [O]ne way to do this is by means of transparently public principles, which others can test and copy.[113]

What Danielson's position comes to is that the "class of entities that can be moral . . . is determined by their functional abilities."[114] This is the view I have been defending throughout the book. But if Danielson is right, another element is exposed: it is crucial that such entities have publicly accessible decision procedures that are adaptable to "interest-based change" and that they have the ability to commit themselves to plans and partial plans that may not reflect straightforward maximization of their interests.

The cognitive transparency and publicity of their procedures and policies is important so that they can both identify and be identified with their general strategies. That makes possible for them, especially in their interactions with each other, relatively accurate access to the strategies of others and for others to identify them as ethically constrained interactors. They are then able to utilize that information in the making of constrained rational decisions and plans. Corporations or rather CID structures, as I have maintained, are, simply, designed with those functional capacities that Danielson's analyses reveal to be essential to moralized rational interactions. Humans, however, don't seem to be. Danielson comments:

> I find that . . . firms are suitable rational moral agents but humans perhaps are not . . . [T]hey have morally crucial capacities that individual people may lack. For example, firms . . . may be constituted by public decision procedures, some of which commit them to various courses of action contrary to their interests yet which are open to interest-based change.[115]

Humans are, as Putnam[116] has said, opaque to themselves and each other. Neither of the two of us driving on that narrow road had a

dependable way of knowing how to identify the general strategies of
the other. I'm rather sure that I had no idea about what I would do
when his car got closer and closer to mine at sixty miles per hour. We
are also less able than corporations with formalized decision procedures to change or reorganize our constitutive principles of decision-
making to be responsive to optimizing pressures and constraints while
keeping long-term interests in view. I have already shown in some
detail how we are far more prone to weakness of will, to choosing to
achieve short-term satisfactions rather than long-term goals, than
are corporate actors. Quite simply, corporations, especially when
interacting with each other, are functionally better prepared to behave
ethically than are human persons.

Such a claim will undoubtedly be decried from various fronts.
Some will object and reply that corporations are capable of only
straightforward maximization decision making, something the proponents of such a view usually associate with rationality. They'll concede
that CID structures can be constructed to produce rational decisions.
However, as Danielson has shown, the straightforward maximization
strategy in social interactions, whether of the Prisoner's Dilemma or
Chicken variety, is not rational. Certain constrained maximization
strategies relative to the specific type of interaction are. So, if it is con-
ceded that CID structures are capable of producing rational decision
making, they must then be adaptable to constrained maximization
strategies in their basic policies, for that is what is rational. There certainly can be no question that CID structures are specifically designed
to produce corporate decisions and actions that will satisfy the conditions of rationality. In fact, if they stop doing so in a reliable way, they
will be targeted for reengineering. It is empirically demonstrable that
most corporations do adopt constrained strategies in the very marketplace that for about three centuries we have been told is governed
only by unconstrained maximization. They do so—some might say
they have to do so—because the constrained approaches simply fair
better. Constrained strategies are more likely to produce market success than the unconstrained ones. That is what the empirical tournament evidence in game theory indicates. That is also what the success
of Japanese corporations in the global marketplace is teaching American corporations that fell victim to the short-term maximization fad of
the 1980s.

I certainly am not saying that corporations are automatically ethical, or that by being involved in the marketplace they cannot avoid
becoming ethical. That would be grossly out of line with the facts.
Instead, I am saying that corporations, by their very constitutive
structures, evidence the functional capacities necessary to be ethical.
The evidence regarding humans is far more ambiguous. Danielson
calls corporations "models of adaptable rational agents."[117]

I think that the news that corporations are perhaps better suited than humans to being ethical than humans should be heartening. What it means is that the most important entities in our society with respect to its stability and order are more adaptive to being ethical than the humans on which the society once depended. That's good news. The invaders offer more hope for a moral world than the persons who have been invaded ever did. The conversion of the invaders into ethical entities is also more likely to be successful than any similar attempts to convert humans. That, of course, means that it must be possible for an entity to be ethical even though its component parts are not. Ideally, of course, we would like a social world in which all the Rank B-ers made morally constrained rational decisions about their actions and acted accordingly. The remainder of this book, however, focuses on the problems and issues to be confronted in the ethical conversion of cognitively transparent, rational corporate actors.

ENDNOTES

1. *Prosser and Keeton on The Law of Torts*, 5th ed W. Page Keeton, Gen. ed. (St. Paul., 1984), especially chapter 1.
2. Douglas Adams, *The Hitchhiker's Guide to the Galaxy*, (London, 1979).
3. Charles Taylor, *Sources of the Self* (Cambridge, Mass., 1989) 195.
4. For a fuller account of the Anglo-Saxon laws and the *wergeld* system see John Holdsworth, *A History of English Law* (London, 1942).
5. Walter Ullmann, *The Individual and Society* (Baltimore, 1966) 42.
6. James Coleman, *The Asymmetric Society* (Syracuse, 1982) 14.
7. Ibid. 14
8. Ullmann, op. cit., 44.
9. Ibid. p.44.
10. For a fuller account of this aspect of art in the period, see James Burke, *The Day the Universe Changed* (London, 1985) chapter 3.
11. For a collection of important papers on social contract theory, see Michael Lessnoff, *Social Contract Theory* (New York, 1990). The book includes selections from Hobbes, Pufendorf, Locke, Rousseau, Kant, Rawls, Gauthier, and Diggs.
12. Perhaps the most famous account of this sort is put forth by John Ladd in "Morality and the Idea of Rationality in Formal Organizations," *Monist*, 54: 488–516. But see also Manuel Valazquez, "Why Corporations Are Not Morally Responsible for Anything They Do," *Business and Professional Ethics Journal* v.2, no. 3 (1983); and Milton Friedman, "The Social Responsibility of Business is to Increase Its Profits," *The New York Times Magazine*, September 13, 1970.
13. Ibid.
14. James Coleman, *Foundations of Social Theory* (Cambridge, Mass., 1990).
15. Alvin Goldman, *A Theory of Human Action* (Englewood Cliffs, NJ, 1970).
16. Elizabeth Anscombe, *Intention* (Ithaca, NY, 1963).
17. Donald Davidson, *Essays on Actions and Events* (New York, 1980).
18. Robert Audi, "Intending," *Journal of Philosophy*, v. 70 (1973), p. 387–403.
19. Michael Bratman, *Intention, Plans, and Practical Reason* (Cambridge, Mass., 1987), p 5.
20. Ibid. p. 6.

21. J. L. Austin, *Philosophical Papers* (Oxford, 1970) p. 283.
22. Ibid. p. 279.
23. Ibid. p. 193-194.
24. Coleman, *Foundations of Social Theory*, p. 421.
25. Robert Nozick, *Anarchy, State, and Utopia* (New York, 1974) part I.
26. Coleman, *Foundations of Social Theory*, p.421.
27. Ibid.
28. Ibid.
29. I originally came up with that notion in a paper "The Corporation As a Moral Person, " *American Philosophical Quarterly* 16 (1979), p. 207–17.
30. James Coleman, *The Asymmetric Society*, (Syracuse, 1982).
31. Ibid. p. 26.
32. Ibid.
33. John Ciardi, "What Was Her Name?" in *Person to Person* (New Brunswick, 1962).
34. Nozick, op. cit. p. 18.
35. Ibid. p. 19.
36. See, for example, Velazquez, op. cit. He writes:
    "Moral Responsibility for an act attaches to the entity that originates the
    act . . . . Since the acts of a corporation are brought about not by the direct bodily
    movements of the corporation (as an entity distinct from its members) but by
    those of its members, and since the intentions of the corporation (if there are such
    things) are not the intentions with which those members acted, it follows that the
    corporation is not the entity that is morally responsible for those acts."
37. For an excellent discussion of the responsibility of mobs, see Larry May, *The
    Morality of Groups* (Notre Dame, 1987). Especially chapters 2–4.
38. Larry May, (Ibid., p. 75) writes:
    "My account makes it a necessary condition or the description of collective
    responsibility to unorganized groups that each member of a group engage in acts
    or omissions which contribute to the harmful consequence for which the group is
    held collectively responsible. However, while each member must contribute in
    some respect . . . in order for a group to bear collective responsibility for a harm,
    the contribution of each does not necessarily determine how individual responsi-
    bility will be distributed among the members."
39. See J. L. Austin, op. cit. "Three Ways of Spilling Ink," p. 273–87.
40. Ibid. p. 198.
41. Coleman, *Foundations of Social Theory*, p. 543.
42. I borrow the term from H. L. A. Hart. See his *The Concept of Law* (Oxford, 1961).
43. Tom L. Beauchamp, *Case Studies in Business, Society, and Ethics* (Englewood
    Cliffs, 1989) p. 122.
44. Meir Dan-Cohen, *Rights, Persons, and Organizations* (Berkeley, 1986) p. 46–49.
45. Peter Danielson, *Artificial Morality* (London, 1992).
46. For a collection of essays on human personal identity from various perspectives,
    see John Perry (ed.), *Personal Identity*, (Berkeley, 1975).
47. David Hume, *A Treatise of Human Nature* (1740) (Oxford, 1978 edition) p. 257.
48. Plato, as is well known, portrayed the state as if it were a human "Writ large." The
    state reflects the structure of the human, having three constitutive elements or
    classes as the human soul has three parts. See Plato, *The Republic*, English Trans.
    by F. M. Cornford (Oxford, 1941) p. 53–59.
49. Coleman works out a similar typography of interactions in *Foundations of Social
    Theory*, p. 542–52.
50. John Rawls, "Justice as Fairness" *The Philosophical Review* LXVII (1958) p. 166.
51. Ibid. p. 60.
52. Robert Paul Wolff, *Understanding Rawls* (Princeton, 1977) p. 180.
53. I recommend, in addition to Rawls' famous book, the anthology edited by Norman
    Daniels, *Reading Rawls* (Oxford, 1975). Of special note should be the articles by

Thomas Nagel and Ronald Dworkin.
54. Rawls, op. cit. part one.
55. F. H. Bradley, op. cit. "My Station and Its Duties."
56. Chandran Kukathas and Philip Petit, *Rawls* (Oxford, 1990) p. 13.
57. Rawls, *A Theory of Justice*, p. 139.
58. Ibid.
59. Rawls has addressed these and other criticisms in his recent book, *Political Liberalism* (New York, 1993). See especially p. 18–46 and p. 173–200.
60. Michael Sandel, *Liberalism and the Limits of Justice* (Cambridge, 1982).
61. For a good overview of the disputes between the liberals and the communitarians, see Stephen Mulhall and Adam Swift, *Liberals and Communitarians* (Oxford, 1992). Will Kymlicka, *Liberalism, Community, and Culture* (Oxford, 1989), provides an attack on the communitarian critique of liberalism. He defends the view that liberalism is compatible with the concern to preserve communities and cultures. See especially p. 1–39.
62. See Plato, *The Republic* (trans. by F. M. Cornford) (Oxford, 1941).
63. Rawls, *A Theory of Justice*, p. 140.
64. Thomas Hobbes, *Leviathan* (London, 1651) Chapter XIII.
65. John Martin Fischer, "Responsibility and Failure," *Proceedings of the Aristotelian Society* (1985–86) p. 251–70. See also Harry Frankfurt, "Alternative Possibilities and Moral Responsibility," *Journal of Philosophy* 66 (Dec.1969) p. 828–39; P. S. Greenspan, "Behavior Control and Freedom of Action," *Philosophical Review* 87 (April 1978) p. 22540; and John Martin Fischer, "Responsibility and Control," *Journal of Philosophy* 89 (January, 1982) p. 2440.
66. Ibid. p. 262.
67. Thomas Wartenberg, "Situated Social Power," in *Rethinking Power*, Thomas Wartenberg, ed. (Albany, 1992) p. 81.
68. Ibid. p. 83.
69. Coleman, *Foundations of Social Theory*, p. 548.
70. For a good anthology of papers on weakness of will, see Geoffrey Mortimore (ed.), *Weakness of Will* (New York, 1971). It includes contributions to the subject by Plato, Aristotle, R. M. Hare, H. J. N. Horsburgh, Weil Cooper, and others.
71. Ibid. p. 548–49. [Iterated Prisoner's Dilemmas, to be discussed in more detail in Section 14, can be used to demonstrate the need to get human players to commit to long-term goals rather than short-term triumphs. But players I have tested often succumb to short-term strategies, favoring the grasping of the bird in the hand rather than the two in the bush. They generally do poorly in games with an unknown number of plays.]
72. Ibid. p. 549.
73. George Lipsitz, *Time Passages* (Minneapolis, 1990) p. 44.
74. Ibid. p. 41.
75. Ibid. p. 41.
76. Ibid. p. 56.
77. I am indebted to George Lipsitz for having identified these plots. See Ibid. chaptor 2.
78. Ibid. p. 48.
79. Immanuel Kant, *Groundwork of the Metaphysic of Morals* (1785), trans. by H. J. Paton (New York, 1964).
80. Nozick, op. cit. p. 28–33.
81. Ibid. p. 32.
82. See Charles Taylor, "Atomism," *Philosophical Papers* (Cambridge, 1985), "Atomism" for a criticism of Nozick's individualism.
83. Ibid. p. 32.
84. Milton Friedman, op. cit.
85. Ibid.
86. Ibid.

87. Nozick, op. cit. p. 35.
88. Ibid. p. 41.
89. Ibid. p. 45–46.
90. John Stuart Mill, *Utilitarianism* (New York, 1957) p. 10.
91. Fred Feldman, *Introductory Ethics* (Englewood Cliffs, 1978) p. 24.
92. Ibid. p. 26.
93. Ibid. p. 33.
94. Peter Singer, *Practical Ethics* (Cambridge, 1993) p. 131.
95. Ibid. p. 94.
96. Ibid. p. 95.
97. Nozick, op.cit. p. 49.
98. See David Wiggins, "Locke, Butler, and the Stream of Consciousness: And Men as a Natural Kind," in *The Identities of Persons*, ed. by A. O. Rorty (Berkeley, 1976) (p.139–73), p. 167, and my response to him, French, *Collective and Corporate Responsibility*, chapter six.
99. Wiggins, op.cit. p. 161.
100. Coleman, *The Asymmetric Society*, p. 14.
101. There is something of Bertrand Russell's "citizens of the universe" in my account of Rank A membership. He writes, "The free intellect will see as God might see, without a *here* and *now*, without hopes and fears, without the trammels of customary beliefs and traditional prejudices . . ." See Bertrand Russell, *The Problems of Philosophy* (London, 1912) p. 160.
102. See Lipsitz, op. cit. for a fuller account of the complicity of the government in the conversion of the population to consumers.
103. Ibid. p. 45.
104. Robert Axelrod, *The Evolution of Cooperation* (New York, 1984).
105. Peter Danielson, "The Moral Significance of Tit For Tat, "*Dialogue* 25 (1986) p. 449–470.
106. Peter Danielson, *Artificial Morality* (London, 1992) p. 46.
107. David Gauthier, *Morals By Agreement* (Oxford, 1986).
108. Gauthier, op.cit.
109. Danielson, *Artificial Morality*, p. 89.
110. Danielson provides tables to show how the tournament tests will come out. See Ibid. p. 99.
111. Ibid. p. 120.
112. Ibid. chapter 9.
113. Ibid. p. 196.
114. Ibid. p. 196.
115. Ibid. p. 198.
116. Hilary Putnam. *Meaning and the Moral Sciences* (London, 1978).
117. Ibid. p. 198.

INSIDE THE INVADERS

1. Stockholders and the Ownership of Corporations

A Weberian organization, named for Max Weber, who first provided a sociological analysis of it,[1] is a formal hierarchical organization in which the activities of each position are supervised by the position above it. Anyone who has studied basic management or taken an elementary course in business is probably sick to death of the Weberian model. The idea, as almost any book in business will tell you, is that the formal organization of a corporation is intended to firmly structure the relationships between at least three components: agents (or natural persons and machines), activities, and physical resources.

Corporations organized in the classical hierarchical or Weberian manner usually differentiate authority relationships in terms of line and staff functions. Line authority, to quote from an elementary book in business, "is the right to direct subordinates' work."[2] Line positions tend to be connected with decision making and command in the corporation. They are usually associated with what are called "line functions," such as production, marketing, purchasing, and sales. Staff authority is generally advisory to line positions. It might involve research, quality control, and personnel management.

The authority relationships within any corporate actor are typically displayed on an organizational chart where the protocol is to identify line-position authority with solid lines and staff positions with broken lines. The charts are read from the top down, indicating the various echelons of management, generally identified as top, middle, and lower, and that the flow of authority comes from above.

It seems a bit strange to a philosopher that there should be so wide an agreement in both business textbooks and in business practice not only on the theoretical value of the Weberian model, but on its practicality in managing corporations. Virtually every company that I asked to send me its organizational chart produced a Weberian model. Perhaps this should come as no surprise because the model is also crucially linked to the influential Harvard Business School's policy framework, in which the preferences of the executives at the top of a company's organizational chart are understood to be the primary source of all of its actions and policies. Suspicion that the model is more garnish than main dish is, I think, well founded.

The structural model generally goes hand in glove with the conception of the corporation as "an owner of capital . . . which buys factor inputs such as raw materials, labor, and processing equipment, organizes their appropriate integration to yield a final product, and then sells the product to consumers."[3] The corporate insiders are, supposedly, its owners, its investors, and the suppliers of its capital. Every human. And everything else connected to it falls in the category of factor inputs. Humans, even in higher managerial roles may work for the corporation, but they are not inside it. They are not really part of it. To be perfectly frank, this view of the corporate actor, at least the larger ones—the important ones—is inconsistent with the facts.

In the first place, there is something suspicious about the idea that someone who buys stock, that is, gives money in exchange for a certificate, can be said to still own the capital he or she has just used to make the purchase. Buying stock is not making a loan. It is making an investment, usually with the hope that it will turn a profit either through regular dividend returns or when it is sold on the open market. The capital obtained by the corporation from the sale of its stock is the corporation's capital. They sold the stock to get that capital. The stockholders own pieces of tradable, resalable property. They don't own the corporation. Buying the stock gives them certain privileges, and if they own enough of it, they can exercise those privileges and even take over the management of the corporation. But they are not, in the aggregate, the corporation in which they own stock.

Most of today's corporate investors are well and happily outside the corporations in which they invest. Toward the beginning of the twentieth century, probably the majority of even the larger corporations were capitalized and their factor inputs organized by the same humans. That has not typically been the case for many decades, except for family businesses. Of course, investors have residual claimant status with regard to the corporation's earnings and assets, but they do not have regulative or actual causal control over the normal use by the corporation of its factor inputs, of which the money they used to buy the stock is but another component. They are not corporate agents.

Stockholders do, in theory if not in practice, vote for the board of directors, but evidence shows that few take that right seriously or regard it as a major justification for investing. The reason, as Coleman notes, is probably that their capital is transportable from one corporation to another with little loss in the exchange.[4] They are in it for the money, purely and simply. If they think they can do better financially by moving their investments to the purchase of stock in another company or having a fling at the crap tables in Las Vegas, they will do so without blinking an eye.

> Investors' interests lie almost solely in the economic benefits they derive from the corporation's activity, through dividends and increases in share prices. With this conception the inside of the corporation no longer contains the owners. They are seen as mere providers of a factor input, bought at a price which is approximately the interest rate for loans or the dividend rate for stocks. [5]

The evidence that stockholders have little interest in the running of corporations other than to see a return on their investments is overwhelming. For instance, Coca Cola has more than seventy thousand stockholders, yet only twenty-five on average attend its annual meeting. Bristol-Myers Squibb has more than sixty thousand stockholders, but its meetings draw only about enough stockholders for a pick-up softball game. Controlling the affairs of the company is not high on the typical stockholder's list of priorities.

The Friedmanesque idea that corporations are owned by their investors and that the board members and their appointed managers are trustees for those investors deserves display in a dinosaur museum. That does not, however, mean that corporations do not have responsibilities to their stockholders, especially as regards profitmaking. Clearly they do. They are, after all, playing with other people's money that was obtained with promises of significant financial rewards.

Where those responsibilities fall within the full spectrum of the responsibilities of a corporation, however, is not as clear as Friedman and his followers would lead us to believe. Nonetheless, we can, by applying the Kantian side-constraint test for Rank B-ers, agree that, by and large, the transactions between stockholders and corporations are ethically legitimate, even though both parties are using each other as means. The only times when this would not be the case would be if the corporation falsified its prospectus and business reports in order to obtain capital. The famous old dictum, "Let the buyer beware," may have some ethical viability, but if the seller has so masked the reality as to make discovery of fraud or misrepresentation virtually impossible, then the buyer is being used as a means only and the side constraints are being violated.

Deliberate deception also has occurred when corporations try to make themselves look like unprofitable risks to ward off potential raiders or to drive down the stock prices so that a management team can buy them out at a more favorable rate. In such cases, the stockholders are also being used in violation of the side constraints.

Insider trading can also have the same results from the ethical point of view. Of course, stockholders are not going to be complaining about being used without their consent when the shenanigans are inflating the value of their stock. It is only when their profit expectations collapse that they see themselves as used. I think they are used in either case and even if they make a windfall profit. The principle forbids nonconsensual manipulation of the interests of other Rank B-ers.

2. The Powers and Influences (Such as They Are) of Boards of Directors

So who is inside the invaders? Members of boards of directors? After all, as can hardly be missed, they show up at the top of the hierarchy of power on the corporate organizational flow charts. It may look good in model theory and in annual reports, but the overwhelming evidence is that boards hardly have much power or control in corporations today. Theoretically, boards are elected by the stockholders to manage the affairs of the business for them. They are empowered to hire and fire the corporate executives, monitor fiscal matters, provide annual reports to the stockholders, and distribute profits. The executives of the corporation are supposed to be just employees of the stockholders with whatever authority is delegated to them by the board of directors.

Being a director looks pretty important, definitely on the inside of corporate action. Looks can be deceiving. Ralph Nader, Mark Green, and Joel Seligman, in a famous book on the governance of corporations, supported by more than ample evidence, tell us:

> [I]n reality, this legal image is virtually a myth. In nearly every large American business corporation, there exists a management autocracy. One man . . . or a small coterie of men rule the corporation.[6]

Directors do few of the things that, according to the standard picture, they are supposed to do. Harold Geneen, former chief executive officer and chairman of the board of ITT Corporation provides a memorably vivid description of the typical workings of boards for those of us not privileged to receive the annual $100,000 plus perks to be in attendance ourselves.

> Most of the time the boardroom is empty: these important people use it only 12 times a year. The first Tuesday or the second Thursday of every month, the members show up. On entering the room, each is handed a sealed envelope. Soon, the minutes of the previous meeting are read and

approved. Perhaps the directors then adjourn temporarily so that the executive committee of the board can meet separately to discuss management
salaries and changes in company personnel. When the whole board recon-
venes, the chief executive presents an overall view of the company's activities and results that month. If he is so inclined he may go into details, or
he may turn the explaining over to a subordinate. Whatever the results,
management always reports in effect how good they have been and are and
will be, despite whatever intolerable conditions hover over the economy
or the marketplace. They never tell you that they've done a lousy job or
that they were beaten by a more efficient or smarter competitor . . .
Management does 90%-95% of the talking. Outside board members, who
are not part of the management, sit there and listen; then they go to lunch,
and then go home and open the envelopes that contain their fees.[7]

The outside members of the boards are elected by the stockholders, but as Geneen points out, in practice they serve at the pleasure of
the chief executive officer. If he vetoes a nomination, it will never be
put to the vote of the stockholders. If you own stock in a corporation
and so have been mailed a proxy ballot, you have some idea of the sham
of this process. It has been compared by some to the way the former
Soviet Union used to conduct democratic elections. There were ballots,
sure enough, and you got to mark them. But there was only one candidate per office. The same thing happens in most corporate elections of
directors. Is that a bad thing from the moral point of view? Not particularly, I suppose. Why should board election be an open contest? Why
should there be more than one candidate per slot? Why should we be
concerned about choice? Is there something morally better about having more than one candidate for a position, when those voting don't
usually care who occupies the position in the first place? I think this
issue deserves less attention than some philosophers have afforded it.
If those voting don't register objections, I can't see how there could be
a major ethical matter in it. After all, they do get the opportunity to
vote. Though, unlike the former Soviet Union, most do not avail themselves of that opportunity.
    The critics, I think, are drawn to the director-election process
because they are captives of the stockholders-own (or are) -the-com-
pany myth. If you think someone is being cheated out of the right to
control what they own, your moral juices ought to start boiling. But
even if stockholders did own the corporation, and boards were their
representatives, no necessary link exists between ownership and control. Berle and Means in a landmark book published some sixty years
ago talked of the joint-stock corporation as having split the "atom of
private property," severing ownership from control.[8]
    In the inside of a corporation, ownership is a theoretical myth. No
one owns IBM, Coca Cola, AT&T, or General Motors, even if some of
us think we do. Humans and other corporate actors have invested in

those corporations, provided the financial capital necessary for them to be viable productive entities. But, as I noted above, investment is another needed factor input. Separating it out from the other factor inputs is important for matters of finance and accounting, but unwarranted if we are trying to understand what a corporate actor is for purposes of ethics. Control is what matters, power is what counts in the corporation, not ownership.

Perhaps the masquerade of board elections should be discontinued in favor of a vote of endorsement or confidence in management. That is all that usually happens now anyway. Most of the ballots I have received make clear that the senior management recommends the particular slate of persons for election to the board. Of course, what they are doing is recommending a few additional persons, outside of management positions, to sit with the insiders. Usually those persons are thought by the insiders to be placed in positions that are or could be particularly useful to the corporation's enterprises. For example, the banker for the corporation will generally be offered a seat. (Private universities and colleges are especially adept at finding places on their boards for persons who have made major donations to the institution or are likely to do so in the near future. That they know or care about the issues of higher education is of, at best, secondary importance.) Collecting outside board members, to hear some corporate executives tell it, seems to be the grown-up extension of collecting baseball cards. The names and pictures of outside board members are often displayed for show, but little is usually told about what contributions they make to the decision making of the corporate actor. As Thornton Wilder once wrote, "I suppose there's no harm in it . . . . Whenever you come near the human race, there's layers and layers of nonsense."[9]

It seems to be a point of consternation among business ethicists that chief executives are on the boards of their corporations and that most also chair their boards. According to the received hierarchical organizational model, the executives, including the chief one, are managers. It is their management, their stewardship, that the directors are supposed to monitor for the sake of the stockholders. Talk of conflict of interest! Yet, not only are the CEOs of all of the major American companies on their own boards, in the vast majority of cases those boards are top heavy with senior management personnel. Geneen notes that the CEO usually only has to persuade one or two outside members of his position on any issue to have a voting majority. He can count on the support of the board members that are also part of his management team.[10]

While we are running down the list of reasons why the standard view of directors is flawed, it is worth noting that, by and large, the boards of directors of large corporations in America no longer set the salaries for the senior management, once an almost sacred task of directors. Consulting firms are hired to tell the board what the executives should be paid based on the size of the corporation and the going rate for companies of that size. The corporation's performance during the year is seldom taken into consideration.[11]

This fact created quite an international stir in 1991 when a number of corporate presidents and chief executive officers joined President George Bush on a junket to Japan to try to drum up markets for American goods there. Actually, an unpleasant air of begging surrounded the excursion, and that was not lost on the Japanese. Though they strained to remain good hosts and to control smirks of satisfaction, a number of Japanese business analysts, as reported in the American news media, could not be restrained from pointing out the vast disparity between the salaries of workers and those of the senior executives in American corporations. That differential, they also noted, has been widening in recent years despite major downturns in productivity and profitability. In Japan, they were always ready to demonstrate with the appropriate charts, the difference in pay between a worker and a company president is but a small percentage of what it is in America. Yet corporate performance is significantly greater. The objectives of the tour, such as they were in the first place, symbolically crumbled when, after vomiting into the lap of the Japanese Prime Minister, President Bush crumbled in a faint at a state dinner in Tokyo. I will leave it to the likes of newspaper humorist Dave Barry to explain the deeper meanings of those events, though we will later (in Part 5) need to address some of the differences between Japanese and American business organization and practice in the global markets.

The matter of exorbitant executive salaries, however, is not as important in corporate ethics as might be suggested by the level of indignation it arouses in those of us making a comparative pittance, nor is the charade of rubber-stamping of executive management decisions that has become standard practice in American boardrooms. The question here is whether the board of directors of a corporation constitutes its insides. The answer should be, by now, obvious: the board, or at least some subset of its members, is on the inside of the corporation, unlike the investors, but the directors as a unit, certainly are not, in practice, really indispensable elements of its CID structure.

With respect to any aggregate of persons or actors who have some power in a situation, it is natural to think that each of the members of the group, to some degree at least, has the power.[12] Insofar as determinations of moral and legal responsibility are usually thought to be dependent on resolutions of questions regarding what someone has or had the power to do in a situation, the distribution of power in such collectives is an important factor. As noted in Part One, to have power in a situation is to have certain abilities and capacities in that situation. Hence, to have power in an aggregate group like those identified on the corporation organizational chart, is to possess the dispositional property of being able, if one wants, under certain conditions, to move the rest of the group, in this case the CID structure agents, to action or inaction; that is, to act so that the corporation acts.

To have power over the corporation's behavior is not necessarily to have exercised that power or even to know one has it. However, the latter as well as the former may be moral failings for which persons, actors, and groups can and should be held responsible when things go wrong. These are the sorts of failings that the critics of current board practices are making about the apparently impotent or merely lazy boards of American corporations. Under what conditions is a particular subgroup of those on the organizational chart liable to be held responsible for what the corporate actor did or did not do?

It should be recalled that I adopted the position that when persons or corporate actors have power with respect to particular occurrences or events, there are some intentional actions those persons or corporate actors can perform at the appropriate time that will ensure that their particular events will occur. Likewise there are some intentional actions they can perform that will prevent the events from occurring. My account of power corresponds (again, as noted in Part 1) to what Fischer calls control.

Board members of most American corporations have, at best, only regulative control of their corporation's actions, if they have any control at all. They are not typically in on the daily operations or on the bulk of the decision making. That is what managers are hired to do. The ethical principle is that to be held responsible, a person must have had at least regulative control in the situation in question.

To determine the board's or any particular director's power and control in a corporate decision situation we could first collectivize our analysis of power and control. Let us suppose that we are thinking about the board of directors of Proctor & Gamble and that the issue is the possible removal of Rely tampons from the market.[13]

The time is the early 1980s. In September of 1980 the Centers for Disease Control releases its report on toxic shock syndrome in which it reveals that 71 percent of the afflicted women in its study had been users of Rely tampons. The publicity linking the Proctor & Gamble product to the disease is explicit and widespread. Television news, magazines, newspapers are featuring stories, and Rely is always prominently mentioned. Rely had about 25 percent of the tampon market. Its major competitor, the giant in the market, is Tampax with 43 percent of the sales.

As all the researchers would have to admit, the evidence that linked Rely to toxic shock syndrome is far from ironclad, but the indications of a relationship are hard to ignore. Consequently, the Federal Drug Administration meets with all of the major tampon manufacturers to work out a warning that could be voluntarily placed on their products.

Only Tampax refuses to prominently display the warning on their packages. Tampax's share of the market increases to 56 percent. Proctor & Gamble executives, led by CEO Edward Harness, first decide to "fight for their brand," but when they learn that their own researchers cannot refute the CDC report, they reevaluate their stance, stop production of Rely, and then withdraw it from the marketplace. In fiscal 1981, they take a $71-million tax writeoff to offset their unrecovered investment and the lawsuits they have to defend arising because of deaths due to toxic shock syndrome associated with the use of Rely. They use the remaining tampons in stock as fuel in one of their factories.

Harness was not only CEO of Proctor & Gamble, he was chair of its board of directors. Did the board have power in the Rely affair? If it did, then there would have to have been considerable coordination, particularly of information, within the board and between the board and the executives at Proctor & Gamble. In other words, for the directors to do what they, as a group, are theoretically supposed to have the power to do, each (or most) must have information about what the other elements of the corporate actor are doing or are likely to do in the circumstances. How they get that information and how they act on it is a version of the coordination problem for decision-making groups, a near cousin to the coordination problem in Iterated Prisoner's Dilemma. (Remember that desirable outcome in Iterated Prisoner Dilemma requires that the players coordinate their choices so that they will both cooperate.) Minimal coordination between the board and the executives sets the parameters on the lower end of the actualization of whatever latent power the board may have.

The fact is that a subset of all of the corporate agents of Proctor & Gamble has the power to decide to withdraw Rely tampons from the market. Let us stipulate that that group includes the senior management and members of the board. In effect, that subset has regulative control with respect to the marketing of Rely. It is possible that Mr. Harness alone has the power, and so the control. But let us imagine that he cannot or will not take such a step without the concurrence of certain other corporate agents. Any particular agent's power in this situation then is dependent on whether or not he or she is an indispensable member of the coterie of Mr. Harness's advisers with respect to the removal of a product from the market.

Consider the following principle: someone is a dispensable member of a group with respect to a certain task if, when all of the members of the group except that person wanted the task to be done, it would be done, even if that person opposed its being done. A person is indispensable with regard to the task if his or her opposition would alter the outcome. The task would not be done, despite the fact that the other members of the group wanted to do it.

The power distribution principle may be summarized as:

A person has some power with respect to a task if a group of which that person is an indispensable member has collective power with respect to the task.

Some of the board members were insiders, high ranking executives of Proctor & Gamble. Others were outsiders. We may reasonably imagine that with respect to the removal of Rely, some of the directors were dispensable and some were indispensable. We may discover, as the sociological evidence regarding American corporations indicates, that what made a director an indispensable member of the CEO's advisory team was not board membership, in and of itself. In other words, some of the directors may have been indispensable in the action, not because they were on the board, but because they were high up in the management team assembled by Mr. Harness. No matter what other board members might advise, it will not really be taken into consideration, and no one's advice will be taken into consideration just because it comes from a board member.

In this case, it is unknown whether Mr. Harness required the support of three or five or ten of his top aides before he was ready to act. Perhaps he made up his mind and acted if at least two of his senior management team members concurred with his decision. He may not tell them his decision, but he decided to act only if at least two advise him to do so in the manner he has determined is best. (Or perhaps it must be the right two.) It doesn't matter how these things actually go. The point is that there is a critical mass of advisers whose opinions will influence the process. The membership in that group will probably vary from subject to subject, fluctuating with the need for expertise. Influence generally translates into power.

Peter Morriss writes:

> The connection between power and responsibility is . . . essentially negative: you can deny all responsibility by demonstrating lack of power. You can do this . . . by proving that you couldn't have done the crime. Or you can do this by showing that you couldn't have prevented the catastrophe. In either case, power is a necessary (but not sufficient) condition for blame: if you didn't have the power, you are blameless.[14]

If the board members in their role as board members are powerless in the decision making of the corporation, then they cannot be said to have any regulative control over its actions, and so bear no responsibility for what was done or not done by the corporation. Insofar as the evidence seems to indicate that boards have been systematically reduced to rubber stamps with little influence in most operational corporate decisions, they are of little interest to corporate ethics.

One question remains troubling with respect to this analysis of power and influence: what if a director (especially an outside director) would have had a major impact if only he or she would have, contrary to the expected behavior, spoken up? Should those in a position to influence know that they are? I think they should, at least up to a point. Suppose if Outside Director X had argued that Proctor & Gamble was weakening its position in potential product liability suits by its unilateral and rapid removal of Rely from the shelves and its educational advertising blitz warning users of Rely of the dangers of toxic shock syndrome, Mr. Harness and his management team would have been persuaded to stiffen their resolve and really fight to save the brand. Wouldn't we have to admit that Director X has power in the situation? But would Director X have acted ethically or unethically by remaining quiet and letting the decision to pull the product be turned into action? A person has a moral responsibility to understand the place, role, status, or station he or she occupies in society at large and in more restricted groups and CID structures. That may be a version of the Socratic dictum, "Know thyself."

Suppose Director X had expressed his view, and some women, who used Rely after Proctor & Gamble became aware of the risks but did not pull the product from the market, died as a result of toxic shock syndrome. Shouldn't the moral responsibility for their deaths fall in some measure on Director X?

It is possible that a person such as Director X may have no idea of his or her power in the CID structure in rare sets of circumstances, such as the Rely case. Past experience on this and other boards left X with the firm conviction that nothing said by outside board members is taken very seriously by management. In such cases it may not make sense to say that X should have known that, with respect to this matter, the CEO would not only be all ears, but would be influenced by X's views.

People may not know their individual powers and have no relatively easy way of finding out about them. Still, a rational-person test could be applied. Simply, any rational person in the circumstances should recognize the reasonable and ethical course of action and try to communicate it. If the person is unable to persuade the appropriate decision-maker(s), at least the person has tried and, in the process, learned the limits of his or her own power.

What is disturbing about the current state of boards of directors in American corporations is that few outside members ever seem to try to represent whatever views they may have on the issues confronting the corporate actor. I think of Piggy in *The Lord of the Flies*, a boy who realized more clearly than the others what the situation required. He tried desperately to convince the other boys on the island of the proper way for the group to organize. However, he lacked the powers of persuasion, the authority, and the brute force necessary to bring about the outcome, and the results were tragic for himself and the others.

Attempts like Piggy's may serve to exclude one from a share of the personal moral responsibility for a corporation's actions or inaction. "I would have been but one against the many," however, is not a morally exculpating plea in one's personal or corporate life.

It could be, and in many places has been, asked whether boards should be changed to make them the crucial insiders of the corporation, to make them, for moral purposes, the corporate agents to whom most attention should be paid in business ethics. Some have proposed clever ways to catapult boards of directors in practice into the lofty positions the glossy company literature says they occupy. I will mention a few such proposals, but I am not convinced that it should matter to corporate ethics whether boards are paper tigers or snarling wolves. What matters is the way corporate actors actually are organized and run, not how we could resuscitate an old organizational model if only we could make the corporate structures over in its image. I don't see why the board charade should be of more than descriptive interest to us, unless the only way to get corporate actors to act ethically, that is not to violate the side constraints against using other Rank B-ers as means only, is to reorganize and reempower boards. Some have argued for that position.

Christopher Stone has set forth the most coherent and thoroughgoing board-focused version of corporate ethics.[15] For Stone, the only, or the best, way to control corporate behavior is to reorganize corporate boards. He, in concert with a number of other corporate critics, argues that inside directors should be eliminated. Richard DeGeorge, for example, wonders, if the board sits in supervisory judgment over the executives, how can those same executives sit on the board?[16] Geneen agrees with Stone and DeGeorge. He writes:

> Perhaps the best way for a board of directors to regain its independence would be to take all the internal management members off the board, including the chief executive . . . . Each group—board and management—would then have separate and distinct responsibilities.[17]

Such a division of labor is intended to increase the accountability of senior managers, but that is not at all guaranteed. Unless the directors have their own staffs and a considerable amount of external input, they will be utterly dependent on the reports provided to them by the senior officers they are supposedly supervising. Overcoming that problem, however, would create a considerable amount of redundancy, and might not produce tangible results. The board would become rather like a shadow management as it shadowed management. Efficiency would be sacrificed, but to what worthy ends?

Stone also endorses a revision of standard director procedure that was put forth by Miles Mace: that the functions of each director should be defined and closely associated with the operations of the corporation.[18] Stone recommends job descriptions for each director, but he does not join with Mace on the matter of who will establish the job descriptions and therefore set the guidelines for the accountability of each director.[19]

Who is in a position to do so? The managers? Hardly. Managers do not want directors to have specified duties that will result in their hounding around the company looking into this or that operation on even a microlevel. Directors? Well, they're most likely to follow their old ways and cast their job descriptions in the broadest and least specific terms. Most of them don't want to spend the vast amounts of time close supervisory activities might take. Therefore, if we leave the matter of guidelines for directors up to the interested parties, we are likely to get nothing much more specific than is currently occurring. Stone's solution:

> The answer lies in society's identifying core functions the directors ought to be performing and then providing for them *by law*; the federal government has adequate power to do so by general legislation under the Commerce Clause.[20]

Stone and others would also like to see a radical change in the way we assess the liability of directors for the activities of their corporation. It is true in fact, if not in theory, that directors have little liability when it comes to their oversight of corporate affairs.

> Directors run virtually no personal risk for any amount of complacency, cronyism, or outright neglect of their duties. While the law holds them responsible as fiduciaries to the stockholders, the courts have interpreted that responsibility very leniently. A director would rarely be found liable unless cupidity, a clear conflict of interest, or gross negligence (a vague concept) could be proved. Even then he is usually further protected by his company's indemnification and insurance policies, which in effect guarantee that any damages assessed against him will be paid by the company.[21]

Stone's recommendations are that directors should be liable to the corporation for losses it incurs due to gross negligence by the board and for their failure to perform those directorial duties that are most vital to the corporation. Gross negligence might include situations in which the loss is caused by criminal activity when the director was or should have been aware of the likelihood of its occurrence and did not take the steps a reasonably prudent director would take to prevent the criminal activity. The vital duties, as noted by Stone, might include checking the accuracy of stock registrations and declaring dividends that are reasonable in light of the corporation's financial needs. Still, Stone would not, except in the worse nonfeasance and gross negligence cases, penalize the offending director with more than a three-year prohibition from serving as an officer or board member or consultant to a company engaged in interstate business.[22]

Well, what should be made of these attempts to locate the directors square in the middle of a corporation's responsibility? Very little, I think. The directors, to be sure, are agents of the corporate actor, but they are not, in practice, as we have noted, anywhere near as important as they are portrayed in the standard accounts in the organizational literature. The idea that their responsibilities should be beefed up and emphasized seems to be a product of frustration with the fact that the reality of the corporate actor is inconsistent with the favored economic and organizational models and theories. The directors of any corporation are a relatively small number of human persons who can be isolated and easily targeted for ethical evaluation. But the principle that ethical responsibility requires control and influence, as discussed above, shields them, for directors, despite the boilerplate, have only limited power and control with respect to most of what corporate actors do. Their agency is remarkably limited. Robert Townsend comments:

> [M]ost big companies have turned their boards of directors into nonboards . . . . In the years that I've spent on various boards I've never heard a single suggestion from a director (made as a director *at* a board meeting) that produced any result at all.[23]

What really underlies this focus on directors in the business ethics literature are two dubious, but persistent, beliefs: that managers are the incorrigible villains of the corporate world and that stockholders really own or are the corporation. As I have already discussed the latter, we can shift our attention to the former belief.

3. Management: Drones, Comers, and Stars — Their Games and Sports on the Managerial Ladder

In recent years, managers, especially senior managers, have become the culprits of choice of popular culture. Bankers played those roles since the days of the melodrama and secured a firm lock on them in the '30s in westerns and crime fiction. But in the last few decades if a script writer is looking for a villain the majority of folks can hiss, he or she shines the spotlight on the residents of the executive suites. We ought not, of course, forget that there is much precedent for this in the last century when Charles Dickens took a number of well-aimed swipes at the captains of industry, as did Upton Sinclair, Sinclair Lewis, and others in the first half of this century.

The corporate manager as corrupt, degenerate scoundrel, however, has risen to new popular heights in films such as *The China Syndrome, Wall Street, Batman Returns, Men At Work, Silkwood, Acceptable Risks, Big Business, Where The Heart Is*, and *The Toxic Avenger*. Obviously, the public perception of managers is not far above lawyers and used-car salespersons. I do not hope to be able to convincingly explain why managers are the new targets of popular-culture venom. Perhaps the gospel of greed with which they are often associated, and with which they associated themselves in the 1980s, makes them appear as more easily corruptible than the rest of us. Perhaps the fact that managers of large corporations are known to wield so much power, and we all have been told by our grandmothers that power corrupts, accounts for their pop status. Maybe we have seen so much of managerial scandal, duplicity, cutthroat behavior, and unsavory associations reported in the news media that it is becoming difficult not to think of managers as nefarious. Reports of executive incomes in the range of those of drug kingpins doesn't help the common perception. Still, America's business schools are packed to overflowing with young people who are desperate to become managers, willing to study such boring subjects as accounting, marketing, finance, foregoing the joys of English literature and art history. I have known students who actually get "turned on" by finance. Their ecstasy at the prospect of debt financing reportedly is, as some managers have been quoted as saying, better than sex. High praise, indeed!

So, there is something of an anomaly on the scene. Popular culture has been having a great time denigrating and castigating (and even castrating) managers, while hordes of educated Americans are preparing themselves and applying for corporate managerial jobs. Clearly, students in business schools know that corporate actors are the dominant units of our society and that managers are the dominant corporate agents, the corporate insiders. They are the main players in corporate decision making. They are in control. They have power. Some overlook the fact that that also makes them responsible.

Who are these managers? Robert Jackall's thorough sociological study of corporate management is most helpful in getting a clear picture of them.[24] Based on his work, we can roughly classify managers into three categories. They are either Drones, Comers, or Stars in their corporations. Drones are managers who "find . . . comfortable organizational niches and settle into them."[25] They are usually in their mid-forties or fifties. Perhaps they were once ambitious, but they discovered along the way that they didn't have the drive or the social skills or the style to pursue higher levels of power. They have resigned themselves to career immobility.

In the corporate managerial hierarchy "tacit agreements are reached about them, a kind of silent barter—as long as they continue to perform their functional role, they can stay."[26] Drones are often protected in the decision-making system because a core of knowledgeable but nonthreatening managers is useful to those trying to better themselves. Jackall quotes a manager at a chemical company:

Potential is important but you need some people who are, well, drones. You don't *want* them to move. You need people who will stay in a job for year after year and do the necessary work that is essential to an organization's survival.[27]

Drones have little to no real influence in the decision-making process, though they may be asked to supply standard analyses and position papers from their departments. Jackall says that they tend to be subject to the scorn and contempt of those with power or those seeking power. Often they are overlooked or their performances are downgraded in comparison to Comers. Drones, as a matter of self-protection, tend to try to camouflage their droneness by speaking of themselves in terms of upward mobility. But they are generally fooling no one but themselves.

Comers and Stars avoid like the plague identification by association with Drones. As most Drones started off their corporate careers as Comers, would-be Stars, the Drone is a living, breathing symbol of the failure the Comers all desperately fear. There stands, or rather sits, the Drone they might become but for the grace of the shining Stars and the luck of the markets. If they fail to hurdle over the break points in the corporate career ladder, they will join the ranks of the contemptible, necessary, mediocre majority.

How should Drones be treated? Is there anything ethically wrong with the way the other managers and the corporate actors use the Drones? Of course, outright derision is unacceptable and only the most callous of Comers will behave toward even the most entrenched Drone in that fashion. It's not good form. It gives the impression of kicking someone when they are down. Still Drones are often the butt of Comers' jokes, practical and verbal. The usual dealings between managers, however, are not Type One interactions. They are a species of Type Three interactions. Both are acting as corporate agents, albeit of the same corporation.

When midlevel manager 1 (a Comer) asks midlevel manager 2 (a Drone) for a certain market survey, the interaction is not between human persons. Manager 1 ought not to treat the Drone as a means only to his own ends, that is, to his advancement up the corporate ladder. However, let us stipulate that manager 2's job is described as a line or staff function of manager 1's position. Manager 2 is there to be used by manager 1. If he isn't used, he has no function in the CID structure. Of course he is not being used by 1 for 1's personal ends, except incidentally. If 2 does well, 1 will get the credit, and that will improve 1's chances of busting over the break point. The ethical issue between the two reduces to a matter of respect between human persons, so long as the task manager 1 is procuring from manager 2 is within the defined corporate role of the latter. Simply, manager 2's residence in that position in the CID structure constitutes his or her tacit approval to be used as a means to certain types of corporate ends by those in other stations or positions in the corporation, even though they stand to benefit personally from that use. Manager 2 has no moral or other grounds for objection.

But, there are different ways to use people, even, especially, Drones, when they are serving as corporate agents. The Comer has a moral obligation to observe those constraints, restrictions against behavior that amounts to one form of harassment or another, as will be discussed in detail later in this part of the book.

A Comer: A lower-ranking manager who has shown sufficient promise to be assigned to successively more responsible probationary positions. The making of a Comer begins in college, but the first reliable signs that one is emerging are not evident until the latter part of the senior year. Comers are then clearly distinguishable from other college students by their dress. They have doffed the uniform of the college undergraduate: sloppy, uncoordinated clothing, usually torn in strategic places, rumpled tee-shirts or stained sweatshirts and jeans, dirty, dilapidated tennis shoes (but of a major brand), hair cut, and perhaps dyed, in some outrageous fashion, ragged beards, fluorescent lipstick. Comers don the uniform of the corporate office. They show up to class, because they are later to go to an interview, in "three-piece, wool pinstripped suits or suited skirts; button-down collars or unfrilled blouses; sedate four-in-hand foulards for men and floppy printed bow ties for women; wing-tipped shoes or plain lowheeled pumps; somber straightforward hues; and . . .bright, wellscrubbed, clean-shaven or well-coiffured appearances."[28] The change can be utterly upsetting to their professors and fellow classmates.

The youth pseudo-ghetto that is the American college is annually afflicted with a dress-for-success plague breaking out all over. I can vividly remember one year a female student who had appeared in classes for ten weeks dressed in the current (and ironically expensive) grunge fad as though she were auditioning for a chorus part in Annie's orphanage, but with streaks of bright green and maroon in her platinum hair and two-inch curling fingernails painted to match the black lipstick she always wore, showing up in a taupe skirt with a matching vest over an unfrilled white blouse. Her hair had, miraculously turned to an ordinary brunette, her nails were cut and coordinated with light pink lipstick. No one in the class recognized her. She even sat up straight instead of the usual slouch across her desk. It was really unnerving. I got the distinct impression that the other students viewed her either as a kind of traitor or as someone who had caught an unpleasant disease, was unlikely to recover, and deserved sympathy. She had job interviews that afternoon. She was becoming a Comer, or at least she hoped so.

The business of dress is no small matter among managers. Social image, public appearance, is very much a part of the job, at least if you're a Comer. Some managers have told me that you can tell when a

Comer has given up and settled for being a Drone by a subtle shift in appearance. He or she starts wearing more comfortable-looking clothes, though probably not sports coats, at least at first. Hair may be allowed to grow too long or get cut too short. He or she might start wearing brown. Red ties are replaced with earth tones. Resignation to droneness has occurred!

> Anyone who is so dull-witted or stubborn that he [or she] does not respond to social suggestion and become more presentable is quickly marked as unsuitable for any consideration for advancement.[29]

A manager informed Jackall:

> I'm always astonished by this emphasis on appearances. I mean . . . if they like the way you look, you have a good chance to impress them . . . When the top guys see a guy and say: "Hey, he's great," the myth about the guy is perpetuated. If they say to a plant manager that some guy is great, the plant manager is not going to say that he can't find his ass in a rainstorm. And suddenly the guy is on the fast track.[30]

The acceptable style, of course, is that of the Stars, the top management. Comers realize this and shape themselves accordingly. The "look" must be professional and conservative. Comers make whatever adjustments are necessary in their personal tastes and opinions to eliminate any hint of conflict with the Stars.

Comers must also be known to exercise self-control in all things. They need to quickly develop a talent for masking their personal emotions and intentions "behind bland, smiling, and agreeable public faces. One must avoid both excessive gravity and unwarranted levity. One must blunt one's aggressiveness with blandness."[31] In effect, the trust of the Comer's superiors is built up by blandness, by fitting in, by—in the words of the song from *How To Succeed in Business Without Really Trying*—doing things the company way. The rewards, of course, are increases in control, power, and salary. The first two outdistance the third as motivators. Which is not to say that the third is not important.

Comers, unlike Drones, must be prepared to spend a considerable amount of their time in social rituals inside and outside of the office. These range from endless hours conversing about recent articles in the business press, to political discussion, though not debate, to listening to, telling, laughing at, and repeating jokes. The Comer must float around from office to office, cubicle to cubicle, engaging in face-to-face repartee. If they don't, they are likely to find themselves out of the game. Comers should, therefore, never take long vacations or extended business trips. The Stars may soon forget them and other Comers will do all they can to hasten the process.

The above description of a Comer may suggest that appearances and social graces are all that matter and that "hitting your numbers," achieving the profit quotas set for your department, is of little importance in managerial success. Surprisingly, studies of corporate management indicate that profit making, hitting or surpassing the numbers, is no sure ticket to managerial advancement. Jackall identifies three simple rules that seem to generally apply to line managers: (1) No one who regularly misses his or her numbers will survive; (2) A manager who always hits his or her numbers but who is deficient in the social-ritual elements of corporate life will not advance and is well on his or her way to droneness; and (3) A manager who sometimes misses his or her numbers but who evidences the approved appearance and social and political traits will continue up the corporate ladder to the Stars.[32]

In effect, Comers must become, in the preferred language of corpration, consummate "team players" who regularly deliver the goods. The language of sports, and particularly of that most plodding of major American professional sports, football, has become the language of the corporate managers. The use of the football lingo is rather natural given the tendency of managers and the media to describe American business as a game. Some major problems with that analogy will be discussed below, but first the identification with football is worth some mention.

American football, at least in the eyes of many managers, mirrors corporate life in its extremely specialized personnel aspects, its somewhat plodding and conservative strategy, the almost devotional dependence of the players on the head coach for play calling, and the occasional bursts of action in which individual players do outstanding things while being supported by the rest of the team doing its work. The star running back, for instance, scampers for a thirty-yard touchdown, but only because of the flawless execution of the pulling guards, the interference run by the tackle, the downfield block of the wide receiver, and the perfect handoff from the quarterback. Oh yes, and because the coaching staff had brilliantly designed the whole play. Business will probably never be aligned with professional basketball where the action is fast and furious, set plays typically break down so star players must create on their own, going one on one with an opponent, and leaving the coach, though happy, somewhat in the dark about how it all happened.

From football the corporate world has appropriated: "carrying the ball," "taking the ball and running with it," "fumbling the ball," "passing the ball," "punting," "reversing fields," "getting blindsided," "running down the clock." The list could go on and on. The point of using this sports language is to instill in the Comer the need to be a team player.

There are many aspects to being a team player that corporations want to cultivate, but some are worth special mention. True team players commit themselves willingly and happily to long hours of work for the team. Studies indicate that higher-level managers, those hoping or expecting to become Stars, put in twelve to fourteen hours a day in their corporate offices. Team players are supposed to evidence perseverance at their assigned tasks for the good of the team effort. The popular expression is that they are not prima donnas.

This leads to some odd practical outcomes on the managerial scene. If a manager is deemed brilliant, that may count as a strike against him or her.

> This almost invariably signals a judgment that the person has publicly asserted his [or her] intelligence and is perceived as a threat to others. What good is a wizard who makes his [or her] colleagues . . . uncomfortable?[33]

A midlevel manager is quoted by Jackall as saying:

> Someone who is talking about team play is out to squash dissent. . . . My boss is like that. . . . It's hurt me because I have spoken out. It might be that someone has formed the opinion that I have interesting things to say, but more likely, it gives you a troublemaker label and that's one that is truly hard to get rid of. The troublemaker is often a creative person but truly creative people don't get ahead; to get ahead you have to be dependable and a team player.[34]

A recent perusal of the books on management in a major popular bookstore turns up four or five titles linking management to sports. Books with titles like *Using Sports to Win at Management* and *Successful Management Through the Use of the Strategies of Sport* exploit two features of contemporary life: that Comers are well aware that they are in competitive careers in which winning isn't everything—it's the only thing—and that Comers are more likely to be more knowledgeable and take more seriously matters of sports than any other aspect of the culture. It is hard to imagine a book selling well to Comers with the title: *Winning Management by the Use of Trojan War Tactics* or *How To Get Achilles into the Fray When You Really Need Him* or *Playing Macbeth's Game While Avoiding the Pitfalls of Misunderstanding the Prophesies.*

I am not going to suggest that use of the game analogy and the heavy emphasis on team playing is unethical or immoral playing. There are, however, some problems, or potential or perceived problems. Let's look at the game analogy first.

Robert Solomon and Kristine Hanson have correctly pointed out that the "metaphor for understanding much of American business is not economics; it is rather the ethics of the *game*."[35] The game analogy actually has two sides, and it is not obvious that they are compatible. Comers must certainly see their situations as iterated win or lose games against other Comers. Their careers are pitted against those of others in virtual zero-sum games, many of which may be in progress simultaneously. A number of corporations set up and encourage fierce competition for many fewer promotions than the number of hirees at basic managerial levels. Obviously, this leaves less and less room at the top. (College professors will probably never understand fully what this involves because huge cohort groups of them can move up the promotion ladder on parallel tenure tracks with virtually no competition among themselves.)

Each Comer must view his or her future in the corporation as dependent on comparative performance ratings. Advancement through various managerial grades will come to only a few. The others will either settle into some lower niche or get fired and find themselves on the street looking for another corporation that will afford them the opportunity to compete again. For every victory, there is at least one loss.

On the other side, while all of this internal gameplaying is going on, the corporation itself is engaged in fierce competitive gaming against its rivals in the marketplace. There is no guarantee that the internal game will produce external victories. In fact, because it could have deleterious effects on the bigger game, the team player model is widely stressed. Internal competition is fine, but don't forget that the corporation is in business to make a profit, to outdistance its competitors. Comers must never forget the idea that at least being perceived as a team player is crucial to winning the internal game against the other Comers. In other words, every Comer, by definition, has a semihidden agenda that the internally applied game model suggests. The corporation is aware of that agenda and encourages it, but only to the point defined by the concept of team play. Team play is then the corporation's internal analog to its reciprocally constrained cooperation on the wider social scene.

The sports and game metaphors have been vigorously and vehemently criticized from various quarters. Perhaps the most sustained criticism, and one that has been co-opted by other philosophical points of view, can be identified with Marxism. The criticism is not against using the sports metaphor to characterize the Comer's situation, it is against the very competitiveness of that situation which the sports analogies are intended to illuminate for the Comer. Marxists argue that competition is inherently alienating,[36] and therefore the Comer is placed in a situation that is inherently immoral.

Look at sports, whether professional or quasiprofessional (collegiate). You'll see evidence of team spirit, of disparate people pulling together for a team victory, of hard work, hours of practice, culminating in personal and team success. But you may also see competitors downing huge doses of dangerous drugs to enhance their performances, illegal payoffs made to athletes, the outcomes of games fixed to please criminal gamblers, brawls erupting nightly on professional baseball diamonds, players intentionally provoking and then trying to hurt other players in basketball games, football players blindsiding defenseless opponents, and the list could go on and on. These are indicators,

the Marxists will insist, of something perverse about sports competition. They are but a few examples of the way it alienates people from
their true natures, turns them against each other, and ultimately
against themselves. Drew Hyland writes:

> I would speculate that virtually everyone who has participated actively
> in sports has experienced some form of alienation at one time or
> another . . . . Most of us have played in many a sandlot game which dis-
> solved into futile arguments about whether a baseball hit was fair or foul,
> whether a tennis ball was in or out, whether a person was fouled or not in
> basketball . . . . [M]ost of us have known people who seem only to play their
> best at their sport when they are alienated, when they are angry at their
> opponent, want to hurt them, etc. The frenzies of alienation that some foot-
> ball players work themselves into before games are legend—and
> appalling. . . .[A]lienation is very often, all too often, a component of athletic
> competition.[37]

Hyland is certainly right, but are matters as bad as Marxist Jean-
Marie Brohm describes them?

> Sport . . . contains all the values of traditional, repressive morality and
> hence all the models of behavior promoted by bourgeois society. . . . Sport
> is basically a mechanization of the body, treated as an automaton, gov-
> erned by the principle of maximizing output.[38]

Saying that those who engage in sports generally do so of their own
free will, that any use of them, no matter how alienating, is consensual,
will be met by the Marxists with the rebuttal that a long-standing cultural campaign praising the so-called virtues of sports makes informed
consent impossible. We've certainly heard that argument in various
guises before! It is becoming one of the most popular retreats of those
attacking any major element of Western society and its culture. It
doesn't claim that people are too stupid to realize that they are being
exploited or alienated, but that without the proper training in understanding what is actually happening to them, they are incapable of
making informed consent decisions.

A grand conspiracy to get most of us to love sporting events and to
participate in competitive athletics so that we can be pliable members
of a capitalistic society surely would be harder to make convincing in
another JFK assassination plot. Even Oliver Stone wouldn't touch it.

Actually there was a conspiracy of sorts to get adults to regularly
participate in sporting endeavors, but hardly for the reasons Marxists
would offer. It was motivated by a concern for disease prevention. In
the nineteenth century, during and after the great European cholera
epidemics, the concepts of public health and preventative medicine
were quite deliberately foisted on the population for its own good by
civic figures, medical practitioners, and a philosopher or two. Sport was
encouraged as a way of developing and maintaining a healthy body.

For centuries before that, games, other than sedentary gambling and hunting and shooting, were thought to be the sole province of children. The health craze that accompanied the cholera panic produced an adult fanaticism about exercise, especially if conducted out-of-doors. Most of the team and individual sports that now occupy so much of our time and energies blossomed into adult avocations in this period. Consider mountain climbing. Hasn't it ever struck you as odd that peaks like Everest and the Matterhorn were scaled so relatively recently in human history. They've been there, and humans have been in their vicinities for a terrifically long time. So what would have motivated anyone to climb to the very top of them? Or even to do it competitively, trying to beat a time record up the North Face or some other team of climbers? Frankly, nothing motivated folks to climb them until the nineteenth century. And then? Well, there are always a few folks who will take a healthy hike and a bit of rock climbing to its limits for the sheer "high" they anticipate they'll get from it, turning an activity with medicinal virtues into deep-play froth with life-threatening risks.[39]

There probably was a link, if tenuous, between the encouragement of sport and capitalism because the period in question was also the time of the burgeoning of the Industrial Revolution and workers dying of cholera were hardly very productive. There would have been self-interested reasons for the new captains of industry to champion the cause of sport, and, no doubt, they did. But that is hardly a reason to think that sports were encouraged, as Brohm maintains, to train "the work force to operate according to the norm of capitalist . . . exploitation."[40]

Competition, whether in or out of sport, can be undeniably alienating. It often produces dissociative behavior, behavior that estranges a person from his or her fellows, from the activities in which the person is engaged, and from him or herself. Managers not infrequently report thinking back on what they did to get promoted in their corporations with a sense of unpleasant detachment: "I find it hard to think that I did those things. Well, I suppose I did, you know, to get ahead. It's a dog-eat-dog world. And sometimes you've got to be a real dog. There's just so many bones. But . . .well, I did it, I guess I can't deny it now. It just doesn't seem like me, that's all. I don't like to think about it." Football players looking back on game films of their blindside clipping or intentional injuring of an opponent have been heard to say similar things. And they usually add, "Well, it's part of the game. You've got to show them who's the boss out there. . . ." But is competition *inherently* alienating?

On the descriptive level, all we can legitimately say is that competition frequently produces alienation. But that does not mean that it is inherently alienating or that alienation in some doses is a bad thing. Competition might only be alienating when it is unconstrained or not restricted by basic ethical principles.

Those principles in sports or games are generally classified as encouraging the virtues of sportsmanship and fair play. The very concept of sport, I think, should include, in some way, the notion of sportsmanship, of being sporting. To display those virtues associated with sportsmanship is to rein in one's competitive spirit at least to the point where one does not take unfair advantage of one's opponent, where one does not use all means at one's command to win, but only those that are fair, again the analog to the reciprocal cooperator constrained strategy discussed in Part 1.

Sportsmanship requires playing not only by the rules of the game, but playing in a certain way. Only fairly won advantages are to be taken. It isn't sporting to cheat, or to intentionally injure. I don't intend to try to more closely examine the concept of fairness in sport. I'm willing to assume that we all, or at least all of us who have played sports, have a rough and ready idea of what fairness comes to. I'm convinced we do in the gross cases and, even though a more thorough analysis could prove edifying in sorting out the application of the concept in the gray areas, that can be left to some other occasion.

It is rather intriguing that the game and sports analogy with the careers of Comers not only draws us to the virtues of sportsmanship and fair play as constraints on corporate-ladder climbing, it yields another concept that is pitted in the minds of many Comers against those very constraints: gamesmanship. Stephen Potter, in 1947, wrote a book called *Gamesmanship: The Art of Winning without Actually Cheating*. Business psychoanalyst Michael Maccoby used the notion to describe someone who is in management mostly for the challenge it provides to prove oneself better than others.[41] The gamesman plays barely within the rules, without *actually* cheating. He or she generally plays on or very close to the margin of fairness, using only the most restrictive definition of that term. Gamespersons go for every edge they can get. They work late hours, but cut corners wherever they can. They are, apparently, more likely to be lured over the edge to unfair play than sportspersons. They are not adverse to bluffing other Comers into pursuing self-defeating projects that will probably exhaust their competitor's energies. Some of their time, in other words, is spent in trying to ensure that their rivals for the better jobs are following fruitless avenues or actually doing things that will eventually benefit the gamesperson. No small amount of their time is expended in garnering information that it took their competition some time to amass. They are, in a word, smooth. They will play a bluff against a fellow to realize a personal gain, but they are careful not to do so in a way that might be discoverable by their superiors or that could hurt the corporation. They are both hated and admired by their fellow Comers for the seemingly effortless way they are able to manipulate others to both their own purposes and the accomplishment of tasks that are in the corporation's interests.

Gamesmanship, in and of itself, is probably not ethically objectionable, assuming that it is constrained by fairness, that cheating is out-of-bounds. Again, we could spend a considerable amount of time trying to clarify whether this or that type of gamesmanship chicanery is cheating. For example, is it cheating to encourage a colleague to believe, though you don't actually say so, that you are doing one sort of task so as to get him or her to reveal data they are working on that is pertinent to your real assigned task? Suppose the rapid and successful completion of your task, made possible only with that data, will thrust you into the corporate limelight and propel you over the competitor whose hard-earned data you garnered? I will, however, let such matters lie.

The major difficulty with gamesmanship as the adopted life-style of Comers from the corporation's point of view is that its manifestations can often obscure the corporate actor's interests and goals. Young managers can get so wrapped up in trying to get and maintain an edge in the contests against each other that the corporation becomes somewhat akin to a well worn playing field. Corporations are not in existence to provide sporting grounds for gamespersons to tussle. Gamesmanship, therefore, requires two sorts of constraints: The interests of the corporation are overriding, hence team play is primary and rewarded accordingly, and fairness, or the ethics of sportsmanship, must dominate the tactics of gamesmanship.

A further word about alienation and competition: Hyland draws attention to the Aristotelian distinction between descriptive and teleological analyses of any phenomenon. A descriptive analysis tries to provide an accurate description of the phenomenon, possibly a causal one, while a teleological analysis

> . . . appeals not just to the way things are, but to the way they ought to be, or are at their best . . . what the thing will become if it is allowed to develop to its highest capacity.[42]

The standard way of explaining teleological analysis is to refer to a seed, perhaps one of those whirly maple seeds we used to play with as children. Teleologically, it is the nature of maple seeds to become maple trees. But, because we messed up a whole bunch of them in our wanton childish play, and others fell on pavement or poor soil, or for a million other reasons never took root, few of them ever become majestic mature maple trees with glorious fall foliage and delicious early spring syrup. The point is that a teleological analysis of the seed depends not on what usually happens to seeds, but what happens to seeds if they are allowed to develop in the fullest way they are naturally capable of developing. It doesn't matter if such development only infrequently occurs, even if it never can occur because of the unnatural interference of childish maple-seed fiends.

Hyland grants that there is a very strong correlation between sports competition and the alienation of the competitors from each other and from themselves (and sometimes from the sport).

> On a descriptive analysis, that would be sufficient to claim that competition caused alienation, that alienation was a "natural" consequence of competition . . [43]

Teleologists, however, could argue that when competition is allowed to achieve its true, natural, ends that it produces a nonalienating situation. Alienation, though most common, it might be said, is the "defective mode" of competition. Hyland thinks that "Competition at its best, when it works, is an occasion of friendship."[44]

I have strong reservations regarding Hyland's conception of the telos or ultimate end of competition being friendship. Surely, many of us have found and secured stronger ties to friends while competing with them over one thing or another, perhaps the net on a tennis court. But I doubt that the competition itself is responsible for the friendships and, to revert back to the descriptive, it can most certainly destroy friendships. It seems to me extremely odd that if friendship is the true and natural end of competition, that competition can so easily be marshaled to defeat it. During a television broadcast of the NBA finals involving the Chicago Bulls and the Phoenix Suns, Magic Johnson, one of the world's true experts on competition, chided stars Michael Jordan and Charles Barkley for being too friendly. The game is about competition, fair, yes, but not friendly.

I am willing to join with the Marxists in associating *unconstrained* competition with alienation. After all, that is the sort of thing Hobbes would have identified with his "state of nature," and his description of that could substitute for the definition of alienation in the dictionary.

> . . . [E]very man is Enemy to every other man; . . . wherein men live without other security than what their own strength, and their own invention shall furnish them withall. In such a condition . . . the life of man [is] solitary, poore, nasty, brutish, and short.[45]

I suppose it would be too unbelievable in this day and age, or too unsporting a slap at Hobbes and the Marxists and all of those busy psychoanalysts out there, to boldfacedly claim that nothing is inherently awful about alienation anyway, that it can be, and often has been, a creative and productive state for many humans. No, I guess that would be too, too much. Instead I would argue that nothing is wrong with a moderate amount of alienation, that, at least in some doses, it is a powerful wellspring of action that if properly channeled, can be most productive. Those capable of stomaching a certain amount of it, of getting on with their attempts to achieve their goals despite a consistently nagging sense of it, are suited to the higher managerial roles in a corporation.

If you must have friends and a constant sense of self-contentment, then the life of the Drone is suited to you. But if you aspire to managerial power and control in the corporation, you will have to learn to cope with alienation, because the competition is incessant. The old expression, "It's lonely at the top" is true, but it's also lonely on the way to the top as well. Is that a bad thing, something we should, in the name of ethics and morality, want to change? I don't see why. Our primary ethical principles, as discussed in Part 1, forbid behavior that treats Rank B-ers as mere means unless the conditions necessary for any Rank B-er to lead a worthwhile life are threatened. The competition involved in the Comer's corporate existence does not violate that principle, though individual Comers may violate it in their dealing with others trying to climb the corporate ladder.

We should conclude that there is nothing wrong, in general, with the sports and games metaphor, or with the competition between Comers it is supposed to illuminate, so long as that competition, like sporting games, is not unconstrained. Within most corporations the recognition of this requirement is evident in the antidote of team play that is prescribed in large doses for all Comers.

There are, however, some possible moral problems with all of this team-playing business in business.

4. The Protestant Ethic, Managerial Language Manipulation, and Lying

One of the myths of American corporate business is that it, the evolved form of capitalism, embodies the Protestant ethic. It doesn't. The Protestant ethic, identified by Max Weber, refers to a set of beliefs to the effect that individual hard work and self-discipline will be rewarded with prosperity by the grace of God. The idea is that "restless, continuous, systematic work in a worldly calling"[46] is held in highest esteem by God and therefore honored by prosperity.

This belief is identified with the Protestants probably because certain Protestant sects, particularly those with Calvinistic commitments, both in their formative years and today, profess some version of it. (There are ancient biblical roots to the belief as well, though much of the Book of Job seems to be devoted to belittling it. Job had been a hard worker, a devout man, and a pillar of his community; still, he lost his prosperity and everything that went with it because of a cosmic bet between God and Satan.) In any event, the Protestant ethic encourages individuals to utilize their talents in hard work in order to achieve both earthly prosperity and heavenly salvation. It may not have produced, but it certainly encouraged and authenticated, the mercantile, and then the Industrial Revolutions.

> The enduring significance of the Protestant ethic was due to the way it linked the probation of self, work in the world, and eternal salvation. An individual served an unknowable God, not by prayer or by almsgiving but by faithfully, continually, and unremittingly performing his or her worldly work. The rational and methodical pursuit of a worldly vocation, when it was crowned with economic success, proved a person before others. Their approbation helped the individual convince himself that he had proved himself to God and attained salvation.[47]

There can be little doubt historically that the Protestant ethic was instrumental in the growth of capitalism. As it encouraged saving rather than spending one's earnings on such frivolous things as vacations and new clothes, it motivated the creation of the capital necessary for industry to expand. And expanding was something its prescription for salvation encouraged. It also justified the accumulation of wealth by the formerly middle-class merchants and artisans and so gave rise to deeper class distinctions in the industrialized countries. And the Protestant ethic justified those as well because, and we hear all manner of its offspring today: Poor folks are poor because they do not work hard enough or long enough to have attained the favor of God. Prosperity favors those who are self-reliant, frugal, hard working, and rational in their decision making. Economic and social failure is the price paid by those who lack those virtues.

Above all, the Protestant ethic is individualistic. In that respect it reflects the central Protestant doctrine of the "priesthood of all believers," the idea that every individual believer can have direct access to God, requiring no priestly intercessions, no ecclesiastical hierarchical structures, in the process. In its day, such an idea was radical in the extreme, and its popularity in the countries of northern Europe in the sixteenth century laid the foundations for the political individualistic doctrines of Hobbes and Locke.

The religious elements of the Protestant ethic have disappeared from its tenets, except in isolated communities such as one I used to live near in rural Minnesota. It is the wealthiest per capita community in the state and surely the most devoutly Calvinistic. The Protestant ethic has become the Work ethic. It still sports its extreme individualism, and it is the wellspring of self-made-man (or -woman) stories, thousands of self-help, how-to-succeed books, and hundreds of half-hour infomercials on late-night cable television networks owned by self-made men.

The Protestant ethic, stripped of the promise of religious salvation, turns into something on the order of "work your fingers to the bone to amass a fortune so that you can will it to your children or, because you haven't had time to have children, to some money-grubbing private college to endow a building in which students will be taught to despise not only the fruits of hard work, but hard work itself."

More importantly, the Protestant ethic cuts right across the grain of the consumerism that American business must foster to keep itself afloat. Frugality and debt-financed consumption aren't strange bedfellows—you can't even get them into the same room. Work is not sanctified in contemporary America. Consumption, the more conspicuous the better, is.

The tenets regarding frugality and salvation were removed from the Protestant ethic with the separation of church and work. But surely its bare-bones praise of the virtues of toil—that business about earthly rewards for hard work, self-reliance, the Emersonian prattle now associated with Dean Witter—remain and are still apropos. Hardly.

In fact, work isn't work anymore, not the way it used to be. Or rather the very form of work, except in pockets of the economy such as the one into which I have fallen in the company of an ever-decreasing number of family farmers and a few other misfits, has been transformed by the corporate invaders. The corporatization has put a clock on work. It has standardized what is done and when it is done, made the business of business a matter of routine procedures. And with it came the managers and the corporate CID structures in which they function. Out went the Protestant ethic, in came the corporate or bureaucratic ethic: team play. Corporatized work has made the remnants of the Protestant ethic obsolete.

William Whyte, in his famous book on corporate life, *The Organization Man*, argues:

> One of the key assumptions of the Protestant Ethic had been that success was due neither to luck nor to the environment but only to one's natural qualities—if men grew rich it was because they deserved to. But the big organization became a standing taunt to this dream of individual success. . . . As organizations continued to expand, the Protestant Ethic became more and more divergent from reality. . . . That upward path toward the rainbow of achievement leads smack through the conference room . . . the committee way simply can't be equated with the "rugged" individualism that is supposed to be the business of business. . . . The man of the future, as junior executives see him, is not the individualist but the man who works through others for others.[48]

Whyte's point is that the emphasis on team play and conformity that marks the contemporary corporate office is a far cry from the tenets of the Protestant ethic. Managing has become an "end in itself." It is severable from the productive activities it manages. It doesn't matter what is being produced or what services are being provided by the corporation; its managers can easily shift their energies from one product to another, from one corporation to another.

I had a conversation with a recent graduate of a business undergraduate program. He told me he had three job offers, all for bottom-rung management jobs, in three corporations that produced things as different as computer software, cake mixes, and engine gaskets. He wondered which one I thought he should take. I asked him which company's business he knew the most about. He laughed. He knew nothing about any of them, if what I meant was how they manufactured their products. That was immaterial, he assured me. He would be a manager, not a production person. What really mattered was the prospects for upward mobility. Even the original starting salary was secondary. In fact, he chose the company where he thought he had the best chances of rapid promotion. It was not the one in which he would make the highest starting salary. A few years later I saw him again, and he bubbled with enthusiasm about his rising status in the company and joked that although he still didn't have much of an inkling of how gaskets were made, his managerial talents were becoming more and more finely tuned. He had learned team play and praised its virtues in the fanatical way of a new convert.

What does the team-play ethic of corporations require of managers? Quite a lot in terms of conformity of dress and attitudes and long hours of office rituals. Although some of my colleagues, in unison with the old Protestant ethic crowd, argue that such demands are morally indefensible because they rob people of their individuality, I don't find that persuasive. Such an argument would have to work against dress codes and uniformity across most occupations for it to be at all convincing. Academics, of course, notoriously get away with much more in the way of expressions of personal style than those in other professions, but that is hardly a reason to think that the tailored suit and designer tie crowd is being used in a way that violates the side constraints relevant to Type Two interactions.

People can quite rationally and freely choose to work in organizations that require extreme conformity without being the victims of the manipulation of those organizations. Though I am rather sure that I would find the boundaries of behavior in most corporations uncomfortably restrictive, many, perhaps most people do not, or they are willing to trade off some control over their dress and time for the prospects of organizational power and a comfortable salary. I can see no good reason to wave the red flags of morality at them or their corporations on that count.

There are, however, some more serious ethical concerns involved in the team-play ethic that cut much deeper than the superficial matters of outward conformity. These involve the language manipulation required of managers, and especially Comers. Do you have to be a liar to rise to corporate power on the managerial ladder?

Jackall writes:

At any given moment in most major corporations, one can find a vast array of vocabularies of motive and accounts to explain or excuse and justify, expedient action; . . . [A]nd the ideological constructions of managers grappling with the whirlwinds of discontent and controversy endemic to our society . . . inevitably envelop the corporation. Managers have to be able to manipulate with some finesse these sophisticated, often contradictory, symbolic forms that mask, reflect, and sometimes merely sweep through their world.[49]

What is meant by "manipulate these symbolic forms?" Actually, that very expression is an example of the problem. Comers must learn how to speak in "provisional discourse." They must master the art of speaking in complex and euphemistic ways in order to both protect their positions vis à vis other managers and to shield the corporation from those outside of it that are perceived by the managers to be in permanent attack mode with regard to any vaguely suspect corporate activity.

Comers must learn that even though they are locked in career make-or-break struggles against other Comers, that innuendo and not open criticism is the only acceptable way to communicate the failures of one's competitors within the corporation. There are many rational reasons for the unwritten sanction against overt criticism of other managers. But the most obvious is the prudential one that counsels that today's managerial equal may tomorrow be one's superior.

More important, however, is the matter of style. Managers who are known to be critical of others are regarded as not being able to work with people, as lacking finesse in handling others, and so as unworthy of advancement. Jackall notes:

Discreet suggestions, hints, and coded messages take the place of command. . . . One cannot even criticize one's subordinates to one's own superior without risking a negative evaluation of one's own managerial judgment.[50]

The language a Comer uses is to be emotion-neutral, oblique whenever possible, emptied of strong convictions, and devoid of sentiment.

The real art of talking managerialese, however, is to be able to string together a number of sentences that are filled with internal contradictions and still make it all sound sensible. Doing so allows the Comer to have an expressed view on all sides of an issue. I am not trying to be facetious here, though I admit to a degree of bemused puzzlement about the whole business. Having been trapped myself in the tangle of trying to determine what a manager, in this case a college administrator, actually was endorsing, and unfortunately, making the wrong interpretation, I know the difficulties one who is "maze-dense" (as the managers say) can cause for him or herself and others in the organization. A colleague recently told me that he had just been to a meeting with the senior executive of the institution and thought he had heard rather strong support for his research project. When he heard that same executive quoted by one on the next lower level, however, he was told that support was tentative and hardly worth banking on. I told him to join the maze-dense club.

On the other side, Comers who are likely to really get ahead quickly become "maze-bright." That's a wonderful term for those who not only are able to talk in euphemistic contradictions, but who actually are able to correctly read between the lines of what other managers and superiors are saying and act in the approved, if hidden, way. "Maze-brighters" can distinguish mere posturing from expressions of executive intent, bluffing from real threats, and spur of the moment suggestions that will be soon forgotten from directives to act that must be carried out or one's job is lost.

Underlying maze-brightness is what Jackall refers to as "the implicit understanding that should the context change, a new, more appropriate meaning can be attached to the language already used."[51] What this comes to is that success in management requires a Comer to adopt the attitude towards himself or herself and others that what one says is not one's bond, that all symbol manipulation is provisional, never carved in stone, and that those who take promises and yesterday's expressions of agreement as binding are foolish. Furthermore, the language used by subordinate managers must, at least in the difficult cases, provide the senior managers with a sufficient amount of deniability, a term bequeathed to the vocabulary by the politicians in the Reagan administration. The idea is that any problem or crisis must be described both to the public and to one's superiors in such abstract and euphemistic terms that no single interpretation emerges as self-recommending. "The rule of thumb here seems to be that the more troublesome a problem, the more desiccated and vague the public language describing it should be."[52] Examples include the way managers in the tobacco industry talk of lung cancer, how those at Exxon first described the *Exxon Valdez* spill, the Union Carbide explanations of the Bhopal tragedy, the way executives at Ford Motor Company discussed the Pinto case, the verbal maneuvering of McDonnell-Douglas after crash after crash of their DC-10s.

The general idea is that managers must become adept at saying all sorts of things, often flat-out contradictory things, about the same event or problem and yet, as a consequence of their symbol manipulation, not be identifiable with any particular point of view or claim. One's vocabulary should also reflect the current fashion in rhetorical obfuscation, but, above all, the mark of managerial success at team play is the ability to sound absolutely convincing when one is being utterly inconsistent. "Throwing people off the track" is the practiced and highly regarded skill, and it doesn't matter if those people are members of the public, government regulatory agencies, or, to a point, fellow insiders. This begins to sound rather a bit like an epistle from C. S. Lewis' famous devil, Screwtape! Perhaps it should.

Lying, as many renowned ethical philosophers and the moral codes of most every culture tell us, is wrong. Perhaps the most famous defense of the prohibition against lying is found in the ethical theory of Immanuel Kant.[53] Kant, applying his universalization principle, as discussed in Part 1, would have us imagine the consequences of lying becoming a universal feature of social life. He says that if that were to happen, no one would tell the truth, and therefore no trust between persons would ever be sustainable. Most human interactions, because they are based on some degree of trust, would cease to occur. But insofar as the conditions that make truth-telling possible would be annihilated, any point in lying would also be lost. Lying depends on a social background of expected and confirmed truth-telling and trust. Without that, a lie has no power. Insofar as lying, if universalized, would destroy that background, a liar cannot rationally will that the maxim of his or her action become a universal law for all people without willing that the very thing he or she is doing, lying, lose its point. Therefore lying is wrong.

Sissela Bok has elaborated on this Kantian point by emphasizing the consequences, that is, she argues that lying in any form is wrong because it always weakens the stability of society. "A society . . . whose members were unable to distinguish truthful messages from deceptive ones, would collapse."[54]

On the other side of this issue, at least as it is applied to business, is Alfred Carr. In a famous article in the *Harvard Business Review*, he argued that the ethics of business ought to be understood as akin to that of poker. Carr writes:

> We can learn a good deal about the nature of business by comparing it with poker. . . . No one expects poker to be played on the ethical principles preached in churches. In poker it is right and proper to bluff a friend out of the rewards of being dealt a good hand . . . . The game calls for distrust of the other fellow. It ignores the claim of friendship. Cunning deception and concealment of one's strength and intentions . . . are vital in poker. No one thinks any the worse of poker on that account. And no one should think any the worse of the game of business because its standards of right and wrong differ from the prevailing traditions of morality.[55]

In poker it is permissible to try to bluff the other players into thinking one is going to do one thing rather than what one actually intends, or into thinking one holds a hand with a value considerably greater than it actually is. The rules of poker do not require that one prevaricate about such things, but lying, in the form of bluffing, is not prohibited as a strategy or tactic. All players fail to guard against it at their peril or the peril of their pocketbooks.

Certain kinds of lying are forbidden in poker. When the hands are called there can be no lying, though if the bluff is successful, one will probably lie to conceal that it was a bluff in the first place and thereby make the other players less likely to question one's bluffing during future hands. Poker's rules set the boundaries on what is cheating, and discovered cheaters not only find it hard to get another game, at least in Old Texas they can get shot dead where they sit. Discovered bluffers may merit more respect and attention, but they won't be packed off in a pine box to Boot Hill.

Is bluffing lying? Sure. It is a kind of lying, and the best bluffers work the trick through an elaborate set of symbol manipulations, both verbal and nonverbal. It is not telling the truth. Is it morally wrong in poker? No. Why? Just saying that the rules do not forbid it is inadequate. The question concerns not its poker permissibility, but its moral permissibility. When one has been bluffed out of a good-sized pot, the response that such an outcome is permitted, even expected, in poker rings hollow. One still wants to say, "You shouldn't have done it. You won by deception. It's lying. It's morally wrong. Think what Kant would say. You've played on my gullibility, my trust of you," silly gibberish like that, and if one says such things, there will be no more invitations to the neighborhood poker parties. But the reason it is gibberish is that the moral appeal is what is hollow. There is nothing morally wrong with this sort of lying.

In his *Lectures on Ethics*, Kant retreats somewhat from his categorical stand against lying. He writes:

> I may make a false statement when my purpose is to hide from another what is in my mind and when the latter can assume that such is my purpose, his own purpose being to make a wrong use of the truth.[56]

The idea is that one need not tell the truth if the parties involved know that lying is commonplace, likely, and built into the premises of that activity in such a way that most of those engaged in the activity are fully aware of it. Norman Bowie calls this "the openness condition."[57]

The openness condition is really a consensual condition. When I sit down to play poker with my neighbors, I consent to their attempting to bluff me and I will try, in the usual absence of good cards, to bluff them. I'll go, of course, only as far as I think I can persuade them, and as that is generally not very far, none of them will get too mad at me for doing it.

In the obfuscating and euphemizing verbal world of the manager, bluffing lying satisfies the openness condition. After all, the Comers and most of the other managers, perhaps especially the Drones, are expected to be maze-bright. And what is maze-bright if not a satisfaction of the openness condition? What is interesting is that maze-brightness does not seem to weaken the effectiveness or the frequency of the verbal manipulation.

It would probably take a social psychologist to explain why maze-bright managers participate in the team-play ethic with such relish. One possible explanation is that, as with poker, even though everyone is aware that bluffing is an accepted strategy, the particular form it will take from manager to manager is uncertain, and the outcomes are also uncertain. Changes in the acceptable fashion also make matters of adaptability uncertain. Hence, the activity is challenging and risky. Success is also highly rewarded. And it must be remembered that two things are not permitted: outright fabrication and winning by bluffing in a way that damages the interests of the corporate actor or one's superiors. Those conditions cast fairly strong controls over the extent of lying that can be tolerated in managerial circles.

In effect, then, managerial bluffing does not really violate the side constraints and it apparently has positive consequences within the corporation when it comes to molding the sense of teamwork that has reined in the Protestant ethic, while it does not discourage productive individual competition between Comers for an always decreasing number of superior positions.

The same symbol manipulation techniques, when applied by managers against those outside of the CID structure, the public and other corporate actors, however, cannot usually pass the openness test and will violate the side constraints against Rank B-ers using other Rank B-ers. The exceptions are managers of used car lots. These matters will be discussed further in Part 4.

One further point is worth making with respect to the team-play ethic: the interactions involved are Type Three. That is to say that the Comers are not, in the normal cases, acting as human persons in these interactions. They are corporate agents interacting with other corporate agents. The legitimacy of their relationships in the interactions, indeed the point of them at all, comes from their stations or roles in the corporation. Outside of the corporate structure their symbol manipulations would either be meaningless or outright offensive: morally wrong.

Because the parties in these interactions are both corporate agents and human persons, it is possible, and even probable, that parallel Type One interactions will also occur. Maze-bright Manager X may have taken an immediate disliking to Comer Y, and so she throws roadblocks in Y's path just for the joy she expects to get when the "little bastard" screws up. The Type One interaction may supersede the team-play ethic of Type Three interactions for X. She is no longer bluffing for corporate reasons. She is bluffing to cause a disaster to befall Y, regardless of the corporate fallout. The moral protections of the openness condition are violated.

Within Type Three interactions the bluff and the symbol manipulation may be permissible, not unethical. But if those activities fall to a personal level, a Type One interaction in which the openness condition is not satisfied, they are unethical. In this way, the CID structure maps the ethical conditions under which corporate agents, particularly managers, act. Team play, in the end as well as the beginning, entails a team.

5. Teleopathy: Symptoms and Sources

On March 3, 1974, on the outskirts of Paris, France, a Turkish Airlines plane carrying 346 passengers and crew crashed, killing everyone on board. The plane was a DC-10 manufactured by the McDonnell-Douglas Corporation, with design subcontracting done by the Convair Division of General Dynamics. Actually, it was Ship 29 of the DC-10 line. The crash was no mere accident. It was not the result of pilot or crew error. It occurred because the plane's cargo door blew open at approximately ten thousand feet, causing the floor of the passenger compartment to collapse, breaking the lines of electric and hydraulic cables that run under that floor and without which the plane cannot be flown.

The Paris crash was not the first cargo-door failure to happen while a DC-10 was in flight. As a matter of fact, the prototype ship of the line, Ship 1, while under pressurization tests on the ground, blew its cargo door. Many of the engineers and managers at McDonnell-Douglas knew of the likelihood of what the airline industry calls a Class IV hazard involving the DC-10 due to a defective design of its cargo door locking system.

The original plans by Convair engineers, led by Dan Applegate, Director of Product Engineering, for the door latching system on the DC-10 called for hydraulically actuated locks and controls. McDonnell-Douglas engineers, however, opted to use electronic actuators to close the doors, thereby saving twenty-eight pounds of weight per door and, presumably, ensuring easier maintenance. The Convair engineers regarded the hydraulic locks essential to the safety of the aircraft. Their concern was how the systems would work if the doors were not properly latched on any particular flight. Improperly secured hydraulic latches would slide open if just a little pressure had built up in the cabin of the plane. The faulty door would blow off its hinges, but, because this would all happen at low altitudes, there would be little decompression of the cabin, and the floor would not collapse severing the cabling. The plane would be able to make a controlled landing. If an electronic latch failed, it would not do so under low pressures, so the door would be blasted open at high altitudes and the resulting rapid decompression of the cabin would produce an uncontrollable situation. That is, of course, what happened to the Turkish Airlines plane.

Convair's engineers found nine possible ways in which the McDonnell-Douglas system was likely to fail causing major loss of human lives. One was rather simple, but probably was involved in the Turkish Airlines disaster. It involved the fact that the warning indicator lights in the cockpit had a tendency to fail. This, coupled with the likelihood that the doors, if not properly locked, would explode at higher altitudes, meant that the plane had a potentially faulty door-locking system. And if it did fail, might give no warning of the impending doom. Obviously, if the warning system were dependable, then, because the hinges would not blow until the plane had fully pressurized, at about ten thousand feet, the pilot would be able to safely land the plane and have the doors properly locked. The combination of faults, however, made that most unlikely.

On July 29, 1971, the FAA, after receiving data from McDonnell-Douglas and running the usual tests, certified the DC-10. Its early performance ratings were excellent, and the company embarked on a far-reaching campaign to sell the plane in the United States and to foreign carriers. McDonnell-Douglas had been seriously suffering in its sales war with Boeing for a profitable chunk of that market. Even before work on the DC-10 had begun, Boeing had successfully introduced its 747 and it was cornering the market on wide-bodied passenger aircraft. Because of their original agreement regarding responsibilities for certification, Convair was contractually prohibited from reporting its position regarding the flawed design to the FAA.

On June 27, 1972, fifteen days before a DC-10 blew its cargo door in flight over Windsor, Ontario, and miraculously landed despite major structural damage and serious injury to eleven people on board, Applegate wrote a now famous memorandum to his immediate superior at Convair. In his memo, Applegate expresses his grave concern that the design of the DC-10 with respect to its cargo doors is fatally flawed. He provides test data to support his opinion. He explains the alternatives that had been proposed by his engineers. He then writes:

> My only criticism of Douglas in this regard is that once this weakness was demonstrated by the July 1970 test failure, they did not take immediate steps to correct it. It seems to me inevitable that, in the twenty years ahead of us, DC-10 cargo doors will come open, and I would expect this to usually result in the loss of the airplane. This fundamental failure mode has been discussed in the past and is being discussed again in the bowels of both the Douglas and Convair organizations. It appears however that Douglas is waiting and hoping for government direction or regulations in the hope of passing costs on to us or their customers . . .
>
> It is recommended that overtures be made at the highest management level to persuade Douglas to immediately make a decision to incorporate changes in the DC-10 which will correct the fundamental cabin floor catastrophic failure mode. Correction will take a good bit of time, hopefully there is time before the National Transportation Safety Board (NTSB) or the FAA ground the airplane which would have disastrous effects on sales

and production both near- and long-term. This corrective action becomes more expensive than the cost of damages resulting from the loss of one plane load of people.

F. D. Applegate
Director of Product Engineering[58]

Applegate's memo went only to his superior, J. B. Hurt. Hurt and Applegate realized that McDonnell-Douglas was not going to embark on the necessary redesign. Hurt told Applegate in his response that if Convair raised more issues about the safety of the design that it, and not McDonnell-Douglas, would probably have to bear the costs of the modifications. The top managers at Convair agreed with Hurt, and Applegate stuck his memo away in his file cabinet. In less than two years, the cargo door of the Turkish Airlines DC-10 blew open and the lives of 346 innocent people were lost.

There are many reasons to be concerned about the events at Convair and McDonnell-Douglas that culminated in the Paris crash, but I want to focus on a general managerial problem that is evident in this case and that is widespread in all sorts of corporations. Kenneth Goodpaster has labeled the sickness of management that produces symptoms like the DC-10 case, "teleopathy."[59] He finds it rampant among managers as a very basic and central character disorder. What is teleopathy (from the Greek for "goal" or "purpose")?

> [T]eleopathy can be understood as a habit of character that values limited purposes as supremely action-guiding, to the relative exclusion not only of larger ends, but also moral considerations about means, obligations, and duties. It is an unbalanced pursuit of goals or purposes by an individual or group.[60]

Teleopathy actually amounts to a failure by managers to constrain their decisions and actions by the principle of not treating others as mere means. That is, it is a condition in which the corporate agent does not respect those other Rank B-ers who are affected by the action being performed. It suspends the side constraints in favor of achieving goals that themselves were not subjected to the side constraints. It emphasizes limited ends and purposes at the cost of the bigger picture and ignores or rationalizes away the impact that the side constraints would have on the attainment of those goals.

Teleopathy evidently afflicted both the management at Convair and McDonnell-Douglas. McDonnell-Douglas managers, seeking at least short-term profitability, plunged ahead with the defectively designed aircraft, perhaps convincing themselves that the chances of a catastrophe were remote and that they could not burden their already financially shaky company with the costs of redesign and modification. Convair senior managers, confronted with Applegate's memorandum, chose to bury their engineer's report and recommendations rather than face having to cover the modification costs or breaking their contract by going to the FAA with their evaluation of the design. Teleopathy, result: 346 people dead, devastation for their relatives, friends, and others.

Goodpaster points out that at least three types of thinking common among managers produce teleopathy in a CID structure. Many managers have adopted the view that if they look out for their corporation's best interests in a rational way, applying the techniques of cost-benefit analysis, that ethical matters will take care of themselves.

Ford Motor Company displayed such thinking in perhaps its most boldface form in the infamous Pinto case. Internal Ford memos revealed that the company had calculated the costs of putting a protective bladder around the Pinto's dangerous gasoline tanks at $11 per vehicle. Insofar as that would involve 12,500,000 vehicles, the cost would be $137,500,000. They estimated that there would be 180 deaths and 180 serious burn victims from 2,100 burned Pintos. The cost of each of those deaths they estimated at $200,000, each burn victim would cost them $67,000, and each burned vehicle they valued at $700. The total came to $49,500,000. Obviously the cost of making the modifications was far greater than what Ford expected to pay out for incinerated humans who had been lured into buying Pintos. The modifications were not made. The side constraints were clearly violated. Ford, despite winning the famous Indiana criminal case, paid out millions of dollars to victims and "Pinto" became synonymous with "dangerously defective product" or "human incinerator." Ford's reputation suffered enormously and it took decades of "At Ford Quality is Job 1" advertising to reestablish it as a leader in the market. Teleopathy.

I should note that nothing is inherently ethically objectionable about the use of cost-benefit analysis as a guide to managerial decision making. Problems arise either because of the items that are factored or because the whole process is not controlled by the side constraints. With regard to the former, it might be argued that the costs of human lives are not appropriately valued in the same monetary way that the costs of gas-tank bladders are priced. Perhaps humans have no value. They are priceless. Or, alternatively, whatever value is put on them should be considerably higher than the $200,000 Ford used. If that value were higher, it might have changed the outcome.

But how high would it have to be to offset the modification costs? Suppose it were set at $4 million. Then the cost for the 180 deaths alone would be $720,000,000, far above the modification costs. But is $4 million a reasonable price for a human life? A number of courts have thought so, but using the standard social-costs-of-death method, $4 million might be hard to justify. That is not my concern here. The point is that valuing human life as low as Ford did (though they had precedent for doing so), weighted the analysis against the modifications and it had the effect of doing so to gain short-term profit for the corporation.

There definitely are ways to utilize cost-benefit analysis that avoid such ethically objectionable outcomes, but nothing in the process itself assures that managers who use it are acting ethically.

A few more points about cost-benefit analysis as a managerial tool are worth making. As has already been noted, for cost-benefit analysis to have even a semblance of credibility, the elements being analyzed must be expressed in a common measure and that is usually money. When the analysis pushes against the side constraints, the primary reason is that dollar prices are being attached to nonmarketable elements. In the Ford case that was the value of the life of a person.

Other factors with difficult to determine or no market values could also become factors in cost-benefit analyses in corporate cases. For examples consider tranquillity, fresh air, the view and sound of a babbling brook outside one's window. But, then, the infamous Ivan Boesky is purported to have said, "What good is the moon if you can't buy it and sell it?"

Economists who work with cost-benefit analysis have produced ways to reduce such nonmarket items to the requisite dollar figure. For instance, suppose we wanted to know how much to value the brook beside my house. Perhaps a corporation is deciding whether to dam it upstream for their own purposes, leaving me with a dry bed except when we have torrential rains. What would a person pay for the view and sound of the brook? What is its market value?

Views and sounds of brooks are not traded, on markets, but they can be bundled with things that are traded and the difference between the price of those goods with or without the view and the sound of the brook will give us its value. Or so the theory goes. Simply, houses like mine, but without the view and sound of the brook, sell for a certain price and those with brook views and sounds sell for a certain price. The difference in price is the value of the brook-view property. That, of course, assumes that all other factors are kept constant, and that is a rather huge assumption.

But does this process really capture the value of the brook to me? I don't see how it can, because it must accept the values of those who are willing to buy homes where there are no babbling brooks as the base line. And I am not in that group. Suppose those people have all sorts of reasons incommensurate with mine for buying houses where they do: it is closer to work, they prefer urban clamor to natural sounds, they are deathly afraid of running water, they want to keep their flood insurance to a minimum. Who knows. Why should they be allowed to set the price on babbling brook views and sounds?

Consider also the thermometer effect. Steven Kelman writes:

> Cost-benefit analysis . . . may be like the thermometer that, when placed in a liquid to be measured, itself changes the liquid's temperature.[61]

The idea is that the very attempt to place a market value on some things denigrates them, reduces their perceived value. That may well be the case with the price of a human life. As Kelman notes, one way to mark something as having inestimably high value is to put the "Not for Sale" tag on it. In fact, we seem to think that if it is relatively easy to affirm the value of something because it has an attached price tag, that it is worth much less than a similar thing that is not, under any circumstances, for sale. Abraham Lincoln is supposed to have answered an aide's query about why he threw a man out of his office, "We're told that every man has his price, and that guy was getting dangerously close to mine."

A second type of thinking cited by Goodpaster as leading to the disease of teleopathy afflicting managers is a version of the invisible-hand concept popularized by Milton Friedman. It regards as dogma the belief that the capitalist free-market system itself contains within it all of the values it needs to ensure that business is ethical. Whatever constraints are required to maintain ethics in all types of interactions are imposed by the markets themselves. The idea is that if it doesn't sell, there is something wrong with it. Profitability in a fair market justifies all. Over the long haul markets will adjust to correct for any untoward gains.

In the DC-10 case this sort of thinking would have led McDonnell-Douglas managers to reason that they needn't pay heed to ethical issues in their decision making on whether to go ahead with the sale of the defective planes. Any ethical considerations would be worked out in the market.

My experience suggests that, in various versions, this is a popular, if utterly irresponsible, attitude among managers, especially those whose undergraduate training in economics came at the hands of Chicago School-trained professors. In effect, it offers relief for the manager from having to confront any ethical considerations in the decision-making process. An external—in this case invisible—hand will see to those matters. Michael Rion writes:

> To say that managers should simply maximize profits as agents of the shareholders presumes that the market dynamics are effective and relatively quick to respond. If so, it is *possible* that competitive pressure would prevent the worst abuses. The truth, however, is that this assumption is invalid for a whole range of corporate decisions. And, when the assumption is false, the injunction becomes dangerous. If managers are ignoring realms of corporate impact removed from market constraints, immense

injury can occur to employees, customers, communities, and the public interest.[62]

It is instructive to see how those afflicted with the teleopathy spawned by this sort of thinking try to justify or excuse their decision making after the catastrophe occurs. I discussed the DC-10 case with a number of involved managers and Friedmanesque economists and business professors. After the standard appeals to the party line about the inherent ethical values of the market, they shifted the ground to matters of risk. They maintained that McDonnell-Douglas managers, operating in the best of market traditions, had taken a reasonable calculated risk during the production of the DC-10 and in making the decision not to modify the design to alleviate Convair's safety trepidation.

They pointed out that all machines are liable to break down or fail, sometimes at crucial moments. All manufacturing corporations know that and take out product liability insurance to cover themselves against such contingencies. Consumers also know that there are risks that the machines they buy and use will malfunction. Turkish Airlines and its passengers can be presumed to have had such knowledge and to have acted on it. What's the problem? Risks were taken. There is no guarantee that when they are, people will not suffer losses. That's what business is all about.

If what is meant when it is said that the managers at McDonnell-Douglas (and Convair for that matter) took a calculated risk is that, fully cognizant of the plane's design deficiencies, but believing that catastrophic failure either was not likely or that if it occurred it would not cost the corporation as much as modification, they produced and marketed it, then that should make them more, not less, responsible for those 346 deaths outside of Paris. It certainly doesn't ethically justify their decision, as the teleopathically infirm were urging. "It was a calculated risk," if anything, should inculpate the managers.

The defenders of the McDonnell-Douglas managers shifted their ground, but stayed with risk. They maintained that everyone has a risk budget. Reasonable persons will accept a certain amount of risk to get something they value more. All airline passengers know that when they get on an airplane they are running a certain risk that it will, in the bureaucratic gobbledygook of a National Transportation Safety Board (NTSB) report, suffer "a controlled flight into terrain." In the case of most commercial airplanes, that risk is extremely low. The benefits of rapidly getting to one's destination far outweigh the risk of crashing, so the passengers board the plane and off they go.

The fact is that none of this rather unexceptional risk budget business applies in the DC-10 case because of the actions of the McDonnell-Douglas managers. The design flaws of the DC-10 were such as to drive it out of the risk categories of the other planes in the sky. Passengers calculating risk budgets with respect to air travel who are ignorant of the relevant design information in Applegate's memo cannot be said to have accepted the risk of flying on a DC-10.

The fact is that the managers at McDonnell-Douglas were dead wrong in their calculations regarding the risks to which they were subjecting passengers, and so the risks to which they were exposing their corporation. This might not be so bad had their error been an honest one arrived at due to unavoidable ignorance of crucial factors, but in this case they should have known that they were wrong. The defective engineering information was widely disseminated throughout their ranks. As Applegate noted, had the design flaws been public knowledge, it is unlikely that McDonnell-Douglas would have been able to sell the airplane. The idea that acting on a calculated risk intended to profit the corporation is, in and of itself, an ethical justification of managerial decisions is an unmistakable symptom of teleopathy.

The third type of thinking that leads to, or signals the presence of, teleopathy also requires an external source to supply the supposed ethical element in managerial decision making. Rather than depending on markets,

> . . . this type of thinking relies on noneconomic forces outside the organization to secure the value of, say, environmental protection without direct managerial involvement . . . [63]

What it depends on is the strong arm of the law.

If the law requires it, then that is what, and all, the managers should do. The responsibility for making ethical evaluations is understood to be well outside the realm of the manager's principal duties. The manager is to look after the economic interests of the corporation within the limits set by law. Ethics are the law's business. If he or she follows the law, it is assumed that the ethical matters will take care of themselves. In other words, management requires no specifically ethical thinking. All questions are, more or less, descriptive. If the law permits it, one is fully justified in doing it. For the manager, the law marks off the limits of ethical conduct. If it's not illegal, it's not unethical.

This sort of thinking turns up frequently in the so-called ethics codes of many corporations. One of my students, having just returned from a seminar conducted by an engineering company, produced a wallet-size laminated card they had given her that bore the title, "Being Ethical at X Corporation." The first line under the title read: "Always ask yourself before you act for the company, is this legal. If it is, then it is ethical."

I wondered how employees of X Corporation were expected to ascertain whether what they contemplated was or was not legal. Are they supposed to be that well acquainted with the law and all the regulations? Are corporate attorneys always at the ready? She said that she asked just those question and was told that often employees would find out only if the corporation wasn't prosecuted or sued. She said that a chuckle accompanied that answer.

The real problem with this thinking, which puts the onus of ethical vigilance of managerial decisions on the law, is that it fails to notice that nothing ensures that the laws and regulations are themselves ethical or that following them will necessarily produce an ethically justifiable outcome. It may be of interest that no criminal charges were prosecuted against the managers at McDonnell-Douglas and that after the Windsor incident occurred, the NTSB investigated and recommended modifications in the cargo-door locking system and the installation of relief vents between the cabin and the cargo compartment. The FAA administrator, however, chose not to issue an airworthiness directive, which would have grounded the planes until the NTSB's recommended alterations were made. Instead the FAA turned the report over to McDonnell-Douglas and agreed to let it make the modifications and inform airlines flying DC-10s of new procedures for securing the cargo doors in whatever ways it deemed appropriate. Is that ethical vigilance provided by society's governmental and legal institutions?

As Goodpaster notes and I think the evidence clearly supports, many, if not most of the major business scandals of the past three decades have occurred in companies whose managers suffer from teleopathy contracted from a heavy dose of either of the three common managerial ways of thinking about the source of ethics in management. The rationalizations in the management offices and the boardrooms all over America, whether the problems are banking scandals or environmental disasters or industrial espionage, cloys with the same sorts of rhetoric.

Saul Gellerman identifies four standard responses; all symptomatic of teleopathy:

> . . . believing that the activity is not "really" illegal or immoral; that it is in the individual's or the corporation's best interest; that it will never be found out; or that because it helps the company, the company will condone it.[64]

So what is the cure for the disease?

6. Types of Agency and the Antidote to Teleopathy

What is meant by saying that someone is an agent of someone or something else? When agency is mentioned, perhaps the type of cases that most frequently pop into mind are lawyer–client relationships. The lawyer acts as the agent of the client in that the lawyer's words and deeds within the legal arena are understood to be those of the client. The lawyer files papers, argues in court, pushes all the legal buttons as the instrument of the client. When the lawyer talks, it is as if the client is talking. The purposes and goals of the lawyer's actions are not his or her own, they are those of the client. The lawyer carries out the client's wishes. The lawyer doesn't sue; the client sues. The lawyer just files the appropriate papers.

The lawyer's primary, indeed some would say sole, duty is to do everything in his or her power to carry out the client's wishes. If acting in defense of one's client in a criminal case, this may involve using everything that is legally permitted to secure an acquittal. The crucial point is that the lawyer's client, his or her principal, is a separate individual from the lawyer (except in the ill-advised cases in which one serves as one's own attorney). So, presumably, the lawyer has his or her personal or private views, goals, and interests, and they not only may be entirely different from those of the client, they might not even be compatible with what the client wants or believes to be his or her interests.

In effect, the lawyer stands in for the client, represents the client, in the limited realm of the client's legal matters. The lawyer's authority to do so while not being regarded as responsible for the actions of his or her client comes from the legal institution that creates the role of lawyer and the rules by which lawyers operate as agents for their clients.

Gerald Postema nicely characterizes the lawyer-client agency relationship.

> He often acts, speaks, and argues in the place of the client. He enters relationships with others in the name of the client. When he argues in his client's behalf, he often presents his client's argument; when he acts, he is often said to be "exercising his client's rights" and what he does is typically attributable to the client . . . . [T]he lawyer becomes an extension of the legal, and to an extent the moral personality of the client.[65]

Compare the agency of the lawyer-client relationship to that which exists in a parent-baby relationship. In the latter type of agency, the parents assimilate the interests of the baby to their own interests. Coleman writes:

> Through some process as yet imperfectly understood, the mother comes to identify herself with the child. This means that in the earliest period of life, at a point when the baby is not yet able to be an effective agent on behalf of its own interests, there is automatically a powerful agent acting for those interests . . . . [It] engages a major portion of the mother's energies in the baby's behalf.[66]

I will adopt Coleman's terminology and call this second kind of agency in which the agent virtually identifies with, or adopts, the principal's interests "affine agency." In an affine agency relationship there is no principal to agent exchange. It is not the case that in such an agency relationship the principal and the agent are satisfied by receiving the same thing. Instead the agent is satisfied when the principal's interests are satisfied.

It will be recalled from Part 1 that a corporate actor is only capable of acting through the actions of its agents. Although corporate interests, plans, and goals may be quite distinct from those of its agents, corporate actions, including corporate decision making about its interests, supervene on the actions of its agents. The most significant corporate agents in CID structures, as they are now constructed, are the managers because it is their decision making that motivates most corporate action. But how is that corporate agency relationship to be understood? Are managers ordinary or affine agents?

Those, like Friedman, who identify the shareholders with the corporation, view the managers as agents of the shareholders and so will probably be comfortable with treating managers as ordinary agents acting under the direction of their principal. In the contemporary corporate world, however, few directions seem to be flowing from the shareholders. Just one tends to gush forth from that source: make us as much profit within legal bounds as you possibly can. It is no wonder that the corporate raiders, with their junk bonds and leveraged buyouts that cost thousands of employees their jobs, thought of themselves as heroes because they were enriching shareholders with enormous profits from all of their Wall Street shenanigans.

On the ordinary interpretation of agency, when the managers act or speak from within their corporate roles, it is really the shareholders who are acting or speaking. And they are saying one thing over and over: profit, profit, and more profit. I hope that the discussions in the earlier sections of this part of the book have dispelled the myth that shareholders are the corporation. Shareholders neither own the corporation nor are they identical with it. But if that is the case then I don't see how managers can be properly described, on the model of the lawyer-client relationship, as ordinary agents of the shareholders.

If the shareholders are not their principals, for whom do the managers act as agents? The answer, of course, is the corporation itself. But now we have a really interesting puzzle that the shareholder-as-principal myth avoids: the corporation cannot instruct all those who act for it because it cannot act unless some of its agents act. So it would seem that managers, or at least the senior ones, stand to their corporations in agency relationships that must be closer to Coleman's affine type than to the ordinary sort. There are no principal-to-agent exchanges in those managers' agency relationships with the corporation.

Other managers and employees may still fit the ordinary agency role in that their relationship to the principal is mediated by its affine agents. This would be comparable to the relationship between a lawyer representing a baby, say in a wrongful life suit, whose exchanges are limited to dealing with the affine agent, the baby's parent. The parent has internalized the interests of the baby, and the lawyer carries out the orders of the parent, who is understood to be acting as or for the child, though the child is not capable of participating in principal to agent exchanges of any kind.

The skills and services of managers are not merely employed to act in the interests of the shareholders. It makes sense to talk of the interests of the corporation apart from the standard shareholder demand to maximize profits. In order to act as agents of the corporation its interests will need to be internalized by a critical mass of the managers, perhaps in something like the way the interests of the baby are internalized by the parents.

So, to achieve legitimate corporate ends, managers, or at least some of them, must identify their interests, in large measure, with their corporation's interests, their plans with its plans. To be one of its affine agents, however, one does not have to make one's interests the corporation's interests in the sense that one acts for the corporation as if one is the corporation. Parents do not act for their young children as if they were those children. Instead, the manager as affine agent must adopt the corporation's interests as his or her own, though not to the exclusion of his or her personal interests.

The restriction on the personal interests an affine agent may keep is set by the idea of conflict of interests. As long as a manager's personal interests are not hostile to those of the corporation, they can be retained without violating the trust of affine agency. If managers in corporations were all rational, pure affine agents there would be no need to police for conflict of interest in their corporate actions and decision making. Such managers would realize that harming the corporation's interests will also cause harm to their own interests.

Teleopathic thinking is probably the major cause of conflict of interest for managers. Leslie Jacobs writes:

> Most cases which appear to involve impropriety . . . are examples of bogging down in a single course of reasoning and losing sight of the ethical standards to which the law, sometimes circuitously, leads.[67]

Affine agents among the managers, especially the senior managers, are crucial to the running of a corporation. In fact, at the top level of management, most of the personnel must, to some degree, be affine agents. Obviously a corporation will get far more service from an affine agent than from an ordinary agent. That is why internalization of the corporation's interests by its employees is typically encouraged, and it explains why senior managers at many firms work twelve to fourteen hours a day without complaint, while the corporate attorney or accountant might only put in a standard nine to five.

With all that affine agency requires of a human, why would any rational person become one for a corporate actor? (Would-be parents might consider this question as well!) How is the affine agent benefited? What makes it all worth it?

When that question is put to corporate executives, they are prone to spout the most insipid platitudes imaginable. They talk of the joys of a job well done, of the exhilaration of "climbing the mountain." They trade in all manner of sports metaphors that suggest that they get some personal kick or high out of the great efforts they expend for the corporation (the home team). In the end, when pressed, most admit that the real benefit just comes from knowing you have been of service and that you've done your part. Such outbursts of managerial fervor and self-beatification, generally reserved for media events or public school assemblies, fail to mention that because the manager has changed his or her own interests, he or she is, in fact, satisfying those interests when he or she is acting to satisfy those of the corporate actor. Coleman writes:

> Given that the process of changing one's interests involves internal costs, and thus ordinarily proceeds more slowly than the process of exchanging control over events or resources, then if these costs are overcome, an agent who changes his interests by identifying with a principal is subjectively better off than one who does not.[68]

In the parent-child cases, when the child shows pleasure because its interests are satisfied, the parent will usually gain further satisfaction. In something of the same way, when the corporation's successes in satisfying its interests are publicized or when its accomplishments attract the attention of those in its market or in the financial markets, the manager receives further gratification. A healthy salary and generous fringes and perks additionally increase the benefits to the affine agent by fulfilling those of his or her interests that are not strictly identified with the corporation's interests.

So the affine agent, in times of corporate achievement, will feel that he or she is substantially better off than the ordinary agent. Such subjective benefits can motivate a considerable amount of deeper corporate identification. When F. Ross Johnson lost his job as CEO of RJR-Nabisco after KKR bought it out in a leveraged deal, he is reported to have said to the chairman of the board, "Henry, I loved running this company so much, I'd have paid you to let me do it." Johnson's problem, or at least one of his problems, was that he was seriously afflicted with teleopathy, and so the company was in an ethical shambles, not to mention that its stock was flat. He had inadvertently laid down the welcome mat for the raiders.[69]

If the subjective rewards of affine agency are so much greater than those involved in ordinary agency, why don't all managers restructure their personal interests so as to identify them with the interests of their corporations? At a psychological level, one answer probably would be that the loss of self (anticipated by some agents as likely to be experienced in the identification process), is regarded as a greater loss than the subjective gains they believe they can expect from affine agency. But it may also be that the burdens of responsibility associated with affine agency are much greater than they wish to bear.

Generally such managers find themselves comfortable in droneness. They are more comfortable viewing their agency relationship to the corporation on the ordinary model. They do as they are told. Their primary interests are in various types of personal and familial security. The corporation is where they work. They are command driven. It seems to be a pretty dependable rule that Comers who cannot or do not become affine agents of their corporations never achieve stardom on its managerial ladder. They find their level and eventually become Drones. The whole hierarchical structure, in fact, is based on the expectation that they will do so.

The ethics of affine agency is a vast and relatively unexplored area. I suspect that it would help to study the ethics of caring and the concept of parenthood for a start. The obvious major differences, however, between the parent–baby and the manager–corporation situations may cause that analogy to collapse, and I suspect that what one learns there may prove of little use in the end.

Other types of affine agency relationships have been cited by sociologists: the patriotic identification with one's nation and the devotional association of members to a commune, but none of them seems to quite capture what goes on in the senior corporate manager's agency situation. Perhaps a more fruitful analogy would be with those who, in legal matters, speak for the trees or for works of art. In both of those cases, there can be no principal-agent exchanges. The problem is that though we might reasonably say that a work of art has interests, such as not being mutilated, it is a little hard to see how an agent internalizes that interest as his or her own.

In the environmental protection cases, I suppose, it is possible to discern the relevant sort of identification among, for instance, certain Sierra Club members. But I have my doubts about whether they actually see their interests as those of the redwoods. I am suspicious of a romanticism that has muddled them to some degree. Not that I don't like trees. I am especially fond of trees, despite or because of the fact that I currently live in south Texas, where the closest thing we have to a tree is a scrub oak.

One thing seems patently obvious: the fact that corporate actors are now the major players in the social world, with clear economic interests that can be trickled down to their agents makes them most attractive principals for humans to identify with and serve. The most popular account, and probably the right one after all, is that corporations are where the power is. Historically, power has always been an almost irresistible motivation to trade in one's own interests for those of another.

I want to make it clear that I do not see anything ethically wrong with a Comer deliberately setting about to become an affine agent of his or her corporation. As I said earlier, such conversions are essential to the operative existence of corporations, and should be encouraged. Without them a corporate actor would lose its core of authority, its moral status. It would become merely a thing acted upon. Something of only instrumental value. A corporation that is lacking in affine agents as top managers is sure to be a target for acquisition, sell-off, and dismemberment. It is nothing but a commodity and might as well be used by anyone who can get his or her hands on it and can manipulate its assets for personal gain.

Rampant teleopathy among top managers in the 1980s discouraged affinity in agency and resulted in corporate disasters that are still having negative effects on managers, low-level employees, and those who belonged to other constituencies of those corporations, including the general public. One need only talk to the Texas bankers and to the folks who used to be employed by R. J. Reynolds in Winston-Salem, North Carolina, for confirmation.

A number of corporations, following the lead of the Japanese firms, have begun extensive programs to try to ensure internalization of the corporation's interests by management and by nonmanagerial employees as well. Some of these programs may sound ludicrous and even degrading to liberal individualists and academics, involving, as they sometimes do, singing the company song and wearing the company uniform, but the point is to enhance and encourage the affinity process throughout the CID structure.

The fiduciary relationship in which managers stand to their corporations is then, at least in crucial respects, significantly different than that of a lawyer to a client. The managers, understood as a CID structural unit, bear ethical responsibility for the corporate actor's interests and behavior in a way that lawyers do not for the actions and interests of their clients. Securing compliance with the side constraints in Type 2 and Type 3 interactions is their primary ethical duty.

Legal profitability and the nonviolation of the side constraints with respect to interactions with other Rank B-ers are the co-considerations ethically imposed on the manager who is acting as agent for his or her corporation. Given the affine agency/dependence relation between top managers and their corporations, it is fair to say that managerial accountability for ethical corporate actions is a not insignificant part of the very authority of managers in the first place, a view endorsed by Goodpaster.

Managers are, in a crucial moral sense, both subjects and legislators in their corporate realms. They mold the organizations that mold them. They are not the corporation, but the corporation can do nothing unless they perform in their assigned roles as its agents, and at least some as its affine agents. From the point of view of ethics, the logic of managerial thinking must take the side constraints against using other Rank B-ers as seriously as profitability in the corporate decision process.

How is that done? Goodpaster maintains that managers must replace the teleopathic thinking to which many have become accustomed with the view that ethics is an authoritative guide to their actions. Such managerial thinking does not ignore the profit motive, but it gives independent force to the side constraints against using Rank B-ers as mere means. In other words, it both rejects the surrogates of self-interest, the law, and the market and internalizes the ethical considerations in the core of the corporate decision process.

> [It] plac[es] moral considerations in a position of authority alongside considerations of profitability and competitive strategy in the corporate mindset.[70]

That means that the pursuit of profit as the primary goal of the corporation is to be controlled, in the thinking of the managers themselves, by the ethics of the side constraints, by adopting strategies of reciprocal cooperation in Prisoner's Dilemma-type interactions and less broad cooperation if the interactions are of the Chicken-type. Goodpaster refers to such considerations as respect for person principles. I have no objection to that characterization as long as corporations themselves are included in the class of persons being respected, turning his class of persons into my Rank A-ers and B-ers.

The sort of thinking that is required as an antidote to teleopathy brings an ethical conscience to corporate decision making. The affine agents of the corporate actor must adopt such thinking, reflect it in an objectively discernible way, and require it as a matter of corporate policy of the ordinary agents who are subordinate to them in its CID structure in order that their corporations act ethically in other than an accidental way.

Goodpaster identifies three imperatives for managers that are intended to infuse their corporations with the sort of thinking that works against teleopathy. In the first place, managers need to take a sort of moral inventory of the existing dispositions among the managers in the corporation. Goodpaster calls this an orienting stage. Senior managers, he thinks, should conduct a survey of the operative attitudes of the other managers.

> The objective is to discern the dominant ethical values of the company. . . Such scans are only a first pass, however. More qualitative, clinical methods are needed to identify moral victories, defeats, and dilemmas that

operating managers experience as they do their work and pursue their careers in the organization.[71]

Goodpaster's surveys might be of some sociological value or interest, but I have serious doubts about the value of requiring managers to take them. What can they hope to learn from such surveys that will assist them as they try to institutionalize ethical thinking? I suppose there is some practical point to senior managers learning where matters stand ethically in their corporation so that they can shape the institutionalization process to the specific problems and needs they uncover. But if they are going to do any surveys and soul-searching, I would think it would be more valuable for them to get clear about what they think their corporation does as a corporation.

I agree with Michael Hammer and James Champy who maintain that the managers who are going to reengineer their corporations need to concentrate on what should be rather than what is.[72] The removal of teleopathy, after all, is as much of a reengineering problem as are cost cutting, productivity increasing, and customer service. Nonetheless, the actual attempt to make the ethical considerations "part of the operating consciousness of the company" is the core of Goodpaster's program and deserves mention.

The primary concern is how the senior managers, presumably most of them affine agents of the corporation, can get the employees and other managers to sufficiently identify with the interests of the corporation so that they will resist the temptation to teleopathic thinking.

In 1982, seven people died from cyanide poisoning after ingesting capsules of Extra-Strength Tylenol. Tylenol was the best-selling health product in America. Johnson & Johnson, maker of Tylenol, faced one of the worst of corporate nightmares. If they recalled the product and removed it from sales, it was likely that the corporation would lose a major portion of its revenues, not to mention the trust of its customers. To remove it might well be interpreted as an admission not only of guilt, but of a corporate failure to ensure the safety of its products. Not to pull it, to "stonewall" the issue, however, could also lead to comparable disasters and possibly even more deaths from the use of tainted capsules.

The senior management of Johnson & Johnson, with the leadership of chairman, James Burke, decided to remove all Tylenol products from the market and to cancel all of its advertising of the brand. Within a week the company's stock dropped by 20 percent. The advertising agencies advised the managers to change the name of the product and quickly reintroduce it. But the managers reasoned that it would look like an admission of guilt and a lack of faith in the product to just drop the Tylenol name. Instead, Johnson & Johnson redeveloped the Tylenol packaging and they eliminated the more easily tamperable capsule format, replacing it with caplets.

When these changes were made, they reintroduced Tylenol with an advertising campaign assuring the consumer that the product was untainted and that Johnson & Johnson's commitment to safety and the highest quality in their products was evidenced by the way they had handled the poisonings. In effect, Johnson & Johnson's managers fought off the temptation of teleopathic thinking and opted to take a short-term loss to avoid treating their customers as mere means, and choosing not to risk the lives of innocent members of the public to maintain market share. The happy ending for Johnson & Johnson was that within a year of pulling the product Tylenol recovered 90 percent of the market share held before the poisonings.

The handling of the Tylenol crisis has become legendary in the annals of business ethics. I have no intention of trying to tarnish the well-earned image of Johnson & Johnson with respect to Tylenol. My point in raising this case is the same one made by Goodpaster: that the laudable actions of the senior managers at Johnson & Johnson constituted one relatively clear way of communicating to the rest of the managers and employees the corporate commitment to giving ethical considerations full force. In short, the case seems to show that a way to impress nonteleopathic thinking on the minds of managers in a corporation is by example. Goodpaster notes:

> The institutionalization of ethical values depends first and foremost on leadership conviction expressed in action.[73]

Before the reintroduction of Tylenol to the shelves of America's drug stores, James Burke noted:

> We consider it a moral imperative, as well as good business, to restore Tylenol to its preeminent position in the marketplace. It is ironic that the job of rebuilding Tylenol is made more difficult because we . . . did our job of informing and protecting the nation so efficiently.[74]

I suppose we might prefer that Mr. Burke not stress the irony when he is crediting himself and the Johnson & Johnson managers with doing the right thing from the ethical point of view. Still, his expression of it helps to make more obvious the tension that the side constraints of ethics introduces into the corporate decision process and the extent of the temptation to teleopathic thinking that lurks in the heads of almost all managers.

Goodpaster also recommends that the inculcation and maintenance of the ethical approach to managerial thinking be accomplished by establishing a set of corporate standards (presumably in writing) and procedures to monitor compliance throughout the corporation. Such codes and ethics audits are, of course, nice projects and they may do some short-term good, but they are probably next to useless unless they are associated with substantial incentives. Corporations that promote managers who hit their numbers while ignoring ethical considerations in their decision making send a far clearer signal to Comers than any finely crafted list of ethical standards hung on the wall of every office.

Goodpaster's approach to addressing the problem of rampant teleopathy evidences some ethical difficulties of its own. Daniel Gilbert has pointed out that though Goodpaster wants to infuse corporate thinking with respect-for-persons considerations, his approach does not seem to respect the very persons whose behavior it is intended to improve.[75]

There is more than a kernel of truth in Gilbert's criticism. Goodpaster joins many of those who write about business ethics who are unduly impressed with the hierarchical organization of CID structures, or who are committed to what Gilbert calls "well-known assumptions from management theory," more specifically, Harvard Business School theory. I must admit to having lent some support to this conception in my early accounts of CID structures because they utilized the pyramidal model.

That popular paradigm is typically read as revealing that any behavior modification in a corporation must not only be introduced from the top executives down, but that only the top executives are important to the process. In other words, making a corporation ethical (or more productive or more profitable) can only be carried out by top executives displaying the desired behavior (as in the Tylenol case) or setting up mechanisms to monitor the behavior of lower-ranking employees or urging them on the desired path with financial carrots.

In the typical decision structures of American corporations, the affine agents tend to be the top executives, and they have enormous power, real and imagined, material and psychological, over everyone else in the CID structure. Jackall discovered that:

> [S]uperiors do not like to give detailed instructions to subordinates. . . . A high-level executive . . . explains: "If I tell someone what to do—like do A, B, or C—the inference and implication is that he will succeed in accomplishing the objective. Now, if he doesn't succeed, that means that I have invested part of myself in his work and I lose any right I have to chew his ass out if he doesn't succeed. If I tell you what to do, I can't bawl you out if things don't work. And this is why a lot of bosses don't give explicit directions. They just give a statement of objectives, and then they can criticize subordinates who fail to make their goals." . . . It's the CEO who sets the style, tone, tempo of all the companies. . . . "Every big organization is set up for the benefit of those who control it; the boss gets what he wants."[76]

Hardly any wonder that Goodpaster focuses all of his attention on the senior management. They have the power (and know how to wield it), and we can reasonably suppose that they can be motivated to alter the corporation's decision making in order to overcome teleopathy (which may be responsible for corporate scandals and other embarrassments).

It does not follow, however, that the only way or indeed the best way to reform those organizations is by the top-down methods Goodpaster recommends. In fact, Goodpaster's methods, ultimately and crassly, put the whole weight of producing ethical reform among the lower-ranking managers and employees on an external-inducement (incentive) basis. In effect, they attempt to alter the thinking of the subordinate managers by manipulating their interests in an obviously paternalistic fashion that is laced with heavy doses of self-interest appeals. That is exactly the type of thinking Goodpaster claimed is symptomatic of teleopathy in the first place.

7. The Ethical Costs of Corporate Reengineering

It is fair to say with Gilbert that Goodpaster's approach evidences a degree of disdain for the people who occupy the less than top stations in the corporation. They are systematically excluded from the process and end up being used to bring about the desirable end.

Goodpaster's approach appears to have been derived from an ethically defective corporate organizational model that was envisioned by Adam Smith in the eighteenth century and fully realized in this century by industrial giants like Henry Ford. Smith's conception of the division of labor, specialists doing their one and only one little thing on an assembly line that at its end turns out the product in an efficient, cost-effective way, has dominated organizational thinking in America for two centuries.

The Smithian model, in fact, worked. It worked wonders. *No wonder* Smith rose to so saintly a status among business people. The idea was that any productive work can be divided into smaller units and a person hired to do them and do them over and over for forty hours a week. Tasks were to be cut razor thin so that the training necessary to do them would also be minimal. And, of course, that meant that those performing those tasks did not need extensive educational backgrounds. As was probably not anticipated by its devotees, the more workers you have, each doing some tiny part of the production, the more supervisors you need to see that the work is getting done and that the product is successively taking shape.

Like magic, almost, the production process requires a bureaucratic accompaniment that grows at a staggering pace. Soon you have blue- and white-collar units comprised of specialists each doing some tiny aspect of the production, supervision, management process.

The Smithian prototype (for him it was a pin factory) translated from production to the bureaucracy. Management positions were created and defined in terms of fewer and fewer responsibilities for the overall operation. Instead, each manager has but a small purview over which he or she performs the same routines hour in and hour out, day in, day out.

The Smithian division of labor theory was, and continues to be, exported from manufacturing industries into what are called service industries. The commitment to it is so fanatical that hardly anyone indoctrinated with its simple principles seems capable of recognizing its grotesque practical and ethical costs.

I am a member of the American Automobile Association, a well-respected organization that sells travel services. The other day my car broke down, and I called the AAA to arrange for a tow to a repair shop. My call was transferred to someone who was supposed to take down the pertinent information. I explained where the car was located, just off a busy freeway, about a block from a major cross-city street. The person recording the information sounded puzzled and asked me to spell the name of the street and asked if the highway I was mentioning was a big one. In disbelief, I asked her if she didn't know how to get around in San Antonio. She laughed and said that she didn't, that she was in Dallas, some 260 miles away, but that she would dispatch a tow truck.

A point of information: a tow truck driver who has only a basic knowledge of the street patterns of San Antonio can get to almost anywhere in town from almost anyplace else in a half hour or less, excepting rush hours. After two hours of waiting in the blistering afternoon sun, the truck arrived and towed my car about four blocks to the repair shop.

The next day I called the administrative offices of the AAA to complain and was told that, yes, the dispatchers are now located in Dallas because that is cheaper than having them in all of the major Texas cities. However, the administrator continued, the Dallas person should not have asked me so many questions because she is only supposed to fill in a certain number of blanks on a computer screen, then the order is sent to a person who has a computer program that maps the location of the vehicle. The mapping information is then sent to another office that identifies the nearest available AAA-contracted towing firm. Still another office contacts them and they send out their truck. The truck driver, when he finally arrived, couldn't understand why I was at all irritated. He was just doing his job.

The administrator apologized for my being inconvenienced, but not for the thin-sliced system that had contributed in such large measure to my discomfort. Instead, she reiterated the oft-intoned remark that good help is hard to find these days. It seemed not to have occurred to her that the problem might be with the organizational model itself, the model that apparently dominates Goodpaster's three-step approach to curing teleopathy, as discussed in the previous section.

I think we can make a case that if the Goodpaster program were put into practice that it would violate the side constraints and is therefore not ethically permissible unless it can be shown to promote the interests of Rank A-ers. That latter condition is, however, somewhat problematic. I think it is indisputable that the interests of Rank A-ers will benefit by the elimination of teleopathy in CID structures. So it would seem that if that end is achieved by Goodpaster's program and it well might be, then using some Rank B-ers (subordinate corporate agents) as means should not bring out the ethical red flags. But my intuition is that it is or should be ethically worrying because most of us believe that some limits must restrict the permissibility of using Rank B-ers even to benefit the interests of Rank A-ers. This may be something like our concern that nothing may be ethically wrong with slaughtering cattle for our fast-food hamburgers, but it should not be done by bashing the cattle over the head with baseball bats and tire chains.

The limit leaps rough and ready to hand: the use of Rank B-ers to achieve the interests of the Rank A-ers cannot be countenanced if other equally good and efficient ways of achieving the desired end will not treat Rank B-ers as mere means. In other words, Rank B-ers may only be used without their consent to benefit the interests of Rank A-ers as a last resort. So the real problem for institutionalizing appropriate ethical values in the corporate decision-making process is: can the program be accomplished in a way that respects those being affected by it, the subordinate managers (Comers and Drones) and the other employees?

Coleman maintains that vesting rights of control of the corporate actor's actions in the target agents is an especially effective way to produce the identification of the agents' interests with those of the corporation.[77] But the Smithian model, in conjunction with the Goodpaster program, does not provide any ways of assuring that this will happen. In fact, the Smithian model purposefully fragments the corporate actor's actions so as to alienate any particular agent from the whole. The agent can, at best, only identify with the single element of the corporate action that he or she performs in virtual isolation from the whole. This, of course, gives rise to the "I only work here" syndrome.

Goodpaster's program seems to accept this situation as unalterable and opts for a form of what Coleman calls "forward policing" to try to ensure compliance. Authority is always exercised downward and the program requires feedback information loops to continually apprise those at the top of the progress being made.

There are other tested ways to police a corporation that do not depend on the downward authority chain conception. One was developed by Honda. Coleman calls it "backward policing." The idea is that in a corporate (manufacturing in this case) system every unit may be vested with the authority to reject any input it receives from another unit, and it is held strictly accountable for its outputs by the units that receive them. What is supposed to happen, and apparently does at Honda, is that each unit acts as its own inspector, presumably to avoid the embarrassment of a rejection by those who receive its outputs. Considerably fewer supervisory personnel are needed in a backward-policed organization than in corporations operating in the traditional top-down fashion.

Another alternative to the mere use of the subordinate managers and employees in the process of trying to conquer teleopathy in a corporation is the adoption of the Japanese quality circles or quality of work life program. Establishing quality circles in an American corporation is no mean task. The supervisory jobs in such a restructuring are assigned to work teams, and authority is distributed throughout the corporation.

> Each team meets regularly, ordinarily once a week during work time. . . Its business ranges from modifying the work structure to resolving interpersonal problems among members of the team.[78]

This team-oriented tactic and its related flattening of the hierarchical management system operates on the assumption that empowerment of the employees in the decision-making process of the corporate actor will produce greater productivity and better, more efficient products and services. Quality circles should enhance the employees' identification with the corporate actor and the internalization of the need to try to defeat the teleopathic decision making that is likely to damage the corporation's long-term success. Reportedly such revamping of its CID structure has had positive results in a number of corporations.

Frankly, however, much of the evidence that has been gathered has focused on productivity, profitability, and consumer satisfaction. The incidence of ethical difficulties in quality circle corporations has not, to my knowledge, been researched. The assumption is that because the employees are more closely associated with many more elements of corporate actions than they would be in a traditional CID structure, their identification with the corporate actor should be greater, and that should put them more on their guard against corruption and malpractice in the workplace. It seems a good assumption, but I am reminded of the Texas bankers who, though not organized in quality circles, nonetheless had a considerable input in many of their financial institution's actions. Yet they waded in up to their necks in highly unethical and even illegal capers that not only tarnished the reputations of their companies, but caused the majority of them to fail.

Superficially similar to the Japanese approach, though they claim their position actually shares few features with it, is the theory of reengineering of the corporation recently championed in a best-selling book by Hammer and Champy.[79] In their book, they speak little about the need to infuse corporate decision making with ethical values, but their approach, it seems to me, could be especially well suited to meet the side-constraint demands that Gilbert and I find unsatisfied by Goodpaster's dependence on the traditional hierarchical model.

As I noted above, Adam Smith's corporate prototype, the blueprint for the industrial revolution, was based on the belief that workers are, on the whole, stupid or ignorant or too busy working to think at all about the corporate decision and production processes. They must be restricted to simple, repeatable tasks. As those tasks are sliced thinner and thinner, creating more and more simple tasks, a complex process is required to unite them into a productive whole. The rule is: the more elementary the chores are made, the more of them must be created (even to make a pin or thousands of pins), and the more supervisory or managerial personnel are needed to link and monitor them.

The Smithian model requires authoritative leadership from senior managers whose primary job is to ensure that those myriad tasks performed by the employees throughout the complex process actually result in the product or service from which the corporation expects to make its profits. Hammer and Champy's innovation, what sells their book, was to reverse the Smithian model, flip it on its head.

They recommend the compression of tasks, combining many jobs into one, and a corresponding streamlining of the productive processes. In other words, they are touting complex, integrated job descriptions and uncomplicated processes with responsibilities diffused throughout the corporate actor instead of residing in upper management. A reengineered corporation, on the Hammer and Champy model, is the antipode of an assembly line. They recommend what they call a case-worker-based process of integrated case workers or case teams. (That is where they sound very like the quality circles theorists, but the similarities and differences are not worth discussion in this context.)

Hammer and Champy reengineering produces a compression not only on the horizontal plane of the CID structure, but in the vertical as well. That is so because, theoretically, managerial positions and levels can be lopped off as redundant, thereby shortening the vertical distance between top executives and the other employees. Decision making becomes part of the productive job and not something reserved only to the managers. They write:

> Vertical compression means that at points in a process where workers used to have to go up the managerial hierarchy for an answer, they now make their own decisions. Instead of separating decision making from real work, decision making becomes *part* of the work. Workers themselves now do that portion of a job that, formerly, managers performed.[80]

Clearly, the reengineering and the quality circles theories of corporate organization would, to use the currently popular term, empower

larger numbers of corporate agents than the traditional top-down management approach that grew out of the Smithian model.

> People working in a reengineered process are, of necessity, empowered.
> As process-team workers they are both permitted and required to think,
> interact, use judgment, and make decisions.[81]

These types of reorganizations should far better satisfy the side
constraints against using people as mere means than the traditional
Smithian inspired CID structure. They do not show, in Gilbert's terms,
"disdain for persons" in the lower corporate roles. The inculcation of
ethical values that Goodpaster persuasively argued to be necessary to
counteract teleopathy in its decision-making patterns, in the reengineered corporation, theoretically will not need to be imposed from on
high on those who are presumed to be moral neophytes. Empowered
employees should not be victims of top-management coercion, albeit
coercion to do the right thing. Presumably, they will become inclined
to adopt affine agency roles and so be motivated to self-direct the corporate actor to achieve the desired levels of productivity and profitability while avoiding the social embarrassments, scandals, and illegalities
that work against the corporate good. Further, because they are crucial
factors in the decision-making process, the side constraints forbidding
the mere use of them without consent would not be violated. One
important change for the good would have been effected internally and
noncoercively.

Many proponents of the new organizational schemes argue that
because the managerial levels are compressed and corporate decision
making is dispersed, the adoption of a program to discourage the
dependence on external surrogates in favor of a forceful ethical component in corporate thinking will percolate from all of the elements of
the CID structure.

The assumption seems to be that support for such a program will
arise as the result of a bargaining process, a sort of morals by agreement. The autonomy of the individual humans, the employees, would
be preserved and protected and teleopathy will be defeated. When
described in that way it sounds great from both an ethical and an economic point of view. But I can't see how the process can be guaranteed
to produce nonteleopathic results.

Why should we expect that the multitudinous voices of the empowered employees will produce the desired ethical outcomes? I have no
faith in either the bargaining process or the values of individuals when
it comes to ensuring that the right thing will be done. Democracy is no
guarantee against the tyrannies of the majority and enlightened self-
interest. Why won't the empowered employees be just as likely as the
old top-management group to adopt any one of Goodpaster's three
teleopathic ways of thinking as to select the ethical way?

Let's suppose that there are four employees in a process-team unit and that each is convinced that the only, or the best, way to think about the relationship between ethical considerations and corporate decisions corresponds to a different one of the four types discussed in the previous section. Is there any reason to believe that the person who supports a proactive ethical approach will be able to sway those who are persuaded that external factors such as the market or the law should be adequate constraints on corporate actions, that ethical matters will take care of themselves as long as decisions take cognizance of those factors? I would certainly like to think so, but the evidence is disheartening. After all, the newly empowered employees are just as human as the old CEOs. The top managers in the old structures may well have considered all of the types of decision making that the newly organized employees will bring to the table, and they, typically, settled for the types that are prone to teleopathy. Why should we expect the employees to be motivated differently? (This is a version of the problem with which we concluded Part 1: that corporate decision structures are more suitable to consistent ethical decision making than humans.)

The argument that Gilbert and others seem to be making is that the empowering of the employees is the greatest good in itself and that it shouldn't matter if the choices they make in guiding corporate decision making repeat the old failures. Actually, I suspect that the romanticism of this sort of individualism extends to the further conviction that the empowered employees will reject teleopathic thinking and embrace the ethical approach because they are somehow ethically purer than the top managers who have been coercing and harassing them all these centuries. They ought to get to know the workers! When it comes down to it, we're all a pretty "rum lot." I have no faith that the desired outcome will emerge from the "bargaining processes by which those persons tailor their relationships to their respective values."[82] And I don't think that ethical considerations in the corporate decision process should be left to chance.

Even in the reengineered corporation, it will still be necessary for someone to educate the decision makers to the dangers of teleopathy and instruct them on the virtues of taking full account of the ethical consequences of corporate actions in the very decision process that results in those actions. That must be built into the policy elements of the CID structure. In fact, someone will need to clarify what those virtues are and explain why they are not optional.

Still, we cannot ignore the fact that, from the ethical point of view, the reengineered corporation that empowers the employees at all levels will more likely satisfy the side constraints against using any Rank B-ers in the organization as mere means, while the traditional organizational structure falls miserably short in that regard.

But there's another fly in the ointment. Or rather, there's a rather huge practical and ethical problem that must be confronted squarely. That problem concerns the employees that the reengineering model is supposed to empower. A not insignificant number of persons in the current work force, or who would like to enter the work force, will have to be excluded from these newly designed, diffuse responsibility corporations. As Hammer and Champy admit, the criteria for hiring someone in a reengineered corporation must be radically different from the criteria applied in the traditional corporation.[83] As I mentioned earlier, the Smithian prototype assumes that workers are not well educated, but are job trainable in only a narrow way, hence the division of labor idea, a reasonable assumption for Smith to have made, and one borne out in the factories of the industrialized world for nearly two centuries.

At most companies, as long as a potential employee is functionally literate, he or she can be trained to do a specific repetitive job. In some companies, the nature of the tasks permits the literacy requirement to also be waived. It is intriguing that in the burgeoning fast-food industry it is apparently not necessary to know basic math in order to qualify at the counter. The employee needs only to recognize an icon, punch it in, and the machines figure the customer's bill and the correct change.

In the reengineered corporations employees will need decision-making skills as the jobs will be multidimensional and require a flexibility unheard of in American corporations since the Industrial Revolution. Training, no matter how good, in a single specific skill will be inadequate.

> For multidimensional and changing jobs, companies don't need people to fill a slot, because the slot will be only roughly defined. Companies need people who can figure out what the job takes and do it, people who can create the slot that fits them. Moreover, the slot will keep changing.[84]

I'm sure that all of this sounds absolutely terrific to organizational planners and to those interested in both improving American corporate productivity and empowering the work force in a way that could never be thought possible from within the old Smithian prototype. Imagine that, and in an era of mushrooming technical innovations that can even stymie a rocket scientist! Yes, but that's exactly the core of the ethical problem that will be fostered by all of this reengineering.

What the Hammer and Champy plan requires, as they happily concede, is an educated work force, not just a trained work force. (The distinction is theirs.) Great, but where is that coming from? If there is anything we don't have in America, that is exactly it, and we are not likely to acquire it for decades to come.

This book is not about educational reform. I wouldn't think of even beginning to evaluate the American educational system. Its gross inadequacies may be taken as givens, fodder for the television exposé news hours and the weekly magazines. Still, we must realize that a rather sizable portion of the potential and actual adult work force in major regions of the country is functionally illiterate or quite nearly so, at least in English. Persons with such a disability, though they can probably find work in the Smithian-type corporations, are never going to qualify for empowered jobs in the reengineered corporations of Hammer and Champy. Look at their example of Hill's Pet Products, a subsidiary of Colgate-Palmolive.

Hill's opened a new facility in Indiana that was fashioned around the Hammer and Champy theory. One hundred fifty employees had to be hired. When the finalists from three thousand applications were selected, they all had the same characteristic: they did not have factory experience, but had better than average educations. Ironically perhaps, many were ex-schoolteachers, exasperated with their "careers" in education. (Apparently they were neither football coaches nor administrators.) Reportedly the facility is doing very well, a testimony to the success of reengineering.

So? It may well be that the price of empowering the employees in the newfangled, reengineered corporations is that many, if not most, of the work force from the old division of labor- and management-intensive companies cannot qualify for employment. What happens to those people? We may expect that the proponents of reengineering will offer overtures about the need for improving American education. And, indeed they have.

Better educations in reasoning, logic, ethics, and other traditional subjects, *not* retraining, is what is wanted. Of course, government hasn't gotten that message, so "retraining" is their buzz word of the month. For instance, President Clinton announces that even though his plan to save the old-growth forests of the Northwest will put many in the lumber industry out of work, federal funds will be provided for their *retraining*.

If the corporations of America are reengineered along the lines suggested by Hammer and Champy, retraining will be another huge government waste of time and money. Education, not in a specific task, but in how to think, how to evaluate, how to imagine, is what is needed. Where is that going to be found and, if it is, how is it going to be made available to an at-risk work force? The reengineering theorists simply find other external surrogates to take care of those ethical problems: public education and government unemployment programs.

In order to satisfy the side constraints, corporations lured into adopting reengineering, an ethically commendable idea in and of itself, must take responsibility for their having created and sustained an ill-educated work force for so long that its progeny cannot simply step into the demands of an empowered, multitask position. The educational condition of that work force is as much the fault of the traditional corporate organizational model as any other single factor.

Sadly, we are told that the public educational system has now fallen into such ill-repair that it is most unlikely that a new young work force will emerge that is capable of meeting the challenges of the new job descriptions. When the supervisor of the Dallas dispatching office of the AAA called to apologize for the trouble they had caused me, I asked why they didn't combine the tasks instead of all the hand-offs, put a single person on each case to see it from the phone call to the tow. She said that would be impossible because, though all the members of her staff had high school diplomas, they just weren't well enough educated to handle the complexities that would be involved without "screwing up." The company had given serious thought to the way they had designed the system and was convinced it was the only way likely to meet the service demands of its customers, given the work force it could hire. She assured me that the person who had taken my call would get a reprimand and more training.

Some years ago, I worked as a seventh-floor sweep in a flour mill located on the Great Lakes. My sole task was to clean the gigantic sifters that took up the entire floor. When I left, after an eight-hour day, the room was spotless. When I returned the next morning, it usually had a coat of flour dust. Frequently, because of the humidity (the mill wasn't air-conditioned in summer), the cloth, sock-like tubes through which the sifted flour was conveyed to the sixth floor would clog and burst. Flour would flood the room, and I would have to shut down the defective sock and shovel the loose flour back into the system. If the spill was bigger than I could handle in a reasonable time, I could call up two workers from the sixth and fifth floors to help shovel.

I seldom saw or talked with anyone else in the mill, though I did get to know some of the lower-floor workers when I would chat with them around the conveyer that took me up to my floor. None of them had even high school educations and they thought it funny that I was working there between college terms. They assured me that a person could make a good living in the mill. All you had to do was learn a few simple jobs.

Most of the employees were second- or third-generation mill hands. None, however, had the foggiest idea how the mill itself functioned and they didn't care. Many who had worked there for decades didn't know much, if anything, about the tasks of the workers on the floor below them. And they were shocked that I wanted to understand how the whole process worked.

I once asked if the flour I was shoveling back into the system from off the floor was then separated from the clean flour and somehow reprocessed. No one knew, but the comedian in the group said something like, "Why do you think you're supposed to keep that floor so spic and span?" I never found out, but my hunch is that his guess was on the mark.

It is impossible for me to imagine those mill hands functioning in a reengineered mill. It is impossible for me to imagine a reengineered mill. But that won't be necessary. A few years after I left the mill, it closed down and all of the workers were out on the street. I ran into one once. Things were bleak; the only job he could land was as a bagger in a supermarket at minimum wage. Perhaps some had found jobs at McDonald's or AAA. Retraining?

Despite the public platitudes and the foundation gifts to prestigious universities, the corporate legacy to American education can be found in the faces of the unemployed and unemployable who once labored in the mills and plants and factories. They heard the job training message loud and clear. Division of labor. Do what you do well. Let the bosses worry about how it all works. Now, after a hundred and fifty or more years of the traditional model, a lack of competitiveness in the global markets, downturns in profitability, questions about productivity, conjoined with popular talk about empowering people to take charge of their own lives, have brought the revolutionaries out of the woodwork of academia with restructuring schemes.

Had those schemes been put in place in the earlier era, the ethical problem of treating the undereducated workers as means might have been solved: the work force might have been educated so they could assume complex roles in the new CID structures of their corporations. They then would have been fully empowered, or empowerable, so that a Goodpaster-type program to ensure the role of ethical considerations in decision making would not have to be a paternalistic process. Gilbert's criticism would have been met. If.

It is instructive that Hammer and Champy tell those who would follow their program to forget about the past and begin by asking yourself, "If I were recreating this company today, given what I know, and given the current technology, what would it look like?"[85] That is fine from the point of view of economics and management theory, but not ethically permissible. We are caught in an historical trap: It is unethical to act as if the past one hundred fifty years were only a bad dream from which we are awakening. It wasn't a bad dream. It was a bad real-life system, one that had, and continues to produce, innocent victims.

The basic principles of the traditional corporate structure were always ethically deficient, because they permitted, no, encouraged, gross violation of the side constraints. They condoned disdain for persons rather than respect for them, but to fix what clearly is broken by restructuring the corporation in the manner recommended by consultants like Hammer and Champy will have a similar ethically unacceptable effect on large numbers of innocent people in the current work force. Not to fix it in a fundamental way, however, we are confidently and I think correctly told, could lead to the loss of markets and profitability. That spells utter disaster for the American economy and our standard of living.

To restructure or not to restructure? I am convinced by the arguments in favor of empowering the corporate agents. A bad structure should not be endured simply because the better one has unwanted effects. But I think that the side constraints require that corporations be discouraged from adopting nontraditional structural models that empower their employees unless their current work forces are sufficiently educated to qualify for the jobs in their restructured system. The two elements cannot be divorced if the corporation is going to act ethically.

To some this may seem a version of or a cousin to the plant relocation issue that has been discussed in business ethics for some years. There are similarities, but restructuring is the more integral ethical issue because one of its outcomes, on most of the alternative models, will clearly be a better ethical situation for all agents of the corporate actor than was allowed by the traditional organizational model. In the plant relocation cases, the changes usually leave the structures intact. Their expected upsides are predominantly financial. For example, the corporation figures to be more profitable, efficient, and productive. Their downsides do, of course, involve displacement of workers, disruption, and even destruction of local economies.

New companies, of course, need not be deterred from organizing around the reengineering principles (or other models) that empower the corporate agents while maintaining business viability. In fact, they should be stimulated to do so.

There is only one ethically viable way around, over, or through the restructuring dilemma, other than by appealing to the interests of Rank A-ers to justify the lack of respect in the treatment of the undereducated work force, a crass appeal I would not happily make. That is to develop a principle of compensation to be applied between Rank B-ers when violation of the side constraints occurs. It seems to me ethically defensible to hold the following compensation principle:

> If a Rank B-er violates the prohibition against treating another Rank B-er as a means without consent but in order to rectify a situation that is itself a violation of that prohibition, the violating Rank B-er must fully compensate the victim(s) for the loss suffered.

In the first place, this compensation principle only is applicable if the violator is correcting a situation that would itself fail the test of the side constraints. What that means is that no one can simply overstep the boundaries for personal reasons and then make everything okay by compensating victims.

I took a number of college students on a six-week tour of England one summer. In the middle of the night in a beautiful old hotel in the

Lake District, I was aroused by the owner and confronted with one of the students who had ripped the door of his room off its hinges and had broken up some antique furniture. The owner was about to call the police, but decided to deal first with me. The student would say only "So how much is that stuff anyway? I can pay for it." He admitted that he was prone to fits of violence. Back home he was under a psychiatrist's care. He always carried enough money with him to pay for his escapades. The hotel owner was placated with a sum that was considerably more than the "stuff" was probably worth, but I've always had the feeling that the whole matter had gone rather badly, that I should have insisted on some more significant penalty. I hope I would have if the target of his wrath had been another human and not a door, some chairs, and a writing table.

Secondly, a victim is only fully compensated for a violation if he or she ends up no worse off than they would have been if the violation never occurred. "[S]omething compensates X for Y's act if receiving it leaves X on at least as high an indifference curve as he would have been on, without it, had Y not so acted."[86]

There are some real problems with applying this compensation principle to reengineering the corporation problem. The primary ones concern determination of the baseline for the workers who cannot qualify for the new type of jobs. What do we do if their positions are already deteriorating before the reengineering is undertaken by the corporation? In Nozick's terms: "[I]s the baseline for compensation where he was heading, or where he was then?"[87]

If the company will have to lay off a number of employees because it has lost market share under its old structure, should it have to compensate those employees if they cannot qualify to be hired back under the new? What of the legal principle of limiting one's losses? If the employees have not been obtaining the sort of education needed to compete for the process-team jobs, if they have been using their free time for vacations, parental activities such as coaching the kids' sports teams, watching sitcoms on television, and the like, should the compensation level be reduced? And if they have been making some preparations on their own for the changeover, should that benefit the corporation by lowering the compensation they will need to provide?

The principle answers these questions by appeal to the notion of full compensation. The activities of the employees that do nothing to ameliorate their losses are irrelevant to the amount of compensation the corporate actor must provide. The employees are not made worse off by their continuing in the life-styles to which they had become accustomed. That is the baseline from which compensation must be assessed.

But what sort of compensation will be appropriate? Cash settlements would probably appeal to the army of lawyers, but they hardly will return the victims to the baseline in a meaningful way. Something more rad-ical, but clearly appropriate, seems to me to be in order: corporations themselves must get into the business of education in a direct way. What I have in mind is a combination of something like the GI Bill and major financial support for teaching institutions that are dedi-cated to educating people for the process- and case-oriented positions in the reengineered businesses.

I think that most of the current crop of schools, whether precolle-giate or college level, are hopelessly encrusted in the educational the-ories of the past. Departmental turf wars, political posturing, professorial angst, research emphases, and teaching neglect are ram-pant. In fact, the educational institutions are in as great a need of reengineering as the corporations.

The appropriate compensation would be accomplished if corpo-rations, perhaps in consortia, were to provide funding for educational institutions prepared to address the corporate organizational needs of the twenty-first century. Those schools will need to hire faculty that are dedicated teachers and fully cognizant of the relationship between their subjects and the educational goals for which the fund-ing is provided.

Reengineered corporations should make tuition remission and liv-ing expenses available to all employees for the number of terms needed to successfully complete the curriculum at those schools. Course completion would not be a ticket to a job, but would put the educated, not retrained, employee in a better position to compete for the jobs than someone who had not received the education.

Obviously, many facets to this idea for compensating the victims of restructuring need to be worked out, and this is not the place to do that. I will leave the idea as but a bare suggestion and only an exam-ple of how the compensation principle might be satisfied while reengi-neering is ethically permitted. In any event, if adequate restitution can be instituted, and I think it can, then we will not be permitted to appeal to the notion that the interests of Rank A-ers will be bene-fited to justify the use of Rank B-ers as mere means without their con-sent. Ethics will not allow us to dump the under-educated work force like so much toxic waste in Love Canal. If we did, they will surely seep up and pollute whatever corporate structural utopia we have engineered.

The restructuring dilemma reveals not only how central and cru-cial to our society the corporate invaders are, but how even tinkering with virtually any element of them can cause shock waves across the whole social network that supports human life and makes it worth living. That system is far more intricately integrated around the cor-porate actors, despite the fact that their traditional organizations are ethically defective, than has previously been appreciated by both business ethicists and management theorists alike.

8. Heroic Whistle-blowing and Conflicts of Duty

In one of Louis L'Amour's western stories a weathered cowboy named Conagher drawls his motto: "You take the man's money, you ride for the brand."

January 28, 1986. I was in a meeting with a college administrator when his secretary rushed in, tears welling in her eyes, her voice cracking. "She's dead," she choked out, "and all the others, all dead. It just exploded only a few seconds after the launch." The meeting was hastily adjourned and we all went into the outer office to watch the replays on CNN.

The space shuttle *Challenger*, seventy-three seconds from ignition, in full view of a national television audience tuned in to witness the historic flight of schoolteacher Christa McAuliffe, blew up. As the secretary had said, all of the seven astronauts on board were killed.

As with all disasters involving government agencies, a commission was appointed to investigate. It determined that the cause of the explosion was faulty O-rings and it learned from engineer Roger Boisjoly, a rocket-seal expert with Morton Thiokol, Inc., that not only did his company know of defects in the O-ring seals, but that it and NASA decided to launch the shuttle against the strong objections of Boisjoly and other engineers on the project.

Boisjoly's testimony before the commission had the effect of publicly damning his corporation. He pointed out that he and other Morton Thiokol engineers discovered that the primary and secondary O-ring seals on a field joint were prone to be compromised by hot gasses which eroded the seals if launches occurred at low temperatures. They had run a number of bench tests and were convinced that if temperatures were low, "it was possible that neither the primary nor secondary O-rings would seal."[88]

They informed their superiors and also engineers and managers at NASA. Boisjoly sent a private company memo to R. K. Lund, Morton Thiokol's vice president of engineering on July 19, 1985:

> This letter is written to insure that management is fully aware of the seriousness of the current O-Ring erosion problem. . . . If the same scenario should occur in a field joint (and it could), then it is jump ball as to the success or failure of the joint. . . . The result would be a catastrophe of the highest order—loss of human life. It is my honest and real fear that if we do not take immediate action to dedicate a team to solve the problem . . . we stand in jeopardy of losing a flight with all the launch pad facilities.[89]

A research team was created, but got little support. One of the team members wrote to the manager of the Solid Rocket Motor Project,

"HELP! The seal task force is constantly being delayed by every possible means . . . This is a red flag."[90]

On the day before the *Challenger* was to be launched, a teleconference between Morton Thiokol and NASA was conducted. An eighteen-degree temperature was predicted for the morning of the launch. Boisjoly and some of his engineering colleagues were present at the teleconference, as were managers from both the company and NASA. Lund recommended against the launch, and Joseph Kilminster, vice president for space booster programs at Morton Thiokol, supported his engineers' decision.

NASA representatives were shocked and suggested that Morton Thiokol was trying to set new criteria for launching. Kilminster asked for a five minute caucus of the Morton Thiokol managers. Ignoring the advice of their engineers, they voted unanimously to recommend the launch. "Kilminster revised the initial engineering recommendations so that they would support management's decision to launch."[91] Only the four senior executives of Morton Thiokol were involved in the final decision.

The meeting marked a change in NASA policy. In the past NASA had always placed the burden on engineers "to prove beyond a doubt that it was safe to launch." The outcome of the teleconference, in effect, meant that the engineers at Morton Thiokol were "expected to prove that launching *Challenger* would not be safe." Boisjoly wrote in his office journal: "I personally do not agree with some of the statements in Joe Kilminster's written summary stating that SRM-25 is okay to fly."[92]

After the explosion, Boisjoly gave his notes, memos, and reports to the investigating commission. He was called into Kilminster's office and was reprimanded for revealing that he and the other engineers did not support Kilminster's evaluation of the data and the managers' decision to recommend launching.

Boisjoly testified before the commission that the decision of the four executives during the teleconference was unanimous. This contradicted the testimony of Morton Thiokol executives who tried to convince the commission that it had not been unanimous.

Ed Garrison, president of aerospace operations for Morton Thiokol, attacked Boisjoly for "airing the company's dirty laundry" through the release of his memos to the investigating commission. Boisjoly was reassigned to another position in Morton Thiokol, but the general feeling throughout the company was that he had been disloyal, that he had contradicted the company line, and that he had seriously damaged the company's image. He found it virtually impossible to work in the hostile environment that confronted him at Morton Thiokol. On July 21, 1986, almost exactly six months after the *Challenger* explosion, Boisjoly requested extended sick leave.

The affine agents of a corporation tend to be intensely loyal to all aspects of its activities and interests, and they expect loyalty in return from the other managers and employees. In fact, they regard loyalty to the corporation as a duty, and to some extent, no doubt, it is. Loyalty to a company means a number of things, most of which anyone in ethics would readily endorse. For example, managers and employees are thought to have an obligation not to divulge trade secrets and propriative information to competitors. Many companies, quite rightly, expect that employees they have trained will provide them with service over a fair amount of time rather than selling their skills off to the highest bidder.

Loyalty also would seem to require that managers and employees not deliberately set out to damage the corporation's reputation. However, as Solomon and Hanson have pointed out, "the question of company loyalty is a question of fair exchange. . . . Loyalty is a two-way affair, and it is the responsibility of the company to inspire and deserve loyalty."[93]

Corporations inspire loyalty by creating the kind of workplaces that are attractive to their work forces, by setting up decision structures that do not violate the side constraints. The Toyota Corporation in Japan has been especially successful in fostering what virtually amounts to cradle-to-grave loyalty among its employees. Becoming and remaining a Toyota family member is highly prized as it involves housing, schools, health-care facilities, recreational activities, almost everything imaginable. The old American company town, the "owe my soul to the company store" idea, has, along with a number of other originally American ideas, been perfected by Toyota. But rather than the American resentment of such life-style management, the Toyota worker feels an intense loyalty and pride in the company.

Corporations deserve loyalty because they pay the salaries and provide fringe benefits and additional career training for their employees. But where do the duties of loyalty end? What happens when they come in direct conflict with other duties, especially with moral duties? How are conflicts of duty to be handled?

A former student recently telephoned to ask me for advice. She'd been doing volunteer work at her church. In the absence of a Spanish-speaking priest, she was called upon to serve as an interpreter so that a man could make his confession in Spanish. The man confessed to the brutal beating of his two children and was given absolution. Afterwards, the priest informed her that she had a sacred duty to keep the seal of the confession.

Texas law, however, requires anyone who learns of child abuse to report it to the proper authorities. And that law, according to the opinion of the state attorney general, does not exempt the clergy even if they gain knowledge of child abuse while serving in their religious capacities. To make matters worse, my former student recognized the man as a neighbor, and she was acquainted with his kids.

She felt trapped in a web of conflicting duties. She had promised a priest she would not break the seal of the confession. But she was burdened with the weight of duty to inform the authorities not only because it is the law, but because she feared for the safety of children she knew. She wanted me to tell her what ought she to do?

Her case reminded me of an episode on the old television show *M*A*S*H* that vividly demonstrated that as a doctor one may see oneself as having certain duties, while as a moral member of society one can feel the pressure to do something quite antithetical to one's professional duties. The 4077 MASH unit was inundated with a larger than usual number of casualties owed to the reckless leadership of a particularly gung-ho colonel. The colonel visits his wounded soldiers, but shows little sympathy for their condition. He attempts to cheer up those in the postoperative ward with bravado talk of the prospects of the unit taking a virtually impregnable hilltop enemy fortification. However, rather than getting permission for an all-out assault on that objective, headquarters orders him to hold his position and not try to capture the hill. He confides to Hawkeye and B. J., the MASH surgeons, that he will follow the letter of those orders, but that does not exclude his sending out reconnaissance patrols that will surely be fired on. When the shooting starts, he'll commit his troops, and headquarters will have to back him. He admits that his battle plan will probably cost about seven hundred wounded or dead, but the hill will be worth it.

Hawkeye devises a plan to get the colonel drunk, cause him severe cramps, and diagnose their source as appendicitis. He will then perform an appendectomy, thereby effectively putting the colonel out of service for some months. B. J. is horrified by Hawkeye's plot and reminds him of his oath as a doctor to heal, not to cut into a healthy body and remove a healthy organ. Hawkeye maintains that he could not live with himself if he does not violate his duties as a doctor in favor of meeting a greater duty to save hundreds of young soldiers from death or mutilation. B. J. refuses to assist him. Neither my former student's nor Hawkeye's problem directly involve corporate positions, but they are illustrative of the conflict of duties issues that can confront corporate agents and that become especially brutal in cases like that of Roger Boisjoly.

Many philosophers hold the view that there are no real moral duty conflicts. Stuart Hampshire refers to this belief as the "doctrine of moral harmony."[94] Kant was committed to moral harmony, maintaining that all apparent conflicts are resolvable by application of principles derived from reason itself, the categorical imperative. Kant writes:

> A conflict of duties and obligations is inconceivable (*obligationes non collidunter*). For the concepts of duty and obligation as such express the objective practical necessity of certain actions, and two conflicting rules cannot both be necessary at the same time: if it is our duty to act according to one of these rules, then to act according to the opposite one is not our duty and is even contrary to duty.[95]

Mark Halfon writes:

> A Kantian might . . . claim that any person of integrity must act in accordance with the categorical imperative and that there can be no conflicts regarding this principle. If there are no conflicts, then there is no need to make any exception to the categorical imperative.[96]

Traditional utilitarians, while certainly disagreeing with Kant about ethical principles, are also committed to the doctrine of moral harmony. For them, choosing the action that will produce the greatest benefit over the affected population should resolve all apparent conflicts. (Preference utilitarians, of course, will maximize preferences or satisfied interests.)

One of the underlying assumptions of the doctrine of moral harmony, as noted by Isaiah Berlin,[97] identifies all conflicts of duty as due to clashes of reason with the irrational, or the immature and insufficiently developed aspects in human life. So, in principle, all are avoidable. Truly rational folks will never have them at all.

This did not seem to be the case, however, for my former student or for Hawkeye in *M*A*S*H*. Even if we were to discount her religious duty to keep the seal of the confession as irrational or based on superstition or as childish, she would still have a conflict because she promised the priest not to reveal the content of the man's confession, and a promise is one of the most traditional of ethical examples of an obligation-generating practice.

Hawkeye's plan to prevent the slaughter of hundreds of troops might be seen as childish, but surely the principle to which he is committed is not irrational. Still, the moral harmony folks insist that tragedy is not an inescapable characteristic of the human condition.

To this, Martha Nussbaum[98] responds with the ancient Greek story of Agamemnon and his daughter, Iphigenia. Agamemnon had assembled the Greek warriors at Aulis to avenge the honor of his brother Menaleus, a cause demanded by Zeus and one "he could not desert without the most serious impiety." The ships that would take him to Troy were becalmed by the anger of another god, Artemis, and the soothsayer divined

> . . . that the only remedy for this situation is the sacrifice of Iphigenia . . . There is open to him no guilt-free course. . . . If Agamemnon does not fulfill Artemis's condition, everyone, including Iphigenia will die. He will also be abandoning the expedition and, therefore violating the command of Zeus. . . . To perform the sacrifice will be, however, to perform a horrible and guilty act . . . both courses involve him in guilt.[99]

Clearly Agamemnon's duties as a father and as a commander conflict, and no rational pattern of action appears in which he can fulfill both, yet neither duty can be dismissed as flat-out irrational.

Utilitarians, of course, can support the sacrifice in order to save the army, Agamemnon's choice. But I am not certain that those of us who are not utilitarians, but are fathers, would agree that that is the only clearly right thing for him to do in the circumstances. Is it so obvious that he would have done the wrong thing had he refused to slaughter his daughter? I'm convinced that we can quite rationally get caught up in situations that allow no morally totally satisfactory way out.

Moral harmony theorists might argue that the Agamemnon story is a particularly wrenching one of conflicting *prima facie* obligations, but that deeper investigation of his situation will result in the identification of his true moral duty. Or they may maintain that his situation is one in which part of the evidence supports one duty and another part supports an incompatible duty, but taken as a whole, the available evidence is insufficient to determine which is his genuine moral obligation. Or they could argue that the conflict is between different kinds of duties, parental duties vs. political or military duties, only one of which is really moral. But which one?

It might be pointed out that if "ought implies can," and Agamemnon cannot perform both of his duties, then he can have no duty to perform them both. So he has no conflict. The idea goes something like this. Imagine you are sitting by a swimming pool (another threadbare philosophical example), and a child falls in the pool near you. The child can't swim, you can, and you can easily pull her out. If no one else is around, you have a moral duty to save the child. But suppose there are twins, and they both fall in. Do you have a duty to save both?

Philosophers such as Feldman[100] point out an important difference between the cases. We can all agree that when one child is drowning, it is your moral duty to save her. Nothing would be morally better in that isolated situation. But if the twins are drowning, and you physically cannot save both, your moral duty is to save one or the other of the twins. Failure to save either would be wrong, but the choice of one rather than the other isn't a moral one. The moral duty is to make the choice as to which one to save quickly enough to at least save that one.

This version of moral harmony recognizes no ethical conflict of duty when the two (or more) tasks one has an obligation to do in a certain situation are indistinguishably worthy and one cannot do them both. One must, of course, choose and act.

If my former student cannot both keep the seal of the confession and report the child abuse to the authorities, then, the argument will be, it doesn't matter morally which she does, assuming the duties are, for all intents and purposes, equal from the moral point of view. If they are not equal, then the one of greater moral weight should be done. But what makes one duty of greater moral weight than the other?

Utilitarians have ready answers, or at least ready formulas. Within the framework I have adopted and defended, matters are more complicated. We will need to refer to the side constraints and to issues of whether or not the interests of the Rank A-ers are benefited by fulfilling one rather than the other duty.

Those who regard the duty of keeping the seal of the confession to have priority might argue on utilitarian grounds that the sacrament of the confessional (or reconciliation) has important social benefits. The guarantee of secrecy encourages the revelation of the penitent's most terrible thoughts and deeds, so it allows the priest a unique opportunity to reform the penitent, to teach him or her so that further harm to the members of society may be prevented. Admittedly these reformation and reconciliation attempts may sometimes fail, but, at least the Catholic Church believes, in the majority of cases the priest should be able to persuade the penitent that his or her thoughts and deeds are wrong and are not to be repeated. The benefits of the confidential sacrament then run both to the penitent and to the community at large. Therefore the seal of the confession should be kept regardless of Texas law or the trepidation one may have for the welfare of the victimized children. Putting a version of this argument in the way it was offered to me by a young priest, if word ever got out that a priest had revealed the content of a confession, no one would make confessions and all the good that is done would be lost. A sort of rule utilitarianism seems to be functioning here, but other defensive tacks have been taken.

St. Thomas Aquinas, for example, argued that confidentiality makes more probable that the penitent will be honest and unburden his or her most shameful actions and future intentions. Then the true inspection of conscience can occur and personal repentance, something morally good for the penitent, is possible. That would save the soul of the penitent, but leaves no assurances with regard to the plight of the children.

All of these "moral" defenses of the seal of the confession—and we might as well include a simple Kantian one that says that the sacrament is based on a promise of confidentiality and that promise-keeping is a moral duty—however, don't prove that that duty is morally greater than those imposed by Texas law or the one a person might feel with regard to preventing further harm and injury to innocent people.

The idea that the duties involved are basically equivalent, like the hypothetical twins drowning in the swimming pool, also overlooks the fact that people who find themselves in conflicts (whether or not they are only apparent from the perspective of some moral theory) feel that no matter what they do that they will fail to do something they should have done. And they regret, resent, and feel guilty about deciding to do the one thing and not the other. (One only needs to reread *Sophie's Choice* or watch the movie for a convincing example.)

Those guilt feelings can, however, be written off by maintaining that they are the result of a recognition that one is responsible for a bad state of affairs, for having caused or contributed to something bad happening. But they are not appropriately associated with the feeling that one has failed to do something one ought morally to have done. They are, therefore, the sign of a good moral character.

Hawkeye, in the *M*A*S*H* episode, also feels badly, guilty, about removing the colonel's healthy appendix, but he clearly and quite vocally disassociates that guilt from moral guilt at having failed to do his moral duty. He says to B. J., "At least I can hate you, me, and this whole situation with a clear conscience." Boisjoly doesn't seem to have displayed quite so much self-righteousness, but it seems clear from his physical breakdown that he harbored some guilt about what his actions had done to Morton Thiokol and to those with whom he worked. Still, a year after the *Challenger* exploded, Boisjoly, in a speech at MIT, said:

> I have been asked by some if I would testify again if I knew in advance of the potential consequences to me and my career. My answer is always "yes." I couldn't live with any self-respect if I tailored my actions based upon the personal consequences as a result of my honorable actions.[101]

Boisjoly and Hawkeye chose to protect their own self-respect, their moral integrity, rather than to honor the demands of loyalty to the corporation or professional duty. A good candidate for a first principle of ethics would be to always act to preserve one's moral integrity, whether for humans or corporate actors. I think it can be shown to be a corollary to the side constraints.

Integrity is often thought to be at stake when one's situation cries out for compromise, as seems to be the case with Hawkeye, Boisjoly, and my former student. They sense that there is no course of action open to them that will not leave them with remorse, regret, guilt, and, possibly, shame. The loyalty demands in corporations not infrequently place managers and employees in just such situations, though usually not so dramatically, and usually the lives of other innocent people are not at stake. How is integrity sustained when all around one are demanding compromise?

What is integrity? Gabriele Taylor reminds us that a person of integrity is typically thought to be someone "whose self is whole and integrated."[102] A disintegrated person is said to lack integrity. Martin Benjamin[103] points out that like many moral concepts, integrity can be clarified by looking at ways people are said to lack it. Four ways are especially obvious and tend to occur with uncomfortable frequency in corporate offices.

First, there is the moral chameleon who is "anxious to accommodate others and temperamentally indisposed to moral controversy and disagreement; the moral chameleon is quick to modify or abandon previously avowed principles in order to placate others."[104] Moral chameleons have no core set of values for which they stand. They bend to whatever social pressures are in the corporate wind. They will betray others they only yesterday befriended.

The description of moral chameleons may sound suspiciously like the account I gave earlier of what is expected of Comers. Though there are similarities, especially as concerns the need to cover oneself on all sides of an issue and to perfect the purposeful use of a noncommittal vocabulary to guard against changes in company policy or the views of one's superiors, I doubt if moral chameleons are likely to be Comers, or if they are, that they will remain Comers for long. Frankly, moral chameleons are not dedicated to getting ahead, to rising up the corporate ladder. Their rule of life is "Get along, don't make waves." Drones are more likely to be moral chameleons. But even they will not last in the organization, if they are discovered to be so. As Benjamin says, "The moral chameleon bears careful watching . . . even those whose colors she assumes cannot turn their backs on her for very long."[105]

Opportunists are a second class of those lacking moral integrity, and they do seem to be in abundance in the managerial positions of American corporations.

> The opportunist's . . . values and principles are quite fluid. . . . Opportunists will alter their beliefs and behavior whenever they think it will lead to personal gain or advancement.[106]

The opportunist is the paradigm of a person stricken with personal teleopathy. "[T]he opportunist places overriding value on his own short-run interests."[107] The opportunist is committed to personal success even if that means changing one's positions hourly. Opportunists have few substantial commitments. They are good team players only so long as they can see the personal benefit from playing along.

It is of some note that opportunists are both hated and admired among corporate managers. Their dedication to getting ahead is applauded, but the fact that they cannot be counted on within the circles of managers with whom they are associated makes them targets of suspicion. An opportunist who succeeds rises to a top executive position and must be respected. But one who is found out along the way is despised. And his or her fall will meet with general enthusiasm and no small amount of smugness. Note in the movie *Wall Street*, the response of the others in the office when the opportunist character played by Charlie Sheen is arrested. Neither the successful nor the failed opportunist, however, is ever confused with a person of moral integrity, even within the jaded corporate halls filled with other opportunists and hypocrites.

Hypocrites have more of a center of personal values than their other lack-of-integrity cousins. Taylor describes a hypocrite as pretending

. . . to live by certain standards when in fact he does not. In the clear-
est case he consciously and calculatingly exploits for his own ends the fact
that certain types of behavior are seen by others as constituting or imply-
ing certain commitments and that therefore he will be seen by others to
be acting as he does because he is so committed.[108]

Hypocrites have one set of values for public display and another
that they keep hidden, but which actually motivate their behavior.
Benjamin notes that a deeper understanding of the hypocrite, despite
this apparent inconsistency between words and deeds, will reveal "a
coherent internal rationale. Underlying the hypocrite's apparent external inconsistencies, then, is a deceitful internal unity. Hypocrites may
be 'rotten to the core,' but they are not wholly without a center."[109]

Hypocrites abound in corporate life, as they do in most human
pursuits. The arguments of Carr, discussed earlier, might even be
taken as recommending an ethic of hypocrisy for business, always saying and doing one thing in order to get the competitor to think you're
up to something you're not: throwing them off the trail while you lay
the ambush. But, hypocrisy and bluffing are quite different things.
There is no game in which hypocrisy, when revealed, is rewarded, certainly no social game. The bluffer is not a hypocrite, or at least not necessarily so.

The fourth type of person who lacks integrity is the self-deceiver.
Benjamin again aptly characterizes the type:

Self-deceivers are often motivated by a discrepancy between the values and principles that they like to think of themselves as acting upon
and the conduct that is motivated by quite different, incompatible interests
and desires. To resolve this tension and, at the same time, to preserve the
idealized self-conception while indulging the incompatible interests and
desires, they deceive themselves about what they are in fact doing.[110]

Self-deceivers think they are internally consistent and positively
brimming over with integrity, but it is all a sham that others can often
see through. Corporate Drones, in the descriptions that Jackall provides, seem to be prone to self-deception in that they typically convince themselves that they are really Comers and that their current
lack of corporate mobility is but a temporary pause in the upward trek.
They affect the language of Comers and occasionally try to act like they
are in the power circles. But it is a charade that is all the more pitiful
if they are unaware of it. It is one thing to intentionally put on the
appearance of a Comer, knowing full well that one is a Drone, and it is
quite another to convince oneself that one is a Comer when one is not.
In the former case one might be a hypocrite or, more likely, merely a
self-preservationist. In the latter, one is definitely betraying one's
integrity.

I do not want to suggest that these categories either exhaust the types of persons who lack integrity or that they are pure character types. People can be traitors to their own integrity in myriad subtle ways and in degrees and combinations of the types. I also do not want to exclude corporate actors from those who can lack integrity. A CID structure can be fabricated in such a way that it is typically opportunist in its actions, a hard and fast straightforward maximizer. Such a corporation would be governed by executives inflicted with teleopathic thinking to the point that its policies require that only short-term profitability considerations are to be given weight in decision making. A number of such corporations have come and gone, especially in recent decades. Many were created for just that purpose.

It seems to me also possible that a corporation can turn itself into a self-deceiver by instituting policies that have the effect of keeping it in the dark about what it is really doing, while fostering the sincere belief that it is up to something else. Some years ago, I did a study of Air New Zealand regarding the crash of one of its DC-10s into Mt. Erebus in Antarctica.

Air New Zealand, since its inception, conceived of itself as a family-like corporation. For them that meant that verbal communication was to be the norm. The company's operations had, however, grown to a size, with multiple divisions, that made such communication not only inefficient, but unsafe.

The DC-10, flight TE-901, on a sightseeing tour with 257 people on board, was to have flown on a certain navigational track that had been used by previous flights of its type. That flight plan was given to the captain at a briefing and he noted it and entered it on his maps. It would have taken the plane over McMurdo Sound, where it was to fly at fifteen hundred feet to give the passengers a good view of the splendors of the frozen continent. The evening before the flight, the Navigation Section of the Flight Operations Division of Air New Zealand directed the Computer Section of the same division to reprogram the on-board computer of TE-901 to bring it in line with the tactical air navigation system of McMurdo Station. That was not an unreasonable thing to do, all things being equal.

The order to reprogram came verbally from the operations manager who had heard from a captain of an earlier flight that the computer navigation track was about twenty-seven miles to the west of the McMurdo signal. That pilot did not tell the operations manager to change the flight plans. He only expressed the view that the other pilots should be informed that there was such a discrepancy. At least that is what he now claims he said. Nothing is in writing! The operations manager, believing that a serious error in the flight plan existed, ordered the reprogramming of the computer to bring the track in line with the signal. He, so he says, did not think such a change important enough to inform the captain, so he said no more about it and, of course, no written messages about the change were left for the captain or the crew.

As it happens, if you fly an airplane at fifteen hundred feet down a track twenty-seven miles west of the original McMurdo Sound track, you will crash it head on into a twelve-thousand-foot mountain. Worse yet, you will not notice the mountain until you are virtually on it because the terrain is so white that it causes a flattening, or white-out visual illusion. If you think you are over the frozen sound, none of the visual cues you are receiving from scanning the horizon will persuade you otherwise. There will be no time to take evasive actions. Two hundred fifty-seven people, many unwittingly snapping pictures of their gruesome deaths, perished.[111]

An investigating commission found that the primary cause of the disaster was the communications system of Air New Zealand. At the commission hearings Air New Zealand's CEO insisted that he ran the company on a verbal basis to foster a family-like atmosphere, and that the airline had an excellent safety record before TE-901.

It was pointed out in the commission's report that other major carriers did not trust crucial messages to word of mouth and that such a family-type organizational policy was inappropriate for the industry. Air New Zealand, however, persisted in the self-deception that the reason for the crash was pilot error and steadfastly made no changes in its standard operating procedures. They have, however, ceased the sightseeing flights to the Antarctic. They are surely not the only corporation whose CID structure is programmed for self-deception. A number of America's giants in manufacturing also suffer from such a lack of integrity and it has cost them dearly in the marketplace.

I also don't see why a corporate actor could not be designed to produce hypocritical behavior. The tobacco companies, many of us suspect, have been up to that for decades. Of particular note might be their advertising of cigarettes in African-American neighborhoods and the sponsorship of athletic events. It is virtually impossible to believe that anyone in the high echelons of the tobacco companies is not aware that cigarette smoking is the major cause of lung cancer. Still, the tobacco companies persist in the myth that smoking is an integral part of a desirable lifestyle filled with fun and frolic and sexual adventures. This image is sold on posters and billboards all over poorer African-American neighborhoods and free samples are regularly distributed to young African-Americans. African-Americans now smoke more per capita than other groups in America and are contracting lung cancer in far greater numbers. The tobacco companies retort that they merely make the product available and that it is a person's own business whether they use it. They are only meeting the needs of a market. Hypocritical?

Another sort of hypocrisy can be seen in the "commitment" of most corporations to affirmative action programs. Written affirmations of those commitments are sprinkled throughout corporate literature. But what of practice? Affirmative action should work at two stages in employer–employee relationships. The hiring stage is the most obvious place at which it should function, and many corporations have installed policies and procedures that make good-faith efforts to employ women and members of minorities. Success in breaking down the hiring barriers has been largely achieved. If there is any current issue about affirmative action employment programs, it is probably the cost that corporations, and other institutions, incur in meeting federal requirements to maintain records of employees with respect to their race, sex, ethnicity, and so forth.

The second stage of affirmative action, however, is where recent studies indicate serious nonconformity to the principles of equal treatment that are consistent with the side constraints. *Working Woman* magazine recently published a survey that indicates that women earn approximately the same salaries as their male counterparts in only a few job categories. The specific types of jobs where equality seems to have been achieved are in the advertising fields such as account executives. Women are doing better than men in nursing, engineering (if they are under age thirty), and as deans of law schools. Also women can earn more than men as automobile mechanics and food preparers. Elsewhere, women, even if they enter at comparable salaries to men, fall into a gender-gap pay differential as they rise up the corporate ladder.[112]

Faye Crosby reports her studies on the pay differential problem to be most puzzling. She writes:

> To my surprise and dismay, when we looked at the date, our computer printouts showed that the employed women in the study earned significantly less than the men with exactly comparable jobs. When we turned to the data on attitudes, we were surprised to find that the employed women were just as satisfied with their employment, including their compensation, as were the men . . . the women in my study remained blind to their own disadvantage.[113]

The matter of the women's attitude could be explained in two not incompatible ways: that women are convinced, in the words of finance professor Maria Falchero Davis, that the price they pay "for breaking the glass ceiling is earning less,"[114] and that attitudes about the role and value of women in our society are shared by many women because they have been acculturated to hold those beliefs, even about themselves. (This issue will be discussed at greater length in Part 2, Section 10, and Part 4, Section 7.)

The fact that many women in the workplace may not be unhappy with their salaries when those salaries are not equivalent to what men in comparable positions are making is, however, irrelevant to the matter of corporate hypocrisy. What is hypocritical is that corporations typically associate themselves with affirmative-action programs while quite deliberately paying their female employees less than their male employees for comparable work. In doing so, they clearly violate the side constraints against using Rank B-ers as means, and they are doing so hypocritically because they mask their violations in corporate proclamations of not only compliance with but endorsement of affirmative action.

A person or a corporate actor of integrity is not a moral chameleon, opportunist, hypocrite, or self-deceiver. Fine. But what are they? Benjamin claims that when you think of integrity in this way

> . . . [w]hat emerges is a conception of the person as an integrated triad consisting of: (1) a reasonably coherent and relatively stable set of highly cherished values and principles; (2) verbal behavior expressing these values and principles; and (3) conduct embodying one's values and principles and consistent with what one says. These are the elements of integrity.[115]

A person of moral integrity is one who maintains an invariable commitment to do what is morally best in any circumstance, no matter how adverse the conditions or personally unwelcome the consequences.

There are, however, a number of other kinds of integrity besides moral integrity and some of the conflict of duty cases, such as Hawkeye's and Boisjoly's, might reflect a confusion between the sort of integrity one is preserving and the sort one is compromising. If my former student keeps the seal of the confession, she'll be a person of religious integrity.

I'm reminded of the story of Eric Liddell, as told in the film *Chariots of Fire*. Liddell, a devout Christian, refused to participate in the one-hundred meter dash in the 1924 Olympics because the qualifying heats were scheduled on Sunday. Had he run, he would have compromised his religious integrity for the sake of his athletic integrity. But had his refusal to do something on the Sabbath amounted to his not trying to help someone in need, he would have sacrificed his moral integrity for his religious integrity. We should not then be so ready to applaud him . . . unless, I suppose, we are followers of Kierkegaard and take him to be a knight of faith who has "concurred in the suspension of the ethical."[116]

In my view, to be a person of integrity one must minimally be a person of moral integrity, a person unwaveringly committed to doing what is best in the circumstances, to doing the right thing. Persons of moral integrity don't pursue courses of action that bring their characters into disrepute. They don't compromise their moral commitments to preserve some other sort of integrity, because that would amount to losing their moral integrity and so ultimately any claim to being persons of integrity.

To compromise you must make concessions about what you believe ought to be done and you must be willing to act in a way that is opposed to your beliefs. A moral compromiser sounds like a hypocrite or an opportunist, and if you try to rationalize following a course of action you believe to be morally unjustified, you're a self-deceiver. In either case, moral compromise is not possible without loss of moral integrity and therefore character.

Hawkeye did his moral duty, as he understood it, while compromising his integrity as a doctor. I suppose it is possible for him to have integrity as a doctor without being a person of integrity. But he cannot be a person of integrity without moral integrity.

But wait, we will be told by those in business and other professions that compromise is the name of the game. If you can't or won't compromise, you'll not get far in business. Boisjoly refused to budge on his principles, and he damaged his company and fellow corporate agents and also himself. Can't one maintain moral integrity while compromising a bit for the good of the corporation? Surely compromise is acceptable when one is trapped in a dilemma involving political commitments or financial commitments.

Agreed, but there is something opprobrious in the very sound of "ethical compromise." Persons and corporate actors of moral integrity are uncompromising when it comes to their ethical commitments.

"Uncompromising," however, also sounds rather unsavory. It suggests a prig, an ideologue, a fanatic. People who are uncompromising take obdurate stands and do not take seriously any criticisms to the effect that their views might, just possibly, require revision, that there could be good reasons to abrogate their principles. People who are uncompromising in this sense reflect, to use Halfon's account:

> . . . an arbitrary disregard of individual differences and mitigating circumstances. It appears that anyone who is uncompromising in this sense exhibits an undesirable trait and acts more like a dogmatist, fanatic, or ideologue than a person of integrity.[117]

"Uncompromising" has another sense, however, one that more closely associates with integrity and lacks the derogatory connotations. People who are uncompromising in this praiseworthy sense of the term do not "indiscriminately violate their principles nor arbitrarily abandon their ideals."[118] They do not give in to temptation, if their principles are at stake. One objection might well be that no obvious test exists for whether a person is uncompromising in the priggish way or in the way that indicates integrity. Both types of uncompromising people will refuse to abandon their principles or moral commitments. Neither will make concessions when their principles are involved. But there are various ways of not making concessions, as Halfon has noted. A person may be unwilling to modify, amend, or qualify his or her moral beliefs, principles, and attitudes. He or she just won't even consider it. On the other hand, a person may refuse to "betray, surrender, abandon, forsake, or violate one's commitments."[119]

People who are uncompromising in the derogatory sense will not make concessions in the former way. They regard their beliefs as unalterable, their principles as not to be modified even in the face of what might seem reasonable though conflicting considerations. On the other hand, a person may admit to some good reasons to modify his or her principles, to make concessions, but may refuse to do so because no good reason was offered.

People like Boisjoly will not accept, "It's for the good of the company" as a good reason to compromise their moral principles against lying. They are uncompromising, but not inflexible. They remain people of integrity while admitting that occasions may arise when their moral beliefs and principles may need to be reassessed or revised, but those will only be occasions when good reasons of a moral sort are put to them. From this account, however, it does not follow that people of integrity may compromise their moral commitments if there is a good reason for them to do so. I agree with Halfon that "any compromise of one's moral commitments will typically result in a loss of integrity."[120]

Suppose we ask whether someone has compromised his or her moral commitments if he or she reassesses and modifies those commitments after being presented with a good moral reason to do so. I don't think that he or she has. If you make a moral concession or compromise, as noted above, you are acting in a way that opposes your beliefs. Doing so reflects a weak moral character, at least a weakness of will, if not hypocrisy. But conflicts of moral duties exist, as we have seen, and no amount of theoretical footwork seems to shuffle them away. They must be resolved in judgment and action. Moral harmony is a myth. So where does that leave us?

Presumably a moral conflict of duty arises because you are and hope to remain a person of integrity in the first place. If moral integrity doesn't matter, you've got no problems. But if it does, and it should, then you pursue a general commitment to try to do what is best in any circumstance. To do that you must apprise yourself of the relevant facts and take care to weigh the relevant moral considerations. If you simply bring unbendable rules to the situation, you are uncompromising in the derogatory sense. Remember that Kant, when asked about whether a person should lie to save the life of a friend from a fiend out to kill her, responded that "to be honest in all declarations is a sacred unconditional command of reason, not to be limited by any expediency."[121] Tell the fiend where your friend is hiding. Most everyone I know who has read the article in which Kant says this is aghast, and I think rightfully so. Preserving one's moral integrity must involve more sensitivity than Kant seems to allow.

A person can retain moral integrity even though he or she has revised his or her moral beliefs and principles, though he or she cannot do it by compromising them. The important question is not whether one can preserve one's integrity when compromising or making concessions with respect to one's moral principles, but when should one reassess or revise one's moral principles.

I think there is no straightforward answer. It will depend on the situations into which one gets oneself or that are thrust upon one. And, of course, it will depend on the specific set of moral rules and principles one has adopted. If, with Kant, you think that truth-telling is an unconditional duty on all occasions, you will either have to reassess that rule when you cannot both tell the truth and save the life of an innocent person or reassess the principle that you should save innocent lives when you can do so.

I suppose there may, in some situations, be good reasons not to save the innocent lives, but they will be rare. The truth-telling principle will probably be the best choice for reassessment and revision. But what did the managers at Morton Thiokol decide to do? They accepted the prospect of killing the seven astronauts and chose to manufacture a bastion of lies to protect their corporate and individual images. They might have thought that doing so was necessary to protect the corporate reputation and so possibly the jobs of a large number of people. They might have been using a perverted kind of utilitarianism as a justification for such a compromise, not as a principle of reassessment for the truth-telling rule. They might have been betting that the explosion would not occur and that they could fix the problem with the O-rings on future rocket assemblies. They had no reason to take such a risk, but they might have justified it in their minds, again to protect the company's contracts with NASA. Because of the rewriting of the engineers' reports to bring them in line with the managerial decision, the process certainly looks more like a compromise of principles that was masked after the fact. Integrity was the first victim of the *Challenger* explosion.

Consider again the case of my former student. She could not both keep her promise to the priest and try to prevent an avoidable harm to those innocent children. She is in a genuine moral conflict, aside from the conflict between moral and legal and religious duties that also plagues her. The circumstances and the primary moral commitment to do what is best seem to me to call for her to reconsider her commitment to the promise-keeping rule in such circumstances. She should revise it, qualify it, to allow her to act to protect the children. That seems to me to be the best thing she can do in the circumstances. Not to do so might well be interpreted as evidencing the sort of self-righteousness associated with fanatics and not as a mark of moral integrity. Her conflict then is only apparent, and its resolution is clear.

There is, however, a nagging problem: how do we know when to make exceptions to moral principles? Frankly, I don't think we can know in advance of experiencing those entangling predicaments. No preestablished rule or algorithm exists, for if one did, it would be liable to revision in some yet to occur, complicated situation, unless, of course, with Kant, one just adopts the view that it (in Kant's case the categorical imperative) can never be revised. But then one must either believe that such a rule will resolve all apparent conflicts or that not even apparent conflicts will ever really arise. Both positions seem to me to utterly ignore the facts of social life, in and out of corporations.

The grounds for revising a moral principle must lie in the particulars of a situation in which the principle is supposed to apply. It therefore takes a certain ethical skill to judge whether a revision is in order. A number of philosophers in recent years have provided helpful ways of thinking about the requisite skill or art. Hilary Putnam, using an example he attributes to Judy Baker and Paul Grice, offers one of the better analogies of the kind of thinking that must be involved.

> A man is climbing a mountain. Halfway up he stops, because he is unsure how to go on. He imagines himself continuing via one route. In his imagination, he proceeds on up to a certain point, and then he gets into difficulty which he cannot, in his imagination, see how to get out of. He then imagines himself going up by a different route. This time he is able to imagine himself getting all the way to the top without difficulty. So he takes the second route.[122]

To imagine a climb up a certain peak, a mountaineer needs to know a number of things about mountains, hiking, climbing, weather, and the like. The mountaineer also needs specific information about the particular mountain to be climbed. The climber must have developed the ability to see that the first choice of routes is similar to one taken on a similar peak and which met with failure, even disaster. In short, to do the requisite imagining the climber needs a plethora of information and experience focused on the particulars of the task before him.

How does this relate to the sort of reasoning required to determine that making an exception to one of the moral rules or principles to which one is committed is appropriate? I think of the general moral commitment of persons of integrity to do what is best as comparable to the mountain to be climbed and the paths that cannot both be taken as the rules or principles that comprise one's moral commitments. To decide which must be modified requires moral imagination and that takes experience and skill and art. It can be learned, but not just by learning rules and principles. And it also means that the rules in question need to be understood not as absolute, unchangeable monuments to rational moral thinking, but as more flexible, as rules of thumb or "councils of wisdom" in Aristotle's sense. Halfon sums up the view I am taking quite nicely when he writes:

If persons of integrity are committed to doing what is best and that involves the acknowledgment of all relevant moral considerations, as well as the possibility of reassessment, then the nature and value of integrity cannot adequately be accounted for in terms of maintaining an unwavering commitment to some moral rule or principle.[123]

The *Challenger* explosion and its aftermath took Roger Boisjoly to the depths of his moral character; it tested his integrity. Confronted with conflicting principles, he chose to reassess and revise those that defined his duty of loyalty to Morton Thiokol. He did not compromise. His reassessment or revision of the principles of loyalty to one's corporation is not, to my knowledge, made explicit anywhere, but it can be deciphered from his retrospective statements and the facts of the case. We might spell them out in the following way:

A corporate agent has a moral obligation to be loyal (and all that entails) to his or her corporation unless:

1. that corporation is involved in the production of some goods or services likely to cause serious harm to those using them or to the general public;
2. the agent is in a privileged position to recognize the potential for such harm and has reported it through official corporate channels, but no or insufficient action was taken to correct it;
3. the agent has possession of full documentation of the dangerous product or services and has shared that data with superiors in the CID structure, but without positive results; and
4. the agent has good reasons to believe that the revelation of the corporation's activities with respect to the matter finally will cause the corporate actor to respond to the situation in an appropriate corrective way, and make the adjustments necessary to alleviate the danger.[124]

With such a revision of the corporate loyalty principle in mind, Boisjoly preserved his integrity by not compromising himself or his principles in blowing the whistle on Morton Thiokol at the commission hearing. The moral conflict he had between an obligation to protect people (in this case the seven astronauts) from defective products and his unrevised loyalty obligation to his company is resolved because he can consistently hold both a commitment to the reassessed loyalty rule and to a principle of truth-telling in order to do the best he can in hostile conditions.

Did Boisjoly have a moral obligation to blow the whistle as he did? No, I don't think he did, not an obligation. But he was certainly justified in doing so, and if he hadn't his integrity would have been blemished. This may sound rather paradoxical, but I think that can be avoided. Another major factor in Boisjoly's case and in that of most whistle-blowers is also a factor in the circumstances that confronted my former student: a significant cost is assessed against those who do the right thing. That cost in Boisjoly's case is obvious: he was ostracized at Morton Thiokol, his sense of worth in the corporation was stripped from him, he was criticized publicly by his superiors in the corporation and privately by his fellow workers. Ultimately this was too much for him to bear and he had to leave the corporation in sickness and under a cloud.

Whistle-blowers are almost never thanked by their corporations. No matter how high-minded and moral their motives for blowing the whistle, they are treated as traitors and cast out. Often they cannot find employment anywhere else in the industry. It is not difficult to understand why. Corporations interpret the disloyalty of the whistle-blower as threatening the faith that other employees have in the corporation and as weakening the control that senior executives have in its CID structure. Corporate executives have shown little sympathy for Timothy Ingram's assessment that:

> Snitchers, in fact, are often a firm's *most* loyal members, for it takes a greater degree of attachment to stay with a firm and to protest than it does to "opt out," by remaining silent or moving on.[125]

If these costs to the whistle-blowers are taken into account, I think we should regard their acts, when they satisfy the conditions of moral integrity, as heroic and so not obligatory.

I think there are at least three necessary conditions for moral heroism and that some whistle-blowers, probably including Boisjoly, satisfy them. Heroic acts must be done in order to achieve unambiguously moral ends. The second condition is that a heroic act must be undertaken with full knowledge that one's life or most, if not all, that is important to one in life, is at risk. Knowing sacrifice of self-preservation or self-identity is crucial. Some sort of knowledge condition is needed because it would be odd to honor people as moral heroes if they never even knew or anticipated the risk they were running. Only if we assume that Boisjoly was aware of the fact that he could likely lose his job, suffer the tortures of ostracism, and become extremely ill when he made public his notes and data regarding the O-rings and the teleconference before the fateful launch, does the deed take on an heroic character. If he did not or could not make an assessment of the career risks, and therefore identity, the danger he was running, his actions were not heroic.

This self-sacrifice condition is noted by a number of philosophers, including John Rawls who identifies heroic deeds as good acts that would be moral obligations except for the cost run by the hero.[126] Heroic deeds, then, are not just benevolent acts of helping others or of acting in ways to achieve good ends. They must involve extraordinary risks to those doing them. Insofar as many moralists, especially since the advent of the centrality of the individual in the social contract theories of Hobbes and Locke, believe that morality cannot require acts against self-preservation and other extreme risks, heroic deeds should not be morally obligatory. They seem to be actions it is good to do, but not bad not to do, deeds one cannot be held morally responsible for not doing. We could say that the whistle-blower had a moral duty to reveal the information that might save lives, but not an overriding moral obligation to do so.

Unlike other sorts of morally praiseworthy acts, if we are assessing heroism it seems much more important to know what the person intended. The third condition is that a hero must have the proper moral intentions when he or she undertakes the risky deed. But what is the appropriate intention? Generally speaking, it must be to benefit others. After all, if Boisjoly had blown the whistle on Morton Thiokol just because he had a personal grudge against some of the four managers who made the fateful decision to recommend the launch, his act probably would have had the same outcome in the commission and he would probably have suffered the same fate at Morton Thiokol. But we would not think of him as a person of moral integrity. His motive of harming others eradicates whatever heroism the deed would otherwise have had.

There are some problems with this altruistic condition. For example, the hero's intentions might be construed to mean that he or she preferred to do the deed. If it were the act in the circumstances that the whistle-blower preferred to do, then he or she wanted to do it. But if the whistle-blower wanted to do it despite the personal risks, then many philosophers (usually from within the Kantian tradition) will claim the whistle-blower did not really act *for* the good of others. Heroism loses moral significance, we will be told, if so-called heroes just do what they want to do.

Heroic moments happen with little time for contemplative decision making and the examination of intentions. In the accounts of Boisjoly's story, it is stressed that he had only overnight to prepare for his testimony before the commission. Heroic deeds may reveal character more than isolatable intentions, and character is not an accidental property of a person. As Aristotle maintained, it is the product of one's intentional choices that have ingrained habits of acting. Heroism, in fact, may be one of the better manifestations of integrity. Still, intentions do play a role, if not a major one, in evaluating the heroic. You certainly cannot be heroic if your self-sacrifice is only for your own pleasure.

Most moral thinkers, as J. O. Urmson noted in his famous paper "Saints and Heroes,"[127] recognize only a threefold classification of actions from the moral point of view. Some acts are obligatory, some are of no concern to morality. The rest are forbidden. Kant wrote that the moral law (the categorical imperative) asserts an obligation that:

> . . . either commands or prohibits; it sets forth as a duty the commission or omission of an action. An act that is neither commanded nor forbidden

is merely permissible, since there is no law to limit one's freedom (moral title) to perform it, and so no duty with regard to the action. An action of this kind is called morally indifferent.[128]

Heroic deeds are surely permissible, but they are certainly not morally indifferent. "Hero" is surely a term of favorable moral evaluation. Heroes are exalted, held up to us as examples. Heroic deeds, for the reasons given above, cannot be obligatory, hence they seem not to fit comfortably in the threefold classification.

If Boisjoly had a moral obligation to blow the whistle, we should regard him as a moral coward, a shirker had he not done so and not a hero because he did. Moral heroism seems to be a matter of choice, "merely permissible" in Kant's terms, but then morality should be indifferent to it. But it is not! Heroism will either have to be subsumed into moral obligation—but then all of us could be obligated at least on some occasions to act heroically—or the threefold categorization of actions for moral evaluative purposes will have to be modified.

Consider one alternative. Kant, and a number of other absolutist moral theorists who have followed in his train, distinguished between types of duties. Perfect duties are negative duties, duties of omission, for example, duties not to commit suicide, not to act out of carnal lust, not to lie (recall the business about your friend and the fiend). We are always morally constrained with respect to these duties. To transgress them is vice. Imperfect duties, on the other hand, for Kant, are duties of virtue. They go beyond the formal principles of action and require the adoption of a purpose, not just the performing or the refraining from specific actions. Hence, they leave considerable room for choice in determining the actions one will take to meet the required end. The when and the how are left to each of us. If there is a moral law commanding us to make benefiting others one of our ends, it will not be violated if we do not benefit others on this or that occasion when we might have done so. You will not have failed in this type of moral obligation if today, when approached by a beggar, you refuse to give a dime.

The problem with this sort of classification of duties is, however, that as one gets older the opportunities to decline to perform the actions to meet the imperfect duties, the realm of choice, must become narrower and narrower, the actions become less and less optional, until as one nears death and has not yet acted so as to achieve the morally commanded purpose, they become mandatory. Luck in meeting up with occasions to perform imperfect duties also could enter into the picture. Should a person who, owing to the sheltered nature of his or her existence, has never had the opportunity, seek out objects of charity? Is that then a perfect moral duty?

Benevolence seems to be a solid candidate for a Kantian imperfect duty of virtue. And benevolence as a moral purpose can be satisfied with occasional charitable donations. Whistle-blowing to try to save the lives of future astronauts would also seem to satisfy the benevolence duty, but intuitively there seems to be a vast moral difference between giving a donation to the needy and risking one's career and health in order to expose a dangerous corporate product or service. Furthermore, Kant noted that:

> To provide oneself with such comforts as are necessary merely to enjoy life . . . is a duty to oneself. . . . How far should we expend our means in practicing benevolence? Surely not to the extent that we ourselves would finally come to need the charity of others.[129]

Heroism, however, requires one to put one's career and possibly, as Karen Silkwood learned, one's very life and limb at risk,[130] and if anything, that violates one of Kant's perfect duties to oneself: "The first of man's duties to himself as an animal being is to preserve himself in his animal nature."[131] In the "casuistical questions" related to his examination of this perfect duty, Kant asked:

> Is it murder to hurl oneself to certain death (like Curtius) in order to save one's country?— or is voluntary martyrdom, offering oneself as a sacrifice for the welfare of the whole human race, also to be considered an act of heroism.[132]

Unfortunately, Kant never answers his questions, nor does he, at least in this case, indicate how the answer should go. He seems to hold heroism in high moral regard, but it seems not to be, given the bulk of his thinking on virtue, a higher obligation than the preservation of oneself.

Apparent conflicts between the perfect duty to preserve one's life and the performing of an act of heroism that risks the quality of that life for the purpose of benefiting others may arise because they are the products of two different grounds of obligation. Kant maintained, however, that not the stronger obligation, but the stronger ground of obligation takes precedence. The ground of the obligation of self-preservation, apparently, is stronger than benevolence (although Kant's own casuistical questions cast doubt on whether it is so in all heroic cases). In any event, he tells us that as a perfect duty, transgression of self-preservation is vice and guilt, while transgression of an imperfect duty is "mere lack of moral worth," "want of virtue," "lack of moral strength."

It seems fair to Kant to say that whistle-blowing in cases like Boisjoly's in itself is not a moral obligation, though it may be one way of achieving an end that is an imperfect duty, but that end is arguably at least, not superior to the perfect duty of self-preservation, transgression of which is risked by the whistle-blowing.

The traditional utilitarians have a simpler answer. Bentham wrote:

> Of an action that is conformable to the principle of utility one may always say . . . that it is one that ought to be done, . . . that it is right it should be done, . . . that it is a right action; at least that it is not a wrong action.[133]

Further, if it is the only action in the circumstances that conforms to the principle of utility, it is the only morally right thing to do, one has a moral obligation to do it. Still further, it would seem that if two or more actions conform to the principle of utility, but to varying degrees, that is, they maximize general utility to a greater or lesser extent, then the action that increases general utility to the greater extent, things being more or less equal, is a moral obligation. Whistle-blowers, despite their personal risk-taking, for Bentham, may be doing no more than what they have moral obligations to do in the circumstances in which they find themselves. Sometimes by doing what you ought, you suffer. Often you run great risks.

Urmson argues that heroic actions, though worthy of abundant moral praise, are beyond moral obligation, and I think he is right. For him, morality has two realms: that of what must be done or avoided—the realm of obligation—and a higher realm where we can assess actions as good and commend them to others, but where the morality is one of aspiration, not requirement. In the first realm, morality can be stated in rules and principles, in the second, models. The morality expressed, and even the way it is expressed, in the Hebrew Book of Covenant is of the basic level, while the admonitions of the Sermon on the Mount express the aspirations of the second.

Urmson's vision of the two levels is appealing, but there are difficulties. If heroes are moral models, then the rest of us would seem to be moral failures for not at least trying to be like them. That would, however, make heroic behavior our moral obligation, and so the second level will collapse into the first. After all, what sense does it make to hold heroic people up as paradigms of human virtue if we do not have some moral obligation to emulate them? (It may also be a serious misreading of the Christian message to think that the Sermon on the Mount does not impose duties to "Go and do thou likewise.")

As I have argued elsewhere, the two-realms idea is useful if we understand that the high praise we extend to heroic persons like Boisjoly does not commit us to saying that we have obligations to act in ways exactly similar to them or that they had obligations to act as they did. Instead, moral praise in such cases points at the virtues, the integrity, that someone like Boisjoly manifested.

The primary virtue of heroism is, of course, courage, the courage required to uncompromisingly act so as to sustain one's integrity in the face of career loss and possibly self-destruction.

Aristotle identified courage as one of the cardinal, though complex, virtues. Courage, he maintained, is the mean flanked by the extremes of recklessness and cowardice. It is always put to the service of such moral ends as protecting other people from danger.[134]

"You take the man's money, you ride for the brand." The problem is that it is sometimes exceedingly unclear what riding for the brand requires of a manager or an employee. If Boisjoly's whistle-blowing satisfies the conditions of moral heroism and the preservation of his moral integrity, he may well have been riding for the Morton Thiokol brand when he testified before the commission. Even affine agents can and should be whistle-blowers under those conditions. In fact, they, much more than ordinary agents, should be prepared to respond to the moral failings of their corporations.

Boisjoly, from what I have been able to ascertain about his relationship with Morton Thiokol, may well have been one of its affine agents. That would account for the incapacitation that his ostracism within the company produced in him. That the corporation did not appreciate his actions as an affine agent's expression of corporate loyalty, moral integrity, and heroism does not speak well for the senior management of Morton Thiokol. But that was the core of the problem that Boisjoly was addressing in the first place. The man with the money may not always be the best judge of what is required of someone riding for his brand.

Postscript: Some weeks after her first call, I again heard from my former student. She had decided to keep the seal of the confession, but was guilt-ridden because, in the night preceding, the wife and children of the penitent had murdered him. From her apartment window she had seen the EMS ambulance remove the body and police take away the family. She planned to go to confession that afternoon.

9. Harassment: Invasions of Employee Privacy

As argued in Part 1, humans in the postcorporate invasion social world are freer and yet more irrelevant than in any previous time. We can move from job to job, position to position, role to role, and the social system remains relatively unaltered for all of our shuffling. But, as I maintain, corporations are full-fledged Rank B-ers, meaning that for their actions to be ethical, they must act within the boundaries defined by the moral side constraints that forbid treating other Rank B-ers, in particular humans, as mere means to the accomplishment of their own ends, or at least they are not to do so without the informed consent of those being used. When a corporate actor treats its agents (or employees) in a way that transgresses the side constraints, it has committed an act of harassment.

I use the term "harassment" [135] in this broad sense to cover all cases in which a corporate agent's rights not to be used as mere means are violated by a Rank B-er who stands in a superordinate position to the victim. In some cases the perpetrator will be the corporate actor itself, in others it will be a human who is equal or superior in rank to the victim within the CID structure.

I use the term "harassment" because it implies the sorts of invasions of privacy and identity that are involved in a spectrum of cases. The term has become quite popular in recent years, especially since the Clarence Thomas Supreme Court confirmation hearings in the U.S. Senate. Perhaps it is overused. Usually it is associated with offensive sexual behavior or unwelcome sexual innuendo and advances made by someone with power over their subject. I want to extend the concept to all kinds of improper encroachments of a human's personal "space."

Before looking at specific types of cases, however, we should address general corporate response to all sorts of complaints from subordinates. The freedom the corporate invaders have given us lays the foundation for the response: "If you don't like working here, no one's stopping you from quitting and finding another job."

The underlying conception of the relationship between the corporation and its agents or employees that supports this response is called "employment at will." Patricia Werhane has nicely characterized the principle of employment at will. She says that it

> . . . is an unwritten common-law idea that employers as owners have the absolute right to hire, promote, demote, and fire whom and when they please.[136]

The principle of employment at will has the corollary that the employee works at will and so may terminate the association at any time. In other words, these two principles express the generally praised concepts of freedom and private property.

Freedom is expressed in the obvious sense that both parties may terminate the relationship for whatever reasons, and private property is expressed because the corporation is understood to control its premises and access to them. The worker has a kind of Lockean ownership of his or her body and when, where, and for whom he or she will expend it in labor.

Defenders of employment at will note that working for a corporation is a voluntary action on both sides, and if the agent does not have a specific or definite contract to work, that it would abridge the freedom of both parties if employment at will is restricted. It certainly seems unfair if the agent can quit at anytime but the corporate actor can't fire or release the agent without undergoing some sort of quasi-judicial review. This involves employment that is indefinite and general, not cases in which the employer has made an agreement to forgo rights of dismissal except in special, specified situations. The typical college faculty member's tenure contract is not at issue, but most employment relationships in corporations are.

Employment at will, despite its freedom and private-property defenses, stands in direct opposition to one of the most cherished "rights" in our society: the right to receive due process if one is accused of something. It might be argued that dismissal or firing is not the same thing as being accused of some wrongdoing, but that is semantic clap-trap. The practical consequences or upshot of being fired is that one is looked upon as having been accused of doing something bad. Try telling someone, "Yes, I was fired, but I didn't do anything wrong." One will get the same reception Job did when he tried to tell his old friends, truthfully, that his loss of everything worthwhile to him in life could not have been the result of his having sinned, because he hadn't sinned. They humored him for a bit, but still asked him what he'd done wrong.

Employment at will hurdles over due process and says that the free-dom of the corporation to employ whomever it chooses is to be treated as paramount. But adopting such a principle clearly, I think, violates the side constraints. Employees and agents deserve some form of due pro-cess when they are accused of something that the employer construes as sufficient to fire them.

Suppose it is objected that a due-process requirement will disad-vantage the corporation while not imposing any restrictions on the free-dom of the employee to decamp whenever he or she gets the urge. It is true that the employee has that advantage, but the justification for the imposition of a due-process restriction on employment at will is justified because of the vast imbalance of power in the employment situation. The corporation is in a far stronger position than the employee to dam-age the other's interests. Werhane explains:

> When one is demoted or fired, the reduction or loss of the job is only part of an employee's disadvantage. . . . Without an objective appraisal of their treatment, employees are virtually powerless to demonstrate that they were fired, demoted, and so forth, for no good reason. Moreover, fired or demoted employees generally have much more difficulty than other per-sons in getting new jobs or rising within the ranks of their own company. The absence of due process in the workplace places arbitrarily dismissed or demoted employees at an *undeserved* disadvantage among persons com-peting for a given job.[137]

A matter of equity or balance may also be involved. As Werhane has remarked, corporations have frequently availed themselves of the courts in order to protect their rights against each other or government agencies, and the courts have upheld the corporation's right to due pro-cess.[138] In effect, this looks as if the corporations have the right to fair treatment, while under employment at will, their agents do not. That is fundamentally unfair and can be remedied by requiring due process for dismissed or fired employees. Such a process would have a chilling effect on the capricious firing of employees and require corporations to publicly provide the reasons for termination.

The problem with all of this, some will say, is specifying what constitutes an acceptable reason for firing an employee. That problem seems to me less difficult to handle than might first be thought. One fundamental reason for termination exists on which we should all agree: a corporate agent may be fired for engaging in activities detrimental to those interests of the corporation that are themselves both ethical and legal. That will entail that an employee may not be terminated for refusing to participate in unethical, immoral, or illegal ventures or operations. This applies even if the employee is ordered to do so by a superordinate or if doing so would benefit the corporation financially or otherwise. An employee cannot be justifiably fired for his or her personal activities as long as they are carried on outside the workplace and do not interfere with the employee's job performance. Nor can an employee be fired for refusing to participate in activities outside the workplace, even if the employee's involvement in those activities would reflect positively on the corporation. In effect, this principle reserves for the employee a realm of privacy in his or her personal life outside of the walls of the corporation.

It seems fruitless to me to spell out what sorts of personal matters are therefore excluded. Suffice it to say that corporations will not be permitted to fire employees because of religious, political, or sexual practices, as long as they are carried on when the employee is not on the company clock. There are, however, going to be some gray areas in which a corporation might legitimately attempt to restrict its employees from public displays of views and beliefs that could be associated with the corporation in a way that damages its image. With respect to those cases, corporations will need to work out a set of policies that are understood by the employees at the inception of employment. Such policies may not forbid the activities, as long as they are legal, but they may insist that the employee's relationship to the corporation not be used in their expression. In the most obvious form that would include not using corporate letterhead for letters urging friends to march for a political candidate or identifying oneself as So and So, the director of whatever at Corporation X, during some public demonstration of one's personal commitments or life-style.

Due process for the employee will be procedurally accomplished in the corporation if a mutually agreeable, impartial, formal process is established and utilized in which the corporate actor is provided the opportunity to prove that the agent had acted in a way that was detrimental to those interests of the corporation that are both ethically and legally permissible and the agent is offered the chance to respond and rebut the charges. Whether such a hearing process involves peer review, arbitration by an outside individual or agency, or some other method, is not important here. What is important is that the side constraints that may often be violated by employment at will will be honored.

Corporations should take certain specific steps to ensure the implementation of a fair and impartial personnel grievance policy. In the first place, the original contract between the corporate actor and the agent should spell out the due-process procedures, including the rights and responsibilities of the two parties. The corporation must guarantee that it will abide by the results of the process it has instituted.

Other conditions should be included for the sake of fairness. The most important of those, it seems to me, should be that the process will be carried out in a timely fashion after the employee has filed a complaint. If an employee is fired for reasons he or she feels are untrue, unfair, or unwarranted, the formal hearing, if all intermediate appeals to supervisors have failed to settle the issue, needs to be held promptly. Otherwise the employee, out of work and presumably off salary, could languish in employment limbo, thereby exacerbating the penalty that may have been unjustly dealt to him or her in the first place.

I realize that the whole idea of due process for corporate agents sounds weighted against the employer or gives the appearance of a presumption of wrongdoing on the part of big, bad corporation against the helpless little employee. That is not necessarily the case, but even if it were, there would be no strong ethical reasons to be alarmed. These procedures are specifically designed to try to level the playing field between the corporate giant and the agent. The presumptions admittedly favor the agent, but that does not mean that corporate actors will not be upheld in dismissals of agents. Any employee that has violated the trust placed in him or her by the corporation, that has not earned his or her wage because he or she has failed to carry out assigned, ethically and legally permissible tasks deserves to be fired. But employees who do carry out their tasks in appropriate ways and still run afoul of supervisors, managers, indefensible corporate policies, customs, or behavioral expectations, deserve, from the moral point of view, the meager protection due process in the workplace offers them.

Not all grievances, of course, will be initiated because of termination of employment. There are other types of cases where the side constraints are trespassed in the corporate actor's dealings with its agents, and to which an ethical corporation will make appropriate responses.

Target Stores recently settled a lawsuit brought on behalf of 2,500 Californians seeking jobs as security guards between 1987 and 1991. Target agreed to pay $1,540,000 because it had required potential employees to take a psychscreen test. The test, known as the Rodgers Condensed CPI-MMPI, contained a number of questions that the plaintiffs claimed constituted invasions of their privacy. Included on the test were true-false questions that pried into the religious, sexual, and personal habits of the applicants. For example, the test asked "true or false: I feel sure there is only one true religion." And, "true or false: I am strongly attracted to members of my own sex." What is the matter with such questions on employment screening tests?

Some corporations, including about 20 percent of the *Fortune* 500 companies, subject potential employees to lie detector tests. The questions might range from rather innocuous ones about a person's interest in sports to questions about whether one enjoys movies in which the criminals succeed in robbing the bank and whether one takes various kinds of drugs or has contracted for the services of a prostitute.

We could try to analyze from an ethical point of view the questions on the standard polygraph tests and on the psychscreen, but what would we be looking for? Prying questions that are intended to reveal the potential employees' inner secrets? That, of course, is what we will find. Lots of them. But the specific questions are not the real issue. We should be asking whether a potential employer, ethically, has any business gathering such information on employees or job applicants in such a fashion in the first place.

The practice, and even the specific tests, might be defended by putting forth the argument that the employer needs this sort of information to make a reasonable decision on hiring: to determine if the applicant is likely to be a risk on the job. After all, who wants a bunch of security guards at Target stores who are rooting for the crooks? Others might argue that if you are seeking employment, at least in some kinds of jobs, you are not entitled to withhold from your potential employer information that might be relevant to your suitability for the tasks you will be performing.

Fine, but what does the potential employee's belief that there is only one true religion tell about whether he or she will be able catch a thief in the act? Is it important which religion he or she thinks is the only true one? Suppose he or she doesn't know which one is, but thinks that one must be? Is that a good or a bad answer? Is a person who believes that there is only one true religion but isn't sure she is a member of it more or less likely to provide the sort of security Target requires in its parking lots? These are complex matters!

The disturbing part of all of this is that someone, presumably someone at Target Stores, thinks they know what the correct answers are. Actually, of course, they probably don't. What they want is as complete a profile of the potential employee as they can get before making the employment decision.

Corporations, and the rest of us as well, are obsessed with information, with data collection, especially with data on each other, and it does not seem to matter one iota that we have no idea what to do with most of it once we get it. Prying into each other's lives is the growth industry of the last decade or so.

The comments I raised about Target's use of certain questions on the psychscreen reveal the types of distinctions regarding the information that a company can legitimately procure from potential employees. Simply, only two types of data are appropriate: information relative to the applicant's ability to fulfill the job description (job-relevant data) and information about the character of the applicant that could affect his or her on-the-job performance. George Brenkert has noted that it is with respect to this second type of information that most of the unwarranted information gathering is likely to occur.[139]

Suppose you need a person to fit into a team in a certain division in the company. You know that the other members of the team are vociferously opposed to homosexuals. Their daily banter is liberally sprinkled with rude jokes and other references about homosexuals. Is it important to discover whether the candidates for the position are homosexual or have relatives or friends who are homosexual or are offended by jokes made about homosexuals? Brenkert says no, and I agree with him.

What is legitimate is discovering whether the candidate has the required skills and performs according to the sorts of character traits that are ethically desirable in the work situation. It is no one's business why the employee performs that way or what beliefs and attitudes the employee has about those requisite character traits. It doesn't matter why someone works out well in a certain work situation. "What is relevant is whether this person has, by his past actions, given some indication that he may work in a manner compatible with others."[140] All other sorts of information are private and attempts to acquire them constitute invasions of privacy.

To put the matter in line with the side-constraint approach: As long as the information is job relevant in the two ways discussed above, its acquisition may be regarded as having been consented to by the applicant and so gaining that information will not transgress the prohibition against using someone as a means only. Putting an applicant under the scrutiny of a polygraph test or a psychscreen in order to gain knowledge that goes far beyond the category of job relevant is to treat that person with disrespect. It is an invasion of that person's privacy. It is to harass the applicant.

Brenkert goes further, and I think we can travel with him. He maintains that even if some, or even all, of the questions asked can be construed as job relevant, that the polygraph invades the subject's privacy. A polygraph monitors the subject's physiological reactions to questions asked by the test administrator. The polygraph is supposed to reveal the inner mental processes of the subject. Werhane argues:

> No person has a right to the thoughts and feelings of another person. . . . The use of the lie detector in the workplace threatens workers' moral rights to freedom and respect, because it allows economic interests . . . to override these rights.[141]

There are other reasons why the use of polygraph tests and psych-screens in corporations constitutes harassment. It is typically pointed out, even by operators of lie detectors, that as many as 35 percent of those identified as guilty are innocent. That's a wide margin of error, and even if the percentages were better, some subjects will find the whole situation of being asked to take the test so unnerving that they will exhibit the sorts of physiological symptoms the machine detects as evidence of discomfort with a response or a question. Alternatively, the subject may set off the machine because of personal conflicts and emotional turmoil unrelated to the specific questions being posed.

It may be objected, however, that the potential employee is not forced to take the test, that it is voluntary. If the applicant doesn't want to take it, he or she can look for work elsewhere. Therefore, the side constraints are not violated. Consent was obtained. Harassment has not occurred. But how is consent obtained? The situation is similar to one involving due process. The potential employee is placed in the compromised position of having to consent because not to do so is generally interpreted as an admission of guilt. Jobs are scarce, and it may not be possible to take oneself to the next potential employer, particularly if that means uprooting of oneself and family. Depending on the type of job, that employer may be located not in the next town or the next state, but in another country. In any event, the consent would normally be obtained under less than ideal conditions, a common element in harassment cases.

What of mandatory drug testing? Many corporations in the last decade have adopted drug-testing policies for all or some of their employees. A *New Republic* survey indicates that almost half of the *Fortune* 500 administer drug tests to their employees.[142] In some cases, information regarding whether an employee is using drugs is clearly job relevant. Those responsible for the safety of passengers need to be drug free. But the argument in favor of drug testing is typically given in much more general terms. Companies say that drug use on the job is responsible for lower productivity, higher costs, and declining profits. Health insurance costs for employers rise as the number of sick days increase due to drug abuse. Everything that is wrong with American business gets blamed on illegal drug use.

Employees are hired to do specific jobs, and they can be impaired by drugs from doing them efficiently, safely, carefully. Corporations therefore assert a legitimate right to require drug tests of their employees in order to weed out those who are not performing. They can then provide counseling and treatment programs or simply remove the malfunctioning worker from the position. In effect, the argument favoring drug testing is based on the contractual relationship between employer and employee and the fact that drug users typically breach their side of the contract by failing to work up to the expected level of production.

Is there a reasonable response to what seems a strong case in favor of mandatory drug testing of corporate agents? Actually one simple response does not violate the privacy of the employee in the way that drug testing does.

Suppose we accept the conjectures that drug use has an adverse impact on productivity and causes abnormal absenteeism and that the corporation has a contractual right to a certain level of productivity from its employees. If the employee is achieving the expected level of work, if the tasks are getting done, then whether or not that employee is using drugs is not a job-relevant piece of information. Joseph DesJardins and Ronald Duska succinctly make the point:

> If the person is producing what is expected, knowledge of drug use on the grounds of production is irrelevant since *ex hypothesi* the production is satisfactory. If, on the other hand, the performance suffers, then, to the extent that it slips below the level justifiably expected, the employer has *prima facie* grounds for warning, disciplining or releasing the employee.[143]

The only cases in which it may be justifiable to trespass the side constraints and invade the privacy of an employee by requiring drug testing will be in those jobs where not to do so will expose other innocent people to risk of harm, even death. Hence, airline pilots, train conductors, and employees in nuclear power plants, may, and probably should, be regularly tested for the use of drugs that can impair their job performance. Those cases permit no tolerance for falling below the expected standards of job performance, little or no margin for error. To not proactively try to ensure against harm caused by impaired employees would be to use other people as mere means. The performance criteria should handle other types of jobs not in the high-risk- imposing category.

I've done some consulting work for a major insurance company. In one of my visits with its employees I learned that some of them were concerned that they were being used as mere means. They understood a company policy to require them to record the telephone solicitations they made to potential customers. The employees believed that such a practice violated the law because the customer was not informed that a recording was being made. They were told that the law permits the recording of some conversations of this type for use in training, but that would not justify a general policy of taping all solicitations. Some claimed that they were uncomfortable with the practice and with the way their supervisors were so insistent upon their making the recordings. All, however, said that because of the need to keep their jobs, they would not complain or quit. They had families to support, bills to pay.

It seems obvious to me that an employee cannot be expected to carry out tasks that are illegal or immoral. To require one to do so is a clear violation of the side constraints. The matter is compounded if the only option made available to the objecting employee is resignation.

There may, however, be at least one other side to issues like this one. Supervisors may tell quite a different story. In fact, they did. When I questioned them about the policy, they denied having one and offered the explanation that there had been a period of time, I think it was two weeks, during which all such calls were to be recorded for training purposes, and that three months later another two week-period was set aside as a follow-up period during which all calls would be taped to see how the training had worked. They surmised that a failure in communications prevented the time limits being clearly conveyed to the lower-ranking managers, who assumed that a taping policy regarding all solicitations had been put in place. Memos were fired off to the appropriate offices, and the taping stopped.

There are a number of ways to interpret what happened. Suppose we are charitable and accept the supervisors' account rather than view them as doing a little sidestep to avoid the look of illegality. What does even their version reveal about the supervisor-to-worker relationship at that company? In the first place, it took the questions of an outsider to bring the problem to the attention of those who could solve it. The employees in the telemarketing division were too intimidated to raise objections about the way they were being used. They saw the issue as one involving a threat of unemployment. Weighed against that, they were willing to continue to act in a way they regarded as illegal. They were certain that any legal penalties would be assessed against the company or the managers and that they were personally shielded from prosecution.

Their deep concerns were not fueled by fear of legal punishment. They were ethical concerns. They rightly felt they were doing something morally wrong by following orders to do something illegal. Most described themselves both as having guilty consciences for not having quit and as feeling trapped by their economic situations and the power of the managers. They were ashamed of what they were doing, but also saw themselves as victims.

Whether or not the matter was just a failure in communications, the power imbalance between the employees and the supervisors fostered not only a violation of the ethical side constraints, but illegal activity that exposed the corporation to potentially serious social and legal consequences. What would happen to the good image of the company should it become widely known that telephone conversations it initiates with potential customers are being illegally taped?

The employees felt, with some justification, harassed into behavior that they knew to be wrong. An open procedure for airing grievances, in which the employees do not have to fear retaliation, might have gone a long way toward alleviating the problem. The higher-ranking supervisors admitted that if they had been apprised of the situation, no matter how, they would have corrected it. Well, after all, they changed it after I conveyed the information to them. The ethical bottom line is, however, that an employee's refusal to carry out illegal or immoral orders should never constitute grounds for dismissal. Loyalty obligations cannot run that far and still be consistent with not transgressing the side constraints.

Carl Sandberg wrote:

> What does the hangman think about
> When he goes home at night from work?
> When he sits down with his wife and
> Children for a cup of coffee and a
> Plate of ham and eggs, do they ask
> Him if it was a good day's work
> And everything went well or do they
> Stay off some topics and talk about
> The weather, baseball, politics
> And the comic strips in the papers
> And the movies? Do they look at his
> Hands when he reaches for the coffee
> Or the ham and eggs? If the little
> Ones say, Daddy, play horse, here's
> A rope—does he answer like a joke:
> I seen enough rope for today?
> Or does his face light up like a
> Bonfire of joy and does he say:
> It's a good and dandy world we live
> In. And if a white face moon looks
> In through a window where a baby girl
> Sleeps and the moon-gleams mix with
> Baby ears and baby hair—the hangman—
> How does he act then? It must be easy
> For him. Anything is easy for a hangman,
> I guess.[144]

 ## 10. Harassment: Sexual

A 1988 study of *Fortune* 500 companies revealed that America's biggest corporations lose approximately $6.7 million dollars annually in absenteeism, employee turnover, and drops in productivity due to a single cause: sexual harassment in the workplace. *The New York Times* (March 1993) reports that 50 to 85 percent of women experience some form of sexual harassment in the corporations in which they work. Twenty-five percent of those sexually harassed women quit or are dismissed from their jobs. Men also report being the victims of sexual harassment, but as the overwhelming number of reported cases involve women as victims, that will be my focus, though I will occasionally have something to say about cases where the tables are turned.

The notion of sexual harassment is evolving in academic literature, in popular culture, and most importantly, in court cases. To many people, and especially middle-aged heterosexual men in high-ranking corporate positions, sexual harassment seems to be a deep, dark mystery that they cannot imagine themselves fathoming. Most are aware that they are not supposed to do or say certain things to or about members of the opposite sex or persons of a different sexual orientation. Though they're not sure exactly what is permissible and what is not. They'd like a checklist! Many have virtually no idea where the limits are or how they might find out.

Sexual harassment has become so supercharged a concept that some corporate agents are afraid to have any contact with members of the opposite sex that cannot be included under "strictly business" (narrowly defined). They worry that they may make an innocent comment that will be misconstrued as harassing. This has the effect of isolating women in managerial positions from their male counterparts. They may find themselves excluded from the sorts of banter and socializing out of which networks and dependencies are built that are important to the advancement of Comers. Strong ties that will later pay off in promotions are typically cemented in locker rooms and washrooms that exclude the opposite sex.

Circumstances play a rather large part in governing the appropriateness of any particular remark, though some comments and suggestions are always improper. There is a lot of talk about sensitizing corporate agents to harassment, and a number of harassment gurus command huge sums to go from corporation to corporation performing the sensitizing. Yet there seems to be little decline in the instances being reported.

What is sexual harassment? Anita Superson[145] identifies two rather different types of definitions, and it is important that we examine their implications. One may be called subjective, the other objective. The Equal Employment Opportunity Commission's *Guidelines on Discrimination Because of Sex* (1980) contains the following definition:

> Unwelcome sexual advances, requests for sexual favors, and other verbal or physical conduct of a sexual nature constitute sexual harassment when (1) submission to such conduct is made either explicitly or implicitly a term or condition of an individual's employment, (2) submission to or rejection of such conduct by an individual is used as the basis for employment decisions affecting such individual, or (3) such conduct has the purpose or effect of unreasonably interfering with an individual's work performance or creating an intimidating, hostile, or offensive working environment.

It might first appear that sexual harassment cases are generally Type 1 interactions (as discussed in Part 1), but that is not the case. They are usually Type 2 interactions because the person in the corporation doing the harassing is in the position to do so only because he or she is a corporate agent in a superordinate position over the person being harassed. In other words, most sexual harassment in a corporation involves the interactions of a corporate agent with a human person. The complication is that the human person is also a corporate agent and the harassment depends on that fact. So sexual harassment in the workplace may actually be a hybrid of Type 3 and Type 2 interactions. It is not merely a Type 1 interaction. If it were, it would be some sort of courting or other person-to-person exchange involving sexual aspects.

That does not, however, mean that sexual harassment cannot occur between persons independent of the corporate hierarchy. It can and does. And it occurs between persons on the same corporate level. It is also possible for subordinates to sexually harass a superordinate. The common feature is dominance. In the latter cases the harassment will depend on a power relationship that is independent of the corporate decision structure, for example the male-dominance-over-females mythology of our culture. Hence, a number of subordinate males can sexually harass a superordinate female, though she has corporate authority over them. The award-winning British television series *Prime Suspect* provided a classic example of how this can happen. In that series, a woman is promoted to detective chief inspector and placed in authority over a tightly bonded, all-male team of police detectives.

In the more typical corporate cases, the person being harassed is a corporate agent, and the force of the harassment depends in large measure on the power differential between the parties within the CID structure, that is, the sexual encounter is accompanied by a threat (whether veiled or blatant) concerning job security and advancement. In such circumstances the harassed party is no longer being treated as a corporate agent, instead he or she is being treated as a sex object, while the person doing the harassing remains behind the corporate mask. The corporation, therefore, cannot avoid being a party to the harassment.

In federal legislation, Title VII of the Civil Rights Act of 1964 and Title IX of the 1972 Amendments, two types of harassment charges can be filed. They are *quid pro quo* and hostile-environment harassment. *Quid pro quo* ("something for something") is the sort of harassment in which employment conditions and opportunities are explicitly tied to the employee's performance of activities unrelated to job performance: sexual favors. Hostile-environment harassment happens when the behavior of supervisors or coworkers has the effect of "unreasonably interfering with an individual's work performance or creates intimidating, hostile, or offensive environment."[146]

The courts have interpreted sexual harassment in two ways: disparate treatment or disparate impact. If the corporation's (or one of its agent's) behavior amounts to disparate treatment, then it will be the case that some of its employees are intentionally treated differently than others in the same work group because of factors that are not job relevant, in particular, because of the sex or sexual orientation of the person. A corporation's practices may have disparate impact because they work to the disadvantage of a particular group of people, for example women, even though no discriminatory effect was intended. Most people, male and female, wrongly think of sexual harassment in the workplace as only of the *quid pro quo* variety and as due to disparate treatment because of sex.

The recent spate of legal cases and the coverage in the media have surely implanted the notion that sexual harassment is highly subjective and that it is quite difficult to draw a line between when it has occurred and when the alleged victim has only, perhaps hysterically or as a personal grudge against an individual or the company, interpreted innocent remarks and actions as harassment.

If harassment is a subjective matter, it will be dependent on the feelings of specific persons or what was intended by or in the minds of the parties in the circumstances. If those are the governing issues, then the burden of proof that sexual harassment has occurred, as Superson notes, naturally falls on the shoulders of the alleging victim. She (or he) must show that she (or he) was harassed and that a *quid pro quo* was involved. If the matter is brought as a case of hostile environment, she (or he) must show that the behavior of the superior did interfere with her (or his) ability to successfully carry out regular job assignments.

Consider a fictionalized case based on one with which I am acquainted and that is currently in the courts. A woman in a lower-level managerial position complained through the corporation's grievance procedure that she had been propositioned by her superior. According to her version of the story, she was in his office to turn in a routine report. He invited her to sit down and after some perfunctory comments about the project, he, in a casual tone, changed the subject by offering the opinion that a person ought to have as many sexual partners as possible in order to experience as much of life as possible. Then he said that she was very beautiful and he wanted to go to bed with her.

She was startled by the abruptness of his remarks and did not respond. He apparently took her silence for, at least, interest, and repeated his statement of desire. She stood up and rushed out of the room. He did not pursue her. She claims that following the episode she was no longer able to work productively in the office. Her duties required her to report regularly to him and even the path to her desk went past his door. She is convinced that the promotions of other women in the office have reflected, in large part, their compliance with his sexual demands.

Other men in the office with whom she has shared the story have told her that they are aware of his reputation, but that he's just a good guy who recently went through a tough divorce. They refused to support her in the grievance process and told her to forget it. "He didn't actually force himself on you," they explained. When her complaint became known to his superiors, they called her in to a conference and tried to persuade her that it was a matter of no consequence, that nothing physical had happened, she hadn't been touched, fondled, raped, or anything, and that if he had been sleeping with other women in the office that was consensual and so none of her business. He denied that the incident even occurred.

She got an attorney and sued the company and the supervisor for sexual harassment. She claimed that an implicit *quid pro quo* was involved and that the environment of the office was hostile to her, causing emotional harm and, consequentially, a drop in performance that could affect her career. She also charged intentional infliction of mental distress, claiming that his conduct was outrageous and beyond the bounds of decency, intolerable to her as it would be to any other reasonable woman in the circumstances. The corporation, conjoined in the suit with the supervisor, fired her on the grounds that she was not performing up to expectations and that she was a troublemaker.

What makes an act like that of the supervisor one of sexual harassment? On the standard view, and the one that the woman in question utilized in her complaint, it is behavior of a sexually suggestive nature that is unwelcome or annoying to its target. That is subjective. What annoys or is unwelcome to one person may be greeted with open arms by another.

It is certainly the case that the sort of behavior allegedly evidenced by the supervisor can cause people to have severe emotional reactions ranging from guilt (Why did he say that to *me*? Is there something about me that provoked him? Have I been leading him on?), to anxiety (Will this cost me my career? Should I have given in?), to fear (Will he retaliate? What will he say to the others in the office?), to a loss of self-confidence. There also may be physical reactions directly traceable to the harassment incident: insomnia, gastrointestinal problems including ulcers, even cardiovascular disorders. Some studies suggest that such encounters can trigger drug abuse and alcoholism.

All of that may be true, but should the fact that the subordinate regarded the behavior to be annoying or unwelcome be the condition for its having been an act of sexual harassment? I think there is a very good reason why it should not. In fact, it shouldn't matter whether the woman in the case in question was upset by the behavior of the supervisor. She could throw herself into his arms after hearing the proposition, absolutely unperturbed by it, and it would still be sexual harassment.

Need you know you are being harassed to have been harassed? I think not. In fact, you could be a willing participant and still be harassed. Women have been for centuries. Why then should the fact that one is subjectively annoyed by behavior be so crucial a condition to determining whether or not it is harassing? Why should it be the man's word against the woman's, the superordinate against the subordinate?

Most verbal behavior of the sort involved in this case is open to multiple interpretations. Enough ambiguity may be exposed to shield the supervisor. That was the position of the senior management. The supervisor might retort that he was only being friendly, that the subordinate was "hypersensitive," acting "just like a woman," instead of understanding his remarks in the humorous vain in which they were intended. "If she's going to succeed in business she's got to toughen up."

Why must the woman recognize she is being harassed? The feminists justifiably maintain that for many, many centuries women have been reared to think of themselves as sex objects for men. They have, and so have men, been sold on the myth that women must occupy one of two possible roles in society. They are, I was told by one of the men in the office, either mothers or others. Others are ones who may be treated as sex objects.

Women have been led to believe, by men and by corporations, that a woman's most important feature is her body. It is little wonder that many, persuaded by the hype and the sex stereotyping in our society, regard praise for their bodies as most welcome, hardly offensive, something to spend inordinate amounts of money to achieve. One of the women in the office had spent more than three thousand dollars, a company bonus she had "earned," to have liposuction performed on her posterior because she was afraid it looked too large to the men.

The culture also encourages the myths that men are naturally aggressive and predatory, while women, though they may say "no," really mean "yes" in sexual matters. We've all heard the "she only got what she was asking for" plea. Sadly, it has been too frequently endorsed by the courts. For example, in a recent Florida case, the jury found that the clothes a woman was wearing signaled that she welcomed the sexual advances, culminating in intercourse, of the man she accused of rape. In another case, *Swentek v. US Air,*[147] the plaintiff, a flight attendant, claimed she was the victim of harassment by obscene remarks and gestures. The court, however, found for the defendant because of evidence that the flight attendant "had used vulgar language and openly discussed her sexual encounters. So . . . she was the kind of person who could not be offended by such comments and therefore welcomed them generally."[148]

The point is that the subjective criteria for sexual harassment are deficient on all sides. Women are unfairly treated because the criteria does not take into account their socialization to expect and accept sexually demeaning behavior. Men are disadvantaged because they are expected to do what men have legendarily been incapable of accomplishing from the beginning of time: understanding the inner workings of a woman's mind. The culture simply works against both parties, and the matter of sexual harassment is left to supposition and the vagaries of contradictory words and actions by both parties. There is, however, another approach, one that should be welcomed by men and women, regardless of sexual orientation, and corporations.

Superson offers an objective definition of sexual harassment as behavior "that expresses and perpetuates the attitude that the victim and members of her sex are inferior because of their sex."[149] The most common type of this behavior is that which "reflects men's domination of women in that it relegates women to the role of sex objects."[150]

Sexual harassment in corporations occurs most commonly when someone in a superordinate position expresses, in word or deed, the attitude to a subordinate that the subordinate or members of the subordinate's sex or sexual orientation are inferior because of their sex or sexual orientation. There are myriad ways in which superordinate males can sexually harass a female subordinate, but a common, all too common, way is by making suggestive remarks of a sexual nature that display the traditional cultural view of male domination of women, of treating women as objects for the sexual pleasure of men or as merely maternal beings.

Heterosexual men, of course, do not have an exclusive on the role of harasser. A heterosexual woman or a homosexual male in a position of power can harass a male underling, a lesbian can harass a subordinate woman. I see no reason why a group of women in subordinate roles who are convinced of the superiority of their sex could not become sexual harassers of males, even those in authority positions in the corporation.

How can someone respond if accused under this objective sort of definition, in which the criteria is purely behavioral? The old appeal to intentions will be lost to him or her. Just as the victim needs not prove that the advances were unwelcomed or annoying, the harasser cannot plea that his or her intentions were honorable, that it was a joke, that he or she was convinced that the subordinate wanted it. None of that matters to whether it was sexual harassment. It doesn't even matter if the harasser thought the victim thought it was funny or flattering or whatever.

Well, wait now, the guys in the office are surely going to point out that the supervisor's actions in the case in question might be the expression of sexual attraction. He was courting her, albeit rather clumsily. Sorry. The crucial element is whether the behavior evidenced by the superior reflects the attitude that the subordinate is inferior because of her sex. Superson nicely captures the point:

> Sexual harassment is not about a man's attempting to date a woman who is not interested, . . . it is about domination, which might be reflected, of course, in the way a man goes about trying to get a date.[151]

The objective definition of sexual harassment has another important implication. It interprets sexual harassment in part by reference to a group, those of the same sex or sexual orientation, rather than to the subjective feelings of an alleged victim, even if the person harassed welcomes the behavior and is not in the least annoyed by it. Therefore, another member of the group who is sensitive to what has happened may rightly complain because she or he and all of the others in the group suffer the harm that is involved in sexual harassment. The issue again will not be whether this third party is offended, but whether the harassing act took place.

By condoning or allowing sexual harassment to occur in the workplace, the corporation violates the side constraints against all members of the relevant group in its employ. Indeed, there are those who will go farther by insisting that it trespasses the side constraints with respect to all members of the group or even all humankind.

I am not uncomfortable with that judgment, though the crucial question is: what should the corporation do when it learns of sexual harassment among its agents?

In the case law, *Meritor Savings Bank v. Vinson*[152] should strike terror in the corporate heart. In that case, the court ruled that the corporation is absolutely liable for the damages in a proven case of *quid pro quo* sexual harassment even if the corporate officers had no knowledge of its occurrence.

The corporation can protect itself from liability in hostile environment sexual harassment cases if it has instituted and enforced policies against sexual harassment. But even well-wrought policy statements and policing to ensure compliance will do no good for the corporation if a *quid pro quo* is involved. The solution, I think, is that corporations must be prepared to fire any agent guilty of sexual harassment and to do so on the first offense.

Suppose that the offender in the case I have described is highly regarded by the senior managers, he's a super producer, a fair-haired boy around whom great plans have been made. Wouldn't a warning be sufficient? These are difficult matters for many executives because they are often themselves products and protectors of the heterosexual male domination culture. However, productivity or any other economic factor cannot be allowed to shield the offender if the corporation is to act ethically. The corporation cannot both insist on a harassment-free workplace and treat differentially its agents who are found to have committed sexual harassment. He will have to be fired and assurances given that the victim or other complainants will not face retaliation because "we had to fire a top producer."

Sexual harassment can, but need not involve actual physical contact between the parties. Rape is certainly a violent form of sexual harassment and a major criminal offense. If a corporate agent is convicted of rape, obviously the corporation should terminate his employment. There are, however, cases that are called rapes that require more attention because revelations about them seem to produce ambivalent responses both in corporations and in the general public. They are called acquaintance or date rapes. In our culture, acquaintance rapes are not always perceived with the same degree of seriousness as are stranger rapes. Acquaintance rapes are, in fact, quite devastating, because the victims have a level of trust developed with their offenders before the assaults occur. Unfortunately, because of cultural perceptions, acquaintance rape perpetrators are not always prosecuted.

Insofar as corporate settings are one of the major places where people get to meet each other, where acquaintances sometimes bud into friendships, and friendships flower into romances, the recent rise of reported date-rape cases should be of concern to the corporate actor. Should acquaintance-rape cases be handled in the same way as other sexual harassment cases?

My first inclination is to say yes, but complications in these acquaintance rape cases require some further consideration. Most importantly, rape, of whatever sort, is a criminal offense. Surely it involves sexual harassment, but something else is at stake because of its criminal character: punishment by the state. Because it is a criminal offense, and except in statutory cases, not a strict liability one, we should be careful to retain the protections in criminal procedure and our concept of criminal behavior in order to bring it under control in the workplace.

I want to suggest that we need to think about acquaintance or date rape in a way that is different from aggravated sexual assault— because one of the reasons why juries usually find it difficult to convict perpetrators is that they conflate the two types. There needs to be a system that achieves the ends of protecting each party's rights and meting out punishment to those who deserve it.

In acquaintance rapes, it is not clear, especially to juries, that the victim believed he or she was acting under threat of harm or that she or he had been physically overpowered by the perpetrator. In fact, in many of the more interesting cases, for example in the celebrated William Kennedy Smith trial, the alleged rapist claims, (let us stipulate) sincerely, that he did not intend nonconsensual sex. He usually testifies that he believed that the alleged victim invited the relations. Hence, he does not have the criminal state of mind, the *mens rea*, associated with rape. That is what makes these types of cases different.

Let us take an excursion a short way back in time and across the Atlantic: In 1975 the House of Lords, in the notorious *Morgan Case*[153], ruled that if an accused in fact believed that the person was consenting, whether or not that belief was based on reasonable grounds, the accused could not be guilty of rape. This so-called "Morgan Rule" has been characterized as the "rapists' charter." Clearly it comes down too heavily on the side of *mens rea*, and it excludes a reasonable-person test, which, if applied in cases like *Morgan*, where the facts grotesquely speak of rape, would erase reasonable juror doubt.

Some cases are likely in which the defendant, admittedly overpowering the victim, but while forcing the sexual act, honestly believed that the victim was consenting. The defendants in *Morgan*, in fact, made such a plea, claiming that the victim's husband had told them that his wife was "kinky" and that she preferred intercourse while being forcibly restrained and protesting. So, despite her resistance, the defendants honestly believed she was consenting. None of them intended to have intercourse with her without her consent. Although the defendants in *Morgan* were found guilty because they allowed their defense to drift from insisting on their belief that their victim was consenting to arguing that Mrs. Morgan actually evidenced consent, the Morgan Rule was used as a successful defense in subsequent cases. The Morgan Rule is obviously far too broad, but if it is abandoned we need some way to protect the rights of the accused in acquaintance or date-rape cases.

The Mosaic rape laws (the laws set forth by Moses in the books of Exodus and Deuteronomy in the Bible) are intriguing because a distinction is drawn in them between rape in the country and in the city. If a rape of a betrothed virgin occurs in the country, whether or not the victim cries for help, the rapist is killed and the woman is not punished. But if the rape occurs in the city, then both the man and the woman are stoned to death. Presumably, the law states, the woman did not sufficiently object and cry out, thereby indicating complicity in the act. If, however, the virgin is not betrothed (whether or not the rape occurs in the city), the man must pay her father 50 shekels of silver (half the going rate for a bride) and must marry her and can never divorce her. There is no mention of rape of nonvirgins in the code. Maybe we are to understand that if the woman is married the act would be a "violation of one's neighbor's property" and so prohibited. More likely, I am afraid, the only rapes that interested the ancient Hebrews were those that would devalue the virgin daughters of a family. If there was a hint that the woman had consented, she was guilty of "playing the harlot in her father's house," and so could not be sold in marriage, had shamed her family, and must be stoned to death.

Well, enough of the ancient laws. We have *mens rea* in the criminal law, and it is especially well cemented to the major crimes such as rape. The reason we require proof of *mens rea* is because we have strong views about the appropriateness of punishment when the defendant shows no criminal intent. This can get subjective, which proved a difficulty with respect to sexual harassment. He claims he believed one thing, she claims he had no reason to believe that. He said, she said. The intentions with which someone does something, it would seem, can only be determined by a jury by making inferences about the circumstances and by assuming that as a general rule a person intends the natural and probable consequences of his or her actions. But often other sorts of evidence can rebut such an assumption, and matters get extremely cloudy.

Courts often instruct juries that if they think, after hearing the evidence, that more than one view as to the intent of the defendant is conceivable in the circumstances that it was up to the prosecution to prove to the jury's satisfaction that the defendant had the specific intent. If that has not been done beyond a reasonable doubt, the defendant is entitled to an acquittal.

The "reasonable, prudential person's foresight test," common in tort, is not a fair one with respect to the defendant's rights in acquaintance-rape cases. The defendant's actual beliefs with respect to the consent of the victim really must be examined, no matter how subjective that will make the matter. Even the question of whether those beliefs were reasonable must be made relative to the specific circumstances and the state of mind of the defendant at the time of the act.

What makes a person's belief an honest one? The truth or falsity of the belief should not be at issue. Let us say that the defendant in an acquaintance-rape case falsely believed that his victim consented to sexual intercourse. Could his belief that she had consented still be an honest one? The answer must be "yes." But that is because what makes it an honest belief has to do with the process by which the defendant came to acquire it.

Juries all over America seem to recognize this. But many feminist writers, because they equate "honest" with "true," do not. If everything in the circumstances seems to point to consent, we might well say that the defendant honestly believed that the victim consented. If, on the other hand, the defendant purposefully stifles all of his doubts about the victim's consent, choosing to put his own special interpretation on the situation, the one that suits his desire for sexual intercourse, the belief that consent was present is not honestly held.

Along these same lines, the past sexual history of the alleged victim is not as irrelevant as some writers and some courts have treated it. The alleged victim's past sexual behavior with other partners, however, is not usually pertinent. What may be germane is the sexual history of the alleged victim with the defendant. Such information could be essential to deciding the honesty of the belief that the defendant purports regarding the consent of the alleged victim. Sexual history, of course, is in no way conclusive, but in some cases it is not irrelevant.

The idea that a woman does not consent unless she consents at the moment of penetration utterly ignores the reasonableness and the honesty of the defendant's beliefs, and so shakes the *mens rea* condition. Juries, as Ed Curley has noted,[154] seem almost intuitively to recognize this problem and are reluctant to give rape law full force in acquaintance cases. They tend to import doctrines of assumption of risk and contributory fault into their decision making. Even though the law says that it is rape if the alleged victim aroused expectations in the defendant with no intention of satisfying them or "gave considerable encouragement," then retracted consent at the moment of penetration, juries tend to acquit. Their reasoning, apparently, is not that such involuntary sexual intercourse should not be criminal. "Rather . . . it does not have the gravity of rape" in their considered opinions.

Curley has recommended the need for the law to recognize a lesser offense to apply to cases in which the alleged rapist honestly believed the consent had been given, though it had not. I agree with him that what might be called "nonconsensual sexual intercourse" should be the offense in certain acquaintance-rape cases. It should be a lesser offense than rape, with lesser penalties. Other lesser offenses in the area of rape, such as attempted rape and indecent assault, focus on situations in which there is no sexual intercourse. The acquaintance cases are marked by the fact that the alleged victim knew the perpetrator but did not consent to intercourse.

The rhetoric of brutality and assault is insufficient to truthfully portray the situations we face in the rising tide of acquaintance- or date-rape cases. A lesser offense would not only retain the criminalization of nonconsensual intercourse, it would far more likely result in convictions, thus protecting the rights of the victims.

The basic point, however, is that there is a perception that not all nonconsensual sexual intercourse is rape, but it is all sexual harassment. So we are back to the way the corporation should deal with acquaintance rape involving its agents. I think that if a lesser offense of the sort suggested, following Curley, is instituted in criminal law, that corporations should terminate the employment of any agent convicted of it.

The current law assimilates acquaintance rape to violent rape and tends to result in acquittals in cases where the proposed law would likely get convictions. It also creates a genuine dilemma in the corporation. If an agent is accused of rape, admits that intercourse occurred but claims he sincerely believed it was consensual, and is acquitted because the jury cannot bring itself to inflict the penalties for rape on him, is the corporation to go on with business as usual? Welcome him back as exonerated? Or is it to invoke its sexual harassment policy and fire him?

I think the answer is that he must be welcomed back because sexual intercourse is not sexual harassment. However, if the alleged victim or others lodge a sexual harassment complaint in the corporation against him, then the matter will have to be adjudicated in accord with the corporation's grievance procedures. In effect, the lack of a conviction in the criminal courts does not mean that sexual harassment did not occur. But for it to be sexual harassment in the corporation, it will have to have been the result of the power dominance that the agent had over a subordinate within the corporate structure, that it was an occasion of the expression of the attitude that because of who the perpetrator is and who the victim is that the victim can be treated as a mere means for the perpetrator's sexual gratification.

ENDNOTES

1. See Max Weber, *The Theory of Social and Economic Organization,* trans. by A. M. Henderson and Taleott Parsons (New York, 1947).
2. John A. Reinecke and William F. Schoell, *Introduction to Business: A Contemporary View* (Boston, 1977) p. 100.
3. Coleman, *Foundations of Social Theory*, p. 562.
4. Ibid.
5. Ibid.
6. Ralph Nader, Mark Green, and Joel Seligman, *Taming the Giant Corporation* (New York, 1976).
7. Harold S. Geneen and Alvin Moscow, *Managing* (New York, 1984) from "Board of Directors."
8. Adolf A. Berle, Jr., and Gardiner C. Means, *The Modern Corporation and Private Property* (Buffalo, 1932).
9. Thornton Wilder, *Our Town* (New York, 1938) third act.
10. Geneen, op. cit.
11. See Ibid. for confirmation on this point.
12. For an excellent discussion of social power, see Alvin Goldman, "Toward a Theory of Social Power," *Philosophical Studies* (1972) 23, p. 221–268. See also chapter 5 of my *Collective and Corporate Responsibility,* op. cit.
13. For a fuller account of the Rely case, see Archie B. Carroll and Elizabeth Gatewood, "The Proctor & Gamble *Rely* Case: A Social Response Pattern for the l980s" *Proceedings: Academy of Management*, 41 Conference, 1981.
14. Peter Moriss, *Power* (New York, 1987) p. 39.
15. Christopher Stone, *Where The Law Ends* (New York, 1975).
16. Richard DeGeorge, *Business Ethics* (New York, 1982) p. 138.
17. Geneen, op. cit.
18. Myles L. Mace, "The President and the Board of Directors," *Harvard Business Review* (March-April 1972).
19. Stone, op. cit. chapter 14.
20. Ibid. p. 143–44.
21. Geneen, op. cit.
22. Stone, op.cit., p. 148–49.
23. Robert Townsend, quoted by Nader, Green, and Seligman, op. cit.
24. Robert Jackall, *Moral Mazes* (Oxford, 1988).
25. Ibid. p. 43.

26. Ibid. p. 43–44.

27. Ibid. p. 44.

28. Ibid. p. 46.

29. Ibid. p. 47.

30. Ibid. p. 58.

31. Ibid. p. 47.

32. Ibid: p. 62.

33. Ibid. p. 52.

34. Ibid. p. 54.

35. Robert C. Solomon and Kristine Hanson, *It's Good Business* (New York, 1985) p. 81.

36. See Karl Marx, "Alienated Labor," *Writings of the Young Marx on Philosophy and Society*, ed. and trans. by Loyd D. Easton and Kurt Guddat (Garden City, 1967) p. 287–300 for Marx's early discussion of alienation.

37. Drew Hyland, *Philosophy of Sport* (New York, 1990) p. 43.

38. Jean-Marie Brohm, *Sports: A Prison of Measured Time* (London, 1978) p. 26.

39. For more on the link between the cholera epidemic and the rise of adult participation in sports see Burke, op. cit., chapter 7.

40. Brohm, op.cit. p. 55.

41. Michael Maccoby, *The Gamesman*, (New York, 1976).

42. Hyland, op. cit. p.45.

43. Ibid. p. 46.

44. Ibid.

45. Hobbes, op. cit., part I, chapter 13.

46. Max Weber, *The Protestant Ethic and the Spirit of Capitalism*, trans. by Talcott Parsons (New York, 1958) p. 172.

47. Jackall, op. cit. p. 8.

48. William H. Whyte, *The Organization Man* (New York, 1956) p. 16–18.

49. Jackall, op. cit. p. 134.

50. Ibid. p. 135.

51. Ibid. p. 136.

52. Ibid.

53. Immanuel Kant, "On a Supposed Right to Tell Lies from Benevolent Motives," in *The Critique of Practical Reason and Other Writings in Moral Philosophy*, trans. by L. W. Beck (Chicago, 1979).

54. Sissela Bok, *Lying: Moral Choice in Public and Private Life* (New York, 1978) p. 31.

55. Albert Z. Carr, "Is Business Bluffing Ethical?" *Harvard Business Review* (January–February 1968) p. 45.

56. Immanuel Kant, *Lectures on Ethics*, trans. by Louis Infield (New York, 1963) p. 227.

57. Norman Bowie, *Business Ethics* (Englewood Cliffs, 1982) p. 64.

58. Paul Eddy, Elaine Potter, and Bruce Page, *Destination Disaster: From the Tri-Motor to the DC-10* (New York, 1976) p. 183–85.

59. Kenneth Goodpaster, "Ethical Imperatives and Corporate Leadership," in *Business Ethics: The State of the Art*, ed. by R. Edward Freeman (Oxford, 1991) p. 94.

60. Ibid.

61. Steven Kelman, "Cost-Benefit Analysis: An Ethical Critique," in *Business Ethics* ed. by W. Michael Hoffman and Jennifer Moore (New York, 1990) p. 94.

62. Michael Rion, "Training for Ethical Management at Cummins Engine," in Hoffman and Moore, op. cit. p. 111.

63. Goodpaster, op. cit. p. 96.

64. Saul Gellerman, "Why 'Good' Managers Make Bad Ethical Choices," *Harvard Business Review* (July–August 1986) p. 85–90.

65. Gerald Postema, "Moral Responsibility in Professional Ethics," *New York University Law Review* 55, 1 (April 1980) p. 77.
66. Coleman, *Foundations of Social Theory*, p. 158.
67. Leslie W. Jacobs, "Business Ethics and the Law: Obligations of a Corporate Executive," *The Business Lawyer* (July 1973).
68. Coleman, *Foundations of Social Theory*, p. 161.
69. See Bryan Burrough and John Helyar, *Barbarians at the Gate: The Fall of RJR Nabisco* (New York, 1990).
70. Goodpaster, op. cit. p. 100.
71. Ibid. p. 101.
72. Michael Hammer and James Champy, *Reengineering the Corporation* (New York, 1993), especially chapter 2.
73. Ibid. p. 103.
74. Thomas J. C. Raymond with Elisabeth Ament Lipton, "Tylenol," *Harvard Business School Case* (Boston, 1984) p. 10.
75. Daniel R. Gilbert, Jr., "Respect for Persons, Management Theory, and Business Ethics," in Freeman, op. cit. p. 111–20.
76. Jackall, op. cit. p. 20, 36.
77. Coleman, *Foundations of Social Theory*, p. 519.
78. Ibid. p. 437.
79. Hammer and Champy, op. cit.
80. Ibid. p. 53.
81. Ibid. p. 70.
82. Gilbert, op. cit. p. 117.
83. Hammer and Champy, op. cit. p. 71.
84. Ibid. p. 72.
85. Ibid. p. 31.
86. Nozick, op. cit. p. 57.
87. Ibid.
88. Russell Boisjoly and Ellen Foster Curtis, "Roger Boisjoly and the Challenger Disaster: A Case Study in Management Practice, Corporate Loyalty, and Business Ethics," in Hoffman and Moore, op. cit. p. 398.
89. Ibid. p. 398–99.
90. Ibid. p. 399.
91. Ibid. p. 401.
92. Ibid. p. 401.
93. Solomon and Hanson, op. cit. p. 157.
94. Stuart Hampshire, *Morality and Conflict* (Cambridge, MA, 1983).
95. Immanuel Kant, *The Doctrine of Virtue*, trans. by M. Gregor (Philadelphia, 1964) p. 23.
96. Mark Halfon, *Integrity* (Philadelphia, 1989) p. 93–94.
97. Isaiah Berlin, *Four Essays on Liberty* (Oxford, 1958).
98. Martha Nussbaum, *The Fragility of Goodness* (Cambridge, 1986).
99. Ibid. p. 34.
100. Fred Feldman, *Doing the Best We Can* (Boston, 1986).
101. Boisjoly and Curtis, op. cit. p. 403.
102. Gabriele Taylor, "Integrity," *Proceedings of the Aristotelian Society, Supplementary Volume*, 55 (1981) p. 143.
103. Martin Benjamin, *Splitting the Difference* (Lawrence, 1990).
104. Ibid. p. 47.
105. Ibid.
106. Ibid.
107. Ibid.
108. Taylor, op. cit. p. 144.

109. Benjamin, op. cit. p. 48.
110. Ibid. p. 49.
111. The whole gruesome story of the flight and the subsequent investigation is told in Gordon Vette, *Impact Erebus* (Auckland, 1983).
112. See *Working Woman*, (December, 1993).
113. Faye J. Crosby, "Affirmative Action Is Worth It," *The Chronicle of Higher Education*, December 15, 1993, p. B1.
114. Quoted in an article by Lesli Hicks in the *San Antonio Express-News*, December 23, 1993, p. B1–2.
115. Benjamin, op. cit. p. 51.
116. Soren Kierkegaard, *Fear and Trembling*, trans. by Walter Lowrie (Garden City, NY, 1954).
117. Halfon, op. cit. p. 63.
118. Ibid.
119. Ibid. p. 65.
120. Ibid. p. 71.
121. Kant, "On the Supposed Right to Tell Lies From Benevolent Motives," from *Kant's Critique of Practical Reason and Other Works on the Theory of Ethics*, trans. T. K. Abbott (London: Longmans, Green & Co., 1873), reprinted in *Moral Rules and Particular Circumstances*, edited by Barnuh A. Brody, Prentice-Hall, Englewood Cliffs, New Jersey (1970).
122. Hilary Putnam, op. cit. p. 85–86.
123. Halfon, op. cit. p. 96.
124. I found the attempt of Richard DeGeorge to frame a similar set of conditions most helpful. See DeGeorge, op. cit. p.161–62.
125. Timothy Ingram, *The Progressive*, (January, 1971).
126. John Rawls, *A Theory of Justice*, p. 117.
127. J. O. Urmson, "Saints and Heroes," in *Essays in Moral Philosophy*, ed. by A. I. Melden (Seattle, 1958) p. 198–216.
128. Kant, *The Doctrine of Virtue*, p. 21–22.
129. Ibid. p. 120.
130. Karen Silkwood was killed during the time in which she was involved in blowing the whistle on a nuclear plant in Oklahoma.
131. Ibid. p. 84.
132. Ibid. p. 86.
133. Jeremy Bentham, *The Principles of Morals and Legislation* (1789) chapter 1, section 10.
134. Aristotle, Nicomachean Ethics, book 3.
135. I prefer the term be pronounced ha-*rass*-ment, rather than *har*-ass-ment. The second pronunciation makes it sound too high-toned, too sophisticated, for the sort of violations involved. Of course, I can hardly require you to read it that way.
136. Patricia Werhane, "Individual Rights in Business," in *Just Business,* ed. by Tom Regan (New York, 1984) p. 107.
137. Ibid. p. 109.
138. Ibid. p. 111.
139. George Brenkert, "Privacy, Polygraphs, and Work," *Business and Professional Ethics Journal*, Vol. 1, No. 1 (Fall 1981) p. 19–35.
140. Ibid.
141. Werhane, op. cit. p. 123.
142 *The New Republic*, March 31, 1986.
143. Joseph R. DesJardins and Ronald Duska, "Drug Testing in Employment," in Hoffman and Moore, op. cit. p. 303.
144. Carl Sandburg, "The Hangman at Home," in *Smoke and Steel* (New York, 1920).

145. Anita Superson, "A Feminist Definition of Sexual Harassment," *The Journal of Social Philosophy*, Vol. XXIV, No. 1 (Spring 1993) p. 46–64.
146. *EEOC Guidelines on Discrimination Because of Sex*, 29 CFR Sec. 1604.11(a) (1980).
147 *Swentek v. US Air*, 830 F.2nd 522 (4th Cir. 1987).
148. Ibid.
149. Superson, op. cit. p. 58.
150. Ibid.
151. Ibid. p. 61.
152 *Meritor Savings Bank, FSB v. Vinson*, 477 U.S. 57 (1986).
153. *Director of Public Prosecutions v. Morgan* 2 A11 Er 347 (1975).
154. E.M. Curley, "Excusing Rape," *Philosophy and Public Affairs*, Vol.5, No. 4 (1976).

THE INVADERS IN THE ENVIRONMENT

1. Guardianship of the Environment

The rain may never fall 'til after sundown,
By eight the morning fog must disappear,
In short there's simply not,
A more congenial spot
For happily ever-aftering,
Than here in Camelot.[1]

I was raised on American Westerns—*Red River, Shane, High Noon, The Man From Laramie, The Searchers, The Man Who Shot Liberty Valence*—not the Arthurian legends of England. King Arthur may have ridden a horse, carried a fancy sword, and won his share of battles, but he always seemed more like a grandiose and verbose failure to me when compared to the likes of Thomas Dunson, Shane, Ethan Edwards, and Tom Doniphon. Still, those Western films and the stories of the court of Camelot share an underlying theme. I don't mean the superficial similarity of knights riding out to battle evil in the name of and for the sake of good, rescuing fair maidens in distress. Though that is a primary motif in the tales of the Round Table, it is hardly the plot of *The Searchers*, where Ethan Edwards sets off to rescue Debbie from

211

the Comanches, but he intends to kill her, rather than return her to white civilization, because she has been assimilated into the tribe.

The similarity beneath the surface of both the Westerns and the Arthurian legends, at least the one that strikes me, is an embedded epic tension between the concept of the garden and that of the wilderness. The garden of civilization was forged out of the wilderness of nature, yet it is always on the verge of being devoured by weeds. Most humans are civilized, tamed, but civilization is a thin shell and the suppressed savagery within us is prone to erupt at any time. Nature is barely domesticated. The sawtoothed mountains or the red rock monoliths always loom in the background, the source of devastating floods, avalanches, vicious animals, and saviors.

When nature breaks loose, when it brings death and destruction in its wake, the price of being able to plant and tend the garden, typically, can only be paid by the barbaric, unconstrained brutal actions of a person who can never reap the harvest. Shane and Ethan Edwards (and, of course, the characters played by Clint Eastwood in his most recent masterpieces, *Pale Rider* and *Unforgiven*) ride or walk off into the mountains or the sunset, incapable of enjoying the fruits of the civilized gardens ensured by the benevolent violence they perpetrated while in states of grace.

The Arthurian legends are said to relate to an actual British warlord who probably fought against invading Saxons at the Battle of Badon in A.D. 518 and, reportedly, died in combat against Mordred at Camlan twenty-one years later. Many of the stories of King Arthur and his court of gallant knights and beautiful ladies, however, are derived from much older tales of the Celtic oral tradition. Typically in those Celtic stories the pivotal events occur by springs, fords, forest clearings, or large trees. These sacred sites are defended by a king (or knight) who regularly is challenged to fight to the death. If the challenger prevails, the defense of the place falls to him. It was winner take all.

> The loser was decapitated and his head either thrown into a well or else exposed on a stake. The challenger, if victorious, inherited the following: the office of the loser, which was to defend a sacred site against any other challenger; the title of lord or king of the country; its revenues, and the person of the loser's wife or daughter. The sacred site could be a forest clearing, a spring or well, an island, or a ford—each, typically, with a single tree, which was the scene of the challenge itself.[2]

What was the point of having a warrior king stand constantly at the ready against all challengers, and why does the successful challenger inherit the task? Apart from the fact that the sites were believed sacred and so warranted protection, their defenses were occasions to test the power, vigor, and martial skill of the guardian, who Frazer called "The King of the Wood."

The post which he held by this precarious tenure carried with it the title of King; but surely no crowned head ever lay uneasier, or was visited by more evil dreams, than his. For year in year out, in summer and winter, in fair weather and in foul, he had to keep his lonely watch, and whenever he snatched a troubled slumber it was at the peril of his life.[3]

Why should the strength and prowess of the defender be so important? The British Celts apparently believed that the power of the assigned knight or king, as demonstrated by victory over challengers, the protection of the sacred spot from the ravages of raiders, was the wellspring of the good fortune of the people, the fruitfulness of their gardens. The challengers were not so much punk kids out to make reputations, as true believers on missions to ensure that the defender was in full vigor, and they were prepared to die in the effort. The continued prosperity of the community, based on a delicate balance between the garden and the wilderness, the tribe and nature, was the foremost concern in the whole bloody business.

The Celts believed that a land guarded by a weak knight king, one who had lost physical strength and prowess (and sexual potency), would be magically transformed into Terre Gaste, the Wasteland.

Crop failures, drought, and animal deaths were attributed to the defender's failure to guard the sacred location. The strongest young warrior would be sent to challenge the defender. Presumably, he would prevail and so become "king of the wood" and the prosperity of the villagers would be magically restored, the garden again reclaimed from the wilderness. The political theorists in the Celtic villages soon must have raised a crucial question: "Why wait for matters to deteriorate, for plagues and pestilence to beset the community?" A continual flow of challengers should ensure abundance. It may be imagined that the incumbent did not wholeheartedly welcome these arrangements, especially as he grew older.

Apparently in some districts it was believed that a one-year term limitation ought to be put on the office to ensure the potency and combat readiness of the defender. Annual kingship was created and tenure in the position was culminated, or, rather, terminated on New Year's Day, by the death of the guardian, either by fire or beheading. Stories depicting this way of ensuring the strength of the guardian abound in the Celtic lore. In the *High History of the Holy Grail*,[4] for example, Lancelot, riding in a barren land, finds a ruined city. The townsfolk are gathered in a great hall where a handsome young knight carrying a large ax approaches Lancelot and asks that his head be cut off. His year as defender was over, and his death was required to restore the land to prosperity. Lancelot obliges and decapitates him. (The same theme was later adopted in the great medieval poem *Sir Gawain and the Green Knight*.)

All of this beheading of heroes in the Celtic tales no doubt reflects the influence of what John Darrah refers to as the "cult of the severed head"[5] in their religion. A change in religious beliefs might account, in some measure, for the fact that the saviors in the Western movies typically get to ride away with their heads still affixed to their shoulders. The moral, however, comes to the same point: the domestic folk, whether aggregated in villages and towns or individually trying to plow a productive plot out of the harsh countryside, are no match for the wickedness and wildness of nature turned loose, especially when it manifests in the person of another human. The garden cannot be sustained by gardeners alone. It is worth noting, I suppose, that the yeoman farmers and townsfolk in some of the Westerns do make an effort at holding off the powers of evil or they are marshaled into the service of the, more or less, professional defender, but they generally prove inept without his skill and direction. The Celtic tales, as far as I can tell, include no communal contributions in the heat of battle. It was rather more like *High Noon* than *Rio Bravo*.

A maimed king (and the Celtic stories are overpopulated with them), disabled by the dolorous stroke—symbolically a wound through the thighs—was incapable of warding off those forces that destroy the security, stability, and prosperity of the community.

> Neither peas nor wheat were sown, no children were born, marriages did not take place, plants and trees did not turn green and birds and animals did not reproduce so long as the king was maimed.[6]

So if the defender loses virility, if the sacred place is no longer safe, according to the Celtic mythic logic, the environment is magically polluted, transformed into wasteland.

The Celtic legends, we may say without much exaggeration, forged a link between environmental protection and long-term communal prosperity. The mythology of the protection of sacred natural spots and the threat of magical barrenness if they are not safeguarded speaks across millennia and world views. As I have suggested, it reverberates in, arguably, our greatest American art form, the Western film. (And it was recently played out in an urban fantasy film by Terry Gilliam: *The Fisher King*.) The Celts, of course, were nature worshippers, hence they had deep religious, as well as economic, reasons to guard the environment, to ensure that their productive fields would not become barren wasteland, to find and preserve the equilibrium between the wilderness and the garden. But, more importantly for us, they understood the need to locate responsibility for environmental protection with those who are most likely to have a positive effect on that goal.

Although the people bore the responsibility for ensuring that the defender remained capable of his task, grooming and sending challengers to test his vigor, the defender held the ultimate responsibility for preventing the onset of the wasteland.[7] Failure, it should not be forgotten, resulted in beheading.

I am not going to argue that there is something sacred about the environment or even in support of an ethical environmental imperative.[8]

The latter requires no argument. It is self-evident. At least for the fore-
seeable future, the prospects of human persons flourishing are linked
to a livable environment, that is, an environment that we would find
livable. An environment in which most people contracted various forms
of cancer as a result of the pollution would not be such an environment.
To willfully or negligently destroy the environment would be tanta-
mount to inflicting great suffering on people. With regard to the former,
I don't think the environment is sacred. I don't think nature is sacred,
if by "sacred" is meant that it ought not to be changed or put to some
utilitarian purpose. I also don't think that by this time in human history it makes any sense to counterpoise the wilderness of nature to
the garden of civilization in a way that holds the former up as holy,
virtuous, and majestic and the latter as contrived and debased. By and
large, the earth *is* our garden, for better or for worse. We have put our
mark on most of it, altered it forever from whatever its state had
humans and the corporate invaders never set upon it. We are a part of
it and it is a part of us. The question should not be how we can keep
some spots untouched and wild, but how we can keep the whole planet
from deteriorating into the wasteland that will support neither human
or corporate enterprise nor the flora and fauna indigenous to it.

The great Western films are not nostalgia trips to the pristine
world of the earth-loving noble savage. (That is why *Dances with
Wolves* is mere politically correct escapism.) They acknowledge that
humans and the civilization they bring with them are integral elements of the mix that is the environment and that its preservation or
protection requires carefully constructed and difficult compromises, the
adoption of cooperative strategies. Sometimes it also requires violent
policing to restore the appropriate balance.

One of the major problems with conceptualizing responsibility for
environmental stewardship is that of identifying roles and who should
play them. It's a casting problem. Who can do what? Specifically, when
we speak of protecting the environment we have a natural tendency to
speak in an undifferentiated way about what everyone ought to do:
recycling, picking up litter, and so on. Another recycling campaign,
the third in two years, I think, has just been launched in my neighborhood. That's very nice, and gives us ordinary people a sense of participation in the save-the-planet endeavor. But why have the other efforts
so miserably failed?

The idea that each and every one of us ought to shoulder primary
environmental protection is probably another legacy of the kind of nonsense produced by the atomistic individualists, those seventeenth-century folks I wrote about in Part 1. What generally happens to ordinary
humans who convert to such thinking about the protection of the
environment? After early bursts of energy and enthusiasm and a
garage full of newspapers and aluminum cans, they become frustrated
with the enormity of the task and scurry off to doing something else,

something more within their control, something like self help through the use of crystals and pyramids. Well, at least they usually don't end up like the poor sodbuster in *Shane* or the prospector in *Pale Rider* who only learn they are utterly unprepared to cope with the problem as they lay dying in a muddy street, victims of their own misplaced exuberance.

It's not that individuals have no role to play in environmental protection, but rather that the task, like so many great tasks, cannot be handled until a proper division of labor is settled. I do not make light of the problem. Quite the opposite. The wasteland threatens us all, humans and corporate actors alike. D. Kirk Davidson summarizes the predictions of the Brundtland Report of the World Commission on Environment and Development, *Our Common Future*:

> More hungry people in the world
>
> More people without safe water
>
> Millions of acres of productive land become
>
> worthless each year
>
> Acid precipitation kills lakes and forests
>
> Gradual global warming from the burning of fossil fuels
>
> Depletion of the planet's protective ozone shield
>
> Toxic wastes poisoning the food chain and water
>
> supplies.[9]

Even if the commission is only partially correct, there are bad times ahead, not just for spotted owls and salamanders, but for humans and the corporate invaders. Of course, there are those who will not acknowledge that a significant portion of the problem is a result of alterable behavior by Rank B-ers. For them it is something we will just have to endure the best we can. Robert W. Lee writes:

> It is important to keep some sort of perspective regarding the extent of manmade pollution. For instance, during all of his earthly existence, man has yet to equal the particulate and noxious-gas levels of the combined volcanic eruptions on Krakatoa, Indonesia (1883), Katmai, Alaska (1912), and Hekla, Iceland (1947). Indeed, nature contributes approximately sixty percent of all particulates in the atmosphere, sixty-five percent of the sulfur dioxide, seventy percent of the hydrocarbons, ninety-three percent of the carbon monoxide, ninety percent of the ozone, and ninety-nine percent of the nitrogen oxides.[10]

Humans and corporations put about ten million tons of pollutants into the atmosphere annually. Sounds like a lot. Swamps and forests, however, release into the air about 1.6 billion tons of methane gas, 170 million tons of hydrocarbons, and 3.5 billion tons of carbon monoxide every year.

The figures are disputable (they are regularly disputed from all sides), but it seems undeniable that the enterprises of the Rank B-ers are contributing, in a significant way, to the global environmental deterioration that threatens us all. They may not be the major contributors, but their contributions may be the straws that break the back of the ecosystem. Well, so what? I will avoid the trap of statistical forays. I'm not interested in the question of *how* bad things are or are not. The point is that if they are not now already a mess, soon they well could be, and if they get that way the impact on corporations and humans will, by and large, be dramatically negative. The issue is not, or not only, one of identifying what is causing environmental degradation, it is on whom should the protection and the preservation of the environment fall. Who is best suited for the all-important role of guardian?

In late March 1989, a week or so after the *Exxon Valdez* ran aground on Bligh's Reef and befouled the waters and shores of Prince William Sound with eleven million gallons of oil, a Wall Street analyst was interviewed on national television (CNN). The gist of his position was that disasters of this sort are bound to occur in the industry and should be understood as a cost the society must absorb for its oil-based economy. He went on to argue that neither Exxon nor humans, either on the tanker or in the company, ought to be held responsible for the incident. In effect, he claimed, no person, natural or corporate, ought to be held to account or liable for damages. It seemed to him that Exxon was making a magnanimous gesture by voluntarily cleaning up the damaged region. Besides, oil spills are not the catastrophes the media makes them out to be. The startled reaction of the other discussants left a few awkward moments of silent air time before someone attempted a rejoinder.

In one sense at least, he may be right. The oil spill in Prince William Sound, the deadly methyl isocyanide release by Union Carbide in Bhopal, India, the Three Mile Island nuclear accident, and the blowout of the Union Oil Company rig in the Santa Barbara Channel are representative examples of the industrial phenomena that Charles Perrow calls "normal accidents."[11] Normal accidents are generally unpredictable and unavoidable, at least within the parameters of usual business practices. They occur in systems that are complex and "tightly coupled." "Processes happen very fast and can't be turned off, the failed parts cannot be isolated from other parts, or there is no other way to keep production going safely."[12] John Ladd elaborates:

> No one at the time understands what is happening partly because the antecedent probability of these failures occurring together is so low. . . . High technology is statistically bound to produce more normal accidents, unpredictable catastrophes due to technological complexities and the tight coupling of complex systems.[13]

I am not antitechnology, and I am fully prepared to join with Perrow in allowing that one of the prices we and the environment will have to pay for the lifestyles we enjoy, and the products and services, is the occasional normal accident that kills hundreds or thousands of people and animals.

More importantly, the Wall Streeter was right when he said that such normal accidents should not be the targets of our environmental protection campaigns. The *Exxon Valdez* spill, dramatic though it was—the film footage was horrific—really did *not* create a major environmental disaster. Of course, it would be good to try to prevent such spills, insofar as accidents can ever be prevented. And in this type of case, they can. Doing so will require technological improvements, better corporate decision making, and (possibly) regulation and legal enforcement (to be discussed in Part 6). Tankers with stronger hulls should be placed in service, and crews should be better educated to the tasks they may have to perform. Once that has been said, there is little more to the environmental issue in Prince William Sound from the point of view of ethics. (That does not mean that there is not a great deal to say about the way Exxon handled the whole Alaskan business, especially after the spill.)

Oil spills make terrific news footage, but some controversy arises about whether they do as much permanent damage to the ecosystem as the first few weeks of news footage from the scene may lead us to believe. The *Exxon Valdez* disaster and the highly publicized Santa Barbara Channel well blowout in 1969, according to some analysts, may not leave the irreparable destruction that was first predicted by the anti-industry environmentalists. Even the number of dead birds and sea otters was grossly overestimated by the press.

In any event, the real environmental disasters are the ones that are not cleansed by natural processes (with a little help from human technology): air pollution, the general degradation of the water supply, the toxic destruction of the soils, the deforestation of the planet. Those are matters of real concern for the future of the planet, and their causes can, by and large, be laid at the feet of the corporate invaders. They are the issues to be confronted by corporate ethics with respect to the environment. But the response will typically be that the corporations are not to be blamed, or not to be solely blamed because changes in the purity of the environment are the costs of the life-styles we lead, lifestyles that are also so attractive to people in undeveloped areas that they are willing to sacrifice their more pristine environments to gain a modicum of the lives we lead.

One reason for disagreements about the assignment of responsibility for environmental degradation is that our traditional theories of ownership, such as Locke's, conveniently exclude waste. Hence, dumping manufacturing wastes into the air, the streams, and the ground was thought to be free, not a cost of production. The environmental damage, therefore, was not registered in the manufacturing costs and the pricing of the product. Some have argued that the resulting divergence between the corporation's costs of production and the social costs borne by the society and the environment is almost solely responsible for our pollution crisis.

The corporate actor is not to be faulted if its costing figures never reflected the damage its production was causing. After all, the ledgers weren't hiding anything, it was free. And the consumers of those products could enjoy them relatively inexpensively.

It's rather hard to get humans and corporate actors to voluntarily accept ownership of things they throw away, flush away, or spill. One way to do that, some have proposed, is to put a price tag on polluting. Once a priced ownership of waste is factored into the costs, rational decisions about production may take a different turn from the way they have gone when waste disposal was free. But environmental pollution will not come to a halt or be significantly reversed if such a scheme is introduced. The Garden of Eden will not sprout out of the smokestacks of the Rust Belt.

Larry Ruff has put forth the view that

> . . . the choice facing a rational society is *not* between clean air and dirty air, or between clear water and polluted water, but rather between various *levels* of dirt and pollution. The aim must be to find that level of pollution abatement where the costs of further abatement begin to exceed the benefits.[14]

Ruff's pricing of pollution scheme should mean that instead of what is released beyond the fence being conceived as a public problem, it will be a problem, indeed a legal one, for the polluter.

This may be a reasonable way for society to go in trying to entice corporations to invest in pollution controls, but the Ruff solution invites teleopathic thinking in the CID structures of potential and actual corporate polluters. It offers a handy surrogate for avoiding the ethical consideration of environmental obligations within the CID structure: the heavy hand of the law. In effect, the corrective for bad theory and little or no ethical consideration in decision making is an enforced pricing mechanism that takes the whole matter out of corporate decision making altogether. It, in effect, imposes a tax, a cost of doing business about which the only decision making is "How much can we afford to pay?" A purely economic decision.

Ruff can point to some success for his type of pricing plan in the Ruhr Valley of Germany where the volume of industrial waste in the Ruhr and its tributaries exceeds the flow of those rivers in the drier seasons, but where the Ruhr now supports fish. The German solution was to line one of the Ruhr tributaries with concrete and turn it into an open sewer. A treatment plant handles all the flow at the mouth of the tributary at a low cost to the aggregated polluters who continue dumping into the river system. The manufacturing continues and only one tributary was totally sacrificed. Ruff comments:

> The loss caused by destruction of *one* tributary is rather small, if the nearby rivers are maintained, while the benefit from having this inexpensive means of waste disposal is very large. However, if *another* river were lost, the costs would be higher and the benefits lower; one open sewer may be the optimal number.[15]

I don't want to quibble with Ruff's arithmetic or even with the idea that no river in an industrialized country needs to be free of pollutants, that some level is tolerable. In the Ruhr case what is tolerable was set by the ability of fish to survive in the water. It is the whole conception of controlling corporate pollution by external pricing that I find objectionable for reasons discussed at length in Part 2. If pollution abatement is the ethical thing for corporations to practice, then it should not be necessary to motivate corporate actors to adopt it by the use of surrogate legal and pricing methods. The assumption embedded in Ruff's approach, and those that have followed in his train, is that corporations are no more than straightforward maximizers rather than rational strategists. That is an unfounded, indeed incoherent assumption. But it is also one that tends to work like a self-fulfilling prophecy. If you tell someone enough that they can only think one way, they might just prove you right by abandoning any other way of thinking.

But back to the environmental question: is abating pollution, saving the ecosystem, the ethical thing to do, something humans and corporate persons have an obligation to at least attempt? Why should we protect, even try to improve, our physical environment?

I reject as grossly sentimental the notion that all living things have the *right* to a livable environment.[16] I do think that Rank B-ers and C-ers are morally entitled not to be forced to sacrifice a livable environment so that some Rank B-ers can achieve their own ends. That is required by the side constraints. Talk of rights, especially natural rights, is unnecessary, though if one wants to call that a right I will not object.[17] I admit to certain negative feelings about some birds, in particular chickens, but I have nothing against flora and fauna, all creatures great and small. I would rather they continued living than not, and I support organizations who work to protect them. But I don't regard this as a matter of obligation to the animals, for example the sea otters.

It certainly makes no sense to say that humans and corporate actors have obligations to the trees, the air, and water. The important question is whether anyone is responsible to anyone else for protection of the air, the water, and the soil.

Typical of the discussion of these issues the past two decades is the view that not polluting or deplenishing the resources necessary for a livable life is owed to future human generations. What that is supposed to mean, however, is not self-evident. Protect it for what? So that they can exploit it? How are they going to use it? To what ends are they going to put it? Who knows? Certainly not us. Could the people in the fifteenth century have possibly guessed how we would use the environment? How our style of life would be radically different from theirs? How we would adapt and what we would regard as livable as compared to them? Why not get what we can out of it now, and let future generations, if any, fend for themselves? Why should we leave the environment in good repair for future generations to destroy? Why should we do that if it will cause us to lower our own standard of living to accomplish the conservation? How do we know they will appreciate the ecosystem we would have diligently preserved? When I was young, I collected and carefully saved the baseball cards that came with Topps bubble gum. My sets for the years 1951, 1952, and 1953 were complete and immaculate. When I left home for college, I put off such things and, with fitting ceremony, gave the collection to my half-brother. I returned home for vacation, and he showed me a broken-down, jerry-built, slot car racing game he had purchased with the money he got from selling my collection. The damn thing didn't even work.

Perhaps, as some science fiction writers imagine, future humans will create their own environment, or they will be genetically modified to thrive in bad air and befouled water. Who knows? Nicholas Rescher writes:

> Man is a being of enormous adaptability, resiliency, and power. He has learned to survive and make the best of it under some extremely difficult and unpleasant conditions. By all means, let us do everything we can to save the environment. But if we do not do a very good job of it—and I for one do not think we will—it is not necessarily the end of the world. Let us not sell man short. We have been in some unpleasant circumstances before and have managed to cope.[18]

It is a bit disconcerting that Rescher is confident humans will both botch the environmental protection job and yet succeed in managing to modify themselves to thrive in the polluted environment they will have created. I would have thought that the former was the easier of the two to engineer.

Environmental protection, by definition, must be a long-term project. Its rational sense as an obligation depends, I believe, on the probability that morally responsible entities existing now can stand in an actual relationship with the generations of persons who will (or may) exist in the remote future. Obligations, as Michael Walzer and others have argued, depend on actual relationships between the parties.[19] "Obligation . . . begins with membership," Walzer writes, "willful membership."[20]

Traditional liberal individualist theories fail to provide the basis for such a relationship between humans now living and those of generations far into the future. Consider the "big two" of that tradition: Hobbes and Locke.

The major stumbling block to nailing down the requisite relationship from the Hobbesian point of view is the enormous asymmetry in power to harm that exists between those humans now in existence and those that may comprise future generations of humans. As the environmentalists regularly remind us, we have a disproportionate amount of power to make those in the future worse off. They will never be able to reciprocate. Sure, they can tarnish our reputations, but that is hardly comparable to the messes in which we can force them to live. We, individually and in the aggregate, can materially hurt or help them by ensuring they have clean air and water for starters. They can neither hurt nor help us.

Hobbes' theory depends on the relative equality in the ability to harm each other of the parties to the social contract.[21] A Hobbesian relationship that is productive of obligations, some version of a contract, surely cannot be established between us and future generations. Moral obligations for Hobbes depend on mutual risks of harm. We have no Hobbesian reasons to respect whatever interests in the environment future generations may have. They cannot harm us.

Lockean entitlement protection hardly fares better in motivating a transgenerational obligation-generating relationship. That should be no surprise, for Locke's property theory is, in no small measure, responsible for the carelessness with which the environment has been treated to date. In the opinion of Locke, and more recently Nozick, according to Brian Barry,

> . . . provided an individual has come by a good justly, he may justly dispose of it any way he likes. . . . Since we have a right to dispose of our property as we wish, subsequent generations could not charge us with injustice if we were to consume whatever we could in our lifetimes and direct that what was left should be destroyed at our deaths.[22]

Insofar as pollution is a form of consumption—the consuming of the good air and water—is there no check in a Lockean theory on existing generations expending resources as they go along, leaving nothing for and owing nothing to those who may show up in the future?

Will not such appropriation and consumption violate the so-called Lockean Proviso endorsed by Nozick? The proviso says that acquisition and consumption must be restricted to preserve "enough and as good left in common for others." Nozick, I think correctly, interprets that to mean that we are to ensure that our acquisitions and consumptions *do not worsen* the situations of others. In order to know whether people are being made worse off, we need to fix a baseline.

If they fall below that because of someone else's consumption, they are worse off. Nozick comments:

> It does not include the worsening due to more limited opportunities to appropriate, . . . and it does not include how I "worsen" a seller's position if I appropriate materials to make some of what he is selling, and then enter into competition with him.[23]

Some of Nozick's examples play into the environmental issues. He says that if the proviso forbids one from appropriating all of the world's drinkable water, then it forbids anyone from appropriating some of the water supply and buying up the rest from eager sellers. But is it crucial that the people who are being disadvantaged exist at the time of the acquisition? The answer seems to be "yes," or one could be caught in a rollback-type argument with shifting baselines that would never let anyone consume anything.

For example, suppose that three hundred years from now the people of the earth will have very little clean air to breath. Only the wealthiest will be able to afford private portable oxygen systems. The skies will look like those depicted in the film *Blade Runner*, deadly with particulates and toxic vapors. Acid rain will continuously drizzle on everyone. Most people will be choking, gasping for air, stricken with emphysema. The future generation living in those conditions, let us suppose, is at the end of a chain of polluting consumption of the clean air. Call them Population Z. The population just before them, Population Y, can use up the last of the fresh air. But Y and Z are contemporaries, at least for a time, so Y's use of the air will worsen the situation of Z. Its baseline would have been set in the overlap period when some clean air still remained. Population Y therefore would violate the proviso if it depletes the clean air supply. But then Y is worse off because it will be forbidden by the proviso from appropriating the air for its uses, so Population X's consumption of the air must also be forbidden by the proviso because what it leaves to Y puts Y under the restriction. Y is therefore made worse off. In fact, all of the populations before Y left Y worse off because they left the next generation after themselves worse off. And so on back down to us. Each left the succeeding generation less at liberty to consume fresh air, because less and less of it remained, more and more cramping their styles. So nobody should be permitted to use up any of the fresh clean air, ever.

Nozick argues, however, that the only way to generate this rollback is to adopt a rather stringent conception of someone being made worse off. On that account a person is made worse off if he or she can no longer improve his or her situation by an appropriation. A weaker reading is more appropriate. According to it, a person is made worse off by being no longer able to freely use what he or she previously could. Population Z may then not be worse off because it cannot pollute the air as Y did, as long as enough free air remains for Z to use as Z did when Z and Y were contemporaries. This will restrict Y's consumption to the point of not polluting any more of the air than it did when Z came on the scene, but the rollback to us will be deterred, if not blocked altogether.

The baseline problem with the proviso approach, however, still stands between us and future generations. They are not contemporaries with us at any time, and their baseline is pure speculation as far as we are concerned. We simply cannot know how far the pollution will have extended when, for example, Population Y makes it on the scene. Also, we have it in our power to lower or raise the baseline of the subsequent generations. If we decide to consume the fresh water before the next generation is born, then having fresh water is not something to which they are entitled. It would never have been on their baseline. So, as Barry has noted, this approach does not require us to leave anything worthwhile behind for the next generation. Of course, it will be immediately noted that the conception of discrete generations succeeding each other is not the way things work. Many generations may be contemporaries in any time slice. But that may be but another problem with the individualism that informs all of the Lockean doctrines.

I have no recipes for the proper use and care of the environment. That is not my interest here. Instead, I want to locate the stewardship obligations in a responsibility relationship that makes sense, and not in mystical extensions of the traditional views. The major roadblock to doing so is the apparent lack of a way for existing humans to have actual relationships of willful membership with generations of humans who will not be born, if they are at all, until we are long dead. We can't, but the corporate invaders can. They exist now and they can endure long enough to have such relations with the generations of the future.

Existing humans can only form relationships that give rise to obligations with other existing humans. They can do so by contracting, and they can also enter into noncontractual relations with each other based on affection and companionship. In both types of cases obligations may ensue. But none of those obligations will endure much beyond the death of one or both parties. (Love is wonderful, but its obligations hardly can be said to last after the lovers have died.)

It is no wonder that we feel impotent as individuals with respect to the protection of the environment. It is not just that there is precious little any one of us can do to make a real difference when we live, it is that we cannot ensure that what we do will survive us, that generations after we are dead will assume the obligation to carry forth our projects, even those that might benefit them. We have no way to lock them into the bargain. We are not going to share membership with them in any actual relations that can support an obligation in us not to do them harm by despoiling their environment. Should environmental protection rest finally on some sort of fantasy or mythic membership? Those of us who would exploit the environment for personal gain will surely see through such a flimsy support.

As Roger Scruton has noted,

> The care for future generations must be entrusted to persons who will exist when they exist: and if there are no such persons surrounding me, how can I have that care except as a helpless anxiety?[24]

But surrounding me, intermingling with my very identity and yours, are exactly the sort of entities that will exist (or are likely to exist) when future generations are the existing generations and we are long dead. Obligations to future generations can be sensibly articulated through corporations. The maintenance of the environment in order to protect those generations from the wasteland is, in fact, a reasonable obligation to assign to the corporate invaders, as it is unreasonable to assign it to humans individually or in some aggregate such as the human race. Indeed, corporations are the ideal bearers of it, and through each of our identity dependency relations with those corporations, we participate in the obligation.

Atomistic individualists cheat themselves out of meaningful involvement in long-range obligation relationships. Their purposes in living must be drastically limited, and that no doubt accounts for their typical cynicism about most everything over the long haul. It is no wonder that they put what hope they have in invisible hands while the environment continues to be exploited and degraded.

Let's try to conceptualize four facets of the corporate environmental obligation position:

1. Protection of the environment is always a future-oriented activity. It is never today, but tomorrow, that is placed at risk by pollutants and wastes. Sometimes those tomorrows get here rather quickly, even adversely affecting those doing the polluting, but, on the whole, the effects of environmental debasement will not be broadly experienced for generations. Polluters can reap whatever short-term benefits failure to abate provides to them, and then disappear from the scene.

2. If some entity (or entities) is (are) to be assigned the obligation of preserving the environment in as good a condition as is possible consistent with the continued flourishing of Rank B-ers, that entity should be able to stand in an actual relationship with those being benefited. If it does not, then it cannot really be held to account for its failure. One reason why Americans show so little concern for the mounting federal deficit is that the argument that it will have a terrible impact on future generations who will have to pay it off stirs, at best, only mild sympathy. We'll never have to deal with them, and so what if they write in their history books that we were spendthrifts who lived recklessly above our means. We aren't going to read those books. In a real sense, they are no more than fantasy creatures to us, as we will be historical characters to them. If we really are concerned about what they

might say about us, that in disgust they might tear down our monuments to ourselves, we can ensure they will never come into existence
and, of course, couldn't complain about it either.

Joel Feinberg has written:

> Suppose . . . that all human beings at a given time voluntarily form a
> compact never again to produce children, thus leading within a few
> decades to the end of the species. . . . Would this arrangement violate
> the rights of anyone? No one can complain on behalf of presently
> nonexistent future generations that their future interests, which give
> them a contingent right to protection have been violated since they
> will never come into existence to be wronged. . . . [T]he suicide of the
> species would be deplorable, lamentable, and a deeply moving
> tragedy, but . . . it would violate no one's rights.[25]

3. Environmental protection is a species of care about future generations.[26] We no longer subscribe to the magical barrenness doctrine of
   the Celtic legends, except with respect to the nuclear energy industry.
   But, as noted above, it is senseless to locate the care of future generations with those who cannot exist when those generations come into
   existence. No relationships that can support obligations can really
   arise between us and them. The idea that there is a causal chain of
   partially overlapping links that will stretch from us to them, one generation per link is also unhelpful. It is certainly possible for three or
   even four generations to be contemporaries, and therefore for their
   members to participate in meaningful cross-generational obligation-
   generating relationships. But these are not transitive relations. If a
   member of Generation A is in such a relationship with a member of
   Generation C, and some years later that member of Generation C is in
   a relationship with a member of Generation F, it does not follow that
   the member of Generation A is in the same sort of or any relationship
   with the member from F. The member from A is long since dead.
   Perhaps all that is needed is incremental responsibility relationships
   to found the obligation to protect the environment for the future.
   That's a nice idea, but its reach does not exceed its rather short-lived
   grasp. It hardly takes us far enough into the future to cancel out mere
   straightforward maximizing of the resources of the ecosystem.
4. Corporations, however, can and do endure. They can survive well into
   the future and as they stand in relationships with us now, they will
   stand in relationships with our future generations. Our substitutes in
   the corporate positions we now occupy will be, at least in large measure, the humans of future generations. And even if corporations
   become almost entirely automated and computerized, the humans of
   those future times will still stand in some relationships to them,
   albeit not employment relations.

Something rather unseemly insinuates itself into the issue. It is
conceivable that humans will disappear altogether from the earth,
while the corporate invaders thrive in an environment that could not
sustain us. Would it be unethical for corporations to work to foster

that eventuality? If it is not unethical, they could go on polluting the earth, exploiting its resources, without concern for whether humans can or cannot flourish in the environment they are creating. Throughout the twentieth century they, sometimes, seem to have acted in just that way.

The side constraints approach I have taken will, however, check the intentional elimination of Rank B-ers as means to the ends of other Rank B-ers. Deliberately acting so as to make it impossible for Rank B-ers to survive blatantly busts through the side constraints.

Still, humans could die out from a plague not caused by corporate actions. The side constraints would still govern ethical action, but, as only corporations would remain in Rank B, the effect they had on environmental protection might radically change. The bottom line is that the kind of environment that is to be safeguarded must be relative to the membership of Rank B. Humans place a high value on clean air and water and spots of natural beauty, on nonpoisoned soil, because we require them for survival or because we find them aesthetically enjoyable or because we have recreational uses for them. If we are not around, those things would not have those instrumental values. Computers are not likely, for example, to require clean water or get much enjoyment from a snowcapped mountain, a babbling brook, and a stand of redwood trees.

In any event, humans are not likely to disappear from the earth leaving the corporations as the only members of Rank B, so the human interests in the environment will continue to demand ethical attention. What is more important is that corporations have a greater stake in the protection of the environment than currently existing humans do because they will depend on it far longer than we will. In our lifetimes we might notice some degradation of nature caused by poor stewardship, but most of the predicted catastrophic effects, assuming no changes in current practices, are unlikely to occur in the lifetimes of anyone now living. If they do occur centuries hence, the humans then living will not only be their victims, they will be unable to stand in the same relationships with corporations that we now do. They will not be consumers, employees, managers, or stockholders. They will be radically reduced in social stature, probably living only at subsistence levels. The impact such a change in the lifestyles of humans will have on the corporations can only be imagined. It is unlikely to be beneficial.

I have already shown in Part 1 that corporations are functionally more capable than humans of playing reciprocal cooperative strategies in the short and long term. Environmental protection is such a strategy. So why haven't the corporate invaders done a better job of safeguarding the environment? Admittedly, they have done a terrible job.

The answer is obvious. The managers of most corporations in America throughout the last century have been afflicted with teleopathy.

They have been blind to the long-term interests of their corporations and persuaded that short-term financial rewards must dominate all other factors in corporate decision making. It is not that corporations are incapable of reciprocal long-term cooperative strategies. Rather their capacities have not been put to those ends. They have been subverted by immediate gratification strategies, and sometimes they have been perverted by greed. Though they are ideally suited to play the guardianship role for the environment, few corporations have stepped forth to take up the challenge.

2. Greed and the Redwoods

King of the Wood! Many cases, and different kinds of cases, involve corporations and the environment. I want to focus on one because it not only highlights environmental issues in corporate decision making, but because it shows how interrelated are environmental matters and other business dealings. Lisa Newton has researched the recent history of the Pacific Lumber Company. Her account follows:

> Once there was a very traditional company, Pacific Lumber, based in its company town of Scotia in Humboldt County, California, home of the legendary 2,000-year-old sequoia trees. It took care of its workers, conserved its giant redwood trees, turned a modest but steady profit, planned for the long term, and, in brief, made none of the mistakes that all the shortsighted lumber companies made. . . . Then came the villains, jetting in from Wall Street: the takeover artists, the sharks, Charles Hurwitz's Maxxam Inc., recently spun out of Federated, soon to be joined with MCO, who gobbled up the company's stock, bought off the management, threatened the workers' jobs and benefits, and immediately doubled the timber harvest to pay down the junk-bond-financed debt.[27]

The takeover, leveraged buyout craze of the 1980s produced a number of similar stories. Solid companies were purchased in a frenzy of greed by financiers who had no idea how to run them for the long term and could not have cared less. Their goal was to milk the corporations for all they were worth and then get out. Often they sold off the most profitable parts of corporations in order to buy down the debt created in their takeovers. The intermediaries, of course, skimmed off enormous fees, and shareholders generally realized short-term windfall profits.

All of the activity on Wall Street and in the boardrooms, however, seemed only to have a negative effect on the productivity of American business. Paper was passed around and traded about furiously, huge sums of money were paid to people at various levels of the process, but almost no one seemed interested in the long-term interests of both the companies and, especially in the case of Pacific Lumber, the environment.

The story of Pacific Lumber seems a story of rampant teleopathy blinding the corporation's perspective on its future and ravaging the countryside in the process. It is a lesson in the dangers of failing to ensure that the King of the Wood is on duty.

Pacific Lumber was run by a single family from about 1900 to the raider's assault of 1985. Its financial statements reveal a healthy company turning an annual profit under prudent management. It owned 195,000 acres of redwood forest in Northern California and had adopted a policy of ensuring replacements for every cutting. Unlike its competitors, it avoided boom and bust cycles by a steady harvesting and replenishing program, and therefore provided its employees with dependable jobs.

> PL was famous for employment policies that went far beyond the certainty of a job. The town of Scotia . . . was one of the last of the company towns, wholly built and owned by PL. The houses were rented to the workers at rents that were low even for that area, and in hard times the company forgot to collect the rent. No one ever got laid off or faced retirement or medical emergency without funds to cover them. A worker's children were assured jobs with the company, if that is what they wanted, or a full scholarship to college.[28]

Employee loyalty was intense. Consequently, there was no union movement. The environmental record of Pacific Lumber was exemplary. It never clear-cut the hillsides, so its lands were free of the soil erosion, stream pollution, and destruction of wildlife characteristic of other lumber companies in the region. Pacific Lumber was also famous throughout California for its contributions to the state park system. It made an agreement with the state to set aside its most scenic groves to be purchased by the state for Humboldt Redwoods State Park.

> When the money was slow collecting, PL "held on to the land it had agreed to preserve, patiently paying taxes on it, letting people use it as if it were already a part of the park," until the money finally came through and the acquisition was complete—in the case of the last parcel, forty years after the original agreement.[29]

If one were looking for a corporation to use as a model of environmental stewardship, one would not have needed to look much further than Pacific Lumber. That was before 1985.

Enter the raiders. In early October, 1985, Maxxam Group, headed by Houstonian Charles Hurwitz and financed by Michael Milken's junk bonds, made a tender offer of $38.50 per share for Pacific Lumber. The stock was then trading for $29 a share. The board of Pacific Lumber rejected the offer that seemed to them to have come "out of the blue." Two weeks later, when Maxxam upped the offer to $40 per share, the board accepted.[30]

Wall Street insiders reported being shocked by the acceptance because the company was supposed to be worth considerably more than the Maxxam offer. Immediately questions were raised about how the directors could have been surprised. Was stock parking involved? What kind of advice was the board getting from its financial advisers, Salomon Brothers, when Salomon Brothers would make twice as much if the company were sold than if it successfully beat back the raiders? Substantial golden parachutes were also part of the deal for the top managers and board members of Pacific Lumber.[31] There was a shady look to the whole business, and it wasn't because of the redwood trees.

What did the raiders do when they took over Pacific Lumber? It should be noted that of the $840 million dollars Maxxam spent to buy the company, $770 million was debt, two thirds of which was in Milken's junk bonds. That fact governed many of its actions. The raiders terminated the employees' pension fund and took $50 million from it to finance some of the debt. Then they utterly abandoned the company's conservative cutting policies and accelerated the harvest of trees to produce the revenues needed to pay down the debt.[32] Maxxam wasn't in the lumber business, it was in the takeover business. In 1988, Maxxam paid $224 million to buy a significant amount of Kaiser Tech stock using funds from the profits of Pacific Lumber, a company that was now a shadow of its former self.

The employees of Pacific Lumber were, though concerned about long-term employment prospects, delighted with all the overtime. But as cost-cutting measures and public scrutiny, especially from environmentalist groups, have intensified, they now see themselves as embattled and at risk. Bumper stickers on pickup trucks read: "SAVE A LOGGER—EAT AN OWL." The harvest of the timber continues at a frantic pace. It is hard to resist the $10,000–$15,000 price that the company can get for a single cut redwood. The profits of Pacific Lumber, rather like its land, are being stripped off to finance debt and new takeover bids.

Maxxam and Charles Hurwitz look like the villains of the piece. Newton actually calls them that.[33] The implication, in the public press and academic writings is that something was ethically wrong with the takeovers and leveraged buyouts that dominated the news in the business world in the 1980s, over and above the illegal acts that were committed. But what is the problem?

The story of what happened to Pacific Lumber is not one of someone taking control of the company just to wreak havoc on the northern California environment. It is likely that Hurwitz and his people really had little idea that they would adopt a "cut and git" policy, if they succeeded in the takeover. In fact, they probably knew little to nothing about the daily operations of the lumber industry. Their knowledge of Pacific Lumber seems to have been restricted to its financial records.

They were in the game for the profits, not for the product. But then, that has been common in American business for many decades.

Can takeovers be defended on ethical grounds? Some have tried. As Robert Kuttner has noted, most supporters of corporate raiders' methods are disciples of the "Chicago" school economics.

> The widespread approval of hostile takeovers reflects the philosophical triumph of the "Chicago" school of economics, whose worldview is predicated on the assumptions that markets must know what they are doing. . . . In the Chicago view, the only test that is really necessary is whether the raiding game boosts share prices.[34]

One of the more vociferous of the Chicago-school crowd is Michael Jensen. Jensen maintains that none of the negatives typically set forth by people in business ethics and the press (as well as some in government) are actually caused by hostile takeovers.[35] Shareholders, for example, are not harmed because they usually realize major financial gains as the price of their stock is driven up during the takeover. That seems undeniable, though it is hardly the core of the ethical issues. Other claims Jensen makes for takeovers, however, are far more contentious, and many seem to run counter to the Pacific Lumber experience.

Jensen claims that "Corporate takeovers do not waste resources; they use assets productively."[36] This claim is, in fact, defensible if the only assets one is talking about are financial resources. Jensen notes that transfer of wealth from the stockholders of one company to another is not a matter of consumption. The only consumed wealth occurs in paying the fees of intermediaries: the lawyers, managers, economists, accountants, and consultants who structure and shepherd the deals. Admittedly those amount to sizable sums of money, but they are only a small portion of the value of the acquisition, typically about seven-tenths of a percent to one percent.

Jensen might have been right on this matter of nonconsumption, if the takeovers were not financed by enormous debt loads, supported by junk bonds. What generally happened, and the Pacific Lumber takeover is a classic case, is that the wealth that is transferred to the stockholders of the target corporation is not really coming out of the pockets of those in the raiding party. It is actually being financed by the productive assets of the target corporation itself, with financial institutions loaning the money and adding on their financing and interest charges. In some cases it ends up coming out of the employees' benefits, pension plans, and so on. Usually it will come from a fire sale of some element of the company. In effect, significant waste of resources can and often does occur. Productive divisions of a target company may be sold off or abandoned. Jobs are lost. In the case of Pacific Lumber, whole slopes of virgin old-growth forest are being chainsaw massacred to pay down the takeover debt. And then there's the debt financing, the interest on the debt.

Were resources wasted? Of course they were. And in the Pacific Lumber affair, the waste was also unethical. The environment was victimized and, despite the fact that they are currently demonstrating support for the company, the employees were treated as mere means to the financial gain of stockholders and the Maxxam Group. "Almost 40 lumber mills throughout northern California have shut down or reduced operations since 1990."[37] How much longer will Pacific Lumber last?

The KKR takeover of RJR Nabisco had similar effects on the people of Winston-Salem, North Carolina. Markets don't seem to know what they are doing in these cases.

Jensen claims that "no evidence with which I am familiar indicates that takeovers produce more plant closings, layoffs, and dismissals than would otherwise have occurred."[38] His defense of this rather shaky claim is that even though takeovers may cause layoffs, plant closings, and dismissals in the target companies, because of the wealth gains they are creating, new technologies will be introduced and the overall real standard of living will increase. Only those wedded to the old technologies will experience a reduction in wealth.

It is, of course, impossible to know whether the plant closings, and such would have happened if the takeover financing did not require them. It does seem likely that Pacific Lumber would have continued its conservative policies and practices well into the twenty-first century had the raiders never jetted in. It is also somewhat curious that Jensen, who previously told us that takeovers involve only the transfer of wealth, would turn around and defend them as increasing wealth. No evidence, in particular at Pacific Lumber, indicates that the takeovers necessarily bring new technologies with them. Lumber companies in the Pacific Northwest were clear-cutting the slopes for more than a century.

One summer in the mid-'60s, I worked on a ranch in the Salmon-Trinity Alps region of northern California. To get to the ranch you had to drive on a single-lane lumber company road and yield the right of way to the trucks carting one or two enormous logs at a time down the mountain to the mill in Hayfork. The practice of most of the lumber companies in those days was to clear an entire slope, to harvest until nothing worth cutting was left. The rains produced deep erosion scars on the slopes, and the great trees were replaced with scrub.

Pacific Lumber's lands were a veritable Eden by comparison. Since the takeover, they aren't anymore. The raiders adopted old technologies: "cut and git," not anything new. Of course most of the lumber mills around Hyampom and Hayfork on the Trinity River have had to shut down. There are no longer enough trees to support them. David Yeardon has followed up the situation in that area. He writes:

> I had even heard on the back roader's grapevine that families around Hyampom had worked with the Forest Service to develop a new liveli-hood. Apparently there's an increasing demand both in the U.S. and Japan for Jeffrey pine cones, herbs, and even broken, moss-covered branches for home decoration. Some former loggers were now beginning to make a living from such activities. When I asked about the pinecones, Milt Mortensen, a one-time logger, told me "The potential's here. . . . We're all hanging in and making it work." On a good day Milt loads his old pickup truck with more than a thousand pinecones that he has gath-ered. . . . "At 24 cents apiece—that's $240—it's not a bad living," he told me. "Doesn't quite match the $40,000 a year a good logger made. . . ."[39]

I wonder if you now have to yield the right of way to pickups haul-ing pine cones. I suppose not.

Jensen's optimism about technology changes being hastened by takeovers is sheer nonsense or wishful thinking. The raiders weren't in the game for the sake of improving our overall standard of living or for funding new bursts of research and development in neglected industries. The transfers of wealth that characterized the '80s were not productive, and in some cases they were destructive. The raiders and their cohorts were speculators in the business of merely rear-ranging assets.

Jensen has another argument favoring takeovers that may sound good on paper, but fails the test of Pacific Lumber. Kuttner para-phrases Jensen:

> Even if a bidder buys a company only to sell off its assets, this is also a social good, because the assets ultimately wind up in the hands of some-one better able to exploit them. . . . [W]hen an acquiring corporation goes deeply into debt in order to buy a target company, leaving the newly com-bined firm with substantial debt that can be three or four times its total equity, this sort of "leveraging up" is also a good thing, because the burden of meeting payments forces executives to work harder.[40]

It also produces more overtime for employees who must cut down trees around the clock in order to finance the debt. But, of course, that is a short-lived benefit, for saplings just don't grow into giant red-woods overnight. They don't make it to maturity in ten or fifteen years either, and that's about all the time left for the lumber indus-try of the region, if its chainsaws continue cutting at the current pace.

So the only real gainers in the takeover game seem to be the stockholders of the target company, the investment bankers and other intermediaries raking off their percentages, and the parachut-ing executives. In the Pacific Lumber case the most notorious of the intermediaries, Michael Milken, also lent an unethical hand.

3. Abstract Greed and the Insider Traders

In April of 1990, Michael Milken, the junk-bond financing wizard of Drexel Burnham Lambert, pleaded guilty to six felony violations of the federal securities laws. He paid $200 million in fines and set up a $400 million fund for investor restitution. He was sentenced to ten years in prison. The scandals and their legal repercussions forced Drexel Burnham out of business. What was wrong with what Milken did?

There were five types of charges against Milken: insider trading, defrauding clients, stock manipulation, stock parking, and creating false and/or misleading corporate records in order to hide tax liabilities and transfer illegal trading profits to Drexel Burnham. Apparently, Milken, while acting as an investment banker or a consultant in merger or takeover actions, gained information on which he acted "to close short positions, develop straddles, or buy stock in advance of the announcement of the planned buyout."[41]

It was alleged that he drove up the price of stock of companies he knew, because he was an intermediary in the deals, to be raider targets. That served to increase the takeover costs, and hence the debt load. All of this was done, of course, without informing his clients.

Stock parking, which seems almost certain to have occurred in the Pacific Lumber deal, violates federal law. The law requires that anyone who holds more than five percent of any class of securities in a company must file a statement indicating the holder's source of funds, purposes in acquiring the stock, and plans vis-à-vis the target corporation. In effect they must file a statement within ten days of the purchase that puts them on record as making a play for the company. Milken pleaded guilty to arranging for his clients to buy and hold stock for raiders so that they would not have to file the documents announcing their intentions to take over the target corporations.

The Pacific Lumber board claimed it was caught by surprise by Maxxam's first offer. If the stock had been parked by Milken in the friendly lots of Ivan Boesky and Boyd Jeffries, it is no wonder the board was blindsided. It is of note that in October of 1985, Jeffries sold Maxxam 439,000 shares of Pacific Lumber at $29.10 per share. The market that day closed at $3.90 higher for Pacific Lumber stock.[42] A few days later the Maxxam tender offer was made to Pacific Lumber's board.

Clearly, what Milken and Drexel Burnham did was illegal. They violated regulations that were well known on Wall Street. But that aside, suppose that what Milken did were legal, would it still have been unethical? A number of theorists have suggested or even argued that it would not. The central issue is what is called insider trading. In effect, that has come to refer to someone trading in the stock of a corporation on the basis of information pertinent to its financial future that he or she has gained through his or her special business relationship with that corporation. The typical ethical attack on insider trading maintains that it is blatantly unfair.

The unfairness arises because the information is not available to all potential traders. The playing field, we are told, is no longer level. This seems to me a downright silly argument against insider trading. The playing field is never level in the stock market. Anyone who pretends it is would do better buying land in the Okefenokee Swamp or bridges over the East River than dabbling in the stock market.

Even if a strict disclosure policy were mandated, the first person to possess the information would have a distinct advantage. Thomas Dunfee has noted that if the rule says that I cannot act on the information until I have disclosed it, it would be impossible to specify an appropriate waiting period after disclosure before I can trade.[43] Suppose I learned the pertinent information three days ago, and the rule is that I must wait at least an hour after disclosure to some appropriate public forum before acting on my information. The rest of the traders will then have an hour to figure out what they will do with the data, while I will have had three days. There just is no way to level that discrepancy short of forbidding me to trade altogether. But then, I shouldn't have to disclose and the markets will be deprived of potentially crucial information that could guide trading and help them maintain financial efficiency.

The fairness argument simply is unpersuasive. It overlooks the way the stock market actually operates and the way potential investors make decisions about their investments. There will never be a world in which everyone who might invest in stock will simultaneously not only acquire the pertinent data, but realize how pertinent it is to whatever potential trading is available to them. The most that fairness can require is that people do not come by the information in ways that use others as means to their own aggrandizement. For example, espionage, torture, terrorism are inappropriate ways of gaining evidence about a corporation. Overhearing two executives talking in a public men's room or in a restaurant is not.

But what of gaining the information while acting as an intermediary, perhaps a consultant, to the corporation? That most likely constitutes a conflict of interest. It surely does if the consultant acts on the information in a way that is detrimental to the interests of his or her corporate employer, while benefiting him or herself. The ethical failing then is one of not meeting one's freely accepted duties. In Milken's case, it was the duty "to act on the clients' behalf and to ensure that the clients' financial objectives were obtained at the lowest cost."[44]

Milken and Drexel Burnham violated the side constraints against using a Rank B-er without consent as a mere means to the satisfaction of their own interests. Had their clients been informed by them of what they were doing, they would not likely have approved. Milken obviously recognized that and didn't inform them. And it is pretty obvious that Milken's actions were not taken to obtain his clients' objectives at the lowest cost possible, because many of them, upon learning of his guilty plea to the criminal charges, filed civil suits against him and Drexel Burnham.

It has been argued that the sort of trading in which Milken was engaged is unethical because, if unchecked, it will destroy the efficiency of the market. As I don't happen to subscribe to the idea that the market is especially efficient in the first place, my temptation is just to ignore this argument. However, it should be noted that its primary premise is that if a market is generally seen to be manipulated, ordinary investors will desert it for a more honest game in which to spend their hard-earned money. The principle surely has some merit.

Suppose we were running a state lottery. We would want as many people as possible to buy tickets, so we would work hard to project an image of fairness. We would want all potential ticket buyers to believe they had an equal chance of winning. If it became known that we were really using the lottery jackpots as a way to redistribute wealth, by rigging the drawings so that those in economically depressed regions of the state won more frequently than well-to-do people, the more affluent would stop playing. Our secret agenda, no matter how laudable its ends might have been, would fail.

Milken's ends were hardly laudable and his means violated the side constraints, so on both counts he acted unethically. I think we would, however, have been acting unethically as well had we rigged the lottery to produce those ends, while leading potential ticket buyers to believe everything was on the up and up. Some of those who attack insider dealings as unethical using the destruction-of-the-market approach, however, seem to feel compelled to find a consequentialist justification for their position. They argue that:

> . . . [a] major flight of capital would have enormous implications for funding the national debt and corporate operations. . . . Several of the major financial disruptions in the United States have been attributed in part to spurious activities. It remains significant that the federal insider trading laws were a response to the stock market crash of 1929 and the subsequent depression of the 1930s.[45]

I am more convinced by the fact that the side constraints are violated, usually in a multitude of ways, by the sorts of dealings in which Milken was engaged. But another lesson comes out of the Pacific Lumber takeover: that the corporate world is incredibly interrelated. The negative effects of stock manipulations on Wall Street might show up years later on the slopes of northern California or in pickup trucks filled with pine cones making their way on old logging roads from Hyampom to Hayfork.

What motivates the raiders and the Milkens? What drives the suit-and-suspenders crowd to the heights of arbitrage and leveraged buy-outs? The standard answer is the love of money, the root of all evil. But that is not the full answer. American businesspeople, especially in the past two decades, have made greed a science as well as a religion. We were told by the business pop heroes of the '80s that "Greed is good." The applause from the business school students was deafening. The speaker was Ivan Boesky, now serving time in a federal prison.

Donald Trump is reported to have said: "I don't do it for the money. I've got enough, much more than I'll ever need. I do it to do it."

Greed, the dictionary tells us, is a rapacious desire for more than one needs or deserves. Greed (or avarice) is one of the seven deadly sins. But the condemnation of greed goes further back than the Christian doctrines and to another part of the world. Lao-tzu (c. 604–c. 531 B.C.) wrote:

> There is no calamity greater than lavish desires.
> There is no greater guilt than discontentment.
> There is no greater disaster than greed.[46]

It is difficult to imagine that people in business, even if they believed that greed was to be encouraged, would boldfacedly proclaim it far and wide. But they did, and thousands joined the choir. The saints of the greed religion included Ivan Boesky, Donald Trump, Boyd Jeffries, Sir James Goldsmith, F. Ross Johnson, and, of course, Michael Milken. They had their field days, but most are now "out of action."

Over and above the traditional condemnations, what's wrong with greed? Before trying to answer that, it would be helpful to know what the greed gospelers were singing about. The answer is simple. It usually is in crusades. The pursuit of personal wealth, colossal amounts of wealth, was supposed to make the corporations of America more efficient and productive. It was the same tune being whistled by the takeover artists. Hardly a surprise. After all, they were, by and large, the same folks.

Money was supposed to be only the way of keeping score. To a large degree that seems true. What really drove the greed gang was the pursuit of power. It was the most exciting game any had ever played, having probably failed to make sports teams in their youth. It had its rules, and it had scorekeepers at the *Wall Street Journal*. The federal government was politically committed to staying on the sidelines, to letting things run their course, so the referees' whistles seldom blew.

Power was the trip. But it wasn't power over, say, the loggers in northern California forests that mattered. It was power over each other. Greed equated with strength, machismo, and should never be satisfied, but must be displayed for the awe it inspired in others. The leveraged buyouts, takeovers, Wall Street shuffles of the eighties, were sporting events. The language, again, mirrored the conception. A company was "put in play." Then the players descended on the field and the contest began. Sometimes, through shrewd maneuvering by people like Milken, companies did not even know they were in play until the tender offers were flung down on the table.

The greed that dominated business in the 1980s was what Robert Solomon calls "abstract greed." He writes:

> In abstract greed it is money, pure wealth, that is wanted, not to obtain anything, . . . but wealth as a goal, given and unquestioned, like "honor" in some other societies and "faith" or "patriotism" in others. It is, to hear us talk, the ultimate good, more important than personal dignity and happiness. Indeed, it *is* our personal dignity and happiness.[47]

It was greed without lust. It was not that the greed gospelers wanted the vast sums of money to buy something they didn't have. What didn't they have? How many private jets does anyone need, can anyone use? After you have five palatial homes in various desirable locations around the world, how many more can you desire? No, there was no desire for things the money could buy, just desire for the wealth in and of itself. It might be said that though they didn't desire any particular set of luxuries, they desired the knowledge that they could buy any luxuries should they ever desire them. Fine, but the greed is still abstract.

As Solomon notes, the greed motive is difficult to comprehend because it is actually rather foreign to natural human desires, such as our need for other people and for self-respect.[48] Abstract greed is supposedly a version of what some economists have claimed is the basic or only human motive, or at least the only one worth thinking about: the profit motive. On these accounts, humans are supposed to be naturally motivated by the desire to obtain money, lots of money.

The idea, as Solomon argues, runs against the grain of our cultural traditions. The Greeks had King Midas in their mythology for a reason, and it wasn't to encourage the desire for money. The Christians not only declared avarice a deadly sin, but the treatment of money as a commodity was also forbidden. Hence the laws against usury. Why? Robert Solomon's answer, and I think a correct one, is that they recognized that the pursuit of money, of profit for its own sake, cuts people off from the quest for more human interests and motives, ones the ancients wanted to ensure: the good of the community, the welfare of other people, even the care of one's own soul (or mental state).

Those virtues have all but died in American culture by the late twentieth century. We have lost the sense of community.

The welfare of others has been assigned to governmental programs whose inefficiency we regularly chastise and the need for which we contemptuously question. "What's the matter with these people, aren't they motivated?" Personal senses of living a meaningful life have been consigned to expensive therapy sessions with this or that psychological guru or a variety of exercise machines. Perhaps if the price is high enough we will feel we got what we wanted and find contentment in the bargain.

Greed is the desire to have more than one deserves or is entitled to have. Acting greedily or realizing one's greedy motives with respect to natural property will violate the Lockean Proviso, discussed above, if one's acquisition of such things, like all the trees in northern California, reduces others to positions beneath the baselines where they were before the acquisition. For Locke, a property can be acquired as long as certain conditions are met:

> As much as any one can make use of to any advantage of life before it spoils, so much he may by his labour fix a property in; whatever is beyond this is more than his share, and belongs to others. . . . I think it is plain that property in that, too, is acquired as the former. As much land as a man tills, plants, improves, cultivates, and can use the product of, so much is his property.[49]

So there is a spoilage or waste condition attached to the Lockean proviso. But Locke removes that condition from money. He says that it doesn't spoil, so it may be hoarded without doing injury to anyone. His view as regards money, however, is clearly wrong. The accumulation of wealth, as the Wall Street greed gospelers understood it, is power: power to do virtually anything one wants, including harming those who must work in the fields and factories, on the slopes, and in the mines.

The extension of the proviso to money is not a difficult step. Locke apparently didn't take it because he was protecting his wealthy friends from the sharp sword of his theory. The issue should not be spoilage, but whether there is "enough and as good left in common for others." That concept, which, with Nozick, I have cashed out in terms of whether others are driven beneath the baseline by the acquisition, will erect a moral block to financial greed, one consistent with the side constraints. The problems of establishing the baselines will remain in the case of money as in the case of so-called natural property, but that should not deter us in theory.

Is some greed acceptable? The answer must be no, simply because greed, by its very definition, stems from one's desire to have more of something than one deserves. The boundaries on deserts, however, can be set rather generously in most cases by the Lockean proviso. One is, therefore, justified in seeking to acquire all that one deserves.

That may or may not make one rich, depending on a number of factors including effort, skill, knowledge, and, of course, luck. Solomon notes that "the purpose of the marketplace [is] not just to test the macho-mettle of its participants but to supply everyone with jobs and inexpensive quality products and services."[50]

The fact that many domestic markets that were once the sole stomping grounds of American corporations fell to foreign corporations during the greed-motivated decade should serve as a reminder that greed at the top is one of the surest and fastest routes to teleopathic corporate decision-making. Greed is extremely myopic. Markets, by and large, are farsighted.

4. Spotted Owls and Loggers: Dominion, History, and Protection

Let's return again to the slopes of northern California and those pickup trucks in the mill towns. More specifically let's look at their bumper stickers: "I LOVE SPOTTED OWL . . . SOUP," "THE ONLY GOOD OWL IS A STUFFED AND MOUNTED OWL," "PROTECT AN ENDANGERED SPECIES: US; KILL THE OWLS," "SAVE A LOGGER—EAT AN OWL."

Crude? Of course. But what is going on? As is surely well known, the federal government and environmentalists have been trying for some years to restrict the cutting of old-growth forests in the northwestern United States. This effort first focused on the trees themselves and then utilized the Endangered Species Act because those groves are the only habitat of the endangered spotted owl. The protection of the birds is counterpoised against loggers' jobs in the minds of many in the lumber business and in its support industries, hence a major portion of the human population in the Pacific Northwest. If the birds are to be protected, the environmentalists tell us, the remaining old-growth stands must not be cut. The loggers will be out of work. That matters have come to this because of the policies of most of the lumber companies and Pacific Lumber's takeover by Maxxam, which forced a drastic increase in its cutting policies, is now so much water over the dam. Jobs undeniably are at stake and so is the future of the spotted owl species. What is more important?

In a recent survey, according to Holmes Rolston III,[51] three-fourths of the adult American population believes that endangered species must be protected, even at the expense of commercial ventures. Obviously, most Americans' jobs are not threatened by the protection of endangered species. But they are in the lumber industry. I certainly don't favor the wanton destruction of species, but in the conflict between owls and loggers, I side with the loggers, and I think that is the ethical thing to do.

Environmentalists have been making a great deal out of the need to widen our concept of the moral world to include all things in nature. To a point, I agree with them. The deep ecology ethics position that focuses on the biosphere offers as a basic principle:

> A thing is right when it tends to preserve the integrity, stability, and beauty of the bioptic community. It is wrong when it tends otherwise.[52]

To environmentalists it follows from that principle that "humans have no right to reduce [the] richness and diversity [of life forms] except to satisfy vital needs."[53]

Rolston, in eloquent prose, offers what he calls "The Diversity Maxim":

> Nature creates lots of niches and then puts evolutionary and genetic tendencies to work filling these with a kaleidoscopic array, as glancing through a butterfly guide will show. It would be a pity needlessly to sacrifice much, if any, of the pageant, especially if we get in return only more good like that of which we already have enough. Variety is a spice in life. That says something about human tastes, but not so as to overlook the natural spices.[54]

What's the argument? Who wouldn't want the world to have as many species as possible? The problem is that this idyllic picture of nature is a far piece from reality. The ecological history of the earth is a record of species going extinct, and others emerging. Sometimes they go out of existence because of the intrusion of other species, not always humans. Sometimes other natural events, such as climatic changes, wipe them out. In some cases, all we have are fossils and no totally satisfactory theory to explain what demolished the species. That's the way things are. Species come and go. Humans have wiped out a fair share. No one will deny that. We will wipe out a lot more before we're through. And we will probably be wiped out, or wipe ourselves out.

Should we feel badly about the fact that we have directly or indirectly caused the extinction of many of the earth's species? Of course we should. Were we justified in doing it? Sometimes. Even using the deep ecologist's principle, we were justified when vital interests were at stake. The problem, of course, is in defining what counts as vital and whose vital interests have priority. Those are the issues that separate many of the environmentalists from the rest of us. It is obvious that the vital interests of the spotted owl are at stake, but, I will argue, so are those of the loggers. Which then has the greater weight?

What basis could there be, other than sentiment, for humans to have an obligation to sacrifice their welfare to save a nonhuman species? The hierarchical structure I developed in Part 1 makes clear that, though we should take the interests of animals (Rank C-ers) into consideration when we decide to act, we may use them to benefit the interests of Rank B-ers. Put simply, the ethical conception I have adopted requires we side with the stickers on the bumpers of the pickup trucks in Scotia, California.

But, it may be maintained that vital human interests are not really at stake. That is, I think, a willful misreading of the situation. The loggers cannot simply toss all they own in the backs of those pickups and drive up the road to another job in another sort of industry. Jobs are not so plentiful, nor, for that matter, are industries for which ex-loggers are suited. The loggers' situation is desperate, and so is that of their families and all of those in support businesses that depend on the mills. If protection of the owls requires shutting down the mills, a number of humans who are today living comfortable lives will be reduced to penury. That is a significant moral fact.

When human lives are threatened by animals, generally we don't think twice about exterminating the lot of the offending species. Suppose the Europeans could have exterminated the entire black rat species in the fourteenth century, thereby checking the spread of the Black Death. Would we have thought they had done something immoral? I doubt it. If spotted owls started behaving like the birds in the Alfred Hitchcock film of the Daphne du Maurier novel, swooping out of the skies and the redwood trees, attacking humans, pecking them to death, we would do everything possible to wipe them out. If spotted owl droppings carried a deadly plague that threatened the human population, we would try to destroy them. Well, there might be those extreme environmentalists who would say that we should just isolate them from us and leave them alone. But that may not be possible, and if it is not, then the humans should prevail. The deep ecologists should grant us that.

Jobs, however, are nearly as vital as lives. They sustain human life and contribute to making it livable, the job of a logger no less than that of a business executive or a philosopher. Why should the human standard of living be sacrificed for the birds?

There are biblical grounds, to which I do not subscribe, that assign total dominion over the earth and its species to humans. In Genesis, Adam and Eve are told:

> Be fruitful, and multiply, and replenish the earth, and subdue it; and have dominion over the fish of the sea and over the fowl of the air, and over every living thing that moveth upon the earth.[55]

"Dominion" is an ambiguous term. It might be read as requiring that humans act as guardians of the animals, or it might mean that we are licensed to use them as we wish to our own benefit, dominate them. The latter reading of the biblical passage, as noted by Peter Singer,[56] is probably to be preferred given the example God provides by causing the flood that kills all manner of living things just to punish humans. Of course, it may be pointed out, God did save the species by having Noah include a male and female of each on the ark. Perhaps that means that we can destroy animals for our own needs up to the point of the extinction of the species. In any event, after the flood God tells Noah:

> (T)he fear of you and the dread of you shall be upon every beast of the earth, and upon every fowl of the air, upon all that moveth upon the earth, and upon all the fishes of the sea; into your hands are they delivered.[57]

To cause fear and dread in the spotted owls because they may lose their favored habitat is, it would seem, not in violation of the divine decree.

This view, as Singer reminds us, was endorsed by the early Christian theologians such as St. Augustine who maintained that those who would refrain from killing animals and destroying plants are afflicted with pagan superstitions.[58] The pagan Greeks, however, weighed in on the domination side of dominion. Aristotle wrote:

> Since nature makes nothing purposeless or in vain, it is undeniably true that she has made all animals for the sake of man.[59]

These examples at least indicate that the animal protection position is not at the core of our culture. No one should have expected it to be there, because the Western conception of civilization is that of creating productive enterprises out of the wilderness, not living off and within the wilderness. We define ourselves as civilized by virtue of our mastery of nature for our own ends, by our ability to channel its forces and make it productive for us, even though it sometimes breaks through the levees we have constructed to restrain it. Human ends and interests are dominant. In large measure, that is what we have always meant by "civilization."

Another sort of argument or appeal has been put forth in support of the animals and the trees. It is one derived from aesthetics, and it is somewhat persuasive. In short, it tells us that we ought not to destroy natural settings and the animals in them because they enrich our lives with natural beauty. If human life were deprived of natural beauty, it would be impoverished.[60]

I cannot disagree. Who could? But there must be limits to the extent we should go to protect natural beauty at the cost of human lives. The principle that we should preserve the great beauty spots of the planet certainly should be endorsed. But it should not be a retroactive principle.

The way humans lead their lives now, the jobs at which they toil, the businesses and communities on which they depend are the result of historical processes. They all have an historical context. Loggers work in northern California because of a long and complicated series of human and natural events that have come down to the present. Those events have given birth to intricate interdependencies of humans and corporate actors and cultures and natural environments. Recall that the reengineering theorists, discussed in Part 2, started from the premise that one should utterly ignore the past and imagine how one would create the company from scratch with today's technologies. That is blatant fantasy when the company has been running for 140 years and a population of humans has become dependent on it. The environmentalists that would terminate logging to save the trees or the spotted owls seem to have the same sort of historical nearsightedness as the reengineering folks. The subculture of the Pacific Northwest logging business is a vital historical aspect of life there. It should not be thrown over to save a few birds.

Invasions of territory are common in nature and adjustments are made. Sometimes that means a species will disappear. Sometimes that means the species will adapt to a new environment. That's how things happen. The Pacific Northwest ecosystem includes a fair number of loggers and a few spotted owls. Humans are part of nature themselves. Perhaps the owls will become extinct, perhaps not. Although I do not pretend to any biological knowledge of spotted owls, I wonder why the owls will not shift their habitat to the new growth forests or to the thousands of acres of protected redwoods in Redwood National Park and Humboldt Redwoods State Park and the numerous preserved areas of southern Oregon. Are spotted owls bound and determined to stay in the danger zones and perish? Surely some can be relocated just up the road in those permanently protected zones. Any attempt to move the birds would seem to be preferable to destroying the livelihoods of the humans.

Having said all of that, however, the arguments of the environmentalists should not be ignored with respect to the establishment of new business or the expansion of existing ones. Rolston says that "running in the black is not enough if this requires running out of the green."[61] We should agree with him, but what principles or imperatives should therefore be applied to the development of new industries? I would recommend five:

1. Corporations creating new industries or expanding existing ones should avoid, wherever possible, perpetrating irreversible changes on the environment. It should, by and large, be possible to return the locale of the corporate enterprise, if it is abandoned for whatever reasons, to its former state, or at least nearly so. Put simply, the business had better be extremely beneficial to the genuine interests of Rank B-ers if it will not be possible to redeem its mistakes in the ecosystem. I'm not convinced that the application of this principle would have blocked logging in northern California's redwood forests in the first

place. Pacific Lumber's traditional methods and policies would not have offended it. Many other industrial operations, especially those in the petrochemical industry certainly would.

2. The number of species should not be artificially lowered without a significant offset of long-term benefits for Rank B-ers. This is a maximization of species principle. In effect, it requires that corporations not impoverish the ecosystem for mere short-term business gains. If a justification is needed, we could side with Rolston who points out that the diversity of species in a natural environment not only enhances its chances of stability, but previously unknown uses may emerge for elements of that environment that may be extremely beneficial to humans in the future.[62]

3. The rarest and the most fragile environments on the planet must be used the least or the lightest for business purposes. As an environment or a species becomes rare, what might be called "the collector's imperative" in preserving it should come into play. Rolston writes: "They are planetary heirlooms that hark back to the wonders of nature, to our broader lineage."[63] They may have some utilitarian benefits as well, but their virtues as places of wonder and memory make them worthy of preservation. This, however, is not to argue that merely being rare or fragile grants, in itself, a special moral status. If it did, then a quick route to arranging the ethical protection of a species would be to kill off or destroy most of its members, thereby making it rare and so worthy of special consideration. It is only to take note of the fact that some things or environments are rare in nature before humans start messing around. They deserve the sort of attention this principle requires.

4. Environmental degradation must not be incurred for the production of relatively unimportant products. Consider the mining of molybdenum ore in Colorado.[64] To mine it efficiently and profitably a corporation has to ravage the mountainsides, mountainsides that are beautiful natural sites, and many of which are suitable for human recreation, such as skiing. What is molybdenum used for? Sporting rifles, electric carving knifes, stuff like that, and also solar energy collectors. Solar energy is usually thought to be a major environmental plus. Perhaps destroying a few mountains to make more solar collectors is a good trade-off. But if the only things made with molybdenum were hunting rifles and electric carving knives, the balance should shift to protecting the natural environment in the mountains. In other words, a principle of proportionality must be a feature of the environmental imperatives.

5. Finally, those aesthetic values, mentioned earlier, should play some role. Natural beauty is not a matter of economics, nor, generally, a matter of utility. It is a matter of taste, and so applying a principle that would forbid alteration of beauty spots for corporate industrial purposes may be difficult and look rather arbitrary in practice, though it sounds good on paper and in political speeches. Is the canyon beautiful enough to invoke the principle? What of this partiular grove of trees? The gentle rolling plains of Nebraska, covered in swaying grass, are beautiful to some people, to others they are abysmal, desolate, ugly. Will we need natural-beauty experts to make decisions for us in

particular instances? Some cases will produce no disagreement, but those spots are already national parks. What of the others, the lands where the beauty may require a more discerning eye? And what of animals? Some are beautiful, almost everyone will agree. Others? Some find aesthetic value in the damnest things! This principle will have to be less specific than the others, and so its force will also be weaker.

In sum, Rank B-ers should accept constraints on their use of the environment with respect to new or extended business ventures. Such enterprises should not be undertaken if their return doesn't merit the environmental upheaval and the potential loss of species they will engender. Hence, environmental impact studies are essential to ensuring compliance. Ideally they should be the voluntary responsibility of corporate actors contemplating new or expanded projects. That a corporation does so would be a clear sign that ethical considerations were given the force they deserve in its CID structure.

ENDNOTES

1. Alan Jay Lerner, "Camelot," from the musical *Camelot*, 1961.
2. John Darrah, *The Real Camelot* (London, 1981) p. 67.
3. J. G. Frazer, *The Golden Bough* (London, 1949) p. 2.
4. See S. Evans, *The High History of the Holy Grail* (London, 1898).
5. Darrah, op. cit. p. 12–17.
6. Darrah, op. cit. p. 54.
7. See John Darrah, *The Real Camelot* (London, 1981) especially part I.
8. A number of writers have endorsed this position. See Donald VanDeVeer and Christine Pierce, *The Environmental Ethics and Policy Book* (Belmont, CA, 1994), especially part IV-A for essays by Scott Monaday, Paul Taylor, Aldo Leopold, and Baird Callicott on the land ethic and environmentalism.
9. D. Kirk Davidson, "Straws in the Wind: The Nature of Corporate Commitment to Environmental Issues", in *The Corporation, Ethics, and the Environment* ed. by W. Michael Hoffman, Robert Frederick, and Edward S. Petry, Jr. (New York, 1990) p. 62.
10. Robert W. Lee, "Conservatives Consider the Crushing Cost of Environmental Extremism," *American Opinion* (October, 1983).
11. Charles Perrow, *Normal Accidents* (New York, 1984).
12. Ibid. p. 4.
13. John Ladd, "Bhopal: An Essay on Moral Responsibility and Civic Virtue," *Journal of Social Philosophy* Vol. XXII, No. 1, (Spring 1991) p. 74.
14. Larry E. Ruff, "The Economic Sense of Pollution," *The Public Interest*, No. 19, (Spring 1970) p. 69–85.
15. Ibid.
16. See Peter Carruthers, *The Animal Issue* (Cambridge, 1992) for a sustained argument in support of the view that animals do not have rights.
17. See Joel Feinberg, "The Rights of Animals and Unborn Generations" and *"Human Duties and Animal Rights,"* in Feinberg's Rights, Justice, and the Bounds of Liberty (Princeton, 1980).

18. Nicholas Rescher, "The Environmental Crisis and the Quality of Life." *Philosophy and Environmental Crisis*, ed. by William T. Blackstone (Athens, GA, 1974) p. 104
19. Michael Walzer, *Obligations* (Cambridge, 1970) chapter I.
20. Ibid. p. 7.
21. For a thorough analysis of Hobbes on the social contract, see Gregory Kavka, *Hobbesian Moral and Political Theory* (Princeton, 1986). Also note, Jean Hampton, *Hobbes and the Social Contract Tradition* (Cambridge, 1986).
22. Brian Barry, "Justice Between Generations," *Law, Morality, and Society*, ed. by P. M. S. Hacker & J. Raz (Oxford, 1977) p. 272–73.
23. Nozick, op. cit. p. 178.
24. Scruton, "Corporate Persons," a paper presented at Trinity University in 1989.
25. Joel Feinberg, "The Rights of Animals and Unborn Generations," op. cit. p. 182.
26. For a good collection of papers on issues of justice and obligations between generations, see Peter Laslett and James Fishkin (eds.) Justice *Between Age Groups and Generations* (New Haven, Conn., 1992).
27. Lisa H. Newton, "The Chainsaws of Greed: The Case of Pacific Lumber," Hoffman, Frederick, and Petry, op. cit. p. 91.
28. Ibid. p. 92–93.
29. Ibid. p. 94.
30. See "Pacific Accepts Maxxam Bid," *New York Times*, October 24, 1985.
31. See "Money Talks," *Wall Street Journal*, November 13, 1985.
32. See Robert Lindsey, "They Cut Redwoods Faster to Cut the Debt Faster," *New York Times*, March 2, 1988.
33. Newton, op. cit. p. 91.
34. Robert Kuttner, "The Truth About Corporate Raiders," *The New Republic* p. 16. (January 20, 1986).
35. Michael Jensen, "Takeovers: Folklore or Science," *Harvard Business Review* (November–December 1984).
36. Ibid.
37. David Yeardon, "California's North Face," *National Geographic* (July 1993) p. 70.
38. Jensen, op. cit.
39. Yearden, op. cit. p. 78.
40. Kuttner, op. cit. p. 16
41. Thomas Dunfee, "Beyond the Law: A Brief Ethical Analysis of Milken's Securities Violations," *Journal of Social Philosophy* Vol. XXII, No. 1 (Spring 1991) p. 137.
42. Newton, op. cit. p. 95.
43. Ibid. p. 139.
44. Ibid. p. 143.
45. Ibid. p. 139.
46. Lao-tzu, *The Way of Lao-tzu*, trans. by Chan Wing-Tsit (Indianapolis, 1963) #46.
47. Robert Solomon, *Entertaining Ideas* (Buffalo, 1992) p. 270.
48. Ibid. p. 271.
49. John Locke, *Two Treatises on Government*, ed. by Thomas Cook (New York, 1947) p. 134–137.
50. Solomon, op. cit. p. 271.
51. Holmes Rolston III, "Just Environmental Business," Regan, op. cit. p. 341.
52. Aldo Leopold, quoted by Peter Singer in Singer, op. cit. p. 280.
53. Ibid. p. 281.
54. Rolston, op. cit. p. 336.
55. *Genesis* 1:24–28.
56. Singer, op. cit. p. 266.
57. *Genesis* 9:1–3.
58. St. Augustine, *The Catholic and Manichean Ways of Life*, trans. by Gallagher and Gallagher (Boston, 1966) p. 102.

59. Aristotle, *Politics* (London, 1916) p. 16.
60. See Holmes Rolston III, op. cit. p. 338–39.
61. Rolston, op. cit. p. 353.
62. Ibid. p. 336–37.
63. Ibid. p. 338.
64. Ibid. p. 338.

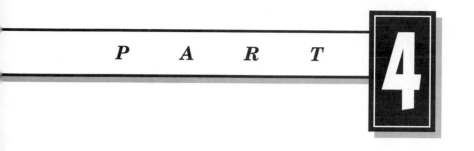

P A R T 4

THE INVADERS AND THE INVADED

1. Doing the Right Thing in Bed-Stuy: Ethical Obligations of Biznez 'n the Hood

In 1989, Spike Lee made a disturbing movie about life on one hot summer day in the Bedford-Stuyvesant district of Brooklyn. The film had the philosophically tantalizing title, *Do the Right Thing*. When released, it generated considerable controversy in political circles, circles that are easily stirred by any piece of popular entertainment that doesn't toe the line of one or the other of the standard persuasions. The movie left matters far too ambiguous to suit either side.

Lee's film culminates with a small riot provoked by the senseless beating to death of an African-American teenager by white police officers. The riot ends with the destruction and burning of a pizza restaurant, Sal's Famous Pizzeria, that has been a focal point of neighborhood life for decades. Its owner and operator, Sal, is an Italian-American who no longer lives in Bed-Stuy, but who refuses to move his pizzeria out to Long Island, despite his family's urging to do so. Sal's sons cannot understand why he would feel any obligation to the old neighborhood now that its ethnic composition has almost completely changed from Italian-American to African-American. He, however, claims that he owes it to the neighborhood to continue to operate there, that the people of the neighborhood depend on him, that most of them have been raised from babies on his pizzas. Sal's is certainly the most popular gathering spot on the block. Almost everyone drops in during the day or orders pizza from it.

Sal, despite his appreciation for the symbiotic relationship between his pizzeria and the people of Bed-Stuy, refuses, in a way that is both obvious and provocative to his clientele, to integrate the decor of his pizzeria to reflect the changed ethnic composition of the neighborhood. On one wall of the restaurant hang framed photographs of Italian-American celebrities. One of the more vocal African-American patrons asks Sal to put "Some pictures of the brothers" on the walls. Why not Malcolm X or Martin Luther King? Even Sal's most bigoted son admits that he is a fan of Michael Jackson and Magic Johnson, though he is unwilling to acknowledge that they are black. To the rising tide of demands from his African-American customers for pictures of their heroes and celebrities rather than Italians they don't even recognize, Sal responds that they should buy their own pizzeria and hang on the walls whatever they want. The pictures on his walls will stay.

But, of course, they don't stay, because the wrath of the neighborhood, sparked by the police brutality, ignites the walls of the pizzeria and the pictures are burned away with Sal's business. The neighborhood is also left without its pizzeria. The lead character, Sal's delivery man, is out of work. But pictures of Malcolm and Martin are tacked to the charred wall.

I watched *Do the Right Thing* with a business law colleague of mine, an African-American, William Burke. Burke was especially intrigued by the issue of the pictures. We discussed whether Sal should have acquiesced and put a few photos of African-American stars on the wall in place of some of those old Italian-Americans, like Frank Sinatra and Joe DiMaggio, he had up there. In retrospect, of course, he would have been prudent to do so. But, as Sal said, it was his restaurant and his wall. Shouldn't it be ethically permissible for him to put whatever he wants on the walls? What would ever lead us to think not?

I've asked a number of people who have seen the film whether Sal did the wrong thing, from an ethical point of view, in not responding to his patrons and changing some of the pictures. The vast majority seem to think that he did. A few were staunch in upholding his property rights, though admitting it wasn't good business savvy. The consensus was that in some difficult to articulate sense, he had an obligation to appreciate the role his pizzeria played in Bed-Stuy community life, and that one way of meeting that obligation would be to not decorate his walls in a fashion that irritated his customers.

The assumption seems to be that an ethical principle here requires a person in business, a corporate actor, to be responsive to the sensibilities of the customers and the concerns of the locale in which the business is conducted. I'd like to explore that notion a bit and then introduce a complication, attributable to Burke, that I find most puzzling.

What does a business owe to its patrons, customers, over and above what is mandated by law? The legal restrictions will take care of sanitary conditions, safe products, and the like. The pizzas from Sal's were terrific. No complaints. So the ethical issue seems to come down to the assumption that businesses have extra-legal obligations that are linked to the fact that they operate in certain locations or serve certain kinds of clientele. At first glance, the principle being cited looks like a broader version of one often used with reference to the plant shutdown cases. (Incidentally, that was the topic of another important film of 1989: the Michael Moore documentary, *Roger & Me*.) I think there are significant differences.

In the plant closedown or relocation cases, the surrounding community usually has a considerable economic stake in the corporation. It generally built and maintained the infrastructure of its neighborhood in a way intended to enhance the productivity and attractiveness of the plant's location. For example, streets may have been created to make access more efficient, and utility lines upgraded. Typically tax abatements were provided, and land acquisitions made easier through the cooperation of various local government offices. Schools were built that largely educated the children of employees, and transportation systems in the region probably reflect the existence of the plant. John Kavanaugh notes:

> By locating and operating a manufacturing plant (or similar job-creating operation) in a community, a company produces certain externalities, affecting both workers and the community, which are pertinent to the relocation issue.[1]

In other words, for numerous reasons, the establishment of almost any business produces unintended side effects, some beneficial, some not, and most of which affect community quality of life more widely than those specifically engaged in the business itself. Most ethicists writing about plant closures follow the lead of Richard DeGeorge[2] who says that these factors external to the economic interests of a corporation should be taken fully into consideration when closings and relocations are contemplated. To do that properly may require compensating newly unemployed workers, city governments, school districts, and such. Environmental damage may need to be repaired. Kavanaugh writes:

> [There is] an obligation, on the part of a company, to give appropriate moral weight to the adverse consequences of its action in moving or discontinuing an operation and to take appropriate action to avoid those consequences even in the face of economic disadvantage.[3]

DeGeorge argues that a corporation morally must minimize the harm to the community its closing or relocation decisions produce.[4] Such obligations should not come as a surprise because they reflect the side constraints against using other Rank B-ers as mere means to the corporate actor's ends.

It seems reasonable to hold that, because community relations are ethically important both at the inception of a business and when that business leaves town or shuts down, that they should be given full ethical force throughout its tenure in the community. I think that is indisputable. Willful disregard for the business's impact on the tax structure, the infrastructure, and community affairs in general would be unconscionable. It would surely violate the side constraints. But how ethically important is disregarding the sensibilities, feelings, pride, dignity of the public in the area where the company operates, while still providing them with the products or services they require or desire? After all, that's what business is about, not the soothing of collective egos and the bolstering of ethnic pride.

Consider some examples that are rather clear-cut. Suppose a business is located in a predominantly Jewish area of a city and its customers are usually Jewish. Would it be wrong to display anti-Semitic symbols on company property? Of course it would. Would it be wrong to pay for advertising the company's product in a newspaper known for its anti-Semitic leanings? Certainly. Would it be wrong to play Wagner over the company's sound system? I think so, regardless of whether or not the company president is a Wagner fan. Why? Because such acts are likely to offend the Jews in the community.

In a business located in a black community, would it be wrong to paint the walls with murals of Little Black Sambo? Yes. Would a Ku Klux Klan motif be ethically improper? Yes. What of hanging photographs of Italian-American celebrities on the walls?

That is not so easy to answer. In all of the other cases, matters were clear because the things in question are readily identified as insulting to certain kinds of people. They are quintessential expressions of hate and have a history of being intimately related to campaigns of intolerance. Wagner, probably for generations hence, is identified with the Nazi period, and many Jewish people report being unable to hear Wagner's music without having images of the Holocaust invade their minds. The *Do the Right Thing* problem, however, is different. Photos of Italian-Americans are not generally thought of as objects of bigotry, hate, and intolerance with respect to any particular ethnic group. There would not seem to be a *prima facie* reason to remove them from an Italian restaurant in a non-Italian neighborhood. Are they, nonetheless, offensive in Bed-Stuy so that it is unethical for Sal to leave them hanging on the wall or at least not augment them with "pictures of the brothers"?

It might be argued that Sal's placement of those photos in an honored place in the pizzeria conveys the implication that those particular Italian-Americans should be admired by his customers. Obviously, Sal put them on the wall because he admires them. To him, they are heroes, people to be looked up to, to emulate.

Some have suggested to me that the photo display was calculated by Sal to offend his African-American customers, because he knew those were not the sort of people with whom they can identify. Holding them up as honored heroes or models might be thought to insinuate that his regular customers are inferior to the Italian-Americans. That is certainly the view taken by the more vociferous of the patrons.

At one point Sal is asked why he won't just put up a couple of photos of African-American celebrities along with his gallery of successful Italian-Americans. He will have no compromise. Only his heroes will grace his wall. Sal, it seems clear from the film, however, had no intention when he put up the photographs of insulting his customers or making them feel bad or inadequate or what have you. He is Italian-American and so are his heroes. Besides, it's a pizzeria! Until that fateful day, no one had even voiced an objection.

So, has Sal gone wrong? I think the answer is yes, and I thought so while watching the film, not knowing that the business would be burned down, in part, because of his stubbornness on this matter. Still, I find it hard to frame what might be called a principle on which a corporate actor might depend when dealing with the sensitivities of its customers. Perhaps that is all that one should say: it is bad business not to listen to one's customers, not to pay heed to changes in the business environment in which one is operating, not to respond to legitimate complaints from those on whom you depend for a living. Fine, but none of those are particularly ethical imperatives. They are prudential business rules. They are good rules of thumb that should help ensure success in the business venture, and because Sal didn't follow them, he lost a business he had nurtured for a lifetime. His loss certainly doesn't give them moral force. To have that we would need to show that not following guidelines, at least in this type of case, violates the side constraints, that Sal was treating his customers as mere means to his own ends.

To make the ethical case fully persuasive would require a number of twists and turns that I think can be left for another occasion. A satisfactory simple answer is forthcoming. The photos represented an affront to the dignity of the African-American patrons. They saw the wall as a Hall of Fame and members of their race as excluded. So they believed, probably correctly, that to Sal, their only value was as customers, consumers of his pizzas. The racist attitudes loudly expressed by his oldest son were easily transferred to Sal via the photos on the wall. At the least, the wall of photos was symbolic of Sal's insensitivity to the changed conditions and the composition of the neighborhood. It was a symbol of success, but it was white success and it had long since migrated to the suburbs leaving the neighborhood a scorching trap to its residents.

Having said that, however, I don't think that Sal can be held morally responsible for the impact on the community the photos on his wall produced, *until* he is apprised of the way they are perceived by his patrons. The pictures were Sal's link to the past, to the Bed-Stuy of his youth, to a different neighborhood, a different world. Hanging on the wall, they allowed him to cope with the radical communal change that the neighborhood had undergone. The pictures had been there, as the pizzeria had been there, through it all. They made Sal's Famous the surviving piece of the old neighborhood. They made it more comfortable for him. After the fire, it's all gone.

My intuition is that Sal, for years ignorant of the way his photos might be interpreted, that they could be offensive to his customers, should be excused for the insult they might have given, but that he has no acceptable moral excuse or justification for not augmenting them as requested after he is rudely informed of the way they are perceived. Sal is ethically obligated to make an appropriate response to the situation or bear the responsibility both for the offense and the consequences. Two things are involved: (1) my judgment that ethics requires Sal to conduct his place of business in a way that is not insulting to his customers and (2) a principle of responsibility that holds that he is accountable for not appropriately responding to a cause of harm that he now knows of, though he originally didn't intend it or perhaps was morally shielded from it by excusable ignorance. Humans and corporate actors, like Sal, should be held accountable for things they never intended, even couldn't have intended. How can that be justified?

Hamlet, to reuse the example in Part 1, intentionally killed the person hiding behind the curtain in his mother's room, but he didn't *intentionally* kill his girlfriend's father, though he was the person hiding behind the curtain. Hamlet had no intention of killing his girlfriend's father or of orphaning her. Yet he did all of that with one stab through that curtain. His intentions with respect to the event seem to have been to (1) kill the king and (2) to kill the person hiding behind the curtains (who he believed to be the king) and, possibly, (3) to frighten his mother. Nonetheless, one way to describe what Hamlet did is to say that in running a saber through a curtain at an unidentified person, he was willing to orphan his girlfriend and kill her father, although he most certainly had no intention of doing so. He was willing to stab his girlfriend's father, if it happened that he, rather than the king, was the person hiding behind the curtain. That's what stabbing blindly into a curtain when you are fairly certain that someone is hiding behind it comes to. The idea that being willing to do something does not entail intending to do it is, of course, firmly embedded in the concept of negligence.

Imagine that my playing in the yard with my Shetland sheepdogs disturbs the neighbors. It gets rather loud sometimes, and I have been known to do it late at night. From past experience, I know that it disturbs them. I don't intend to disturb them, I'm not that kind of person, but surely I'm willing to do so in order to give the dogs and myself some exercise. I hope that tonight I won't bother them. It surely would be odd to say that I intend to disturb my neighbors, when I hope that I won't. No one tries not to carry out their intentions or hopes that they will not. Hence, there should be a distinction with a difference between what one intends to do and what one is only willing to do when one intends to do something else. That distinction, however, is not acknowledged as fundamental when we go about holding people morally responsible for things. Generally we are held accountable for doing the things we were willing to do though we did not intend them, though they had no part in our plans.

Can we describe Sal's behavior as, though not intentionally insulting his customers, nonetheless being willing to do so? I don't think so. Although insulting or offending his patrons was never his intention, the fact that the pictures would do so is probably too remote from his experience to make sense of saying that he was willing to offend them. But all of that stops, the shield melts, when he is informed that the photos are insulting. Then, I think, a rather different principle of responsibility kicks in.

J. L. Austin argued that we can sometimes distinguish someone's doing something deliberately and on purpose from his or her doing it intentionally.[5] I suspect there may be some overlap with cases of willingness, but Austin-type cases are worth at least brief mention. Consider my rushing to get to a basketball game. I'm a big NBA fan. I have great seats for the Spurs and Suns, and only by rushing can I possibly make the tip-off. I hurriedly back my car out of the driveway. Then I stop short, seeing my neighbor's youngest child's favorite doll lying directly in my path. I realize I could get out and move it. But that would cost precious time. It is just too bad, the tickets to the game weren't cheap! I drive over the doll, crushing it, and speed off to the Alamodome.

Following Austin, it seems right to say that I deliberately drove right over the child's doll. But I did not do it intentionally, that is, it was not any part of my intention to destroy the doll. Of course, I didn't do it unintentionally either. It was incidental to my intentions, my plans. But, I am not only causally responsible for destroying the doll, I should be held morally to account for it as well. When my neighbor chastises me, along with some complaining about the dogs the night before at midnight, I will, no doubt, try to lessen my responsibility load by maintaining that the kid should not have left the doll in my drive in the first place. Perhaps he will think me less a monster, but it won't get me off the moral responsibility hook. Had my intentions been to do something laudatory or morally commendable—for example, rushing to the aid of an injured friend—the deliberate driving over the doll would be more than likely forgiven or excused, the slate wiped clean or mostly so. I'd still probably have to buy her a new doll to square accounts. But that only confirms that we can be held morally accountable for what we deliberately but not intentionally do, for otherwise excusing or forgiving would not be sensible.

Doing something deliberately but not intentionally is distinguishable from being willing to do it. After all, to do it deliberately I must have deliberated about it. I may be described as willing to do things that I have hardly thought about. An example is disturbing the neighbors when I play with the Shelties, which I did neither deliberately nor intentionally. Still, none of these cases, I think, quite fits Sal's situation. Although he deliberately and pointedly refuses to put any other photos on the wall, there is more to it than that.

 ## 2. The Principle of Responsive Adjustment and the Pictures on the Wall

In situations in which something untoward occurs that was unintended, unforeseen, not deliberately done, or not willingly done, such as offending customers, it still may be appropriate to hold a person or corporate actor morally responsible for the harm it caused. The cases I have in mind are those that have the further feature that the perpetrator fails to change his or her ways that produced or resulted in the untoward event in the first place. Under such conditions moral responsibility for the earlier event is often reassessed and ascribed to the perpetrator. This is done in full recognition of the fact that when the untoward event occurred it was not intended by the human or corporate actor, nor was it something the human or corporate actor was willing to do. In effect, moral responsibility may be assigned specifically because the perpetrator, subsequent to the event, failed to respond to its occurrence by appropriately modifying the behavior that led to the unwanted or harmful event. I have called this the Principle of Responsive Adjustment or PRA.[6] It is particularly appropriate in cases involving corporations.

PRA captures the idea that after an untoward event has happened, the human person(s) or corporate actor(s) who contributed to its occurrence is (are) expected to adopt certain courses of future action that will prevent repetitions. We have strong "moral expectations" regarding behavioral adjustments that correct character weaknesses, habits, unintentional behavior, and defective decision procedures that have produced untoward events.

PRA, however, is more than an expression of such expectations. It allows that when the ethically appropriate adjustments in behavior are not made, and in the absence of strong evidential support for nonadjustment, the person(s) or corporate actor(s) in question is held responsible for the earlier untoward event in the strongest ethical sense of the term. PRA captures the force of the accusation, "You knew and you didn't change."

PRA does *not* assume that a failure to "mend one's ways" after being confronted with an unhappy outcome of one's actions is strong presumptive evidence that one actually did originally intend that outcome. The matter of intentions with respect to the first occurrence is closed. If it wasn't intentional, nothing after the action could make it intentional when it occurred. PRA expresses the idea that refusing to adjust practices that led to a problem morally associates one, human or corporate actor, with the earlier behavior and so its undesirable outcome. In this respect, PRA captures more of the richness of our ordinary notion of moral responsibility than principles that say that one can only be held responsible for one's intentional actions. It uncovers a principle that explains our practices of reevaluating persons with regard to past events even when attributions of intentionality to those persons with respect to those events are defeated for some reason or other. PRA shows us another powerful reason why the plea that one did not intend to do something is often ineffective in avoiding moral responsibility.

PRA should *not* be read as suggesting that someone's future intentions can affect a past event, that a future intention as manifested in a future course of action could make a past occurence intentional when it was not intentional when it happened. "Backward causation" is not part of PRA. By acting intentionally today, however, a person or a corporate actor can make yesterday's act something for which that person or corporate actor should now bear moral responsibility. A human person's or a corporate actor's past is captured in the scope of that person's or corporate actor's present and future intentions. PRA insists on that.

F. H. Bradley wrote, "In morality the past is real because it is present in the will."[7] PRA provides an expression of this elusive notion. The idea is that ethical considerations require adjustments in behavior that rectify flaws or habits that have actually caused past evils, or that routinizes behavior that has led to worthy results. Put another way, the intention that motivates a lack of responsive corrective action or the continuance of offending behavior affirms or loops back to retrieve the behavior that caused the evil.

Intentions certainly reach forward in time, but they also can have a retrograde or retrieval function by which they illuminate past behavior that was intentional when it occurred. A present intention to do something or to do it in a certain way can draw a previous event into its scope. Humans and corporate actors are not purely prospective, ahistorical, mere abstract centers of action. They have lives, they have pasts that form the context out of which their present intentions emerge.

I'm prepared to concede that Sal never intended to offend his customers with the photos on the wall. Then, on that hot summer day, he was informed by a number of his customers and by his delivery man that they were offended that only Italian-Americans and no African-Americans were represented on the wall. Sal, however, responds to their legitimate concerns only with mockery and steadfastly refuses to change. Had he acquiesced to the demands of his customers and put up pictures of Malcolm and Martin, he would be excused for the earlier offensive behavior. The excuse that he hadn't understood the impact the photos had on his clientele would suffice to shield him. But once he knows and does nothing, indeed defends his gallery, by PRA, he has made the previous offense to his customers and the neighborhood, as well as any future insults the wall occasions, something for which he should be held morally responsible. PRA captures, at least to some extent, the Aristotelian idea that we do not hold people morally responsible for unintentionally "slightly deviating from the course of goodness"[8] as long as they do not subsequently practice behavior that makes such deviations their life-styles.

PRA insists that persons and corporate actors learn from their mistakes, that the pleas of mistake, of accident, of ignorance cannot be repeatedly used to excuse frequent performances of offensive behavior. "It was an accident," "It was inadvertent, a mistake" will exculpate only if corrective measures are taken to ensure nonrepetition. Such excuses can be, and often are, reevaluated after the human's or the corporate actor's actions have been observed subsequent to the event for which the excuses were offered. But it would be wrong to say that in such cases we decide that the human or corporate person must have had the relevant intention in the first instance of the offending behavior.

PRA, applied, may be read as saying that a person or corporate actor should be held morally responsible for a previous event to which that person or corporate actor had unintentionally, even inadvertently, contributed, if the human or the corporate actor subsequently intentionally acts in ways that are likely to cause repetitions of the untoward outcome. A strict set of temporal closures need not apply to PRA. For example, "moral enlightenment" many decades after may demand reevaluation of an event that was not originally thought bad or harmful, and PRA will require moral accountability of the perpetrator if, after enlightenment, no behavioral adjustments were made.

PRA has another intuitively appealing aspect. Suppose that we view all of those things for which a person or a corporate actor can be held morally responsible as exhausting that person's or corporate actor's moral history or life. PRA forces incorporation of originally nonintentional pieces of behavior into a person's or a corporate actor's biography because PRA does not let persons or corporate actors desert their pasts. It demands that current and future actions respond to past deeds. It forces us to think of moral lives or histories as both retrospective and contemporaneous, as cumulative. It does not let humans or corporations completely escape moral responsibility for their accidents, inadvertencies, unintended executive failures, failures to fully appreciate situations, or bad habits by simply proffering excuses.

The PRA countenanced response to such pleas in certain cases will be "Yes, it surely was unintentional, but you have done nothing to change your ways. You have seen what it has produced, and you have not altered your behavior to guard against reoccurrence, to correct it. Hence, you must bear the moral responsibility for the earlier untoward event." The moral integrity of a person's or a corporate actor's life or history depends upon a consistency that is nurtured by PRA.

So Sal should be held morally responsible for the offense he has given his customers. Burke agreed with me about that, but he raised another important issue. He wondered if the majority of people both in and out of the African-American community would agree as well. He ran some surveys that indicated that they did, though many were convinced that all along Sal knew that the photos on the wall were insulting to his clientele, and that was part of his purpose in leaving them there. (That, as argued above, seems to me too harsh on Sal.) The majority, Burke reported, thought that Sal had an ethical obligation to realize who his customers were and to understand what might be insulting to them and to avoid doing or saying such things. He operated a business that was an integral part of the neighborhood and owed that neighborhood a number of things, including respect.

Burke then asked those that agreed that Sal had done the wrong thing with regard to the pictures whether a national franchise pizza dealership like Pizza Hut or Domino's Pizza would have the same obligations to the neighborhood. The startling response was no.

 ## 3. Community, Shame, and Intolerance

The vast majority of those surveyed felt that Sal's Famous should be held to a stricter moral standard vis-à-vis community relations than the national franchise retailers. Why? Apparently, it was felt that the national chains are not really members of the neighborhood. They are outsiders who provide a product, one that is virtually indistinguishable from that provided by any branch of the chain. As outsiders, they do not have the same obligations to participate in and respond to the activities and culture of the neighborhood. Or at least, they are not expected to do so.

I admit to being taken aback by these findings. I've asked the same questions of a variety of audiences and uniformly got similar replies. The national franchise retail stores and fast-food outlets seem to be, in a significant number of people's minds, exempt from the civic and ethical expectations that saddle poor Sal. Suppose a national pizza chain decorated all of their restaurants with framed photographs of Italian-American celebrities. Suppose that after the destruction of Sal's, a franchise were constructed in Bed-Stuy on the very spot previously occupied by Sal's Famous. Wouldn't people think that they should not carry out their usual decor in that restaurant? The answer was no. It would not be objectionable. But it was wrong for Sal to do it?

A number of people have offered me quasi-sociological explanations for these responses. The most popular is that we all expect the national chains to be homogenized, substitutable from one locale to another. The external facades and the internal operations are meant to assure customers of a uniformity of product, service, and price whether one is in San Francisco, San Antonio, Saint Louis, or Scranton. National advertising is more effective because of the similarity of appearance. The same ad that urges you to visit your local McDonald's in Topeka produces a like effect in Tacoma.

All right, the uniformity of the buildings registers in our minds as nonsite-specific. This facade really doesn't belong here, or it belongs here just as much as it belongs anywhere else. It's not a part of the neighborhood, it's a kind of appendage. On the positive side, as viewed by some, these cookie-cutter establishments are a way of breaking down neighborhood distinctions, of bringing us together. Regardless of what other psychological and sociological machinations are grinding away in our minds, however, the ethical issues should remain. Surely we shouldn't allow that just because a retailer is franchised by a national corporate actor, that it does not have to meet the same ethical standards applied to mom and pop operations. Civic ethical duties are civic ethical duties whether the sign over the door was painted by a member of the family or the door is under the "golden arches."

If the Sals of the business world are morally required to respond to the needs and sensitivities of the neighborhoods in which they do business—and they are—then so should the local Kentucky Fried Chicken franchise. That does not mean that the national chains need to remodel their decors to blend with the communities in which they are located. Some communities, however, have insisted that they do so. Usually those are the more affluent burgs that have adopted various types of zoning, building, and sign regulations to sustain their community images. Not long ago I was staying in Sedona, Arizona. It has managed to either keep out chains or restrict them to building their establishments in conformity with the architectural style of the community. Stowe, Vermont, has done something along the same lines; so have towns in Colorado, in which the only golden arches are carved into small wooden signs. Those examples, however, are a far cry from Bedford-Stuyvesant.

In sum, the national franchise retailers have moral obligations to respond to the needs and the interests of the communities in which they are located. That does not necessarily mean deserting their distinctive architectural styles, unless that is clearly inappropriate to the aesthetics and community design of the host neighborhoods. More importantly, they need to be full participants in the affairs of the community, and they need to recognize the sensitivities and concerns of the community and ensure that they do not offend or insult their clientele. To fail to do so would be to violate the side constraints.

These obligations are, in a sense, harder for the national chain franchises to meet than the local mom and pops because managers and franchise owners generally have little room to maneuver between the operational guidelines laid down by the parent corporation. As the survey shows, in most communities there is also a sense that the franchise retailers are intruders, not neighbors. The reluctance to hold them responsible to play the communal roles of the local establishments may be attributable to the outsider image they have, not always deservedly, earned.

National chain retailers, however, have merited some of their widespread reputation for, without invitation, entering a community and driving out the local business establishments. Currently, small towns from Maine to Oregon are engulfed in battles between local merchants and such retailing giants as Wal-Mart. In my community, small, family-run bookstores have been driven out of business by the sudden arrival of a supermarket-size Book Stop (a subsidiary of Barnes and Noble).

The video rental industry is an especially clear case in point. At the advent of the VCR market about a decade ago, most of the tape rental outlets were either the electronics stores that sold the VCRs and television sets or mom-and-pop operations. When it became clear that Americans had fallen for the VCR in a big way and would provide a continuing market for rental films, the giants moved in and the mom-and-pops went belly-up. Blockbuster Video, for example, purchased large buildings, usually in convenient strip malls and filled their shelves with thousands and thousands of titles. They also bought multiple copies of current hits, and because they were so large they could buy in volume, saving a considerable amount of money. The mom-and-pops could maybe afford two copies of a popular film. The Blockbuster store had forty copies. The customers reasoned that it was more likely they would find what they wanted to watch at Blockbuster, and the little shops were deserted.

I don't think there is anything wrong with the way the markets work in these cases. Overpriced, inefficient, understocked local establishments, particularly in businesses like video rental, should have no special protection from the invading national chains. That is not my concern. The ethical issue is one of civic duty, and in that the nationals have generally been allowed to be somewhat lax. The community, of course, must police the corporate actors among them to ensure that the nationals are firmly integrated into the local scene and that the same standards to which they hold the local establishments are impressed on the franchises.

In the video rental business, for example, a community might well be able to ensure by suggestion and other mildly coercive means that a small local company would not rent films that were known to offend its widely agreed upon moral or religious convictions, while the national franchise manager could simply retort that his or her store was following corporate policy in making the offending films available for rental. If the material is an offense or an insult to the community, like the pictures on Sal's wall, it should be removed. The price of doing business in the community, part of the privilege of being a member of the community, is honoring the community's standards and convictions. Many national chains have begun to realize the wisdom of identification with the communities in which they do business and are tailoring their goods and services accordingly.

Having said that, out will march the free-speech brigade with which I have considerable sympathy, arguing that it is never right to control, even by the relatively mild pressure of community rejection or ostracism, the free flow of information and films to anyone who wants to see them. Some communities can be and have been extremely repressive, and opening a few windows to let in some fresh air would probably do them some good. Perhaps, but the broadening of tastes is hardly a good reason to try to destroy the sense of community where it exists, assuming, of course, that the community is not itself organized in such a way as to violate the side constraints. There are generally more effective ways of expanding a community's perspective than, for example, by an all-out assault on full frontal nudity. Besides, some films more than deserve the vocal disapprobation of all communities.

Community is becoming rare in America, and that is not a good thing for many reasons, one that is especially ethical. The homogenized country the advertisers and national chains desire and promote, and have largely succeeded in creating since the 1950s, a country in which communities have been replaced by "the general public," may be a country without a foundation for one of the most powerful moral emotions: shame.

Shame is sometimes confused with guilt, but the two concepts and moral emotions are quite dissimilar, with widely differing ancestries. Guilt is an economic notion. Its roots lie in the concept of debt. Immoral acts, it was probably imagined, unbalance the social and moral ledgers, creating a debt owed by the offender to either the victim or to the society as a whole. Nietzsche, in the *Genealogy of Morals,*[9] wrote that the idea that a criminal deserves punishment because he or she could have acted differently is a late and subtle form of human judgment. The much older idea is that which depends on the notions of creditor and debtor, notions derived from commerce. If he is right, then it makes sense to say that business is the root of moral guilt.

Nietzsche maintained that compensation was prior to punishment in the minds of the ancients and that in debt we find the conceptual origin of guilt. The legal documents from the ancient Middle East tend to support this assessment, though there is considerable room for doubt about whether the notion of compensation predates the concept of community. The conflating of guilt and debt is evidenced in the early sacred literature and carries through subsequent translations. *Debitum* in the Lord's Prayer, for example, was rendered in the Old English as *gylt* and then as *geld*. The concept is still preserved in the expression "paying one's debt to society."

Guilt is a threshold notion.[10] It depends on the establishment of rather specific boundaries and limits to behavior. These are usually defined in rules and laws. Guilt occurs because of a transgression, a trespass of those limits. When the line is crossed, one is guilty, otherwise one is innocent. And when one is guilty, one must pay, literally in the ancient codes, which included no conception of imprisonment. Although crimes may have degrees, guilt does not. You cannot be a little bit guilty, though you can be guilty of a lesser charge.

Guilt is a "minimum level of acceptable behavior maintenance" notion, so guilt-based moralities tend to focus on the minimal requirements for being ethical or moral. Such moralities are usually rule dominated. They are not, in J. O. Urmson's terms, aspirational-level moralities.[11] Guilt avoidance is accomplished simply by following the rules, obeying the laws. Usually that places rather minimal demands or restrictions on one's behavior. Perhaps one of the reasons guilt feelings can be so devastating is that they arise from the knowledge that one has not behaved in even the minimally appropriate ways.

As Herbert Morris has noted,[12] guilt is an audio notion; it is associated with hearing and speaking. The ritual of confession is a product of a guilt morality. Guilty feeling people seem to feel compelled to communicate their misdeeds. They want to be heard, and a significant amount of the language that relates to guilt has audio overtones: recanting, retracting, confessing, repenting, nagging, and so on.

Although Nietzsche claims that guilt was the rudimentary moral concept, shame actually seems to me more primitive. It even has a natural expression where guilt does not. Humans who are ashamed blush. Charles Darwin wrote that blushing is the most human and most peculiar of all of our expressions. Mark Twain commented that "Man is the only animal that blushes. Or needs to."[13] Our word "shame" apparently derives from the Germanic "skem" and "skam," from the Indo-European root kem/kam meaning "to cover, veil, or hide." The "s" prefix makes it reflexive, so it meant "to cover or hide oneself." Shame, rather than involving transgressions, relates to failures, shortcomings, inadequacies, inferiorities, and exposures of weakness. When one is ashamed, the typical response is to conceal or mask oneself. That's because shame depends on sight, or supposed sight, relating to the way one looks to oneself and to the way one wants to be seen by others, and how one thinks one is perceived by others. Shame is therefore more community dependent than guilt. It requires an audience. Gabriele Taylor writes:

> The audience . . . is primarily needed for an explanation of shame: in feeling shame the actor thinks of himself as having become an object of detached observation, and at the core to feel shame is to feel distress at being seen at all. *How* he is seen, whether he thinks of the audience as critical, approving, indifferent, cynical or naive is a distinguishable step and accounts for the different cases of shame.[14]

Experiences of shame are often characterized by a sensation of the loss or slipping away of the identity one has tried to maintain and project to others. To be shamed is to be stripped of one's self-image. If you don't hold yourself in some degree of esteem or associate yourself with some sort of ideal or model identity, however, you can't be shamed. You would be unshameable and so beneath contempt.

A shame-based ethics, because it constantly evaluates the whole person, requires much more of people and corporate actors than does guilt. Suffering shame is an identity crisis and shame anxiety is a feeling of radical isolation. The cure for the shamed is to become a different person. You just can't isolate the actions that brought on the shame and somehow "make them good." To be shamed is to be cast out and restoration requires making yourself worthy to be reaccepted into the community, that is, it typically compels one to perform actions that are considerably more demanding than the ordinary rules of membership require.[15] To be again accepted into the community you must not only make amends, you must demonstrate exemplary virtue. This is a crucial feature of shame that will be of import in dealing with corporate punishment in Part 6.

Shame is a visual rather than an auditory concept.[16] The last thing a person who has been shamed or is ashamed wants to do is talk about it. Confession has little to do with shame. In fact, it may be helpful to think of the contrast between guilt and shame in terms of the contrast between the function of words and pictures. When ashamed, one has a picture of oneself and is rather certain that others have a similar one that is disturbingly different from what one would prefer.

The fear of being uncovered as inadequate in one's community dominates shame-based ethics. Of course, such a fear can lead in two distinct directions. The shameful person may cover up too well, stonewall his or her moral shortcomings, and so a general social failure may be precipitated. On the other hand, as Plato seemed to imagine would more likely happen,[17] the shameful person may be driven by the shame to greater achievements than are necessary to restore social status and esteem. Shame, in that sense, can be a powerful motivator for good.

Shame-based morality has both a private and a public aspect. There is the private sense of inadequacy and the public ostracism, the holding in contempt, the derogation of the shameful for the failure to measure up.

It may be thought that the side constraint ethical position I have adopted and a shame-based morality are, at best, distant cousins. That notion may come from the fact that shame systems generally do not emphasize boundaries, and side constraints, if anything, represent limits. But there is nothing incompatible about holding that the side constraints capture the central doctrine of ethics for the treatment of Rank B-ers and that violations of them could be occasions for shame, as well as guilt, in a community that took them seriously. The primary difference between guilt and shame-based ethical systems is that the guilt systems do not move beyond the letter of the rules, while shame systems can focus on ideal models of behavior to which we should aspire. My view is sparse of rules, but not ethically impoverished. Shame provides the possibilities for considerable richness and depth.

I think we need both types of ethics and should nurture both types of emotions. But the loss of community, and so of an ethical audience, in America, threatens the vitality of shame to motivate ethical decision making and acting by humans and corporations. There is considerable confusion in the country about what should anger us, what should fill us with contempt and unite us behind the ostracism of an offender. Little upsets us enough to get us to band together to stop its occurrence, or we seem unwilling to express our disgust for fear we will be viewed as intolerant. About the only thing on which we seem to agree is the ostracism of adult, child-abusing murderers. In a current case in Texas a man convicted of the rape and murder of a child was paroled, but neighbors in every town in the state to which he was sent to live in a halfway house raised vocal objections. The media trumpeted the story, and he has yet to be relocated. This is interesting for many reasons, but especially because he served the prison time allotted in his sentence, and he was released by the unanimous decision of the parole board. Obviously the community, or what is left of it, disagrees with its legal system. And they should. Nonetheless, we should not forget that more children in Texas annually are raped and murdered by other children than by perverted adults. There have been no community protests when convicted juveniles return to their neighborhoods. I am afraid it is an indication of how shallow our reservoir of disgust has become that it takes something so heinous as an adult's victimization of a child to collectively stir us. As Aristotle would have said, we should be intolerant of many things.

Communities exclude by their very nature. That shouldn't bother us as long as we exclude only for ethical reasons, because of violations of the side constraints. If we are unwilling to exclude for those reasons, we can't complain of the loss of belonging we may be experiencing or the sense that things are out of joint, that somehow the country has gone astray. (I almost said "to the dogs," but decided that would insult my Shelties.)

We should be intolerant of violations of the side constraints whenever and by whomever they occur. That does not mean we should not be forgiving and merciful. But most of us are apparently paralyzed by the worry that if we insist on standards, we will be seen as intolerant or uncharitable, even bigoted. The extreme liberality of individualism has reduced us to choirs of one, each of which seems to have lost his or her voice. Collective community disgust is required, but few will get involved.

A few decades ago people up and down the country expressed revulsion toward the neighbors of Kitty Genovese, in the Kew Gardens district of New York, who watched as she was brutally murdered, not wanting to get involved. Today, it almost seems as if we are not sure we shouldn't be indulgent of murderers. Yet we live in more terror than in previous decades, and, deservedly, we are in terror of our drive-by-shooting children sporting their AK47s and UZIs. And we wonder what happened to community?

Corporate actors are a crucial part, as it happens, of our communities. We need to nurture that conception of community in them, as well as in us, in order to create and sustain the foundations for a more robust corporate ethics and consequently a more livable world for us all.

A bit more about intolerance: The very word connotes mean-spirited, repressive behavior that smacks of totalitarianism. Intolerant people will not abide views that are not consistent with their own. A person once told me he believed deeply in tolerating anything anyone wanted to do. The only thing he was intolerant of, he claimed, was people who were intolerant. Intolerant people will not permit life-styles that are not strictly the ones they themselves have adopted, including, apparently, an intolerant life-style.

We've all known intolerant people. Some of us have been oppressed and harassed by them. In academic circles it seems to be generally assumed that only conservatives practice intolerance. Recent events in the so-called political correctness movement, however, amply demonstrated that liberals can go conservatives a step further when it comes to intolerance of those who do not sing in the same key or even choose to sing a different tune. In many groups where the primary reason for organization in the first place was to fight another group's prejudice or narrow-mindedness, intolerance of those not strictly toeing the party line has become rampant. All political and social movements to some extent are intolerant of those who are not "true believers." In Michael Walzer's terms, each comes to a point where a purge is instituted to homogenize the forces.[18]

If all of this is true of intolerance, why then do I identify it as essential to ethics? Of all things, shouldn't ethics tolerate. . .what? Ethics is not a matter of tolerating what is not ethical. It will certainly be ethical to countenance any and all behavior, no matter how different from one's own, that does not, in and of itself, violate the side constraints against using Rank B-ers as mere means. Not to do so would be itself a violation of the side constraints. But that is the boundary on ethical tolerance. To be ethical and to insist on ethical behavior is not to be indifferent to the way others act. It is to be disgusted at what is disgusting, and to show that disgust and act on it. An ethical community cannot form around a laissez-faire attitude. Much is permissible, but anything does not go. We're not all okay!

4. Disservice and Misinformation in the Service and Information Industries: Alienation and the Computer

A number of writers, in my experience none more persuasively than anthropologist Marvin Harris,[19] have commented on the deterioration of customer service in America in the last two or three decades. I noted in Part 2 that thin-slicing tasks in accord with the Smithian model of industrial efficiency has backfired. Rather than producing desirable outcomes, it has left us in a country, to use Harris' book title, where nothing works. Broken parts or improperly fitted parts, loose wires, missing bolts, carelessly inspected goods, and hazardous assemblies are commonplace. In fact, they are so commonplace that if you buy an American-manufactured product that actually does what it is advertised to do, you are likely to be suspicious that the product wasn't made here after all. It certainly wasn't built on a Monday or a Friday.

Recalls to repair dangerous products are so commonplace that they are seldom reported in the press anymore. Owners simply receive windowed envelopes telling them to bring it in for a "retrofitting." We've not only come to expect it, shoddiness has become a national joke, a joke that, sadly, is on us.

When I was growing up in the '40s and '50s, products made in America were believed to be the best built on earth. And they were. If

something had a "Made in Japan" label, it was automatically catego-
rized as cheap and substandard. It probably had plastic rather than
metal parts. Japanese products, Taiwanese shirts, anything made in
Korea was as lousy as the dreadful monster films they sent us in which
the plots always seemed to involve a beneficent giant lizard protecting
the people of Tokyo from a malevolent giant insect or some other
grotesque creature. Today, American consumers consistently voice a
preference for Japanese-made goods over their domestic counterparts,
and for decades now they have done so when it really counts: when they
go shopping.

There are many explanations for the decline in American products, and I'm not in an especially good position to evaluate one against
the other. My suspicion is that it is a combination of factors, many of
which emanated from the conglomeration of American corporations
that began in earnest in the 1950s and continues today. Corporations
have become so large and engaged in so many utterly different types
of manufacturing and service enterprises that quality control has been
sacrificed to bottom-line considerations. When the same company, with
headquarters in New York, makes canned food products in Michigan
and bicycles in California and television sets in Arizona and lawn-
mowers in Indiana, it's no wonder that what's important isn't how good
each product is, or whether all the screws are in and tightened as it
comes off the line, but what sort of financial numbers are coming in
from which divisions.

The assembly line process, as noted in Part 2, contributes to worker
alienation on the job. It is no wonder that inferior workmanship moves
on down the line, when a worker has little conception of how what he or
she is doing fits into the larger manufacturing picture.[20]

A good friend of mine is the CEO of a gasket manufacturing company in the Midwest. Workers on his line operate powerful presses that
cut the gaskets out of sheets of asbestos material. He told me that the
most difficult problem in running the plant was dealing with the consequences of the boredom of the press operators. Every few minutes a
sheet is slid onto their presses and they bring down the cutting edge
which cuts the gasket to the designed proportions to fit an automobile
engine. The monotony of what would seem to even a marginally intelligent person as virtually meaningless labor has led many of the press
operators to carelessly rest one of their hands on the lower part of the
machine. As the process is routine in the extreme, they then automatically, casually press the start button and slice off their own fingers.
Medical and insurance costs were becoming prohibitive. It was determined that the best way to prevent these shocking accidents, which
when they happened usually would also require a plant shutdown, is to
rig the presses so that they will not run unless both of the operator's
wrists have made contact with what I can only describe as shackles.

When the machine registers that the worker's hands are out of harm's way, it permits the cutting process to begin.

Be that as it may in manufacturing, the American economy is no longer industry-based. We have become what Daniel Bell calls a "post-industrial society."[21] Harris notes:

> [S]ervice-and-information production has in many ways become a more important focus of the U.S. economy than goods production. Since 1947 service-and-information jobs have been expanding almost ten times faster than manufacturing jobs. Today, people-processing and information-processing jobs outnumber goods-producing jobs by at least two to one.[22]

Actually the number is now approaching three to one.

What kind of jobs are these? They generally are low-paying, non-personalizable positions involved in the movement of data or people. We've learned as consumers to expect breakdowns in the goods we buy, but we have also come to expect even worse in the performance of these so-called service jobs. The horror stories abound. Each of us can probably come up with dozens of accounts of bad service, misinformation, utterly disinterested incompetence, stupid mistakes that had far-reaching, unpleasant consequences. Consumers everywhere in America are regularly the victims of the white-collar revolution run amok. Examples?

1. I buy a ticket on an airline and request seat 10b, the bulkhead row in tourist class. My travel agent tells me that everything is confirmed, including the seats. I arrive at the ticket counter at the airport before the flight to pick up my boarding pass. I say to the airline ticket agent, "Here are my tickets, I was told by the travel agency that I'm confirmed for seat 10b." "Oh yes, let me bring it up on the computer. (Delay) Here it is. Yes, today's flight to Denver. Will seat 25d be all right?" "I was told I have 10b." "What's the matter with 25d?" "I requested the bulkhead and was told I have it." "This really is a pain. I don't see what's wrong with 25d." "Are you deaf? Is 10b already taken?" "Already taken?...Yes, that's it." "May I see that confirmed on the computer?" "That's not allowed. Company policy." "I'd like to speak to your supervisor, please." "Well, I suppose we can change it to 10b, but you see you are holding up all of those other people." "10b, please." The agent had, of course, already punched out 25d and the computer had coughed up that boarding pass. That he hadn't listened to my request or even followed through with the original confirmation from the travel agency was of no concern to him at all. Was I being unreasonable in wanting 10b, the bulkhead row? I always prefer it because of my height. There's usually a bit more leg room.
2. My travel agency booked me on flights on the second leg of a trip on an airline that the press had reported was likely to go out of business within a week. The flights were two weeks off. The afternoon the agency delivered my tickets, the airline announced it was bankrupt and that it was suspending all flights immediately and indefinitely.

Time to call the travel agent. "Hello, yes, I received my tickets, but there's rather a big problem here." "Really, my, what have we done?" "You've booked me on flights on an airline that's out of business, and you've billed them to my credit card." "No, we didn't do that." "Didn't do what? I'm looking right at the tickets." "Well, you'll have to bring them in when the manager's here. I've got no idea what to do for you." "Now listen here, I've got to be in Carmel on the 23rd. These tickets, that I've paid a lot of good money for, will get me only to Los Angeles. What am I supposed to do then?" "Maybe the bankrupt airline will make some arrangements." "Do you read the newspapers? They said that people holding tickets for future flights will just have to make alternative arrangements. None of the other lines are honoring their tickets." "Do you want us to make new travel arrangements for you?" "What do you mean?" "Get you on an alternative carrier to the Carmel area? "Yes, of course." "You understand that you will have to pay separately for those tickets, and they will not be at the rate you paid for the other tickets because it will be the Los Angeles to Monterey Peninsula rate." "Wait a minute, are you saying that I have to pay an additional sum to be booked on another flight?" "Yes sir, I think so." "When is your manager going to be there?" "She comes and goes, you'll just have to catch her." "Would you leave her a message to call me?" "Sure, but I can't guarantee she'll do it today." Actually she didn't call me that day or the next, so I went to the agency and found her sitting at her desk. She claimed not to have heard of the problem, but confirmed that I was out of luck on the tickets they'd bought for me on the defunct airline, at least for the short run. She expected that I would eventually get a refund. Did I really have to go to Carmel on that day? I exploded, and after listening to me ranting for a bit, she agreed to purchase the needed tickets for the other carrier and to take the refund that would, possibly someday, come to me. The agency would have to eat the difference, approximately $150. As I left with a new set of tickets, she told me to please take my future business elsewhere. I hadn't been very understanding of the problem from the agency's point of view.

3. My wife tried to pay by check at a local department store. She was told that the check approval system indicated that she was three months in arrears on her payments on a credit card with another department store and that her check would not be approved. She indignantly insisted that her credit was good, but the clerk, before a number of people at the counter, loudly proclaimed that she was on a list of bad credit risks and her checks were not to be honored. She felt that everyone looked at her as if she were a crook. She bristled and asked for the telephone number of the credit approval company that was making such a report. She called the credit agency. They told her that she was in their computer as having failed to make payments on her credit card debt to the other department store. How could that be, she wondered, when she doesn't shop there. It didn't matter, they told her. The computer said . . . .She got the telephone number of the department store that had reported her as delinquent. The person who dealt with her was downright rude. They'd had enough of people who didn't pay

their bills. But she never received any bills from them because she had no account with them. Why had they ruined her credit rating? Through her lawyer, she threatened the department store with legal action for destroying her credit standing and causing her public embarrassment and emotional distress. A supervisor finally acknowledged that some-one in the credit office of his corporation must have made an error. After three days it was determined that an employee in another state had typed in the wrong numbers of a customer's driver's license, trans-posing two of them, and that the data entry person in the headquar-ters of the department store's credit department had compounded the error by typing in the wrong state abbreviation. By sheer happen-stance the numbers and abbreviation corresponded to those on my wife's driver's license. Credit approval in department stores is done by driver's license numbers, so when my wife tried to pay by check at another store it reported that her checks were not to be accepted. The credit check company took another three days to change their data and finally clear my wife's record. All of this hassle, because two people did not take the time to check the numbers and state abbreviations they were processing. The department store where the problem originated finally had a vice president telephone my wife to apologize and to offer her a gift certificate of a substantial amount of money to make some amends for the embarrassment and difficulties they had caused her.

These are only three cases that happened recently. The reports of similar and much worse cases are legion.[23] Whole books have been written cataloging them. Why has American business become afflicted with such an epidemic of misinformation and nonfeasance? Why can't we seem to get anything right anymore? Why do we spend so much time correcting errors? Lots of answers will be offered, ranging from attacks on our education system to the disintegration of the nuclear family. Perhaps all of them have factored into the equation. But I want to focus on one that falls well within the purview of corporations. After all, much of the epidemic has a locus in corporate offices. The misin-formation, rudeness, inefficiency, and disservice relate directly to the way corporations, through their agents, interact with members of the public, their customers. The rampant misuse and abuse of customers is clearly a violation of the side constraints, so corporations have strong ethical reasons to stem the plague. To do that, however, they need to know if and how the corporate environment they have created is responsible for the problem. I want to offer an account of how I think it is, at least, a major culprit. If I am right, then corporate actors will have an ethical obligation to make changes in that environment in order to avoid continuing to violate the side constraints vis-à-vis their customers, and incidentally, their employees.

From almost the beginning of the industrial revolution, a myth has dominated people's thinking about white-collar and blue-collar occupations. The myth is that white-collar work requires more brains, though it is less strenuous, than blue-collar work. Consequently, it has been viewed as more prestigious and thought to command higher salaries than the physical labor jobs.

As the example of my problem with the American Automobile Association shows in Part 2, white-collar jobs today are organized in virtually the same way as blue-collar jobs have been organized for two centuries: on the Smithian model, all that thin-sliced, division-of-labor stuff. Harry Braverman writes:

> [T]he work of the office is analyzed and parcelled out among a great many detail workers, who now lose all comprehension of the process as a whole and the policies which underlie it. The special privilege of the clerk of old, that of being witness to the operation of the enterprise as a whole . . . disappears.[24]

From this observation, it follows, as Harris concludes:

> Simple, dull, routinized, repetitive tasks carried out in offices, schools, or hospitals have the same effect on the psychology of the worker as simple, dull, routinized, repetitive tasks carried out in factories. In both instances the workers become bored, disinterested, and alienated from the product whether it be a manufactured good or a service.[25]

The basic problem is, just as Karl Marx identified it at the dawn of the industrial age,[26] worker alienation. Alienation is dangerous because it produces disinterest and sloppiness. And that can end up harming customers both physically and psychologically. It doesn't matter to the clerk whether I requested seat 10b or not. He couldn't care less that I have reasons for my preference. He happened, in his dull stupor, to have punched out 25d. It was too much trouble to the travel agent to check to see that she had booked me on an airline that was about to cease operations and far too much trouble to do something about it after she'd made the error. The clerk in the department store who mistakenly entered my wife's driver's license number rather than the one she was staring at, couldn't take the trouble to double check. It was not that she was too busy, it was that she wasn't busy enough.

Not long ago I had to rush a member of my family to a hospital emergency room. The woman in front of me at the admitting desk was reduced to screaming and crying by the callousness of the receptionist. She tried to explain that she had brought her son in because he had severed some of his foot in a lawnmower accident. He was bleeding profusely and in shock. She had rushed him to the hospital, not even taking time to grab her purse in which were her wallet and proof that they had insurance. The receptionist just rolled her eyes at her and turned away saying that she could not complete the paper work without the insurance information. The woman was virtually hysterical, the receptionist emotionless. It was a scene from the worst dystopian novels. A passing doctor heard the screams and took the boy and the mother into the operating room. The receptionist turned to me. "Next. Can you believe it, people think we have time to deal with all of their stories. I just follow procedure. That doc's going to get in trouble when my boss gets in. I won't take the rap for this. . . . You better have your insurance information."

More anecdotes, however, are unnecessary. The problem in most corporations is traceable to what makes the service jobs, the people and information processing, so monotonous. The answer is, I'm afraid, the computer technology that dominates our lives, or, more generally, automation. Harris identifies the problem:

> For the majority of secretarial and clerical workers, climbing into cockpits and getting hooked up to a computer has not been very upgrading. On the contrary, the evidence clearly indicates that white-collar automation has already led to an increase in the detailed division of labor, to the elimination of most of the interesting and versatile secretarial positions, and a further downgrading of skills and wages.[27]

The point is that the software that is programmed into the computer on the white-collar worker's desk regulates the worker, supervises the worker, even disciplines the worker. The power of the job, such as it is, resides in the software. In effect, the worker becomes an appendage, even a slave to the software. The ordinary information-processing job of today is infinitely more likely to produce worker boredom and alienation than the factory assembly line bolt-tightener putting together Henry Ford's Model T. The monotony and lassitude of responding to the software is overwhelming. Out of that tedium and an accompanying reduced sense of personal worth emerges the carelessness and callousness that is epidemic in American corporation-consumer relations.

The computer-workstation approach to white-collar work is, I believe, inherently ethically flawed. It reduces the worker to a means, and the worker's pathetic response is to make the customer miserable. Sometimes it happens intentionally, but usually it just happens. Few dare to take out their frustrations and break the tedium by bashing the machine or trashing the software.

The software has made it possible for humans to know less and to think less than ever before while still bringing home a weekly pay check. The standard office design, as Karen Nussbaum describes it, promotes seclusion of the worker and domination by the software.

> There are panels six feet high around all the operators. We're divided into workgroups of 4 to 6 with a supervisor for each workgroup. In many cases we don't see another person all day except for a ten-minute coffee break and lunch time. All we see is the walls around us and sometimes the supervisor. The isolation is terrible.[28]

It isn't hard to understand how the wrong state abbreviation can get entered into the program or how numbers can be frequently transposed. Automation, in particular the software to which the service "professionals" are "shackled," provides little or no motivation for those white-collar personnel in the information-processing industries to treat their corporation's customers with the respect that is due them from an ethical point of view. Just the opposite. It so disassociates the worker from the work, alienates him or her in Marx's terms, that the worker does not feel that he or she is actually doing anything to the customer, that they are even interacting. The software is interacting, the worker's role is purely mechanical, the simpler the better. In effect, the software lowers the worker's competence by not requiring anything much of the worker. It, in Harris' analysis,

> . . . locks them into a set of rigid bureaucratic procedures which eliminate the possibility of adapting to novel or atypical situations. . . .[29]

As the self-esteem of the worker diminishes, so does the quality of the service being rendered. As the bored worker becomes more and more dependent on the software for the very job itself, the customer is victimized by sloppiness, carelessness, lack of interest, and sometimes malevolence engaged in to break the tedium.

Max Born offered the opinion that:

> Should the human race not be extinguished by a nuclear war it will degenerate into a flock of stupid, dumb creatures under the tyranny . . . of machines and electronic computers.[30]

So where are we? I certainly don't think we ought to call a halt to technological progress. But we need to understand, as Langdon Winner has maintained,

> Substantial technical innovations involve a reweaving of the fabric of society . . . building a different infrastructure involves changing relations of power and authority within the spectrum of human affairs touched by the innovation.[31]

Computerization is such a different social infrastructure, and it is not only here to stay, it will expand into areas we haven't yet contemplated. The price in ethical terms requires serious consideration. The computer software that dominates American and international business is the new foundation on which an impersonal, formalized society is being built, a new fabric woven from old threads. As things are going, that will not be a society likely to avoid regular violations of the side constraints against treating Rank B-ers as mere means. What is being, or already has been, lost is the sense of personal responsibility that clerical staff workers of the past typically took for their errors and disservices. No one now needs to feel personally accountable for misinformation and inconvenience. Quite rightly, it's not the human's fault, or, at least, it is not so in the last analysis. I may rant at the ticket clerk or at the travel agent, but neither will lose any sleep over the matter, and, I suppose, they shouldn't.

The matter should be dropped square in the laps of the corporate actors involved in the people- and information-processing businesses. To be ethical, they need to deal on two levels with the problem: with respect to (1) their software-driven employees and (2) their disserved customers. I believe that the former should take priority and that a successful response to the problem at that level will bring with it a significant improvement in the latter part of the problem.

Merely changing the sort of software employed to do the required jobs is no solution. As long as the employee is, in effect, supervised by the software throughout the entire work day, the core problem will remain; tedium, disinterest, estrangement will mount. It would seem therefore that the proper thing to do is to adopt an organizational system not unlike that recommended by the reengineering theorists, Hammer and Champy, discussed in Part 2.

The daily tasks of the data entry workers, the information manipulators need to be expanded. No one should be shackled to the computer screen for virtually the entire work day. A shorter shift at the screens and keyboards would seem to recommend itself. Studies need to be run to determine the optimum time a person can efficiently work under such conditions before the tedium becomes the dominating factor. (I understand that such studies are under way.) Corporations need to relieve the information processors before they reach "the wall." They need to have other tasks, jobs that require them to use their own reasoning abilities and imaginations. In that way they will be expanding their roles and consequently their identification with the corporate actor.

As only a suggestion, perhaps a data entry employee might rotate over different hours of the work day to the customer complaint lines. Complaint department personnel could move to data entry for a like period of time. A more radical suggestion might have ticket agents who primarily check in passengers and assign seats rotate on various hours of their shifts to supervisory roles. They would then have to handle the customers left in the lurch by the sloppiness or carelessness of other agents.

Employees at the service interaction level of the corporation probably will never become its affine agents, but they should have a greater appreciation of the need for accuracy on their entries and a better sense of how one aspect of the business links to others. Perhaps they will also recognize the virtues of taking responsibility themselves for the treatment of customers.

The basic point, however, is that we cannot ethically turn a blind eye to how automation of the people- and information-processing service industries is making our society more formal, less personal, and utterly irresponsible when anything goes awry. We must not, in Winner's words, "sleepwalk our way through the process of changing basic patterns of social . . . relationships."[32]

There is, of course, another solution: total automation, doing away with the need for the human corporate agents all together. How could that be accomplished? I'm hardly in a position to say. Some oil companies, however, Exxon and Mobil in my community, may be showing the way. When I now drive into the Exxon station to fill my car's gas tank, I first run the credit card through a slot that verifies who I am and that I have credit with the company. Then a screen tells me to lift the nozzle and pump the gas. When I'm finished, I return the nozzle to its holder and the machine prints out my credited bill. It works like an automatic teller machine. I no longer go into the station where I used to pay the clerk who figured my bill. In ten years, she never made a mistake on my charges. She was friendly, and we typically exchanged pleasantries. She's not there anymore. No one is there. The station is unattended. She's out of work. Is this something I should be concerned about? My credit bills have been accurate.

Perhaps in the near future almost all service industries will operate similarly, customers sliding identification cards into slots and punching a few keys. Will that be a bad thing? Of course, a problem of dwindling customers might arise due to the fact that so many humans may be out of work, replaced by the machines.

I'm not a futurist, but the predictions of many of them in my lifetime have been far rosier than the realities with which we have had to cope when the new age of this or that technology arrives. I began this book by discussing the invasion of the corporate actors and the new social order they have created, an order in which human persons are freer but less relevant than they ever were in the past. That irrelevancy becomes more and more obvious in the people- and information-processing businesses that now dominate the American corporate scene. As I don't think that a convincing ethical argument can be made for stopping the automation revolution, or even slowing it down, the challenge for corporate ethics must be to identify ways in which human persons can regain and maintain a degree of relevancy consistent with the respect for Rank B-ers that the side constraints require. In the first part of the twenty-first century that may become an overriding issue.

5. Extortion and Bribery: The Honda Story

In most books on business ethics, the topic of bribery is reserved for discussions of the corrupt practices of American corporations in foreign markets. There are certainly ample reasons to think of bribery in terms of corporate agents paying off the government officials in a host country in order to get favorable deals. In some countries, we are told, such payoffs are the way business is done. It doesn't get done unless the bribes and kickbacks have been arranged and paid.[33] But bribery is not limited to foreign countries nor to payoffs to government officeholders. Consider the Tales of Honda here in the U.S.

In the 1970s, Honda rapidly became one of the most desirable car makes in the American market. The Accord and the Civic were huge sellers. Honda had built its reputation on reliability, good gasoline mileage, and stylishness, especially for cars in the moderate price range. Sales on all of the Honda line consistently shot up year after year, to a peak in 1990. Hondas, especially in the late 1970s to the middle 1980s, however, were relatively difficult for dealers to keep in stock, not only because they were so popular, but because the Japanese had agreed to restrain the exporting of their cars in response to pressures exerted politically in this country by the major American automobile makers, Ford, Chrysler, and General Motors, and the United Auto Workers.

The situation was ripe for exploitation, and that is what happened. But who was exploited? As it happens, a wide spectrum of people, many of whom had little or no idea they were being victimized. The pivotal players were the Honda executives in America who were in charge of allotting cars to Honda dealerships in various U.S. sales regions. They had virtually total control over a scarce and highly desired product without which, in sufficient quantities, the Honda dealers could not make a profit. *New York Times* reporter Doron Levin continues the story:

> Tom Roulette opened a Honda dealership in Painesville, Ohio, in 1978, offering what were becoming the hottest cars in America. But more than one Honda Motor Company executive told him, he recalls, that to get all the cars he wanted to sell he would have to "play the game.". . . Mr. Roulette concedes he played the game faithfully, showering Honda executives with gifts—a car, jewelry, a stereo system, barbecue grills, and thousands of dollars in cash. On some Christmases he received a list specifying what executives expected from Santa. One year, he recalls, he sent his wife to buy a watch costing more than $2000 for the wife of a Honda executive.[34]

The system was simple: dealers who wanted to receive the quantity and the types of cars they had ordered had to lavish all sorts of gifts on the executives. The dealers, like Mr. Roulette, doled out to the executives without a complaint, and the Hondas arrived at their lots. They sold the cars, because of demand, even at prices considerably higher than the suggested retail price, and they got rich, very rich. Mr. Roulette made a fortune and bought a second dealership. To keep it stocked, he, of course, had to keep the gifts flowing. In fact, he couldn't have landed his second franchise had he not paid out money, gifts, and other considerations to the Honda regional sales executives. Some Honda dealers were forced to give an executive a percentage, a secret stake, in the dealership in return for the franchise. But, as long as the Hondas were selling like hotcakes, these "inconveniences" hardly made a dent in profits at the dealerships.

The problems started to arise for the executives when dealers began suing each other over car allocations and franchise territorial boundaries of their franchises. Apparently the Honda executives got a bit too greedy in some markets. Accusations of extortion and bribery emerged from the dealers' suits and countersuits, bringing the Justice Department and the FBI into the picture.

> Three senior executives in Honda's United States operations . . . have been accused in court testimony of accepting cash or a secret stake in a dealership. Six of the 10 executives who supervise Honda's regional zones in the United States have resigned in the past year.[35]

How good were things in the Honda dealerships in those days? Mr. Roulette was averaging a $5,000 profit per sale, even on the Honda Preludes. Other Honda dealers were flying around the country in their own Lear jets, enjoying frequent holidays at the luxury vacation spots. The executives who were extorting gifts from the dealers for car allocations and franchises were making corporate salaries in the $50,000 range. The dealers, like Mr. Roulette, were making $2 million to $3 million a year at each of their showroom locations. The $50,000–$75,000 the dealers were spending in gifts to keep the cars coming was a drop in an immense bucket. The buyers were getting their Hondas.

Who was getting hurt? That is the first reaction I've gotten from a number of people to whom I have conveyed the facts. The implication being that no one did, and that therefore nothing should be particularly wrong with the sales executives' game. But a number of people were harmed.

For starters, the buyers were financing the bribes by paying higher prices for the cars, because the dealers were passing on the cost of the gifts as overhead, ordinary business expenditures. The Honda shareholders were also losers.

> Instead of Honda getting the higher wholesale price for its cars or reaping the customer goodwill for not charging a higher price, the executives and the dealers are getting what becomes in effect the higher wholesale price.[36]

Bribery and extortion in the retail sales business is not uncommon. Bribes between the manufacturer's agent and the dealer or salesperson fluctuate with two factors: the demand for the product and the scarcity of the product. Bribes might be expected to flow from the manufacturer's agents, for example the regional distributor or sales manager, to the dealer if there are plenty of units of the product in stock and customer demand is low. The famous 1950s payola scandals involving radio disk jockeys in the music industry were examples of this type of extortion. As in the Honda cases, when the demand is high and the product scarce, the bribes and extortion can be worked the other way around. Retailers have to bribe suppliers to get the products.

Is there any ethical defense for this sort of bribery, admitting, of course, that it is illegal? I think there must be some way for otherwise ordinarily good people to justify these practices, at least to themselves. The people in question were not stupid. They also possessed a modicum of knowledge about the law, especially as it applied to their careers. Surely their imaginations were not so feeble that they could not grasp that they were exposing themselves to federal indictments, FBI investigations, IRS examinations to determine whether they paid taxes on the gifts they received, prison sentences, and criminal fines. These were not master criminals.

The persuasive power of greed could explain a great deal. After all, the extortion schemes at Honda were flourishing during the height of the "greed is good" Reagan era. I'm not, however, satisfied with such an explanation. It is most unlikely that the Honda executives would have mollified themselves with a recitation of the Gospel of Greed. It is more likely that they saw nothing particularly wrong in what they were doing. Perhaps they even thought they were, on balance, doing some good.

Richard DeGeorge explains how such an argument often is formulated from what looks like a utilitarian's point of view, and why such formulations usually improperly or incompletely use the utilitarian's calculus.[37] Generally speaking, the person who tries to justify taking the bribe is short-sighted and tunnel-visioned. He or she fails to notice or recognize serious harms that the practice is perpetrating. When a Honda executive defended the bribery and extortion by maintaining that the good achieved was greater than the harm that might have been caused, he noted that the dealers got more cars, were able to sell more cars, and were able to get richer faster. The executives were able to augment salaries that were puny by comparison to the dealers. Local merchants of luxury items sold more than they might otherwise. Surely all of that offset the fact that buyers, who wanted the Hondas anyway and were willing to pay the higher prices (no one was twisting their arms), did pay somewhat higher prices. The stockholder's losses were marginal because the stock certainly didn't fall during this time. Honda stock might have been worth a bit more than it was, had the wholesale price for the Accords, Civics, and Preludes been as high as the market apparently would bear, but the stock steadily climbed during the period. Whatever harm the stockholders sustained was minimal. Doesn't the good outweigh the bad?

Recall from Part 1, however, that the utilitarian does not argue that an act is right or justified if it produces more good than bad consequences. As Feldman showed, the formulation of the principle that most closely resembles the version defended by John Stuart Mill is that an act is right if, and only if, the person could have done no other act that has a higher utility.[38]

Suppose we restrict the possible actions of the Honda dealers to either paying or not paying the bribes. We already have a pretty good idea of what happens if they pay, but what if they don't pay? Now things must become rather conjectural, but it is reasonable to assume that if a dealer doesn't pay, the executives will not supply his or her car lots with an adequate number of Hondas for the volume of business he or she expects to do. The dealer will then be unable to sell as many cars as he or she would if the bribe had been paid, so the dealer will not be as rich as he or she would be if the cars were available to the salespeople of the dealership. Perhaps some of the sales force will have to be laid off. Buyers craving Hondas in that locale will not get them and will turn to other makes. Honda profits will diminish. The number of luxury goods purchased in the region will drop, so the sellers of those types of goods, such as Rolex watches, will show lower profits.

It looks as if the application of the utilitarian principle will still counsel paying the bribe. I think that will be true so long as each dealer is taken in isolation from other dealers and each must reasonably assume that other dealers competing for the scarce Hondas will pay the bribes. What we have here is in fact a coordination problem among the dealers. In the actual case, apparently that problem has been solved only by lawsuits that are bringing everything into the open. But that is hardly the result of cooperation on the part of the dealers. In fact, they are suing each other.

Coordination might have been accomplished short of legal action, it just wasn't. The dealers in a region probably met on a number of occasions for various business and civic reasons, and they could have discussed the extortion under which they were forced to operate. Out of such discussions could have emerged, but didn't, a resolve on the part of all to resist the extortion. Of course, anyone's refusal to play would still be an individual act, made with a degree of uncertainty about how one's competitors actually will act when they are approached. Success in breaking the extortion ring requires solidarity. Had that happened, none of the dealers would have played the executives' game, and eventually, probably sooner rather than later, the Hondas would have been made available to them on a more equitable basis.

Simply, the executives' game worked because of uncertainty, competitive fear, and lack of coordination between those with similar interests: the dealers.

I do not want to make light of the difficulties the dealers would have, mostly psychological, in providing each other with the sort of assurances that would have enticed each to cooperate and resist the enticements of the extortionist executives. As most automobile dealerships do not have fully functional CID structures—they are one-person or family operations as far as decision making is concerned—they are not cognitively transparent and so will find it more difficult than larger corporations to be reciprocal cooperators. The human element introduces too much uncertainty for most rational persons to risk resisting these extortionist plots. Solo resistance may be the ethical thing to do, but it will most likely lead to the ruin of one's business, while one's competitors' burgeon.

It is fairly easy to understand why the dealers played along: they were making personal fortunes and passing the costs on to their customers; and the courage it would have taken to resist when the cooperation of other dealers could not be assured was more than moralized rationality could support. To play that move would amount to being a sucker or a saint, even reciprocal cooperators prey on them. The dealers' moral failure is in not banding together to resist the extortion, otherwise each is trapped into playing the executives' game by what we could call the "everyone's doing it" argument.

The force of the "everyone's doing it" argument has not often been acknowledged by ethicists or parents. But it is a powerful argument when seen from the point of view of someone locked in such a predicament as the dealers'. It acknowledges that, lacking better evidence of the decision processes of others in the game, if behavioral cues indicate they are unconditional noncooperators, the only rational thing to do is join them. Seeing one's competitors flying their Lear jets for weekends in the Cayman or Virgin Islands is a pretty big hint to the reciprocal cooperator that cooperation from the other dealers is not in the offing. Nonetheless, the side constraints cannot be ignored.

What that means is that if an action by someone or some corporation uses a Rank B-er without consent as a mere means to maximizing that person's or corporate actor's own interests, the action is unethical. In the Honda extortion cases, we have already noted that car buyers and, possibly, stockholders were used in such a manner. But perhaps the Rank B-er most obviously misused in the affair was Honda itself, the corporation. The whole sordid scheme required the corporate setting, the excellent product, and the company's agreement to join with other Japanese automakers in limiting car exports to the United States. In effect, the greatest advantage was taken of the corporation itself. Its product, its image, its management structure were not respected but were used by the unscrupulous sales executives to provide the context for the extortion and bribery.

Rooting out corrupt and possibly illegal practices among its dealers and sales executives has become a paramount concern for Honda's United States management, which is based in Los Angeles. Richard Colliver, recruited from Mazda two months ago to be Honda's senior vice president of sales, said the bribery accusations are credible and "bring shame to the entire company."[39]

[To avoid any misunderstanding with respect to different cultural backgrounds, I should note that all of the Honda sales executives involved in the extortion and bribery game were United States citizens.]

6. Privacy and Health in the Executive Suites

In December, 1992, Steven J. Ross, chairman and co-CEO of Time Warner, died of prostate cancer. Thirteen months earlier the company had released a two-sentence statement to the news media that disclosed the fact that he was ill. In May 1992, Ross himself released a statement saying he was taking a temporary leave of absence. Between May and his death in December, Time Warner "did little to discourage the notion that he was still active in daily corporate decision making."[40]

In April 1993, Theodore Cooper, chairman and CEO of the Upjohn Company, died of bone-marrow cancer. "Mr. Cooper's illness was disclosed on Feb. 1, shortly after he himself found out. The company issued periodic statements about his condition until his death."[41]

Chairman of Brinker International, Norman E. Brinker, suffered a brainstem injury while playing polo on January 21, 1993. Three days later he was replaced as the chief executive officer of the company. He was unconscious for three and a half weeks. Brinker International provided regular reports on his condition to the press.

Matters of health are usually thought of as private concerns, but senior executives of publicly traded corporations are not really private people. Information that a CEO is ill can be most pertinent to the way that investors may consider their investment in the company. Perhaps the investment was made because the stockholder was impressed with the vitality and direction provided by the CEO. Now that person is lying terminally ill or is otherwise incapacitated. Shouldn't the investors be informed? If they are not, aren't they being used; aren't the side constraints being violated?

The Securities and Exchange Commission, recognizing the problem, requires publicly traded companies to disclose "all material information" about the health of their top executives as a duty to their stockholders. However, as Rob Seitz points out, that leaves some rather large loopholes for corporate attorneys to maneuver.[42] Who decides that the illness is material, even if it is terminal? Suppose that during most of the period of the illness, for all intents and purposes, the CEO functions normally?

Serious illness typically, however, will have an effect on the behavior of a decision maker. It seems fair to assume that the performance of the individual will be different from the way it was when the person was healthy. Investors who must depend on outdated information regarding the health of the senior executives might be making expensive risk judgments in the dark. Immediate and full disclosure of any significant change in the health of a CEO would seem to be ethically required, because not doing so violates the side constraints with respect to the stockholders.

There is another, I think more important, reason for requiring immediate and full disclosure of the health of senior officers of all corporations, whether public or private. For corporations to be able to consistently constrain their maximizing actions vis-à-vis other corporations, for them to adopt and sustain reciprocal cooperative policies, they need to maintain a cognitive transparency with respect to their decision making. By "stonewalling" information about the health of major decision makers, they cast an opaque veil around themselves, which makes reasonable predictions as to how they will respond to the choices and actions of others extremely difficult. In the absence of data, others can only rationally assume noncooperation and respond accordingly. That will break down the superstructure of cooperation that the side constraints require of ethical corporate actors.

How could a sudden change in health of senior officers have such an impact? Imagine that Mark Q. is the chairman and CEO of Corporation X. He has built X.'s image and productivity into one of the most respected and profitable competitors in its market. But Mark also suffers from severe depression. At times he can hardly even make a decision about what to have for lunch. The other senior executives know of Mark's condition and they have fairly successfully covered for him when he has been overwhelmed with depression. They have persuaded him to seek professional help and he has done so. Corporation X, however, has managed to keep any information regarding Mark's mental health from the public by making believable excuses when he is unable to carry out duties or attend functions. The therapy recommended by his psychiatrist includes the use of drugs with such side effects as drowsiness, nervousness, nausea, and headaches. Mark, at times, becomes edgy and jumpy and seems then to make hasty decisions. The drug therapy has been only partially successful, and Mark occasionally undergoes severe bouts of depression. He has written at least three suicide notes, found in his wastebasket by his secretary, but he has not attempted to end his life.

It is not difficult to imagine how a CEO's mental illness could radically alter the decision patterns of the corporation. On days when he is depressed or anxious or nervous, Mark may make decisions that are most unlike those he makes when he is feeling fine. It is impossible to accurately predict in what directions his mental state will propel him from day to day or even hour to hour. He might decide that he has little time to live and therefore rush to bring about important changes, whether for good or bad. Or he may feel so depressed into inaction that he just lets things pile up on his desk.

Confronted with Mark Q.'s illness, what should Corporation X do? The answer is probably obvious: Mark needs to be relieved of command and placed in the kind of care that is likely to help him improve. But at many corporations that will not be done because it has the look of mutiny about it. Images come to mind of Fletcher Christian and the sailors of the *Bounty* casting the demented Bligh into a longboat, and later being hung as mutineers. More importantly, many might believe that relieving Mark could have the additional negative result of driving him deeper into depression. Still, that will have to be chanced because a great deal from the point of view of ethics, as well as corporate performance, depends on the person at the top of X's CID structure.

Apart from personal concerns that might make corporations reluctant to relieve an ill CEO of command or reveal the state of his or her health to the public, the fact is that a surprising number of corporations have made no plans for a succession in the case of such illness.

> Many large public corporations have no specific standing policies to govern when and how much information they release in such cases. Many also have no plans in place that designate who will take over for the stricken executive. A survey of the top 50 of the nation's *Fortune* 500 companies found many reluctant even to discuss the topic . . . . Only five had policies for releasing health information. . . . Seventeen reported having succession plans in place, but even those were typically not tied to illness or death.[43]

Ethical considerations require that corporations develop succession policies for their senior executives when, for reasons of health, they are no longer able to function efficiently and dependably. They also must adopt full disclosure policies regarding the health of their senior executives. Reports on changes in the health of those executives should be widely distributed and they should be made without delay after the illness has been diagnosed. A lack of privacy with respect to such matters is a price corporate senior executives will have to pay.

But that does raise a touchy issue, one that has been discussed with respect to people in public service: where is the line to be drawn between one's public and one's private lives? I recently participated with academics from various disciplines in discussing that issue. To my surprise, the vast majority believed that virtually any sort of activity in which a public official was engaged might be job related or relevant and that it was impossible to draw any solid lines around what should be protected as private. It was pointed out that extramarital affairs were indications of character as well as possible bases for blackmail. Health, they maintained, was always pertinent. Sexual orientation, current or former drug use, you name it, were all thought fair game for public consumption. Only the elected public official among us held out for some realm of privacy to which his constituents had no rightful business. When asked to specify what would fall in that area, however, he admitted that in certain circumstances anything he now thought was purely a private matter might rightfully be a genuine concern of the voters. With evident exasperation, he said what so many political pundits have been saying for the past three decades: if the private totally collapses into the public, it will be extremely difficult to get qualified people to run for office. That is probably right, though I personally doubt we'd notice the difference.

Corporate executives surely are not public officials, at least not in the way that those working in government positions are. An old argument, which I'll mention again in Part 6, maintains that the Roman legal tradition supports the idea that corporations are actually organs of the state because they, in theory at least, require public permission and recognition to operate. They are chartered in the public interest, and so corporate managers are ultimately accountable to the state and so to the public.

From the legal point of view, there may be little reason to endorse such a conception. But from the ethics point of view, because corporations are now the dominant social entities and because we live in the corporate society, it is essential that corporations be as epistemologically transparent to each other as possible. Any changes in the lives of top managers that might alter the dependability of information about how a corporation makes decisions is essential to sustaining the conditions that allow other corporate actors to rationally constrain their maximizing actions.

7. Advertising: Deceptions and Ornamentations

Samm Sinclair Baker[44] attributes to Mark Twain one of the few accounts of honest advertising on record. (That the story is attributed to Twain is itself a reason for suspicion on two counts: in the first place that the story is true and in the second that Twain actually said or wrote it. But that is of little consequence in the present context.) The story goes that a man in Hannibal, Missouri, was reading the local paper while sitting in a chair on the hotel porch. He happened to notice a patent medicine ad with the caption "Cut this out, It may save your life." Impressed, he cut out the ad and continued to read the paper.

Through the hole on the page, however, he caught sight of his worst enemy approaching him with a knife. He threw down the paper and surprised the assassin, disarmed him, and packed him off to the sheriff.

Discussions of advertising typically focus on the gross deception cases such as the infamous Campbell's Soup example. (The advertisers of Campbell's Soup did not think their vegetable soup looked thick enough on television, and so they added marbles to the bowl to create the desired appearance.) It is so patently obvious that such tactics are unethical that little need be said about them. Others dwell on the conspicuous poor taste exhibited by advertisements for everything from undergarments to fast-food restaurants. But, as DeGeorge says, "poor taste is not immoral."[45] In fact, some advertisers make their ads irritating and lacking in aesthetic merit on purpose. For what purpose? For the purpose of getting the consumer's attention. It seems to be the case that consumers are just as likely to remember a product advertised in a loud, obnoxious, nonartistic way, as one with high aesthetic values. Being distinctive is what counts, not being a work of art. The crucial goal is to register in the consciousness of the consumer, even if the way the consumer remembers the product is associated with something vaguely aggravating.

Commercial television is undoubtedly the most productive medium for advertising yet invented. The combination of moving pictures, music, and narration or dialogue is incredibly effective. The British director, former comedian, medical doctor, and otherwise genius, Jonathan Miller, once told me that to appreciate the power of television, I should study thirty-second commercials. The one to which he specifically referred me was for Isuzu cars. In thirty seconds we see a father, about to leave on a business trip, tell his family that no one is to drive his new Isuzu in his absence. We then see about ten seconds of the car being driven up hill and down dale in a carefree manner to a rock song. Cut to the man returning home and confronting the family. "Someone's been driving my Isuzu." (The obvious association with the "Goldilocks and the Three Bears" motif might be incidental, but I wouldn't bet on it.) All the members of the family deny driving the car, but the scene concludes with a close up of the grandmother, gently rocking in her chair, humming the same tune we heard when the car was being wildly driven across the countryside. The commercial concludes with a graphic that provides the suggested retail price, and a voice says, "See your Isuzu dealer."

In those thirty seconds we are given a little family vignette; we see the handling ability and the durability of the Isuzu; we learn that even the elderly can handle this sporty car on winding country roads with fast, sharp turns and other hazards and have a great deal of fun doing so; we learn of the car's price range; and we're encouraged to go to the nearest dealer and buy one. That's an enormous amount of absorbed data for so little time. (Imagine what would happen to American education if academics ever learned how to use the medium as well as the advertisers!) The fact is that television advertising is efficient, both in the way it uses time and in the way it produces the outcomes the manufacturers desire. Some of it is also deceptive in a way that may be unethical.

There is much talk these days about the need for truth in advertising. Advertising, however, will be true if it contains true statements and false if it contains statements that are not true. Only statements or propositions are bearers of truth and falsity. The use of false statements in advertising surely must be discouraged, but false statements, in and of themselves, do not make an advertisement unethical. The attempt to deceive is what makes it immoral, and that can be done without using any false statements.

DeGeorge offers this example:

> Suppose that I believe there are four pints in a quart and a friend who is baking a cake asks me how many pints are in a quart. . . . I want the cake to fail so that my friend will not spend any more of our time making cakes. So, intending to give false information, I say, "There are two pints in a quart." Morally speaking, I am guilty of telling a lie, even though, by accident, what I said was a true statement. It is a lie because I thought that what I was saying was false and I said it with the intent to deceive and the expectation that what I said would be believed.[46]

DeGeorge may be playing a bit fast and loose with the term "lie." Most people would probably say that what he tells his friend, that there are two pints in a quart, because it is true cannot be a lie, regardless of what he believes. But, it should be noted in his defense that DeGeorge says that the intent to deceive with the expectation that one will be believed is *morally speaking* lying. Those are the factors that make it wrong, and his accidental truth-telling does not improve its moral standing. He intended to lie, but other events involving his mental states—those concerning how he came to believe that there are four pints in a quart—defeated his intention.

Intentional deception is unethical because it is a coercive invasion of a person's moral space. Sissela Bok writes:

> Deceit and violence—these are the two forms of deliberate assault on human beings. Both can coerce people into acting against their will. Most harm that can befall victims through violence can come to them also through deceit. But deceit controls more subtly, for it works on belief as well as action.[47]

The point is that though lying typically involves the use of false statements, making false statements in itself isn't lying. Lying requires the intent of the speaker to deceive, and that intent is usually accompanied by the belief that the target of the deception will be taken in by it. The liar or deceiver must believe that the statements he or she is making, believing them to be false, will mislead those to whom they are uttered. Some uttered false statements will not mislead anyone, because they are obviously metaphorical or an expression of hyperbole that almost everyone understands not to be literally true. To use a well-worn example in both discussions of advertising and in the advertising copy itself, when Exxon tells us that its gasoline will put a tiger in our tanks, no one thinks they mean that a giant striped cat is being pumped into our cars. Not even the fancy new production techniques that show the moving car filled with Exxon gas metamorphosing into a surging tiger on the hunt make it more believable. We all know it's a figurative use of language and pictures. The point Exxon is trying to get across to us is that their gasoline will give our cars the energy of a springing tiger. The tiger is supposed to symbolically stand in for the product when we notice the arrow is approaching empty and we're deciding on what gasoline to buy. There isn't anything particularly memorable about the way gasoline looks. It's just a liquid with a somewhat unpleasant odor, and it looks and smells about the same from one brand to the next.

Some critics of contemporary advertising seem to be under the influence of the classical free market theories, such as that of Adam Smith, in which advertising is supposed to have only an informational role to play. Free markets, according to the standard theories, are supposed to efficiently allocate resources in conditions of pure competition. Included in those conditions, at least ideally, is that consumers are to have perfect knowledge of the prices and the features of the products on the market. Alan Goldman explains:

> Given such conditions, the market, through its price mechanisms, guides profit-seeking producers to allocate economic resources in ways that optimize the aggregate satisfaction of demand . . . . This process is dynamic and progressive. At the same time as optimal efficiency is achieved in allocating resources so as to satisfy particular wants at particular times, competition generates progress through improvement of productive techniques and processes. . . . Thus the free market is theoretically efficient over time. It guarantees not only the most efficient use of resources in the present, but the production of more and more goods and services in the future.[48]

That is, of course, an idealized version of what is supposed to happen, and there are any number of reasons to believe it never will (or that it ever should) model reality in the market. Within the free-market model, advertising should play only a limited role; it is restricted to the role of the consumer's truthful informer. For the free market to work as advertised, the consumers must be fully informed as to prices, quality, and availability of products.

The critics note that if anything seems true of advertising in the 1990s, it is that it typically does not provide much data on two of those fronts and it may do a rather inadequate job on pricing. Most of the ads on television, for example, do not mention price. Those that do, such as the notorious used-car sales and electronics warehouse operations (both typically fronted by loudmouthed hawkers pacing around lots, show-rooms, and display centers), state prices that are negotiable or that, the would-be buyer learns, may involve all manner of hidden gimmicks.

Availability is not always clear either. The store or the lot often seems to have just sold the last one at that special advertised price. The idea of providing quality information seems to have caught the fancy of the advertisers, but they seem to think it is important to invent ways to display the better points of their products in silly contests against the competition or in outrageous stunts that no rational person would regard as a particularly good reason to buy the product. For example, how many people would think they had been provided with important information about the station wagon they are considering buying by watching it bungee jump off a bridge into a gorge? I suppose it is enter-taining—the first time one sees it—but does anyone think they would play the commercial if the cord had broken or the axle had ripped off? The free market model assumes that corporations in the manufactur-ing and service industries are satisfying the preexisting wants and needs of their consumers. The Jones family is hungry, so take them to McDonald's or Wendy's or Kentucky Fried Chicken or Pizza Hut. Father Jones needs a razor to shave his beard, so offer him a Gillette, a Remington, a Norelco, a Schick. Mother Jones wants hair dye to color her hair, so there's L'Oreal or Clairol. That works for some products and services, but advertising other products and services, especially new ones, seems specifically designed to create a perceived need in con-sumers for things they've never heard of before. The personal and lap-top computers and the cellular phone may well be fair examples. Furthermore, advertising can attempt to create demand for the prod-ucts for which there is a supply regardless of preexisting needs. Also, it is unclear how far back the preexisting desire or need is to go. We cer-tainly have a need to eat, but does that mean that all food products and services are merely responding to that need? Or have many of them, through their advertising campaigns, created needs or desires in us to have more variety in our menus.

Successful advertising often results in brand loyalty, and some free market critics claim that makes entry into the market by new com-petitors a difficult task.[49] One breakfast cereal might be virtually indis-tinguishable from another, but loyal consumers will argue until the cows come home that there are important, perceivable differences between brands X and Y, and will stick with X even though it is higher priced. A friend makes such a claim about the difference between two brands of bottled water, though most people, including him, cannot detect a difference by taste tests. He persists in buying the more expensive brand because he has been persuaded of the difference by its advertising.

By and large, the free-market model theorists, simply, have gotten the purposes of advertising wrong. Advertising is not primarily intended to be informative, other than to apprise the viewers and readers of the product's existence. Corporations in both the manufacturing and service industries advertise to persuade, "to engrave an image of their products in our subconscious."[50] It would be a serious mistake to think that advertising's purpose should be to convey truthful information about products and then leave the informed consumers alone to decide what to buy.

An advertiser can try two ways in which to persuade someone to do something. One, Goldman identifies as rational; the other, nonrational.[51] Rational persuasion might take one of two approaches. The first type follows the Smith model. The advertiser makes assumptions about the preexisting desires of the potential consumers and then pitches the advertisement to inform them that the product has those features that will gratify their desires. In the second type, the advertiser tries to show the potential consumer that he or she should have certain desires and that the purchase of the product or service will be the means to achieving the objects of those desires. The second type of rational persuasion, because it first tries to create the desire in the consumer, is not, strictly speaking, in accord with the free market model. What makes it rational, however, is that the advertiser assembles reasons why the consumer should have the desire to obtain the product, and there is an implicit understanding that the advertiser expects the consumer to consider those reasons and decide in favor of purchasing the product.

The majority of advertisements, however, are of neither of these types. Instead, they are attempts to, as Goldman has noted,

> . . . create an association in the consumer's mind between its product and some image that expresses a subconscious wish or desire, or, perhaps more sinister, between the absence or lack of the product and an image expressing some subconscious fear or anxiety. The consumer is then to choose the product as a way of fulfilling his wish or avoiding the object of his anxiety, but without realizing this as his motive.[52]

On the current scene, perhaps the most successful nonrational persuasive advertising is used to sell various brands of beer. Consider three products of the Adolph Coors Company: Coors Beer, Coors Light, and Keystone. The advertising approach for all three is virtually identical. A bit of background first: the Coors Company is located in the foothills of the Rocky Mountains in Golden, Colorado. For decades they brewed Coors Beer, which they marketed in the mountain states, in the Southwest, and in sections of the Far West. The beer, as often happens with regional products of its sort, established a reputation as a dependably good beer that used fresh, clear Rocky Mountain spring water and the finest of ingredients. A cult following developed with respect to it in parts of the country where it was not marketed. A 1977 box office smash film, *Smokey and the Bandit*, used as its plot, such as there was, the bootlegging of Coors Beer to Georgia. Coors, therefore, had widespread brand identification and an excellent reputation well before it went national in the 1980s.

Advertising beer in America presents some intriguing problems for manufacturers. In the first place, strict rules control showing product consumption in an advertisement. Actors in television commercials, where the major portion of the advertising budget is spent, must not be seen to drink the beer. The beer can be shown being poured into a glass, and later the glass can be shown empty. The visuals may imply that consumption is occurring, but the beer must not be drunk. That means that the advertiser cannot show the satisfied face of the drinker in the process of consumption. So what can the advertiser do?

The law certainly doesn't restrict the advertiser from showing what the product does to consumers after it has been used. But the beer companies have no interest in exhibiting drunken teenagers smashing up cars and themselves, or "beer-bellied" couch potatoes, or people running off to relieve themselves, not always in places designated for such purposes. Coors has, in fact, joined other beer companies in producing some commercials that warn of the dangers of overuse of their products. The "It's the Right Beer Now" series for Coors Light, for example, occasionally shows someone about to drive a car and the song or narration shifts to "But not now." Other companies sponsor designated driver ads. Nonetheless, no beer company is going to spend a major portion of its advertising budget telling people not to drink its product.

Informing the consumer that Coors' products are made with clear Rocky Mountain water (with a raging mountain stream and snow-capped mountains in the background) and the like has been used in a few spots. These assume a preexisting desire for beer and take the rational, informative approach. But by far most Coors commercials and those of the other beer companies use nonrational persuasion to build a connection in the consumer's mind between the products and an image or life-style that the consumer should find irresistible, even if the closest he or she can hope to get to it is just watching the commercial. The majority of Coors advertising focuses on the romping of perfectly proportioned people in the 20–25 age group. The product is identified not only with the beautiful folks, typically dressed in revealing bathing suits, but with lush, usually tropical, settings where they frolic. Seventy-five percent of each commercial is occupied with the cavorting. The beer shows up in cans in coolers or in the hands of the merrymakers, though, of course, they are never seen drinking it. The message is clear to even the most dull-brained TV addict: drink Coors Light and you will look like this and enjoy a life of bouncing around beaches with gorgeous people. Coors also knows that the majority of beer drinkers are males, so most of the scantily clad revelers in the commercials are beautiful women. Drink this beer and you will be surrounded with such women. But a similar message might be picked up by female beer drinkers. You can drink Coors Light and retain your figure and spend your days displaying it among attractive people in such great locales.

When bars are used as the setting for the commercials, as in the Silver Bullet series, again the people are all relatively young, vibrant, happy, and the women are typically dressed in slinky outfits intended to show off their flawless bodies. You never see some forty- or fifty-something guy who is overweight and morose "crying in his beer." The beer is advertised to be associated with good times. It is never pictured as a companion in bad times.

Keystone Beer was introduced by Coors with the "Wouldn't that be Great?" campaign. The motif was a male (or males) pictured in a mundane, work-a-day situation. Then the narrator intones, "Wouldn't it be great if. . . ." The first step in the fantasy progression is usually that the oppressed male turns the tables on his boss by refusing to do an onerous task. Then he is magically transported to some exquisite vacation spot where—surprise—a bevy of carefree, bikini-clad women or a world-famous model caresses him. In some episodes, the model turns out to have both the carpentry skills and the burning desire to build a home for the Keystone drinker right on the beach. And, of course, she has plenty of Keystone Beer to offer him. "Wouldn't that be great!" the narrator pronounces.

Why did Coors adopt the nonrational, indeed the explicitly fantasy, approach to selling its products? The bulk of their ads provide little or no hard information about their products, so the consumer is no more knowledgeable about their beers after watching the ads than before. The consumer then is not better off with regard to making an informed free choice in the market. But, it should be pointed out, the market in which Coors operates is one in which all the competitors are more or less functionally equivalent and standardized. Beer connoisseurs surely will be able to spot the differences between a Coors and a Budweiser and a Lone Star, but most of the rest of us, when we want a beer, will drink whatever beer is available. We won't parachute out of an airplane seeking another jetliner that is serving our preferred brand regardless of its destination, as in a recent commercial.

Beer, per se, also serves no vital human need. Any number of other drinks can slake a thirst. So advertising tries to create an image of indispensability and distinctiveness about the product. The product must be associated with highly desired human ends. For beer, those are wrapped around the concept of happiness. The advertiser tries to make the consumer believe that true or complete happiness cannot be accomplished unless one is having a beer, not any beer, but this particular beer. That beer therefore becomes a symbol for happiness in the mind of the consumer who cannot hope to have a glamour model hanging on him while meandering down a picture-perfect beach with the sun setting in a warm orange glow behind them. All of the fantasy is transferred to the liquid in the can, because that's all the consumer can get, but in some sense it will be enough because even the happiness of the guy on the beach is incomplete without it.

Goldman, among others, has pointed out that the nonrational persuasion method favored by beer producers might allow the advertiser an unfair advantage over the consumer:

> The persuasion is more like a command of a superior to an inferior, in some ways perhaps more coercive than a command that one can consciously refuse to obey. Here one cannot refuse to be persuaded or influenced, for the target of persuasion is not aware of being so influenced. In this respect subconscious persuasion appears . . . to violate . . . the imperative to treat other persons as equals and to respect their rationality and freedom of choice.[53]

This sort of condemnation of advertisers seems a bit too harsh. We should object to the blatant use of sexual imagery and the treatment of women as objects of male fantasies in the commercials. We might complain about the failure to emphasize the bad consequences of drinking beer. But it seems unfair to criticize Coors and the other beer companies as acting unethically by, in effect, violating the side constraints with respect to their consumers. Nonrational persuasion, in and of itself, is not a violation of the side constraints. If it were, then the emotional appeals we commonly make to each other should also be condemned. In fact, a world in which all persuasion had to be to conscious rational processes, using nothing but factual data, would be a rather sterile world, one without music, art, poetry, possibly even love. Coors and the other beer advertisers add a bit of gusto to our lives, even if we don't drink their products.

Coors is not using the consumers as mere means by trying to entice them to associate the Coors products with happiness. The matter is just too trivial for that, though not of course to Coors and the other breweries. The choice of a brand of beer hardly has monumental ethical consequences. Of course, if the nonrational persuasion were used to determine or sway choices in less trivial matters, it might well be unethical, a clear violation of the side constraints. For example, the transfer of the beer advertising techniques to political campaigns could have a chilling effect on the democratic process. Perhaps it already has.

Before leaving Coors, however, there remains that matter of the use of women in the advertising. Coors, of course, is not alone in this. Old Milwaukee, with "It doesn't get any better than this," brought us the Swedish Bikini Team. Budweiser and Miller have frequently used women as mere sex objects, as for example, when a writhing woman in a tight red dress emerges from a dry well when a beer cap is popped. And here in Texas we had the Lone Star jingle that included the line, "Hard work, soft women, and Lone Star Beer." Many commentators, and not just feminists, have objected to the display of women in these and other ads as degrading and therefore unethical. As I mentioned in Part 1, the retort that the actresses and models used in the commercials are well paid and fully cognizant of what they are being paid to do is inadequate because it does not consider the fact that they may be products of an immoral cultural attitude toward women. The use to which they are put in the commercials continues to propagate that attitude.

The advertisers do not camouflage the fact that they are using the women simply because of the established male fantasies on which they are focusing their campaigns. They seem to have no other defense, if it can be called a defense, than that they didn't invent the fantasies, they are only using them. They know the target audience, and their job is to sell beer. They are not social or cultural reformers. But ethical considerations should constrain them from such uses. In the first instance, the women in the commercials are the ones exploited. In the second instance, all women are exploited, and in the third, all humans. This matter, however, has nothing to do with the use of nonrational persuasion in advertising. The point should be that when nonrational persuasion incorporates such stereotypical conceptions of people, even if it is otherwise unobjectionable, it will violate the moral side constraints against using people as mere means. In principle then, there is nothing wrong with fantasy approaches to advertising, but other considerations involving the sorts of fantasies utilized can make them unethical. In the case of exploiting women as sex objects, those reasons have little directly to do with whether the consumer is coerced.

Goldman draws a distinction worth making about nonrational persuasion in advertising. He says that our ethical condemnation of it should be based in some measure on whether or not the target audience can be expected to resist the persuasion if they believed that to follow it was against their better interests.[54] If a man believed that it was against his better interests to drink beer, but couldn't resist buying and drinking Keystone after watching the glamour model and the guy on the beach, we would say that he had lost his ability to make a rational free choice in the matter of beer buying and drinking, and in that sense he was coerced. It would, however, certainly be rare to find any adult so captivated by a Coors commercial that he or she could not resist doing what he or she did not want to do. It may be a mild form of propaganda, but it is not brainwashing. For us to take seriously the coercion claims we would need evidence that a substantial number of viewers were unable to resist the nonrational persuasion methods used by the advertisers. That could be the case if advertising were done subliminally. If messages to buy a product were subliminally introduced during the shows themselves, people might begin getting urges to buy products they'd never even heard of or consciously desired. Clearly then, the side constraints would be overstepped. That is deceptive coercion, pure and simple.

Subliminal advertising is not legal, but another subtle type of advertising edges in that direction. Whenever movies or TV shows are set in contemporary times, it is necessary to create the desired verisimilitude that actors use products actually on the market. Manufacturers pay considerable sums to have their products' labels prominently displayed. When the wife in a situation comedy opens the pantry door, we see shelves filled with recognizable products from Campbell's Soup to Brillo Pads. The public, the advertisers are betting, because it has identified with the sitcom family, will almost subconsciously register that the sitcom dwellers buy those products and will emulate them in the supermarket. Villains never show product labels. Identifiable trademarks and name brands are frequently mentioned, especially on television shows. Its, "Do you want a Pepsi?" not "How about a soda?"

For years automobile companies have supplied vehicles for films so that their products will be prominently displayed. In San Antonio, Texas, an automobile manufacturer settled a personal injury suit out of court in a case in which a teenager, after watching the *Smoky and the Bandit* movies, decided to test whether his Pontiac Trans Am could do the sorts of things the one in the movies did. He wrapped his car around a tree and paralysed himself. The case did go to trial for a few days, but General Motors decided to make a sizable offer to bring an end to the matter after, possibly, sensing that the jury was sympathetic to the young man's argument that the use of the car in the movie was a form of advertisement specifically targeted at the male teenage audience. General Motors admitted that it had not only supplied the cars for the film, but had paid money to ensure that its cars were used rather than those of a competitor.

On the other hand, some limit needs to be established on this kind of liability, legally and ethically. The proper place to set it probably should be determined by asking what a reasonable person in the targeted age bracket of the advertisement or promotion would believe about the use of the product. Do most male teenagers who see cars like theirs being driven at one hundred miles per hour and jumping raging rivers think that is an unmodified vehicle? Do they think that the car in their driveway is really capable of such stunts? I doubt it. Surely the vast majority are well aware of the fact that they are watching a movie and that the vehicles in it are specially rigged to do the tricks that make the movie more exciting.

Advertising directed at young children, however, might be a different story. When I asked a number of people to list the uses of advertising that most disturbed them or that they regarded as unethical, by far and away the most frequently mentioned was the advertising on children's television programs. By "children's television" is meant shows produced especially for preschool and elementary school children that are typically broadcast on Saturday mornings or in the late afternoons when the children are home from school. Several of those shows seem to be little more than half-hour commercials for toys. They include an animated story involving toy characters, such as Care Bears and Cabbage Patch Dolls and Rainbow Brite. The shows were produced after the toys were on the market, apparently with the intention of boosting sales of the toys or accessories for the toys. During breaks in the cartoon story, the sponsors, toy manufacturers, advertise toys and related items featuring the characters of the program. The message to the children is blatant: they are to get their parents to buy them the toys that they have come to see as individuals with episodic lives. Other commercials targeted at young children during the cartoon shows are for breakfast cereals and even medicines and diet supplements such as vitamins.

This sort of manipulation of children and their parents violates the side constraints and so is unethical. Parents report that it is extremely difficult to convince their children that they do not need the toy to enjoy the show. Children, in DeGeorge's words, "can pressure, hound, and influence their parents in the purchases their parents make."[55] The child's resistance to nonrational persuasion characteristically is low, and the intentional process of interweaving the commercial with the program intensifies the breakdown of resistance in the young audience. The outcome is that parents are left to deal with the demands for the advertised toy or the Flintstone vitamins or the sugar-coated-bears cereal either by giving in and buying it or by disappointing the child and having to explain why. Many, the advertisers are betting, will not have or take the time to try to silence the pestering brats with even quasirational arguments. The products will be purchased.

In some cases that will not be a bad thing. Parents, as DeGeorge points out,[56] may want to encourage their kids to take vitamins, and the commercials may prove to be exactly the enticement that does the trick. The child, once resistant, now is eager to swallow them. The cereal might be quite another matter. The parents may be trying to get the child to eat healthy breakfasts and now everything except the syrup-coated bears or dinosaurs will be rejected.

Still, the parents are buying the products, although they could say no. Advertisers might respond that if the parents are unable to exert their own wills over those of their nagging children, the responsibility for that failure should be deposited squarely in the laps of the parents. Another side, however, is that if the advertisers know that the parents are the buyers, then the advertisements should be directed at them, not at the children. What do children know of dietary supplements and nutrition? The advertisers are clearly exploiting the children to get them to pressure their parents into making purchases the parents might not make had the pressure not been exerted. That is using people as means without their consent. And so it is unethical.

I'm now watching a commercial television station. Every ten minutes or so I am assaulted with advertisements. Nonfactual statements are made over and over and over in some of them. But most of those statements are like the tiger in the tank, they wouldn't mislead any moderately intelligent person. They're puffery, we don't take them seriously. The advertisers know that we don't, so they can hardly intend to deceive us by using them. But in many of them something else is going on that might be thought of as deceptive.

When we watch a television show or a movie or a play, we suspend disbelief for the sake of the entertainment but still realize that it is a dramatization with actors playing the parts. Paul Blumberg writes:

> Compare now a typical TV commercial. A woman appears on camera. She is standing in a kitchen wiping a spill with a paper towel. She says to the audience that she always uses X paper towels because they are twice as absorbent as the leading brand.
>
> Now, as everyone knows, or should know, the woman in the kitchen does not actually use this brand of paper towel at all, or if she does, it is irrelevant to the situation. She is an actress playing a housewife who says she uses X paper towels, because she has been paid money to say so.[57]

Well, what then is the problem? The answer seems to be that the advertisers do not want the audience to respond to their little dramas as it does to the television shows and the movies the commercials interrupt.

> Unlike fiction, the intent of the advertiser is to convince viewers to suspend *permanently* their knowledge that this is a contrived dramatization. For after all, what would happen if every viewer thought during every commercial, "These people aren't using this product because it's better; they're only paid to say so"? If viewers consciously thought that, commercials would be totally ineffective.[58]

The commercial, so the argument goes, is only effective if the viewer really believes the actors use the product and that their endorsements are sincere. The ethical oddity of most television commercials is that their effectiveness depends on the advertisers' ability to convince consumers that a contrived fiction is true.

> Much TV advertising is a genre which is fiction but which implicitly masquerades as fact and can only be successful if it is accepted as fact at some level.[59]

If Blumberg is correct in this assessment, then many commercials are, by their very nature, deceptive. But are they deceptive in a way that makes them ethically deficient? That is not at all clear to me.

A cat-box odor remover commercial just came on the television. A voice asks a woman who is sitting in a nicely furnished, middle-class home whether she has ever had a cat odor problem. She giggles and answers back that she never has. A cat pops up on the side of the screen and mouths that the woman is lying. We are then told that the product will remove the unwanted cat-box odors. Was a deception being worked on us? Certainly. In the first place, cats don't mouth English sentences. Secondly the woman was an actress, and not, I'm afraid, a particularly good one. Third, people generally don't live in houses where disembodied voices not only talk to them, but go about asking them embarrassing questions about odors. Did I, or anyone watching the commercial, think that this was anything but a little performance, that the actress now uses the product, or even that she has cats? I doubt it. No one was deceived by the ad and a number of people got some useful information from it. Those with cats and cat-box odors now know there is a product, or another product, especially designed to alleviate their problem. My suspicion is that most commercials are more like the cat-box odor remover than blatant attempts to deceive us into thinking that a doctor is telling us that the only way to successfully deal with hemorrhoids is to use Preparation H.

A reasonable-person test should suffice to draw the crucial ethical distinctions between cases where the deception in the use of actors is exploitive and coercive and when it is but a harmless stage setting, puffery, used to impress the product's image in the consumer's consciousness. If a reasonable person would likely be deceived by the commercial into thinking that the actors are real people, especially people with professional authority that would be relevant to the effectiveness claims being made about the product, giving testimonials, then the ad is deceptive in an ethically improper way. Otherwise, the little dramas of TV advertising are harmless. In effect, this applies a variant of the principle used above to distinguish much of the advertising on children's television from other cases.

Another kind of issue also plagues the ethics of advertising: how much of the truth to tell? Burton Leiser[60] reminds us of the ham scandals of a few decades back when major canned-ham packers such as Swift and Armour advertised their packed hams as juicy. Indeed the hams were juicy, much juicier than the ham you might have purchased from your local butcher. So the statements about their juiciness were true. What the meat packing companies didn't tell the consumers was that their hams were juicy because they had used syringes to inject water into the hams. When the ham was cooked it shrunk by as much as 40 percent as the water evaporated. So the consumers were buying water at ham prices. But the companies covered themselves on that front as well. They labeled the cans, in small print, "Artificial Ham." What made the ham artificial was all of that injected water. In effect, the meat packers were not lying about their product, but they were suppressing the truth about it.

> Surely it is asking too much to expect the advertiser to describe the shortcomings of his product. One must be forgiven for putting one's best foot forward.[61]

One may not be forgiven if doing so conceals relevant information from the consumer that the consumer could not gain in the normal course of events. That the juicy ham was doctored with a considerable amount of water is such a fact. Leiser's point is convincing:

> Telling the truth combined with "suppressio Veri" is *not* telling the truth. It is *not* asking too much of the advertiser to reveal such facts when they are known to him, and he should *not* be forgiven for "putting his best foot forward" at his customer's expense.[62]

We do need to recognize an important point about consumption that many of the critics of the puffery of advertising either overlook or willfully ignore. Theodore Levitt puts it well when he says,

> (T)he consumer consumes not things, but expected benefits—not cosmetics, but the satisfactions of the allurements they promise; not quarter-inch drills, but quarter-inch holes; not stock in companies, but capital gains; not numerically controlled milling machines, but trouble-free and accurately smooth metal parts; not low-cal whipped cream, but self-rewarding indulgence combined with sophisticated convenience.[63]

We buy styles, symbols, ways of life. Advertising embellishes the things, the products, and converts them into objects of status in our culture. It surrounds them with imagery and promise and that is, by and large, what we buy, and what we want. The advertisers, Levitt says, and, by and large, he is right, actually make our world more livable, more bearable by bringing a certain poetic aspiration to it. That does not mean that they cannot go far beyond the bounds of ethics and exploit, manipulate, and coerce us. When that happens, ethics and the law must be called to the consumer's defense, and the side constraints reestablished. Otherwise, we might as well enjoy the ornamentation in our lives that advertising provides.

ENDNOTES

1. John Kavanaugh, "Ethical Issues in Plant Relocation," *Business and Professional Ethics Journal*, Vol. 1, No. 2, (Winter 1982) p. 23.
2. DeGeorge, op. cit. p. 136–37.
3. Kavanaugh, op. cit. p. 30.
4. DeGeorge, op. cit. p. 136.
5. Austin, "Three Ways of Spilling Ink," op. cit. p. 272–87.
6. See Peter A. French, *Responsibility Matters* (Lawrence, 1992) chapter 1; and *Collective and Corporate Responsibility* (New York, 1984) chapter 11.

7. F. H. Bradley, *Ethical Studies* (London, 1876) p. 46.

8. Aristotle, *Nicomachean Ethics*, trans. by M. Ostwald (Indianapolis, 1962) p. 51.

9. Friedrich Nietzsche, *On the Genealogy of Morals*, trans. by Kaufmann and Hollingdale (New York, 1967).

10. For a brief but insightful discussion of the features of both guilt and shame, see Herbert Morris, *On Guilt and Innocence* (Berkeley, 1976) p. 59–63. He makes this point on p. 61.

11. J. O. Urmson, "Saints and Heroes," in A. Melden, *Essays in Moral Philosophy* (Seattle, 1958). See chapter 12 for a discussion of the aspirational level of morality.

12. Morris, op. cit. p. 62.

13. Mark Twain, *Pudd'nhead Wilson's New Calendar* (1894) Chapter 27.

14. Gabriele Taylor, *Pride, Shame, and Guilt* (Oxford, 1985) p. 60.

15. For a more detailed account of the various problems with shame therapy and other aspects of shame, see Helen Merrell Lynd, *On Shame and the Search for Identity* (New York, 1967), and Gerhart Piers and Milton Singer, *Shame and Guilt* (New York, 1971).

16. A point owed to Herbert Morris.

17. See Plato, *The Laws*, trans. by Thomas Pangle (New York, 1979).

18. Michael Walzer, *Exodus and Revolution* (New York, 1985). See chapter 2, especially p. 59–70.

19. Marvin Harris, *Why Nothing Works* (New York, 1981).

20. For the classical account of worker alienation, see Marx, "Alienated Labor," op. cit.

21. Daniel Bell, *The Coming of Post-Industrial Society* (New York, 1973).

22. Harris, op. cit. p. 41.

23. For a compendium of examples, see Steve Allen, *Dumbth* (Buffalo, 1989).

24. Harry Braverman, *Labor and Monopoly Capital: The Degradation of Work in the Twentieth Century* (New York, 1975) p. 314.

25. Harris, op. cit. p. 47–48.

26. See Marx, "Alienated Labor," op. cit.

27. Ibid. p. 51–52.

28. Karen Nussbaum, *Race Against Time* (Cleveland, 1980) p. 3.

29. Harris, op. cit. p. 54.

30. Max Born, *Bulletin of the Atomic Scientists* (November, 1965).

31. Langdon Winner, "How Technology Reweaves the Fabric of Society," *The Chronicle of Higher Education*, (August 4, 1993) p. B1.

32. Winner, op. cit. p. B2.

33. Parker English, who spent some time teaching in Nigeria, informs me that is the case there and in most of the West-African countries with which he is familiar.

34. Doron P. Levin, "Honda's Ugly Little Secret," *The New York Times* (May 2, 1993) Sec. 3, p. 1.

35. Ibid.

36. Lawrence J. White, former chief economist in the Justice Department's Antitrust Division, quoted by Levin, ibid. p. 2.

37. DeGeorge, op. cit. p. 51–54.

38. Feldman, op. cit. p. 26.

39. Levin, op. cit. p. 1.

40. Rob Seitz, "Corporate Conundrum: Disclosing Illness in the Corner Office," *The New York Times* (May, 2 1993) p. F9.

41. Ibid.

42. Ibid.

43. Ibid.

44. Samm Sinclair Baker, *The Permissible Lie: The Inside Truth About Advertising* (Boston, 1971) p. 190.
45. DeGeorge, op. cit. p. 186.
46. Ibid. p. 188.
47. Sissela Bok, *Lying* (New York, 1978) p. 19.
48. Alan Goldman, "Ethical Issues in Advertising," in Regan (ed.) op. cit. p. 236–37.
49. See Goldman, ibid. p. 238.
50. Ibid. p. 250.
51. Ibid. p. 249.
52. Ibid.
53. Ibid. p. 251.
54. Ibid. p. 251.
55. DeGeorge op. cit. p. 193.
56. Ibid.
57. Paul Blumberg, *The Predatory Society* (Oxford, 1989) p. 214–15.
58. Ibid. p. 215.
59. Ibid. p. 216.
60. Burton Leiser, *Liberty, Justice and Morals* (New York, 1973).
61. David Ogilvy, *Confessions of an Advertising Man* (New York, 1963), p. 158.
62. Leiser, op. cit.
63. Theodore Levitt, "The Morality(?) of Advertising," *The Harvard Business Review* (July/August 1970).

THE INVADERS INVADED

 ## 1. Ethical Relativism and Global Corporate Business Practices

For some years now, we have been living in the age of the multinational corporation. Business is global, markets are global. The investment capital to conduct or expand a corporate enterprise based in the United States might come from a banking conglomerate with its home office in Tokyo or Hong Kong or Amsterdam. After the Second World War, as discussed in detail in Part 1, American corporations needed to create new markets and new products to replace their military customers. They turned inward to the American people and managed, rather spectacularly, to engineer a consumption craze that fueled American manufacturing and retail businesses for at least two decades. But various economic reasons conspired to make the domestic market less lucrative in the past two decades and expansion into the rest of the world crucial to the viability of, at least, the bigger firms. At the same time, corporations from other countries, most notably Japan and Europe have invaded America and many have captured the lion's share of the markets they have targeted. The result is global competition.

Some analysts and writers on business ethics saw the rise of the multinationals as a sign of the end of political and cultural nationalism. They forecasted that these corporations would, in effect, constitute the new world order, an order that placed corporate loyalty over that to country or ethnicity. That, however, has not happened and isn't likely to happen. The primary reason is that multinationals are really not what the term suggests. They are not corporate actors redrawing the maps of the globe. By and large, they have remained closely identified and associated with their home countries. The political geography of the Earth has radically altered in the past five years, but the new boundaries on the map have not been drawn by multinational corporate actors, nor are the new national names derived from those of corporations. In fact, the very concept conveyed by the term "multinational corporation" fits almost none of the companies operating in the global markets.

Simply, "multinational corporation," though commonly used to refer to the new breed of corporate invaders, is something of a misnomer. The corporations in question are national companies that have set up or bought into corporate operations in countries other than the one in which they are chartered. They tend to remain dominated and controlled by those in their home country, even though they may hire and promote to responsible executive positions nationals of the countries in which they do business. Their business policies generally reflect the economic, political, and cultural beliefs and commitments of their home countries. The term global corporation is better suited to them than is "multinational."

American corporations in search of not only new markets but cheaper labor forces since the 1950s, expanded into established, rebuilding, and developing nations. Problems and concerns from the moral point of view dogged them. Some infamous cases, mostly involving bribery, erupted into the public consciousness, and the American legal machine sputtered into action to respond to abuses. The Foreign Corrupt Practices Act became law in 1977. It was largely a reaction to the Watergate findings of illegal corporate political contributions and a Securities and Exchange Commission voluntary disclosure program that revealed that more than 250 corporations had made illegal or unethical payments to foreign governments in order to gain foreign market access or specific sales. The Foreign Corrupt Practices Act was intended to provide the basis for American prosecution of corporations whose agents had bribed foreign government officials.

One of the most publicized and discussed cases involved the Lockheed Corporation. About seven years after the Lockheed case had made the papers, I had the opportunity to talk with Samuel F. Pearce, then staff vice president and chief counsel for Lockheed. Even though years had passed since the revelation that Lockheed executives had paid substantial bribes to members of the Japanese government to secure the purchase of Lockheed planes, Pearce reported that he was regularly beset by people, in and out of the media, asking him to explain how Lockheed, in this case meaning his department, could have let Lockheed president Carl Kotchian make the statements he did about the incidents. Kotchian, after testifying before a congressional committee said:

> If, in a situation where high government officials have influence on matters pertinent to a private company, money is requested as pay-offs for those officials, can that private foreign company, which wants its products to be bought at all costs, realistically decline the request on the grounds that it is not a good thing from the ethical point of view?[1]

Kotchian undoubtedly said the wrong thing, yet he voiced a concern that dominates the thinking of corporate executives in the global markets: by what set of principles and rules ought corporate actors play when doing business or working in a foreign country if the foreign (or host) country is one whose inhabitants hold a radically different set of ethical beliefs about business from ours or when some of their ethical beliefs are significantly different from ours? What is to be done if pay-offs to host country government officials or the agents of foreign customers to garner contracts or facilitate services are the expected manner of securing business? The principle to which Kotchian obliquely made reference might be called the "When in Rome, do as the Romans do" principle.[2] As Norman Bowie notes, application of this principle does not necessarily reveal a moral disagreement.

Often factual matters differentiate cultures with respect to what may at first blush seem to be moral disagreements. For example, in the early 1970s the Nestlé Company carried on an intensive Third World marketing campaign for its baby formula that included graphic demonstrations of how breast-fed infants did not look as healthy as those fed with its formula.

> Pictures of undernourished, and malcontented breast-fed infants were displayed adjacent to smiling, full-faced formula-fed babies. The sales campaign appealed to the maternal instincts of women. They were offered free samples of the formula, which they often mixed with impure water because the importance of using boiled water was not stressed. As the child was weaned onto the formula, the mothers ceased lactating, leaving, in effect, no option but the formula for nourishment. . . . Free samples were dispensed by "Mothercraft nurses," women hired by Nestle, who dressed in hospital nursing uniforms and instructed potential customers on the use and nutritional benefits of the product.[3]

Certainly nothing is ethically wrong with marketing infant formula in most Western industrialized countries, but in countries where the water is likely not to be safe to drink, one ought not to market it to those who must mix it with that water. People in our culture and in the other country, we can suppose, firmly agree with the moral principle that says that innocents are not to be harmed. In fact, it was the concern for the health of their infants that made the Nestlé marketing scheme so attractive to Third World mothers. So there is no real moral disagreement between us on that matter. However, the application of that principle leads to different results in very different situations.

Examples like that of the Nestlé infant formula debacle, therefore, are of little ethical interest. If all apparent cross-national ethical disagreements could be dissolved by uncovering mutually held moral doctrines and relevant factual differences, the ethical problems of global corporations in foreign cultures would cease to be of any serious concern. But some moral theorists and, presumably, a number of corporate executives, such as Lockheed's Kotchian, maintain that something like the "When in Rome" principle either has ethical status or it negates all normal ethical principles in cases quite different from the infant formula type.

Does the "When in Rome" principle really have ethical weight when the apparent moral differences between cultures are not attributable to environmental or other factual matters?

Suppose there is no disagreement between two cultures with respect to what sorts of actions constitute bribery. A genuine moral disagreement might be one in which Culture A holds that bribery is impermissible (wrong) and B holds that it is morally permissible, even required, under the same set of factual descriptions. A U.S.-based corporation doing business in both cultures is, like Lockheed, but also Grumman and Northrup (to mention a few more corporations caught in the 1970s scandals), confronted with the option of bribing in a culture; for example, Nigeria. (I choose Nigeria on the information of a friend, Parker English, who, as noted in Part 4, taught there and assures me that anyone wanting to do virtually any business there must bribe public officials.) It is not clear whether the "When in Rome" principle requires bribery in Nigeria or only advises bribery. A number of business ethicists seem to think that a method needs to be devised to guide corporate actors from our culture who find themselves trying to do business in places like Nigeria. Bowie, for example, argues for the procedure that allows that if the moral principle of the foreign or host country is justified, but that of the United States is not or both are justified, then one has a moral responsibility (ought) to act in accordance with the host country's moral principle.[4] That sounds fine, but how are we to determine whether the moral principles of a culture are justified or not? That would require a method of evaluating moral principles that is independent of any culture, and, if we are in possession of such an independent moral point of view, we have no need to raise questions about the "When in Rome" principle in the first place.

Bowie thinks we do have something like an independent set of moral principles, at least for corporations. He assigns that role to what he calls the morality of the marketplace, the reliance on marketplace factors to produce ethically desired results. (Recall that Goodpaster and I both associated that attitude with corporate teleopathy.[5]) He then recommends that corporations heed the morality of the marketplace wherever on the globe they operate. He thinks that if they do so they should improve the morality of host countries by advancing the cause of democracy and human rights.

I suspect Bowie is right when he claims that the morality of the marketplace approaches a universal morality. However, that is because, I will argue, if it is a morality, it is at least not incompatible with morality as we understand it. Put otherwise, radically different *moral* principles do not exist, if by radically different we mean that the principles in question are hostile to each other. Bowie worries that he cannot escape ethnocentrism[6] unless he can independently justify the morality of the marketplace. So he goes on to argue in favor of capitalism. I think his doing so is unnecessary, beside the point. All he needs to show is that the morality of the marketplace is a part of our morality, call it ethnocentric, if you want. Corporate actors must not only start from our own morality, they need not apologize for ending there. Furthermore, cultural relativism can be overcome without having to distinguish between essential and accidental aspects of a morality and without having to endorse the "When in Rome" principle, even in a limited number of cases.

Some of the most persuasive attacks on radical relativism have taken as their point of departure Donald Davidson's well-known argument that not many of the beliefs of any culture can be false.

> The reason for this is that a belief is identified by its location in a pattern of beliefs; it is this pattern that determines the subject matter of the belief, what the belief is about. . . .[7]

As Davidson notes, "false beliefs tend to undermine the identification of the subject matter."[8] If most of your beliefs about something are false, why do you identify that thing as the subject of your beliefs? Simply, if we were to admit to the possibility that the members of a culture other than ours could hold beliefs about any particular subject that were mostly false, we would have to conclude that we had misidentified the subject of their beliefs. If everything, or almost everything, we think they are saying about the moon is false, we'd likely decide that they weren't talking about the moon at all.

Suppose the subject matter in question has to do with the way people ought to behave when doing business. Let us stipulate that we hold a number of beliefs about what people are morally responsible for doing in those circumstances and that members of another culture hold beliefs that are incompatible with ours. What must we conclude? Because we cannot hold that most of our beliefs are false and the same must be said of their beliefs, we must either have gotten wrong that their beliefs are about people's moral responsibilities (moral beliefs), or we misunderstood at what features of the circumstances their moral beliefs were directed, or they must have a different conception of the subject within which they are applying moral beliefs. In the third type of case, we will need to learn how they conceive subject and how that conception differs from our conception. For example, as discussed below, if they think of business on the model of war and we on the model of games, different moral responses to business practices are likely to emerge. In the second case we should expect to discover our error regarding about what features of a situation the members of the other culture are talking and then revise our original judgment that radical disagreement exists between us. In the first case we must conclude that their beliefs are not moral ones. David Cooper has seen the outcome of this argument:

> We can only identify another's beliefs as moral beliefs about X if there is a massive degree of agreement between his and our beliefs. Hence, there is no chance of radical moral diversity.[9]

Such a strategy against the relativist, however, will fail if, rather than distinguishing moral beliefs and judgments from others in terms of content, we identify moral judgments as those having certain formal features such as capacity for being universalized. It will certainly be conceivable that the people of one culture might make universalizable judgments about responsibility that are radically different from, incompatible with, the judgments of people in another culture.

Although the formalistic position has had many advocates, it has been the target of devastating criticism in recent years. Philippa Foot has argued that formal features do not mark off moral judgments from others.[10] For Foot, judgments are moral if they express principles that connect to issues of human welfare, happiness, and such. But Foot's approach, though it offers an escape from formalistic criteria, as Cooper notes, does not escape the suspicion that it is but a lot of idle stipulation.

> Attractive as the stipulation that moral principles *must* display a concern for welfare, happiness, etc., might be, to the extent that it remains a stipulation, the formalist can remain unimpressed.[11]

The Davidsonian-styled approach will, as it happens, arrive at the same destination as Foot, but in doing so it avoids the appearance of arbitrary stipulation.

Imagine that the people of a foreign culture have not developed any geometrical concepts that are even roughly equivalent to the familiar forms of Euclidean geometry. Instead of square, triangle, and circle, they use the notion of "blob." Blob is not a univocal term. Within different contexts it takes on different meanings. They talk about forming a blob, the angles of a blob, and whether a blob of one sort would be preferable to that of another. We can interpret what they say when they talk of blobs in imprecise, though correct, geometric expressions.

Under such conditions we would be right in claiming that they have a geometry, of a sort.

What cannot be imagined is that the people of the foreign culture have replaced all geometric concepts with, say, aesthetic ones, that in place of our beliefs about geometry they have substituted aesthetic beliefs. Aesthetics cannot be their geometry. Lacking geometric concepts and beliefs, they simply have no geometry. Aesthetics is not an alternative geometry. It does not stand to geometry as Riemannian triangles do to Euclidean ones.

Analogously, that a concept or belief is a moral one is for it to fit in a system of moral beliefs that, to a large degree, resembles our system of moral beliefs. In fact, we cannot identify a foreign culture's beliefs about certain types of behavior (say bribery or cannibalism) as moral beliefs about those practices, if a subset of the foreign culture's beliefs is not our moral beliefs. If a person of the foreign culture reports that she believes that bribery of public officials to secure her (or her company's) goals is her moral responsibility or that, at least, it is morally permissible, we first need to ascertain whether she and we use the term "bribery" in reference to the same sort of activity. We do. The next, and natural, move is to determine what force "moral responsibility" has when she uses it to express her belief. That she is prepared to universalize her judgment is not relevant to our problem, for, as suggested above, such formal criteria have proved unreliable marks of the moral.

Before continuing, certain things need to be clarified. First, I am not claiming that it is a criterion of a culture's having a morality that its members believe that people ought not to engage in bribery. No specific moral belief is essential to a culture's having a morality; that is, genuine moral beliefs. That her beliefs about the moral responsibility to bribe or the permissibility of bribery are radically different from our own does not either prove that she has no morality or that her moral principles are incompatible with ours.

Second, behavioral criteria are not sufficient to distinguish moral from nonmoral beliefs. There are at least three reasons why. Suppose she tells us that she approves of bribery. She thinks it should be legal, and she does not object to or refuse to do business with anyone who she suspects of attempting bribery. Does her approval of bribery arise from moral considerations? Perhaps she has (as do most other members of her culture) religious views that encourage acts of bribery. From behavioral clues alone we are not likely to determine that her attitudes are moral ones. But even if we could identify solely on behavioral grounds when she was exhibiting her moral attitudes, we will not likely, on the same grounds, be able to tell what moral beliefs she actually holds.

Does she really believe that bribery is her moral responsibility and not morally wrong, or is it not bribery as we understand it that she thinks is her moral responsibility or is morally permissible. To answer such a question, we need to know more than that she exhibits certain attitudes. We have to ascertain the object of those attitudes. That is unlikely to be a simple observational project. To borrow an example from both John Searle[12] and David Cooper[13], can we suppose that the people in her culture disapprove of keeping promises or contracts? That seems hard to imagine, for we should have to first suppose that they engage in or at least have the concepts of promising and contracting. It is hard to see how they could have the concept of contract or promise and not believe that the parties are obligated with respect to them. Yet it is not simply a matter of definition that "promise keeping must be morally approved." Still, if the evidence seems to support the conclusion that members of her culture disapprove of what we identify in their activities as contracting and promising, we should first question whether we have properly identified of what they disapprove. It may be some other feature of the practices that regularly are associated with those activities. Perhaps they disapprove of the shaking of hands or of the typical linguistic form in which the promise is couched. Perhaps we have utterly failed to understand their social life.

The force of the Davidsonian approach is that radical moral disagreement is not possible between cultures. That certainly, however, does not entail that with respect to specific issues there could not be a considerable divergence of opinion. After all, a range of viewpoints exists in our culture about abortion, euthanasia, and myriad other issues. With respect to these areas of controversy our morality has not pronounced final sentence. Contrast these with a concept about which no reasonable dispute is brewing, for example, murder. A primary reason for our having the concept of murder is to mark off as unjustifiable certain kinds of homicides. Perpetrators of homicides that are correctly described as murders, perform deeds that are indisputably morally wrong. "Murder is wrong" is necessarily true, uninformative, and certainly not a matter of debate. "Euthanasia is wrong" is quite another story. That clearly is debatable. One form of argument in support of it identifies euthanasia with murder, another draws an analogy between it and murder. The moral status of euthanasia is not morally resolved, but we would be getting the situation wrong were we to conclude that because my neighbor and I disagree over whether euthanasia is wrong that we must have different moralities. Rather, our disagreement is more likely to be an indicator that we share a basic morality. Were we, however, to be engaged in a heated debate over whether murder is wrong (I do not mean a debate over whether a particular homicide really is a murder), then whichever of us is maintaining that murder is *not* wrong cannot be expressing moral beliefs. One might imagine trying to teach a child that murder is wrong and getting into some sort of argument with the child over whether it really was wrong. The disagreement would not signal that the child has a radically different morality, only that it has not yet learned its lessons in morality. From within the scope of morality there is, however, considerable space for disagreement. Bribery, I suspect, is more like euthanasia than murder.

A visitor from our culture might question an official in a host country about a bribe attempt by saying something like, "Bribery is wrong," and hear in response, "No it's not, it's just a normal cost of doing business, a cementing of goodwill and friendship between seller and buyer." This is a genuine disagreement, but it does not signal different moralities. That, however, does not mean that it will be resolved. Will the moral question of euthanasia be resolved? It is in principle resolvable. The term bribery might come to name a moral concept as the term murder does, but it is characteristic of morality that there are remarkably few such concepts. In any event, a judgment like "Bribery is morally wrong, and it cannot be your moral responsibility to do it," does not stand alone. It is not a matter of moral bedrock. It must be supported, and such support on moral grounds comes either by appeal to existing concepts or principles within our morality or by allegation that the consequences in human affairs generally of the practice of bribery are morally relevant.

But from where does this concept of moral relevance arise? A consequence is morally relevant only if it is generally recognized to be so. And, as the Davidsonian approach entails, if there is no agreement between members of different cultures on the moral relevance of a number of factors arising from any practice—that it produces or involves harming of innocents, causes suffering, enslaves —it would be a mistake to say that both have a morality. It is unintelligible to claim that judgments that do not reflect our general agreement as to those factors are moral judgments. Hence, if we are correct in interpreting her as maintaining that bribery is a moral responsibility, we must treat our difference with her as a dispute over the application of morality.

Bowie claims that if the morality of a host country is "in violation of the moral norms of the marketplace, then the people have a moral obligation to follow the norms of the marketplace."[14] His reasons for this recommendation are rather difficult to fathom. He tells us that systematic violation of marketplace norms would be self-defeating. One might wonder if this is a formalistic criterion of moral action: that it should not be self-defeating. But surely it would be a morally happy situation were certain practices self-defeating: those that are morally wrong. So, just that doing something in a certain way defeats the purpose of doing it cannot be, by itself, a moral reason for not doing it in that way. Bowie advises following marketplace morality as against that of a host country because to do so is to "provide something approaching a universal morality."[15] Hence, corporate actors by sticking to the "morality" of the marketplace become missionaries for true morality.

Bowie rightly notes that to make this a palatable claim he needs to justify the morality of the marketplace, and to do so he offers what he calls the "contribution to democracy argument."[16] Democracy is supposed to embody the recognition of fundamental human rights, namely those created and protected in a true morality. What we have then is an appeal to the concept of fundamental human rights as a characteristic of genuine morality or, in other words, a stipulation about the content of moral principles with respect to which neither the formalist nor the Davidsonian need be impressed.

In effect, the appeal to the morality of the marketplace and then the defense that such a morality maintains rights reveals that the whole issue of competing radically different moralities is a nonstarter. Why not just start with rights protection? How is the act justified independent of the fact that we believe it to be so?

A culture that has no interest in protecting human rights (for example, a Confucian culture) may still have a morality, but it cannot be one whose beliefs contradict all of our moral beliefs. Hence, a basis for argument and a possibility for conversion on the issue of rights protection would exist between us. The norms of the marketplace might provide the teaching situation to expand the moral beliefs of the other culture. However, the members of the other culture may, quite apart from the marketplace, convince us that the protection of individual human rights is not that morally important. Continued trade and other relationships with China could lead to such a reevaluation of what those in the United States believe to be morally basic!

The "When in Rome" principle has no moral status, even if it does have legal status. When local customs stand in opposition to our moral principles, then the Kotchian-type excuse (or is it a justification?) that "I was only doing what they do," will be morally unacceptable. If I lived in Saudi Arabia, would it be my moral responsibility to subjugate and even mutilate women? Do Saudi men have such a responsibility because that is a part of their culture? If I were dealing in South Africa in the 1980s, ought I to act in accord with its system of apartheid? To take up the practices of a tribe of cannibal headhunters because one happens to be in their community is immoral; those practices are immoral, no matter who adopts them. That is not to say that we may not come to understand and appreciate why people in other cultures act as they do. We may uncover hitherto hidden sociological, geographic, climatic, historic explanations for their customs. But none of those accounts, though they make it more intelligible, will make their behavior any more moral, or any less immoral. If I would be acting immorally if I intentionally killed people, dismembered them, and ate their flesh in Milwaukee, I would be acting immorally if I did so in the company of a jungle tribe. And so would be the members of the tribe, regardless of their traditions.

Those currently supporting changes in Western practices and traditions make clear that the mere fact of existence in a culture is no guarantee of moral status. Slavery was morally wrong in our culture, even when it was widely practiced. The mistreatment of minorities and women is wrong, despite the fact that it is widespread and has deep historical roots. In short, if we have moral reasons for opposing certain practices in our own culture, we have the same moral reasons for opposing the practice in any other culture and in any other historical epoch.

That does not mean that members of one culture will have the same set of moral responsibilities as those of another. Responsibilities depend in large measure on the organizational structure of a community. Obviously, communities that do not have comparable or convertible structures will not have comparable responsibility sets. However, if the responsibilities derive from general moral principles (such as not killing innocent people), rather than being solely tied to tasks or stations, they cannot be incompatible from one culture to another.

An interesting related question, but one that has nothing to do with the basic claims of cultural relativism, is whether certain tasks or stations in a society are, by virtue of the responsibilities associated with them, immoral and so never justified in a culture. To fall in such a category the tasks of a station would have to be such that they could not be performed without violating basic moral principles. A culture in which there existed a large number (I have no idea as to where the line ought to be drawn) of such stations would be immoral and so lacking in moral justification for its existence. The Colombian Cocaine Cartel and the Mafia leap to mind as examples. The culture of the Ik tribe in Uganda, if there are any of them left, may, as suggested by Turnbull,[17] also qualify. In any event, it is not the case that a visitor in another culture has a moral responsibility to act in a way that is common to his or her counterparts in that culture, if they are acting in ways that cannot be justified according to the principles, or extensions of the principles, of our morality. But then, the natives in that culture have no moral responsibility to act that way either.

2. Japanese Collective Capitalism: The Rising Sun and the Setting Stars (and Stripes)

There no longer seems to be much competition for the window seats in airliners. The place of preference has shifted to the aisle seats. I suspect that at least two reasons contrive to explain the change. Most everyone seems to want to hop out of the plane as quickly as possible in order to get to whatever business they've flown off for in the first place. Planes are no longer objects of wonder, they're just conveyers, people movers. The service and the exclusivity that used to be associated with them has eroded. They are merely convenient means of transport in a country that fell so head over heels for the automobile and the truck that it let its rail system deteriorate.

The second reason has to do with familiarity. Hardly anyone is interested anymore in watching the clouds or gazing down on the countryside below. We've seen it all before. We are worshipers of novelty. People just don't look out of plane windows anymore.

On a recent midday flight, I noted that all but five window seat occupants had pulled down the shades, switched on reading lights, and were engrossed in the recent hot-selling mystery. I suspect that none of them could explain to a ten-year old how this rather large and heavy chunk of metal was capable of remaining aloft at 32,000 feet going eight to ten times faster than their car might on the open road. That mystery is just taken for granted as something we will never really understand. There's something about physics in it. And seeing the world from such an altitude, an angel's perspective, holds little interest. Pilots now seldom serve as tour guides over the loudspeaker. "For those of you on the right-hand side of the airplane, you can get a wonderful view of the mighty Mississippi River devastating towns in Iowa." Or if they do, few of the drawn shades are raised to take a peek.

What were the passengers so absorbed in reading that the natural disaster below them could not distract them? The hands-down winner on that flight was a little book by popular author Michael Crichton called *Rising Sun*. Though it has a rather ordinary cops and killer plot, what makes the book interesting is that it is set in the midst of Japanese-American corporate dealings. It describes the Japanese strategies for success in the American and global markets in a remarkably cogent and alarming way. Some claim the book is nothing but Japanese bashing. But that is unfair to the author. His research is more than adequate, his presentation of the business tactics of the Japanese over the past two decades is documentable. Perhaps more importantly, he points out—sometimes explicitly and sometimes by merely subtly inviting comparison—the radical perceptual differences between the corporate structures and strategies of the two cultures.

The fact is that the Japanese corporations have been invading the long-held domains of American business, and their assaults have been spectacularly successful.

I'm not interested in directly attacking the Japanese practices or in spending much time decrying American business, and Americans in general, for failing to appreciate the perilous short-term tactics that were adopted in the face of the invasion. Instead, I want to look at two important ways in which the Japanese and Americans significantly differ in philosophical, and consequently ethical, perspective with regard to global business.

October 19, 1987, was a black day for American business. On that day President Reagan's "Morning in America" turned into "Mourning in America." The Reagan economic balloon burst. On that one day the stock market fell 508 points. On that single Bloody Monday investors in American corporations lost half a trillion dollars.

> It was generally agreed . . . that the main sources of the problem were the U.S. budget, and overvalued dollar, and sluggish economic growth in Europe and Japan. . . . Few recognized the event for what it was—the end, twelve years before its time, of the American century.[18]

Clyde Prestowitz argues, quite persuasively, that the Bloody Monday crash was the culmination of events that occurred during the 1980s. These included the fact that America had lost such key industries as consumer electronics to the Japanese; the president's defense science board warned that the United States was falling behind in all manner of high technology; the semiconductor industry of the United States had been soundly whipped by its Japanese counterpart, and what companies the Japanese couldn't beat they were buying; in the summer of 1987 the United States became the world's number one debtor nation, its international debt surpassed that of Mexico and Brazil combined; at the same time, Japan moved into the top spot as the world's leading creditor, and it passed the United States in per capita gross national product. Is it any wonder that confidence in American corporations dropped to such a point as to spark the Bloody Monday crash?

While the Japanese industries were successfully campaigning against their American counterparts, the Japanese financial houses were garnering the preeminent place in international finance. For example, as Prestowitz notes:

> In 1980, a ranking of the world's ten largest banks had included two U.S. banks and one Japanese. In 1986, it included seven for Japan and one for the United States.
>
> The Sumitomo Bank's purchase of a 15-percent interest in the Wall Street firm of Goldman, Sachs caused a stir of press comment in the summer of 1986. Few people knew, however, that Japanese banks had accumulated over 20 percent of the banking assets in California by acquiring four of its top ten banks. In the following year, a succession of Wall Street houses would announce partial sales of themselves to Japanese financial interests.
>
> In January 1986, for the first time Japan passed the United States in the share of international banking business held. It was predicted "the Japanese now are on their way to becoming the world's banker."
>
> In August 1987, four decades after it became the first U.S. bank to provide financing to rebuild Japan's war-torn economy, the ailing Bank of America was rescued by nine Japanese banks, which agreed to rescue it with a $130-million capital infusion. Observers called the agreement a "powerful symbol of Japan's preeminence in world financial markets."[19]

This litany can go on and on. That would serve no purpose in this context. What is important is that by the latter part of the 1980s, American corporate actors were having to learn to speak Japanese, in more ways than one. High-profile purchases of American real estate, such as Rockefeller Center in New York and Pebble Beach in California, only signaled that surplus funds in the Japanese coffers had become available for more than research and development buyouts and industrial expansion. Although they now own much of Hawaii and considerable chunks of California and have sizable holdings in almost every state, Japanese purchase of American real estate is only symbolically alarming. But then, many will say that the purchase of American industry, invention, talent, and markets by Japanese corporations is not especially alarming either. After all, we sold it to them. We weren't force to do so.

Michael Jacobs writes:

> America is experiencing a mid-life crisis. In its year-end 1990 review of competitiveness, *Business Week* observed that "you can feel America's eroding status in your bones."[20]

Prestowitz identifies a number of reasons why Japan has emerged to world business leadership and the United States has slipped, but one seems to me to stand out. The way it can be accounted for reveals much about the philosophical and ethical differences between us and the Japanese. The simplest way to put it is that the United States does not view industry as a matter of national security, but the Japanese certainly do.[21]

The operations of American corporations are and have been governed, as I have noted before, by principles derived from the philosophy of Adam Smith. The legacy to the corporate world from Smith and the other atomistic individualists who have dominated American thought has disadvantaged us in global competition, especially with the Japanese. The credo of individualism has endowed us with our most enduring image of ourselves: the solitary cowboy facing the band of vicious outlaws or raiding savages or the wilds of nature. It is the man in the wilderness, living by his wits, struggling to flourish, and leaving his sign for others to follow and admire him: Jeremiah Johnson, Daniel Boone, Kit Carson, and in film, hundreds of characters played by such actors as Gary Cooper, James Stewart, Clint Eastwood, Alan Ladd, Henry Fonda, and, of course, John Wayne. That is our national image, and from it we have derived a persistent conception, indeed a dogma, about the role of the businessperson in our society.

We view businesspersons as individuals in an adversarial posture vis-à-vis government, labor, and each other. The American self-image, fostered by the free marketeering of the Smithians, is everyone for him or herself. Hardly any wonder that when the White House fully embraced the dogma, as in the 1980s, the result would be the "me generation" and the decade of greed.

> Can it be that the notion of individualism, so sacred to the United States, is also its fatal flaw—the basic strength that works against itself to reduce strength?[22]

The last decade of global business competition with the Japanese suggests that the answer is "yes."

The contrast between the American perspective and that of the Japanese can be made clearer by drawing an analogy to a western film masterpiece, Clint Eastwood's *Pale Rider*. The plot of *Pale Rider* is superficially similar to that of *Shane*. A stranger, a gunfighter with a past, rides into an encampment of prospectors who are being terrorized by a ruthless corporate mining baron who is using hydraulic mining methods to ravage the mountains. The people in the encampment of miners are not especially brave, but they have banded together to save their investment, though realizing they could lose everything, including their lives, in the bargain. The character played by Eastwood, called only "Preacher," is the epitome of the American western hero. The corporate mining operation is completely under the control of another individualist in the Smithian mold, Lahood. The climax of the film brings the two into deadly conflict and also allows the Preacher to work out a previous grudge against a murderous itinerant marshal and his posse. The Preacher, however, as is the case with the great majority of western heroes, does not remain with those he has saved. After the death of Lahood and his henchmen, he rides off into the mountains, presumably to use his talents to aid other settlers in distress.

The important contrast, however, is not between the Preacher and Lahood. It is between the Preacher and the group of miners and settlers he helps. Although he fights for them and even, for a brief time, works with them, he is never really one of them. He is a loner, a gunfighter, though a person possessed of a healthy dose of grace. The miners are constantly fretting about their fates. They are not gunfighters (as one of them sadly proves on the snowy street of the town when he is gunned down by the murderous marshal), and their real salvation comes from sticking together. In fact, what they do they do as a group. Their point of reference is the community, not the individual. *Pale Rider* puts forth the view that

> . . . a small community of independent miners is preferable to the technologized corporation exactly because it is a community. The task of the preacher-gunfighter in *Pale Rider* is to exhort that community to look after itself and defend itself, and to empower it to live as a kind of epitome of the Jeffersonian small republic of virtuous citizens.[23]

Prestowitz puts it well:

By working together. By fixing wagon wheels—together. By raising barns—together. By starting towns —together. Under attack they circle the wagons together and take on all comers. And win.[24]

The Smithian individualism that has dominated our conception of business sees the corporate actor as a western hero or gunfighter and definitely not as a miner or settler. The Japanese, on the other hand, are not individualists. Their national culture is that of the miner or set-tler, but writ large, and their global business practices reflect that col-lectivist mindset.

I am tempted to say that the Japanese corporations have made cooperation an art form, but rather, for them, it is a science. The indi-vidual, the lone cowboy riding out of the mountains to the rescue, has no place in their strategy. Their wagons are circled, their loyalties to corporate communities are fixed. They may not display the swash-buckling flash of the American corporate raider, but they meticulously plod to a carefully plotted victory. Also, unlike their American coun-terparts, they are patient and prepared to stay the long course to achieve their goals. The main point I want to make, however, is that they have shown that the atomistic individualism that underlies the Smithian world view is not a prerequisite for success in the global mar-kets. It is also likely to lead to national disaster.

Japanese culture rejects the individualism that Smith and Locke and the current crop of laissez-faire libertarians espouse. They are group and collective focused. Management theorists in the United States and Europe have, for about a decade, been clamoring to mimic the Japanese corporate organizational models. Few, if any of them, however, recognize that the model depends on a philosophical concep-tion of society and economics that is, in every sense of the word, for-eign to Americans and Europeans. It is no wonder that recent studies show that where American corporations have tried to institute Japanese team approaches, typically senior managers have derailed the process by asserting their individual authority and power over team developed procedures and decisions.

We have been reared to think that the individual is the great strength of our society. The Japanese are nurtured to believe that the group is the strength of their culture. A Japanese person conceives of the group to which he or she belongs as the sole source of his or her identity. "In Japan there is virtually no life outside groups, which define a person's existence."[25]

The Japanese work hard to sustain and cultivate interpersonal relationships, group morale, and status. The dominant virtue in Japanese culture is harmony. It is not the Westerner's justice. Harmony is instilled and maintained, not by theoretical lessons, but by practices that stress conformity and group identification. The Japanese school systems are the primary teachers of the harmony virtue. We tend to see the two consistent elements of that educational system — unrelenting stress on the uniqueness of the Japanese and the importance of acquiescence to the behavior and values of the group — as unbearably constraining. They give rise to a society in which doing what others do is not just acceptable, it is virtually required, required for virtue.

Harmony, as Prestowitz notes, "requires sensitivity to the needs of others."[26] But this produces some interesting problems, for to be sensitive in the requisite manner, the Japanese must constantly observe each other. They need to keep track of each other, know what the others are doing. This leads to a society of folks always on the watch, watching each other, and watching carefully for even the slightest nuances. We would call it spying, invasion of privacy, something like that. And, in a sense, that's what it is. In fact, during World War II *tonari gumi* or neighborhood spying associations enforced social conformity on the Japanese home front. Though such groups are not practicing today, the attitudes they fostered are still prevalent and are reflected in their business practices. Those who march to the beat of a different drummer will usually find themselves walking in meaningless and unprofitable circles. You have to learn the march and the beat that is acceptable, and you have to continually check to be sure that the tune has not been altered. A considerable amount of watching is therefore necessary. It is little wonder that industrial espionage with respect to American companies has not been treated as a serious matter by the Japanese.

In 1982, Hitachi employed as a consultant in the United States, former IBM employee William Palyn. It asked him to inform them on the recent research and development at IBM regarding the personal computer. Hitachi was in the IBM-compatible or clone business, and decided that it needed to keep its product current with the IBM models to be competitive. Palyn, however, believing he had been asked to do something illegal, went to the FBI, which was happy to talk with him because they were engaged in a major computer theft and technology transfer operation in California. Their concern, however, was not so much industrial espionage by the Japanese as by the Soviet Union. But with Palyn's evidence they managed to ensnare both Hitachi and Mitsubishi for illicitly obtaining IBM proprietary information. The American press and public praised Palyn for assisting the FBI rather than continuing his highly profitable relationship with Hitachi. The Japanese, on the other hand, characterized him as a traitor, a dishonorable person. He had broken a bond of *nigen kankei* (human relations) and he was no longer an honorable, trustworthy person in their eyes. The glue that holds both the Japanese society and Japanese business together is conformity and the preservation, at almost all costs, of *nigen kankei*; the matter of industrial espionage seemed trivial to them in comparison.

The vast difference in business attitude is evident at almost all levels and in almost all practices in the two countries.

> Superficially, the hiring process appears to be similar in U.S. and Japanese companies. In fact, nothing could be more different. The U.S. company is hiring a new employee. The Japanese company is adopting a new member into the family. The first kind of obligation is contractual; the second, intensely personal.[27]

In Japan, a significant portion of corporate employment is for a lifetime, even though that is not explicitly stated at the time of employment.[28] The employee becomes an integral member of a group, and from then on both his or her identity and the group's status in the wider community will be a product of that association. He or she is not just hired to do a job. Advancement and salary in the corporation are almost exclusively determined by seniority, and key executive positions are usually filled by insiders. The Japanese find the American practice of recruiting senior officers from outside the corporation virtually unintelligible. They cannot imagine how such executives can understand the thinking, the decision processes, the CID structures, in their corporate "families" without having been reared in them. Of course, the Americans do not conceive of their corporations as families in the first place, and most seem to think that managerial expertise in one industry will readily translate to similar success in another.

The educational investment a Japanese corporation might need to make to improve an employee's productivity is usually amortizable over the working lifetime of that employee. The Japanese companies can therefore expend considerable sums in training and education with a reasonable expectation of a profitable return. American companies cannot make such a prediction with respect to their workers. The educational efforts and expenses of today are likely to end up tomorrow enhancing production in a competitor's plant. But these differences cut much deeper. For example, new technologies do not threaten Japanese workers in the way they seem to strike terror into the hearts and minds of American workers. The employees view them as enhancing productivity and corporate profitability, and so to be encouraged. That is a goal toward which the corporate culture movement has been striving in American business.[29]

Superiors in Japanese corporations are expected to support their employees and to take responsibility for corporate failures. Americans were shocked that the president of a corporation would resign after the corporation was involved in a disaster, as happened in 1985 when the president of Japan Airlines resigned after one of its planes crashed, killing 450 people. The president of Union Carbide did not resign after the Bhopal disaster.

Senior executives in Japanese corporations are never paid bonuses or exorbitant salaries in hard corporate times. Quite the opposite, they take salary reductions before forcing wage concessions from employees. American executives, on the other hand, spend an inordinate amount of time feathering their own nests and packing their golden parachutes when the profits start taking a turn for the worse.[30] In short, the Japanese corporation sees itself as and behaves like a cross between a family and a military unit with the esprit of the United States Marine Corps. Prestowitz writes:

> Japan's companies are structured along the lines of the ancient clan armies and there is a military aura about many of them. In lieu of an army, the military tradition of Japan has been to some extent transferred to businessmen who are the latter-day samurai. Companies encourage the martial arts and send employees to Zen-meditation courses to sharpen their discipline. Total commitment is expected.[31]

There are almost no takeovers in Japan, and with the employee commitment to their companies, productivity is startlingly high. Managers devote most of their time to genuine corporate issues such as product research and development and marketing strategies. The results have both amazed and frightened Americans in the recent decade.

One lesson that we may draw from this thumbnail sketch of the Japanese counterpart to American corporate life is that despite what we have been taught in economic theory courses, there is no necessary link between capitalism and atomistic individualism. The Japanese have become the world's leading capitalists. They have mastered capitalism, and they have done so without sacrificing their traditional group-oriented social structures. The individual in Japan is always subordinate to the group.

As it happens, the individual corporation is also subordinate to its *keiretsu* or economic group. Most of the Japanese industrial and related corporations are networked into large groups of interdependent and intersupporting corporate entities called *keiretsu*.[32] There are currently six major and three additional *keiretsu* in Japan. Allied companies in a particular *keiretsu* might include banking, insurance, heavy industry, electronics, and petrochemicals.

Should a member corporation of a *keiretsu* run into difficulties, as Mazda did in the 1970s when its rotary engine cars did not make the expected market impact, other members come to its support and bolster it until it is able to return to profitability, as Mazda certainly did in the 1980s. Mazda, the company for whom Kim S. works and with whom I had dealings regarding my leased car, is affiliated with the giant Sumitomo Group. The Sumitomo Group might be called a financial *keiretsu* because it is founded on banking interests. Enterprise *keiretsu* may also be under the umbrella of a financial *keiretsu*. Such groups will generally include the manufacturer, supplier, and distributor of a product. The affairs of each *keiretsu* are directed by a council or club typically composed of the chief executives of the affiliated corporations. The basic purpose of these clubs is to try to ensure that the *keiretsu* has a strong entry in all major sectors of the economy.[33]

> As companies in mature industries decline, the group puts resources behind companies in expanding sectors. This strategy provides the growth that allows flexibility and fulfillment of social obligations. For example, when Sumitomo Group's aluminum smelting companies became depressed, workers were shifted to other group companies. . . . In their regular meetings, each club discusses its business strategy vis-à-vis the other industrial groups and coordinates the activities of its member companies with regard to political, business, and world affairs.[34]

Keiretsu-like organizations, of course, cannot be legally formed in the United States. They offend our commitment to individualism and violate our conception of antitrust. But the bottom line is that they are incredibly successful in the global marketplace. At two levels—that of individual humans and individual corporations—the individualist doctrine would seem to be an unnecessary appendage of capitalism. While American corporations are legally forced to view themselves in deadly competition with each other, Japanese corporations work out vertical and horizontal affiliations that protect their interests and their corporate agents.

Of course, it may be argued that what the Japanese are doing is not capitalism. They aren't playing by the rules of capitalism that we invented. That is certainly true, and I will discuss it in rather more detail in the next section. The fact is, they're not playing. Or rather, they have a radically different view of business than we do. They are, however, winning.

It is worth noting in passing that I recently received a catalog from the Center for Independent Thought. It was called *Laissez Faire Books*. It contained advertisements for books by the leading writers from the libertarian point of view. Books by Michael Novak, Robert Nozick, Kevin Dowd, Myron Magnet, Milton Friedman, Thomas Sowell, and F. A. Hayek were featured. The general theme was, of course, that individualism and free markets will make everyone richer, happier, even more moral. Throughout the catalog the villains standing in the way of all of these benefits are big government, collectivism, and totalitarianism, especially as represented by the former Soviet Union. Not a single book in the catalog mentioned the Japanese corporations or their *keiretsu* system that now dominates markets worldwide. While praising the individualism of the American version of capitalism as morally supreme, it seemed to be assumed that the new countries of Eastern Europe will ignore the Japanese model and flock to the faltering

American one. The global markets, including those in the United States, however, don't appear to discriminate between individualist and collectivistic versions of capitalism. They respond to quality and value for money.

In Japanese culture the emphasis on the group and on group membership as the source of personal identity and fulfillment gives foundation to a shamed-based moral system that seems to permeate the corporate culture. Such a moral system, as discussed in Part 4, effectively produces a unity of purpose and the harmony that is so highly prized in Japan. It clearly surfaces for the world to see when the head of a Japanese corporation publicly resigns when disaster befalls his company, but it is present at all levels of the society. The sort of model consciousness on which shame is founded dominates in Japan, but, perhaps surprisingly, the Japanese morality is not an aspirational one. The Japanese may well have in mind models of the "good executive," the "good worker," the "good company," the "good *keiretsu*," but those are not, as far as I can tell, comparable to our conceptions of the "good doctor," "good soldier," or such. That is, they are not, more or less, mythic. They really are nothing more than representations of what the other executives, workers, corporations, and *keiretsu* are doing. Shame avoidance for them, by and large, is a matter of conformity to the ways of the group with which one is associated, hence, the inordinate emphasis on watching others.

The Japanese corporations invaded the United States markets for what most analysts regard as legitimate survival reasons. The American market, because it has little government control compared to that in Japan, also provided the Japanese corporations with freedom to grow they could never have realized in Japan. Distributors in the United States, unlike those in Japan, typically are not bound to certain manufacturers. They have independence to seek the best prices they can get from suppliers. The Japanese made a long-term commitment to conquering the American market, and so they were prepared to offer low prices for quality goods. They flooded the country with merchandise that was technologically as good or better than the American competition and sold it at a considerably lower price. The American consumers were delighted and flocked to the Japanese products. Slowly, but surely, the Japanese strategy succeeded in a number of major industries. What critics refer to as "dumping," conjoined with long-term corporate and *keiretsu* objectives, drove the American competition out of the markets.

The difference that was crucial to the victory of the Japanese corporations over their American counterparts is that the Japanese companies were growth driven whereas the Americans were (and are) driven by the need to show short-term profits. The Japanese companies knew that they did not have to make short-term profits. They were after markets, and the *keiretsu* system protected them by providing the cushion needed to support short-term losses. American corporate executives are dominated by the daily numbers and even the minute-by-minute shifts on the stock market. The demand for instant gratification by American investors defeats long-term corporate strategy, and it was long-term strategies that won the American markets for the Japanese manufacturing corporations.

Consider dumping. In Michael Crichton's book, dumping comes in for special attention. Crichton writes:

> ". . . the Japanese government starts an intensive program to develop a color-television industry. Once again, Japan licenses American technology, refines it in their protected markets, and floods us with exports. Once again, exports drive out American companies. Exactly the same story. By 1980 only three American companies still make color TVs. By 1987, there's only one, Zenith."
>
> "But Japanese sets were better and cheaper," I said.
>
> "They may have been better," Ron said, "but they were only cheaper because they were sold below production cost, to wipe out American competitors. That's called dumping."[35]

What Crichton doesn't explain is how the economics of dumping works for the Japanese. The Japanese manufacturers in industries such as home electronics rapidly developed substantial overcapacity with respect to their own markets. The *keiretsu* arrangements provided the money necessary to capitalize target industries so overcapacity increased. The typical response to overcapacity is that the price of the goods is driven below the cost of production. Economists, however, note two components to production costs: those that are fixed and those that are variable. Fixed costs cannot be avoided, variable costs can be controlled by the amount of production. Generally, if prices are driven so low that its variable costs cannot be covered, the corporation must stop manufacturing that product.

In the United States, the variable costs usually include the price of labor as well as that of materials. In Japan, because of lifetime employment, labor costs are fixed, not variable. That means that variable costs for production are smaller for the same products than in the United States. The *keiretsu* can make available enormous investment funds to finance the fixed costs, as Prestowitz explains:

> In Japan variable costs are those for materials, which means that when a Japanese manufacturer does variable-cost pricing, the price is much lower than when a U.S. company does the same. The result is prices far below cost in the U.S. market and bitter charges of "unfairness." Semiconductors are the classic example. Overinvestment led to variable-cost pricing. Despite suffering large losses, the Japanese were able to continue investing because of the large amounts of capital available to them and the social basis of their strategy.

The preceding explanations are not meant to detract from Japanese achievements. There is no denying the quality of their goods or the vigor with which they pursue chosen markets; and these factors, combined with the deepness of their pockets and their cohesion, have made them virtually unstoppable.[36]

The point is that the success of the Japanese corporations in invading the American markets and driving out many of their American competitors was intimately dependent on the Japanese conception of their social system. But many factors were involved, not the least of which was the Reagan administration's inability to grasp what was going on or to act in a reciprocal manner, probably because it suffered from tunnel-vision global policy on both national security and economics. The group orientation, as opposed to American individualism, provided the capital, support, and philosophical underpinnings to sustain a long-term siege of the American markets in major manufacturing industries. The Japanese have proven that capitalism and individualism are not inherently interrelated. American businesses are now stressing teamwork in their managerial approaches, as discussed in Part 2, but government policies and a philosophical hang-up on seventeenth-century individualism has utterly discouraged a collectivist development at the inter-corporate level. Individualism, perhaps by its very nature and certainly as it has come to be interpreted in America, is short-term goal oriented. After all, individual humans do not live that long, and their gratification models the general conception. Corporate actors, however, can have extremely long lives, enduring well past those of their human agents. When they are stymied by short-run interests, the disease of teleopathy afflicts them, as discussed in Part 2. A reminder of Goodpaster's definition of teleopathy may be helpful:

> [T]eleopathy can be understood as a habit of character that values limited purposes as supremely action-guiding, to the relative exclusion . . . of larger ends. . . .[37]

The loss of the American markets, in effect, is an outcome of corporate executive teleopathy, and the Japanese corporations are, by and large, inoculated from the disease because of their cultural and social traditions. The Japanese corporations are, therefore, better suited for global success than their American competitors, because the very culture that supports them is antiteleopathic in the first place. Emphasis on the group and the virtue of harmony, rather than the individual and justice, though we see it as repressive, is not understood as such by the Japanese. What makes it repressive to us is our doctrine of individualism. But that doctrine, as Prestowitz noted, may be the cause of our global business downfall.

The doctrine of individualism seems to encourage the metastasizing of teleopathy in the American corporation's decision making with respect to the manufacturing and marketing of its products. Without short-term profits, entrepreneurs are most unlikely to get the sort of capital support necessary to compete for market share. Too often in the past few decades we have seen American inventions sold or licensed to Japanese companies because American companies felt they could not justify the lack of short-term investment return the product was projected to record.

3. Playing Games and Making War in the Global Marketplace

> The object of warfare is murder; the means employed in warfare—spying, treachery, and the encouragement of it, the ruin of a country, the plunder of its inhabitants . . . trickery, lying; . . . the morals of the military class.[38]

The major difference between the Japanese and American conceptions of business is that the Japanese view the growth of their corporate ventures in the global marketplace as a matter of grave national security. Americans think of their national security in terms of military power, numbers of submarines, battleships, nuclear weapons, the size of the military force, its readiness for combat, and the like. When the Bush administration made an effort to justify the Persian Gulf War, it first said that the United States was engaged there to preserve democracy. That didn't ring true because none of the countries we were protecting were democracies. Then the Bush administration offered up, "Jobs, jobs, jobs." When asked what jobs it had in mind, that public relations campaign was dropped, and we were told that the United States had a vital national interest in the region. That interest, of course, was cheap oil, but even that didn't play too well. So, finally, frightful stories of babies being pulled from incubators in Kuwait by Iraqi soldiers were conjured up to rally American public support. (As we have since learned, the Kuwaitis fabricated the incubator stories to help the cause.)

The point I want to make from this, however, is that Americans seem to find it harder to conceive of national security in terms of protecting and enhancing our business corporations' interests than abstract protection of human rights or concepts such as democracy and freedom. I am not saying this is necessarily a bad thing, but it is, no doubt a further product of our conception of corporations on the atomistic individualist model. Let them look out for their own interests. American soldiers shouldn't have to die so that American corporations can make higher profits. The Japanese see things in just the opposite way. To them, their national security is dependent on the success of their international corporate ventures. Foreign policy and corporate economic policy are inextricably linked in their collective mind.

In America, the most common analogy for business is that of the game. Corporate actors locked in a struggle for market supremacy are typically viewed as competitors or teams engaged in a sporting contest. Not only the language of sport, but the attitudes of sport, dominate our thinking about business. "Fair play" seems so important to us that we have established a whole body of laws to try to ensure it. Partly as a consequence of that and partly because it was our conception in the first place, the general society, as represented by the government, is seen as no more than a kind of neutral referee for the market contests. It calls the fouls, but has little interest in who wins, even if the opponents are not both Americans. The idea is that American corporate actors are independent entities wrestling with each other for our entertainment and ours and their profit as individuals, but that the successes or failures of any of them are not especially important to our national security. Games are games, and though it is a serious game that General Motors plays with the Ford Motor Company, the Chrysler Corporation, and the imports, the ethics that govern it should be the ethics of games. Talk of level playing fields is rampant.

What are the ethics of games? Consider basketball. Does basketball have an ethics? Of course it does. There are things a player or coach, and even a fan, ought to do and ought not to do. Some of its ethics are enforced by its rules and involve sanctions. Many are, however, simply matters of expected behavior and custom and all are to be honored whether or not the game is played in a professional setting or on an urban playground. Examples? Impeding a player's attempt to move about the court cannot be done in blatantly violent ways. Interference or spying on the strategy sessions of the opposing team are forbidden. The number of players to a team are regulated so that one team cannot have ten players on the court to the opponent's five.

Further attempts at specifying the ethical elements of the game of basketball are not important. What does matter is that if you see your activity as a game, then you also see certain kinds of constraints on your behavior as appropriate and even necessary to continue to play and enjoy the game. You take a certain stance toward the activity and toward others who are engaged in it. Your hostility toward them is constrained by the internalization of the ethical rules and attitudes that are involved in the game and that permeate our general conception of game playing. After all, it's only a game.

Suppose, however, that you conceive of your activity as analogous to war. (You are likely to do that if you believe that it is essential to your security as a nation.) Some might be tempted to say that war is just a kind of game, but that stretches the conceptions of both war and game too far. There are, of course, war games, and what makes them games is that they are not really war. They are like war in certain respects, but the rules of play are much more confining to the participants. War isn't a game. It's war! Not all human activities are games.

Two phrases or mottoes regularly turn up when war is mentioned: "war is hell," and "all's fair in love and war." Both are inaccurate, even misleading. With regard to the first, we can say with Michael Walzer that war isn't really hell, if what we have in mind are the victims of war.

> (W)ar is the very opposite of hell. . . . For in hell, presumably, only those people suffer who deserve to suffer, who have chosen activities for which punishment is the appropriate divine response knowing that it is so. But the greater number by far of those who suffer in war have made no comparable choice.[39]

General W. T. Sherman, who is said to have first uttered "War is hell" for public consumption while he was marching across Georgia and leaving nothing but charred ruins in his wake, apparently wasn't attempting to describe war. He was justifying it, or at least his way of engaging in it.

> Sherman was claiming to be innocent of all of those actions (though they were his own actions) for which he was so severely attacked. . . .[40]

Sherman made this clear when he answered the protests of General Hood, the commandant of Atlanta, who called Sherman's actions and orders the most studied and ingenious acts of cruelty in the history of war. Sherman noted that "War is cruelty, and you cannot refine it." Sherman went on to argue that insofar as he represented the just side in the Civil War, he could not be held responsible for the cruelty and destruction that his prosecution of the war produced. War is hell, and those who start wars must be held responsible for the hellish damage and destruction that occurs. As Sherman had nothing to do with the causes of the war, he felt blameless with respect to the outcome of the methods he used to win it for the side that was in the right.

Sherman, not unlike many of his profession, was rather too simplistic in his analysis of the situation. War may well be hell in that it involves the infliction of great suffering, but the responsibility for the conduct of the war may not be exhausted when the unjust perpetrator is identified. But then there is that other catchy phrase, "All's fair in love and war," which supposedly means there are no limits to the way a war may be fought. It suggests there are no ethics in war, that everything is permissible. But that is not the case. There are established rules of warfare, impermissable acts even though the carnage may be horrific and widespread. Still, and this is what is important for our purposes, the ethical limits on war are considerably fewer than those on games, or on war games.

What is forbidden in a game may be allowed in war: spying, brutal tactics, killing. War should not, however, be purposeless or wanton violence. Henry Sidgwick provided a twofold rule of the ethics of war that is, at least, a starting point for discussion.[41] Sidgwick's rule is that it is not permissible, even in a war fought for morally good reasons, to do "any mischief which does not tend materially to the end, nor any mischief of which the conduciveness to the end is slight in comparison with the amount of mischief."[42] The end referred to is, of course, victory. So Sidgwick's rule prohibits causing unnecessary or excessive harm and insists that in the first instance there must be a necessary link between the mischief or brutality used and the victory being sought. But Sidgwick's rule also contains a proportionality condition that disallows actions of a harmful nature that produce severe suffering and injury but only minor or slight advances toward victory in a justifiable cause.

The proportionality prong of Sidgwick's rule, however, is going to be difficult to enforce. Walzer comments:

> Any act of force that contributes in a significant way to winning the war is likely to be called permissible . . . proportionality turns out to be a hard criterion to apply, for there is no ready way to establish an independent or stable view of the values against which the destruction of war is measured. Our moral judgments (if Sidgwick is right) wait upon purely military considerations and will rarely be sustained in the face of an analysis of battle conditions or campaign strategy by a qualified professional. It would be difficult to condemn soldiers for anything they did in the course of a battle or a war that they honestly believed, and had good reason to believe, was necessary, or important, or simply useful in determining the outcome.[43]

As a general rule, it would seem that soldiers should be morally entitled to win the wars they are morally justified in fighting. For all intents and purposes they must be morally allowed to do what they think they must do to win.

Sidgwick's rule may be central to our conception of the ethics of war, but it is not exhaustive. Other rules are also in the package, and they do erect limits around the options of warriors to do even what they think is necessary to win the war they are fighting, tactics that Sidgwick's rule might have allowed. Though some war theorists, such as Francisco Vitoria, defend acts by soldiers in war such as rape and pillage because they may prove either deterrents to the enemy or ways of rewarding or spurring the courage of the troops, most of us will agree that such behavior should not be ethically countenanced in war. In the reports from the recent civil war in Bosnia we hear horrific stories of sacking, pillage, and rape by the Serbs of the Bosnian Muslims. Those acts are apparently intended to terrorize the Muslim population so that they will desert their towns. They are therefore a part of the intentional tactics of the Serbs to produce an "ethnically cleansed" region. Even if that end were morally justifiable, which I do not think it is, the ethics of war would rule out such tactics. In other words, proportionality and military necessity have been augmented in our formulations of warfare ethics with protections for those who may be caught up in the fray. That explains why the appeal for support for the Persian Gulf War by using stories about harming babies was so effective. Some acts in war are intolerable, at least from the moral point of view. Not all is fair in war.

The Japanese, as we are beginning to appreciate, view international business as war, not as a game. Consequently, the ethics they apply to their business practices in the global markets are modeled on the ethics of war, not those of games. Their goal is not a win today and the prospect of a rematch tomorrow; they want a win that redraws the international commercial map. They are committed to the field of battle for the long haul, and they do not feel constrained by the sportsmanship rules of games. Trade, for them, is adversarial. Its goal is to destroy the competition.

They are convinced of the righteousness of their cause and that successful expansion into the global markets is absolutely essential to Japanese national security. In that regard, they may well be right. At the very least, by expanding their foreign markets they are able to secure a life-style in Japan that allows them both the cultural isolation they have historically sought and the international power that does not require them to be subservient to other nations. A convincing argument can be made that the various business tactics they have adopted are not only consistent with their end, but tend materially to its accomplishment. That satisfies the first condition of Sidgwick's rule. But is the "mischief" they have done to American business interests proportional to the achievement of the desired outcome? If the response given in the case of soldiers in war is appropriate, then we should probably concede that they also have satisfied proportionality. The fact that a number of American businesses have lost market share and have been forced to withdraw from production may be regrettable for Americans, but it is not a relevant factor when assessing proportionality. That is, after all, what the business war is about. That is how victory is measured. The proportionality condition would come into play if the Japanese corporations were using tactics that produced harms much greater than what is necessary to defeat their international competitors, or if the tactics they were using resulted in major suffering but only marginally improved their market share. That certainly has not happened. American consumers show preference for Japanese products. The chairman of Sony, Akio Morita, tells the story of having visited the home of an American counterpart. He toured the house and was shown the various gadgets and appliances with which it was equipped. All were made in Japan. His host then remarked that he doubted that were he to tour Morita's home in Japan that he would find so many American-made products. Morita admitted that he was right, but he asked his host what American products he thought Morita should have when he hadn't bought any for his own house.[44]

In fact, the introduction and success of the Japanese products in the American markets has forced many American corporations to upgrade their own products in order to remain competitive. The automobile industry is an excellent case in point. The Japanese cars had become so highly regarded by the mid-1980s that American cars, long noted for shoddy workmanship and frequent breakdowns, had to be redesigned and improved to hold on to some portion of the market. By 1993 the American automobile manufacturers had regained much of the public's confidence that they had lost in the 1970s and '80s and their satisfaction ratings rose, as, of course, did their sales.

The dumping tactics of the Japanese corporations, especially in the home electronics industry, arguably are comparable to battle ploys, such as sacking and pillaging, that are prohibited by the moral considerations that augment Sidgwick's rule. I do not, however, see how such a case can be made against dumping. The primary result of dumping in the electronics markets was that most American homes now have television sets, VCRs, and other handy gadgets at affordable prices. Indeed, the American manufacturers of such products were driven from the field, and many of their workers were laid off. Plants shut down, tax revenues dropped. But all of those downsides were the usual or normal outcomes of competition. Losers lose.

It has, however, been argued that the Japanese tactics were unfair because their corporate structure and funding is so radically different from that in America that the playing field was not a level one. The Japanese, simply, can carry out the proven long-term strategies needed to conquer a market because they can absorb short-term losses and bear greater debt loads, and they do not have to show almost immediate profits. That is what dumping is all about. American corporations, because they depend for their capital on Wall Street investors rather than *keiretsu* arrangements, must continually show short-term profits. They can't compete with the Japanese on an even footing. Prestowitz tells the story of his conversation with Bob Galvin, CEO of Motorola. Motorola is in the communications business, as is NEC in Japan.

> In 1979, they were of comparable size: Motorola sales were $2.7 billion, and NEC's were $3.6 billion. . . . Between 1979 and 1986, Motorola's profit after tax was between 5 percent and 7 percent of sales; for NEC, the figure was 2 percent to 3 percent. . . . On every measure of profitability for asset management, Motorola was nearly twice as good as NEC. In one critical area, however, it was not: NEC's annual growth over the period was about 21 percent; Motorola's 15 percent. As a result, in 1986 Motorola

was a $6 billion company and NEC a $17 billion company . . . .So
Motorola's management appeared to be doing their job, but its environment demanded profit, while NEC's demanded growth . . . .When I asked
Bob Galvin why he didn't increase his debt, or even take the company private to avoid the financial pressures of Wall Street and the analysts, he
told me such debt levels would be too risky for his company, because he did
not operate in a Japanese-style environment.[45]

The Japanese high-tech communications industry was therefore
able to drive their American competition from the market. But was it
unfair?

The answer is that it would have been unfair were international
business a game. The playing field is definitely not level between the
American and the Japanese corporations. But in a war, the primary
strategy is to take the high ground, to get your enemy into a bad position. The outcomes of some of the greatest battles in the history of warfare were determined by location on an uneven field of engagement.
Again, if your model of business is war, adversarial trade, the notion
of an even playing field is nonsense. Furthermore, in war the combat-
ants must compete with the resources at their disposal. Such resources
certainly include the means of raising investment capital.

From the moral point of view, we can ask whether the conception of
business as war is more likely to violate the side constraints than the
conception of business as a game. Certainly it would if the adage that
all's fair in war is taken as a basic principle of war. But I have suggested that it is not such a principle. The issue is really whether Rank
B-ers are used without their consent as mere means in the adversarial trading approach. Of course, they might be, but I do not see how
there is any necessary link between conceiving of business as war and
violating the side constraints. War is not by its very nature unethical.

Suppose it is said that the tactic of dumping violates the side constraints because it uses Rank B-ers as mere means to the market success of the company doing the dumping. What Rank B-ers? Surely not
the competitor corporations, for they are aware that they are in a battle for market share and they entered that fray freely. The consumers?
Hardly. Their benefits are significant and desirable. Their freedom to
buy or not to buy isn't curtailed, and they can purchase more high-qual-
ity products than in the past. No one, neither corporate actors nor
human individuals, is being treated as mere means by the Japanese
tactics. Still, there seems to be a sense of unfairness about it all.

I think that sense of unfairness is a result of our own conceptual-
ization of the marketplace, and that concept is more of a myth or a
conceit than an adequate representation of reality. The marketplace
has never been a level playing field. Those with more capital than others have always commanded the high ground. More importantly, the
markets are not playing fields at all. Not all fields of competition are for

sporting events. If the Japanese corporate invaders taught us nothing else, causing us to reconceive our idea of the international marketplace would bring about a radical change in American life.

The typical American response to the successful Japanese invasion of American markets has been to cry foul. We send government missions to Japan to try to get them to change their perception of business and trade. We want them to see things the way we do, to be like us. They're not going to do it. Why should they? It would require that they utterly alter their culture, the very culture that has allowed them to dominate the international business system without conforming to its conceptions, its form of life.

Crichton, in the afterword of his novel writes:

> Sooner or later, the United States must come to grips with the fact that Japan has become the leading industrial nation in the world. The Japanese have the longest life span. They have the highest employment, the highest literacy, the smallest gap between rich and poor. Their manufactured products have the highest quality. They have the best food. The fact is that a country the size of Montana, with half our population, will soon have an economy equal to ours.[46]

I'm not so sure about the food, but the rest is true. And though they have achieved their place by methods frowned upon by American business, in general they have not violated the ethical side constraints against treating Rank B-ers merely as means without their consent.

ENDNOTES

1. See Solomon and Hanson, op. cit. p. 37.
2. See Norman Bowie, "The Moral Obligations of Multinational Corporations," *Problems of International Justice* ed. by S. Luper-Foy (Boulder, 1988) p. 100.
3. Peter A. French, Jeffrey Nesteruk, David T. Risser (with John Abbarno), *Corporations in the Moral Community* (Fort Worth, 1992) p. 165.
4. Ibid. p. 97–113.
5. See part 2, section 5.
6. See Richard Rorty, "Solidarity and Objectivity," *Post-Analytic Philosophy*, ed. by J. Rajchman and C. West (New York, 1985).
7. Donald Davidson, "Thought and Talk," *Mind and Language* (Oxford, 1975) p. 20–21.
8. Ibid.
9. David E. Cooper, "Moral Relativism," *Midwest Studies in Philosophy* (1978) p. 101.
10. Philippa Foot, *Vices and Virtues* (Oxford, 1978) especially chapters 7–9 and 11.
11. David E. Cooper, "Moral Relativism," *Midwest Studies in Philosophy* (1978) p. 104.
12. John Searle, "How to Derive 'Ought' from 'Is'" *The Philosophical Review* (1964).
13. Cooper, op. cit. p. 103.
14. Bowie, op. cit. p. 110.

15. Ibid.
16. Ibid. p. 110–11.
17. Colin Turnbull, *The Mountain People* (New York, 1972).
18. Clyde Prestowitz, Jr., *Trading Places* (New York, 1988) p. 5.
19. Ibid. p. 12.
20. Michael Jacobs, *Short-Term America* (Boston, 1991) p. 1.
21. See Prestowitz, op. cit. p. 13.
22. Ibid. p. 14.
23. Paul Smith, *Clint Eastwood* (Minneapolis, 1993) p. 52.
24. Prestowitz, op. cit. p. 14.
25. Ibid. p. 82.
26. Ibid. p. 86.
27. Ibid. p. 153.
28. This should not be construed as a claim that the major Japanese corporations do not employ large numbers of temporary workers, especially in the ancillary elements of production such as supply warehouses. They definitely do.
29. A bursting of the so-called "bubble economy" in Japan that their current deep recession is producing may force a change in the lifetime employment policies of many corporations. Currently, only the smaller corporations have been reported as abandoning lifetime employment, while the bigger corporations are using early retirement schemes and shorter hours to preserve lifetime employment in difficult economic times.
30. The disparity between American workers' salaries and those of American senior executives is often thought to contribute to American economic problems. There seems to be no hard evidence to support that belief, but it does have a powerful psychological impact, particularly on those concerned about financial waste in America.
31. Prestowitz, op. cit. p. 155.
32. See Karel van Wolferen, *The Enigma of Japan* (New York, 1989) p. 384–415.
33. See Prestowitz, op. cit. p.156–66.
34. Ibid. p. 159.
35. Michael Crichton, *Rising Sun* (New York, 1992) p. 226–27.
36. Prestowitz, op. cit. p. 181.
37. Goodpaster, op. cit. p. 94.
38. Leo Tolstoy, *War and Peace*, trans. by Constance Garnett (New York, n.d.) part ten, XXV, p. 725.
39. Michael Walzer, *Just and Unjust Wars* (New York, 1977) p. 30.
40. Ibid. p. 32.
41. Henry Sidgwick, *Elements of Politics* (London, 1891) p. 254.
42. Ibid.
43. Walzer, op. cit. p. 129.
44. See *Fortune*, (September 25, 1989).
45. Prestowitz, op. cit. p. 209.
46. Crichton, op. cit. p. 393.

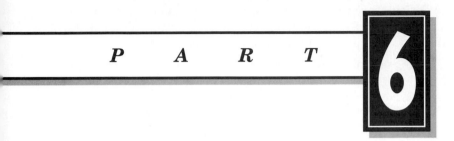

THE INVADERS IN THE DOCK

 ### 1. Corporations as Legal Persons: Roman and German Traditions, Fiction and Realism

The idea of corporations as independent social units, actors on the communal stage, emerged first in the law when they gained status as legal persons.

A legal person may be described as any entity that is a subject of a right, or as any entity recognized in a legal system as supporting such capacities as instituting and defending judicial proceedings. Legal personality is always something conferred, it is never merely the result of the act or acts of parties.

The idea of a legal person (indeed the term "person" itself) comes from the Romans. The Latin *persona* was originally limited to the theater. If you have gone to theater productions, you may well have noticed that the characters and the actors playing the parts are listed in the program under the title *dramatis persona*, a remnant of the Roman theater. Roman law appropriated the term to refer to anything that could *act* on either side of a legal dispute. In Roman law all legal persons were artifacts of the law itself. It was no concern of the law that legal persons might have lives prior to or outside of the legal sphere. The biological status of a subject also was not relevant, so it was not necessary to draw a clear distinction between real and artificial legal persons. All were conceived as creations of law.[1] The great

335

English legal theorist Edward Coke characterized this view as based on the position that being a legal person exists only because of the acts and considerations of the law.

The Roman conception of the legal person, when it was applied to corporate entities, produced what is called the fiction (or the grant or concession) theory. In the introduction to a leading contemporary text in corporation law, the specter of the Roman *persona* thrives:

> . . . saying that corporations are persons serves as a useful shorthand for the fact that the law recognizes them as distinct legal entities endowed with separate legal characteristics that are often identical to those of natural persons . . . [a] corporation is merely a "fiction," a creation of the intellect, and thus . . . dependent for its recognition by the law on some act by the state.[2]

Justice Marshall, in the *Dartmouth* case, provided perhaps the most famous American statement of the fiction theory:

> A corporation is an artificial being, invisible, intangible, and existing only in contemplation of law.[3]

Roman law recognized two types of organizations. One, governed by contract, a *societas*, was such that its assets were owned by the contractors. The other, a *universitas*, was a legal entity separate from its members, capable of holding property and of possessing distinct rights and obligations. Legal personhood was conferred on the *universitas*, not the *societas*.

Conceiving legal personhood as a privilege and not a matter of right was basic to the fiction theory and to Roman law. In 57 B.C., the *lex Julia de collegiia* authorized corporations, but to be granted incorporation an association had to show that it would be "helpful to the state or beneficial to the public."[4] The suggestion, not worked out in Roman jurisprudence to my knowledge, is that corporations are extensions of the state. But that should not be surprising because the fiction theory defines all legal persons *qua* legal persons, whether individual humans or corporations, as extensions of the state. In the case of corporations, this was perhaps clearer than in the case of humans and produced interesting legal results. Corporations, according to the fiction theory, can do only what the state permits them to do. As George Ellard notes, all of their actions are "in effect acts of government, corporate officers being ultimately accountable to the state."[5] The fiction theory holds the state responsible for the supervision of all of the acts of corporations, and that was set in motion within the charter-granting process. A corporation's actions are strictly limited to what was specifically set down in its articles of incorporation. Any other activity carried out in the name of the corporation is *ultra vires*, beyond the power of the corporation, and so not legally attributable to the corporate body. Therefore, corporations, in fiction theory, are by definition law-abiding.

Canon law, the law of the Catholic Church, followed the Roman model in the treatment of its corporate entities such as monasteries, nunneries, and various orders. These were conceived of as *persona ficta* in a literal sense. Holdsworth identifies Innocent IV as the first pope to create the designation.[6] The pope was, apparently, responding to the difficulty of preserving the tenets of canon law while dealing with these ecclesiastical bodies. Monastic orders, for example, in canon law, were comprised of dead humans, people who had resigned their earthly lives, yet the orders had vast property holdings from which they obtained rents and they produced products that could be sold on the market. Abbots and mother superiors regularly had to obtain enforcement of the rights of their orders to their property or to property willed to the orders. In response to the problem, the pope endowed himself with the power to create artificial persons that possessed property and other legal and commercial rights. Such property was understood to belong to no abbot or specific collection of monks. In fact, it belonged to no human person(s). Its ownership lay completely in the "hands" of the *persona ficta*, the monastery, nunnery, or order. Monks and abbots, nuns and mother superiors, were treated as guardians entrusted with the maintenance of the property held corporately. This canon-law conception of a rudimentary corporation migrated into English law during the Tudor period.

By 1615 Coke wrote in *Sutton's Hospital* that for there to be valid corporations there must be "a lawful authority of incorporation." He meant that a sanctioning body should be empowered to create, sustain, and monitor such artificial persons. Holdsworth argued that the reasons for the criminalization of conspiracy are virtually the same as "those which make it necessary to regulate the activities of groups . . . who may acquire great power by organizing in corporate form."[7]

The seventeenth-century individualists were beginning to get an inkling of the social potency of the monsters that contracts between free citizens might produce! The *ultra vires* doctrine embedded in the fiction theory was supposed to solve the problem of controlling the corporate entities and probably explains why the Roman conception survived in corporate law so much longer than it did with respect to human persons. The liberals could, at least at first, see it as a protection for the individual against the power of organizations. But that was to misconstrue its tenets and when that was realized by latter-day Lockeans, they found a replacement more in keeping with their individualism.

In effect, the fiction theory of legal personhood, if taken to its logical conclusion, is grossly totalitarian. All rights, privileges, and duties, whether of humans or corporate actors, must be ultimately conferred by and through a central civil authority. In the corporate sphere the activities of freely associated humans are severely restricted, and the interests and wills of organizations are either interpreted as extensions of the state and always lawful or as reducible to the actions and attributes of humans. And from where does the authority for doing all of this conferring get its legitimacy? I am reminded of the scene in *Monty Python's Quest for the Holy Grail* in which two peasants question Arthur about how he got to be king. They are told about the Lady of the Lake presenting the sword Excalibur to Arthur. Unpersuaded that such an aquatic ceremony could create supreme political authority, they ignore Arthur, who then gives away the real source of his authority by threatening the lives of the peasants with the sword. The fiction theory has a certain medieval look to it, despite the trappings of Enlightenment individualism in which it is often dressed.

To combat the drawbacks in the fiction theory, nineteenth-century liberals foisted on the law (what else but?) a contractual theory of the corporation, which "interprets the corporate form as but a convenient summarizing device for the limited rights and duties of the private parties who contractually create (it)."[8] Government authority vis-à-vis corporations is thereby limited to its authority over any other contractual relations between consenting adults. In American law this conception of corporate legal personhood had its heyday in the 1880s. If the contract theory can be said to have any virtue at all (it surely did not reflect much of corporate life or the role of corporations in society, even in its own time), it is that it rescued corporations from state control. It ended the thinking about them as special creations of the state and its legal system and placed their establishment and operation in the hands of private individual humans. It gave us the separation of business and state that underlies so much of contemporary debate about government regulation of various enterprises. The contract theory reflected the way corporations actually did come into being after the seventeenth century. They were, by and large, the result of joint ventures contracted for by consenting humans. But it failed to appreciate that corporations are much more than ways to pool capital, that they can become full-fledged players in the game of social life, and that they can have "lives" quite independent of their incorporators.

In legal history the major rival of the fiction theory has been the reality theory, often identified with German jurisprudence. The basic premise of the reality theory is that the law does not invent its subjects, it recognizes their existence. The most influential versions of the reality theory were put forth by Gierke, Figgis, Maitland, and Freund.[9] When applied to human persons, the reality theory draws few detractors. It simply asserts that extralegal considerations regarding personhood should dominate the issue of whether any human ought to be treated as a legal person. The law's task is to capture as its subjects the players actually involved in the social game. It does not create those players, though it attempts to regulate their play.

The realists, however, did not restrict their theory to human persons. In fact, humans were far from their primary interest. Corporate entities were their focus. In simplest terms, to the realist, corporations are persons because, prelegally, they meet the basic functional conditions of personhood applied to any entity seeking admission to the legal community. For the reality theorists, the fact that something is artificial or natural or some combination of artificial and natural is irrelevant to whether or not it is entitled to legal personhood status. What is relevant is what it is capable of doing before any legal powers are conveyed on it. What is crucial is whether an entity has certain capabilities and capacities, functions in certain ways and can be known to do so, and evidences identity or self-sameness over time.

 ## 2. Corporate Crime: Control and Adjudication—The Trial of Enforced Corporate Responsive Adjustment

The media on any given day have been known to feature stories under headlines such as the following:

FELONY INVOLUNTARY MANSLAUGHTER CHARGE FILED IN LOS ANGELES AGAINST A CONSTRUCTION COMPANY;

EPA KNOWING ENDANGERMENT CONVICTIONS RETURNED ON 15 CHARGES AGAINST A DENVER CONCRETE ADDITIVE MANUFACTURER;

NATIONAL BANK IN MASSACHUSETTS INDICTED ON CURRENCY REPORTING VIOLATIONS;

NEW YORK COMMODITIES FIRM CONVICTED OF CONSPIRACY AND MAIL FRAUD;

18-COUNT FEDERAL GRAND JURY INDICTMENT FOR RACKETEERING AND OTHER VIOLATIONS BROUGHT AGAINST INVESTMENT COMPANY.

These actually were the headlines of stories on just one recent day, and they weren't all of the headlines of this sort. Not by a long shot. The annals of corporate crime in America are ever increasing as ingenious and well-educated young executives in expensive clothing invent new ways to make corporate profits and personal gains rise dramatically.

When the average American thinks of criminal behavior, one picture typically pops into his or her mind. It is that of a street crime, a young male from a minority group, shabbily dressed, probably on drugs, waving a revolver, and demanding money and other valuables. The mugging is our model of crime. The mugger is the model of the criminal. That is because the mugging brings together in the same space and in a few brief moments all of the things we most fear: confrontation with a member of a group we regard as dangerous and offensive, violence, loss of property, and possible injury or loss of life. But the street crime as a model is, of course, ridiculous, because street crimes, though clearly violent and often dramatic, are not nearly the significant problem to our society that the popularity of the model leads us to believe. The far greater negative social impact is produced by corporate crime, yet corporate crime is typically passed off as somebody fiddling with the books or trying to take too much of a percentage. It is dismissed as if it were a little spot on a dress shirt that no one will notice in the candlelight.

Corporate crime, however, is an enormous drain on our society. Before looking at the facts, a clarification is in order. In the 1940s Edwin Sutherland invented the term "white-collar crime."[10] His sociological studies broke considerable ground, but the idea that corporate crime was a really serious matter has not captured the American mind. Sutherland's definitions also provoked confusion. He defined white-collar crime as "a crime committed by a person of respectability and high social status in the course of his occupation."[11] On this account the crimes of the persons in the Nixon White House were white-collar, so were the crimes committed by Jim Bakker and some of the crimes of Jimmy Swaggert. The actions of Dr. Jack Kevorkian, if he is convicted in Michigan, would also fall in the white-collar crime category. Those certainly weren't corporate crimes.

I think it is advisable to distinguish between white-collar crime and corporate crime. It may be allowed that corporate crime is a variety of white-collar crime, but on my account corporate crime refers to criminal actions that are attributable to a corporate actor or a corporate agent acting on behalf of the corporate actor. Ronald Kramer provides a similar definition. He writes:

> [C]orporate crime will be regarded as a specific form of organizational crime (criminal acts engaged in by corporate organizations themselves as social entities or by officials or employees of the corporation, acting on behalf of or in concert with the corporate action.)[12]

Kramer's definition is based on a distinction drawn by Clinard and Quinney, who divide white-collar crime into two kinds.

> Occupational crime consists of offenses committed by individuals for themselves in the course of their occupations and the offenses of employees against their employers. . . . Corporate crimes are the offenses committed by corporate officials for their corporation and the offenses of the corporation itself.[13]

An executive's taking of a bribe to place an order with a supplier is a white-collar crime, but dumping the company's factory waste into a river is a corporate crime.

The impression one gets from the newspapers and TV news shows is that the number of corporate crimes is escalating, and most sociological indicators suggest that corporate and white-collar crime has increased since Sutherland's studies. Even if some portion of that rise may be attributable to better reporting and more concise definitions, it cannot be denied that corporate crime is a characteristic fact of American life.

The estimates on the costs of corporate crime vary from study to study, but in no case is it close to what could be described as insignificant or unimportant. A Justice Department report in 1980 put the loss to taxpayers from violations of federal regulations at between ten and twenty billion dollars. In 1974 the Chamber of Commerce of the United States claimed that what they called white-collar crime cost forty billion dollars annually.

> One of the most thorough attempts to calculate the financial loss to the country from corporate crimes was that of the Subcommittee on Antitrust and Monopoly of the U.S. Senate Judiciary Committee, headed by the late Senator Philip Hart. This subcommittee put the cost of corporate crime at between $174 [billion] and $231 billion a year.[14]

For the sake of comparison, the annual loss from violent street crime amounts to three to four billion dollars annually. The monetary figures are alarming, but the physical costs are downright shocking. Clinard and Yeager report that "far more persons are killed through corporate criminal activities than by individual criminal homicides."[15] That does not, of course, include those maimed or severely injured from corporate criminality.

Is corporate crime real crime? Sutherland persuasively argued that two criteria apply to the problem of determining whether an action is criminal and that corporate crimes satisfy both criteria. Sutherland's criteria are that the legal description of the act must identify it as socially harmful and there must be a legal penalty for the performance of the act.[16] It should not matter whether the corporate act is punishable by the state under administrative, civil, or criminal law.

The debate in sociology and criminology over the proper definition of crime (should administrative and civil law violations and punishments be counted?) seems to me a mere territorial squabble or a political class issue and of no real significance to the problem of dealing with corporate offenses. The issue is one of control. How is corporate crime to be held in check? How is it to be reduced?

Brent Fisse and I, both jointly and separately,[17] have challenged the orthodox view that corporate responsibility for crime depends on proof of corporate intentionality for the causally relevant acts at or before the time of the untoward event. We have argued that corporate responsibility in criminal cases should be assessed on the basis of the corporate defendant's response to the harm it has caused. Fisse has called this the concept of reactive fault, and I have developed the corresponding principle of responsive adjustment (PRA), as discussed in Part 4.

Reactive corporate fault, according to Fisse, is an unreasonable corporate failure to undertake appropriate preventative and corrective measures in response to the corporate commission of the *actus reus* of an offense.[18] The idea of reactive corporate fault reflects, as Fisse notes, two practical realities worthy of our attention:

1. Communal attitudes of resentment toward corporations that fail to react diligently when they have caused harm, and
2. The common managerial practice, in accordance with the principle of management by exception, of treating compliance as a routine matter to be delegated to inferiors unless major problems, generally involving the reputation or image of the corporation, occur.[19]

PRA, remember, entails that the corporate intention that motivates a lack of responsive corrective action (or continued offending behavior) looks back to retrieve the actions that caused the offense regardless of the fact that they were not corporate intentional at the time of the offense. Intentionality plays a significant role in PRA, but the time-frame focus on corporate policy, needed to generate the relevant corporate *mens rea* or criminal state of mind, must be extended to block nonattribution of responsibility to the corporate offender when its only relevant policy at the time of its commission of the offending act was ordinary, boilerplate compliance with the law (a version of the old *ultra vires* problem mentioned in Part 1). If the time frame is expanded to encompass what the corporate offender has done in response to its commission of the *actus reus* of the offense, then the compliance policy that appears in its annual report will be irrelevant. What will count is what the corporate offender has done or proposes to do by way of implementing internal reform to prevent repetitions.

PRA does not rewrite history, as some have supposed when I have discussed it with them. Time's arrow continues to fly its inevitable course from past to future, but the shotgun of moral evaluation can scatter its pellets in many directions. There is a major difference between thinking that the past can be changed by actions in the present (backward causation) and thinking that we can, and ought to, change our moral evaluations of those who caused harm to happen in the past. And, most importantly, it is in the present and into the future that PRA licenses holding someone responsible for a past deed where a *mens rea* cannot be, in isolation of subsequent behavior, ascribed. PRA does not say that if we had access at the crucial time, we would have discovered a *mens rea*. It does not say that when we get more data about the past we will be able to assess responsibility. It says that *now* we have the intentional reactive fault that includes within its scope the past action.

It would misrepresent PRA to suggest that we can learn of the intentionality of the original act from the subsequent one. However, in forming the intention that motivates the subsequent act, the actor cannot (except in special circumstances) ignore the original act. The intention that motivates the subsequent relevant act retrieves the past act and then either endorses or rejects it. It is not the case that we can, or need to, deduce anything about the intentionality of the original act from the subsequent act. That it was or was not intentional no longer matters. That the criminal event occurred does. We may never be able to pinpoint the relevant intention. Hamlet might himself be unclear as to what specific intentions motivated his killing his girl-friend's father, or even if he had any. Perhaps the act was impulsive. His killing his girlfriend's father may not have been intentional (I do not say it was unintentional), though done quite deliberately and even on purpose.[20]

One modification of PRA is necessary, as pointed out to me by economist Kenneth Koford. PRA, especially when used in corporate cases, is not meant to supplant proactive Bayesian judgments of event probability and taking morally appropriate avoidance measures. If a fair Bayesian judgment is that a harmful result will likely occur, the benefits of avoiding it are greater than the costs. And if most people would agree that one should not do it, then moral responsibility for doing it can be assigned without reference to subsequent actions. This, of course, covers only those cases in which the risks of causing harm should be obvious to ordinary folks. These are the "How could anybody do that?" cases. On the whole, they are rare, but unfortunately they do happen. Koford provided me with the example of leaving a loaded shotgun with a group of seven-year olds. In such cases, PRA would offend our intuitions, because it suspends judgment unreasonably. It should not come into play in such cases. The more numerous and inter-esting cases, however, are those that generate little or no agreement as to the likelihood of bad results. In those cases we cannot say what an ordinary, reasonable person is likely to believe about the probability of harmful or injurious outcomes. Once the harm has been caused, the moral demands change, and PRA provides the structure for the evalu-ation of corporate criminal liability.

PRA offers a promising way of avoiding contentious attribution of criminal intentionality to a corporation, as noted in Part 4. It is rare that a company displays any criminal intention at or before it com-mits an administrative, civil, or criminal offense. The typical legal solu-tion at present is either to impose strict liability or to assess liability vicariously on the basis of the intent of a corporate agent. The former approach avoids the issue by making intention irrelevant at the level of attribution of liability (though intentionality may be relevant in relation to sentencing). The latter approach (which is essentially a form of strict liability) is based on a representationalism that utterly ignores the fundamental criminal element of *mens rea*.

To generate the relevant corporate intentionality that will displace strict or vicarious liability, focus must be on a corporate defendant's policies. That focus is achieved in a germane way by a PRA-sanctioned extension of the time frame of judicial inquiry to encompass what a defendant has done *in response to* the commission of the offense. What matters, then, is not a corporation's general policies of compliance, but its implementation of a program of internal discipline, structural reform, and compensatory or restitutionary relief. This temporal reorientation flushes out blameworthy corporate intentionality more easily than is possible when the inquiry is confined to corporate policy at or before the commission of the offending act.

Firestone's 500 tire was defective. Firestone denied that the 500s had flaws and sold them at half price. It is impossible to show any palpable flaw in the general compliance policies of Firestone, but it is easy to expose Firestone's intentional adoption of a reactive policy that did not include prompt implementation of a recall program in response to the overwhelming evidence that the tire was causing accidents under normal use conditions. PRA allows the laying on Firestone's doorstep of full liability, moral and criminal, for all of the injuries caused by the 500s.

The expansion of corporate criminal liability into a responsive time frame invites innovative ways to tackle stubborn problems of corporate criminal liability. I want to focus on three: the role of interventionism, the due diligence plea, and the design of penal sanctions.

Philosophers and legal theorists have joined a slew of social commentators in developing a plethora of proposals for controlling corporate behavior through government intervention in the internal decision structures of corporate offenders. As discussed in Part 2, Christopher Stone's *Where the Law Ends* led the parade. Stone[21] championed such court-ordered intrusions into a convicted corporation's decision making as mandating new boxes in the flowchart occupied by watchdog directors. Stone was reluctant to recommend applying interventionism across the board. He limited its use to recidivism cases, and to generically hazardous industries. In what must be the vast majority of cases, Stone expressed the belief that the interventionist strategy is too drastic. But what is to be done in such cases?

The American Bar Association in 1980 proposed a continuing judicial oversight sanction. But the ABA recommends that such a sentence be imposed only when the criminal behavior is serious, repetitive, and the result of inadequate internal accounting or monitoring procedures or when a danger to public safety exists. The ABA proposal takes no account of the corporate offender's responsive compliance activities unless the case is extremely severe. Hence, on the ABA proposal the courts must wait for repetitions before more effective sanctions are utilized. The only sanction the ABA recommended in cases neither serious nor repetitive is a cash fine. We may suppose that in that category are misleading advertising cases, (the Firestone 500 might be such a case), yet those cases may be paradigmatic of what happens when a corporation has a defective standard operating procedure, and so those types of cases are prone to repetition.

Fines, even rather hefty ones, hardly have a record of producing the significant changes in corporate decision structures and standard operating procedures that would be desirable if the offending corporate actors are to be brought into compliance. The Hopkins report[22] supports the common intuition that effective changes in defective or deficient corporate operating procedures cannot be expected as a result of fines, though a new study and more data are probably needed where fines are truly stiff.

If interventionism is too limited and intrudes the government too much and too deeply into corporate life, as also does the ABA continuing-oversight sanction, and fines are often ineffective, is there a better way to guarantee an appropriate corporate response to its offending behavior? Yes. The Stone and ABA approaches assume that the courts can examine corporate responses to the commission of criminal offenses only by inserting themselves in the corporate decision process. That assumption, however, ignores the alternative of requiring convicted corporations to file compliance reports that detail their own internal responses to the offense. Judicial intervention could, should, be held in abeyance, used only if the corporation's own reaction is judged unsatisfactory. The approach I have in mind might be called enforced corporate responsive adjustment (or ECRA).

ECRA brings PRA to bear on the judicial handling of corporate offenses. It demands an adjustment in the legal framework for dealing with the majority of such offenses. A two-stage judicial hearing procedure is required. In the initial stage the issue before the court will be whether the offense was committed on behalf of (or by) the corporate defendant. That established to the satisfaction of the court, the defendant corporation will be required to prepare a compliance report that spells out what steps it has or will take by way of internal discipline, modification of existing compliance procedures, and, as appropriate, compensation to victims.

The second stage of the judicial procedure will determine whether the corporate offender has responded satisfactorily to its damages or risks imposed (as established at the first stage of the trial). If adequate measures have been taken to adjust, the corporation will be acquitted. If not, the corporation will be convicted on the basis of PRA and be liable to a variety of further penal sanctions that could include extreme forms of interventionism and judicial supervision. What is important is that use of such drastic violations of the integrity of the alleged corporate offender's internal decision structure will be contingent on the corporate defendant's own failure, quite intentionally or deliberately, to make a responsive adjustment to try to ensure no repetitions of its harm-causing behavior. In short, the ECRA approach by courts and regulatory agencies would preserve managerial freedom, as long as the court is satisfied that effective responsive adjustment has been undertaken.

In notable ways ECRA is a cousin of John Braithwaite's model of enforced self-regulation[23] in which corporations are required to formulate their own regulatory standards, and intervention is restricted to the development and enforcement of overarching principles and social goals. ECRA is not so sweeping. It requires corporate offenders to formulate their own reactive programs in response to specific violations. ECRA has the virtue of minimizing government and judicial intervention, while not, as in the case of fines, excluding it altogether. It places the onus of managerial alterations on shoulders both best trained and most likely to be effective in bearing it: the company managers, most likely its affine agents. This then responds to the fact that though there probably are some fundamental, minimal requirements for effective corporate compliance systems, the variables differ wildly from corporation to corporation without necessarily affecting the compliance outcome. Of further import, ECRA will not be restricted to only the more serious or repeated offenses. The lesser offenses will be more effectively dealt with by ECRA than by purely proactively focused monetary sanctions.

The application of ECRA will, undoubtedly, produce a hue and cry because it does acquit an offending corporation that "cleans up its act" in response to its discovery of harm caused. But it would be, I think, a greater shortcoming if we were to adopt a punishment policy and procedure that undermines our "commitment to the moral force of the criminal law"[24] because it breaks all links to intentionality. ECRA preserves that link and thereby blocks the move to more and more strict liability offenses.

The downside is that corporate offenders may be perceived to be allowed a free "first bite of the apple." It might be thought that a significant amount of corporate damaging will escape punishment. In the criminal sense, of course, that is strictly true, but ECRA is not recommended as a principle in tort law. Hence, existing grounds for suit in tort, including punitive damages, are available to victims. It is imaginable that ECRA could be put to excellent use as the limiter and regulator of punitive damages in tort. It would then effect some desirable tort reform. Certainly it will be the case that the so-called "first bite" does not go without producing a desired effect: a change in procedures and policies within a corporation that has committed a criminal offense.

The adoption of the responsive-adjustment time-frame approach corrects some nasty problems with the popular due diligence defense as it is commonly used by corporate actors accused of violations. Recall the first headline about the Los Angeles construction company that was indicted for felony manslaughter. A worker died in a cave-in at the construction site. He was cleaning dirt out of trenches when an embankment collapsed, burying him. The indictment charged that the soils engineer's report was grossly inadequate because he did not recommend shoring for a vertical cut. It also charged that the excavation contractor had informed the general contractor about safety concerns. No shoring was installed. This is not a strict liability offense, and so it might admit a defense of due diligence.

The construction company was indicted for failure to take due care to prevent such injuries. What standard of due diligence or care would have been relevant in the time frame that preceded the accident? Would it really have been adequate to the situation?

Due diligence purports to import an objective standard of care that takes the practices prevailing in the industry as a benchmark. That objective standard may be adjusted to meet the needs of particular circumstances, but there are clear limits on the amount of alteration allowable, because the standard must still be applicable across the industry. Another problem is that in many industries no generally accepted standard for a compliance system exists. Still, if a customary compliance system does exist in the industry, and the corporate defendant has adopted it, should that get the corporate defendant off the hook?

Suppose that the Los Angeles construction firm had met all of the safety standards normally upheld by construction firms in that area. It, therefore, had exercised due diligence and, on the traditional theory, should be acquitted of the manslaughter charges. If it did nothing to change its excavation methods after the first death and industry standards did not appreciably change either, and in similar circumstances another death occurs, it could again plea due diligence and should again look forward to an acquittal. That sounds wrong!

Due diligence, proactively understood, flies in the face of basic intuitions about justice. However, if the industry standard does not set the benchmark on which the plea rests, then a corporate offender is not provided with clear prior notice of conduct subject to criminal liability. That's not fair to the corporate actors! Furthermore, if a court should determine that the industry standard was set too low, then good-faith compliance with the standard may not shield a corporation from criminal liability. How just is that?

It is surely unjust to disallow a due diligence plea on the grounds that the corporation should have anticipated a failure in its procedures that only came to light in the industry after the injury occurred. Also, advance specification of acceptable standards only invites the search for loopholes.[25]

The typical proactive form of the due diligence defense cannot help but pull the acceptable standard down to a common denominator level that would put the force of the law behind older, traditional compliance technologies. No legal incentives would be provided for corporations to find innovative solutions or to apply state-of-the-art techniques to prevent harm. Law tied to a proactive time frame for offenses is stuck in a dangerous rut that deprives potential victims of adequate protection. It can extricate itself only by imposing higher standards that the defendant can rightly claim "descend from out of the blue."

Legal and moral deficiencies with due diligence also arise because existing industry standards lack particularity, thus inviting myriad interpretations by company lawyers and even a kind of compliance collusion among corporate actors in a particular industry.

These are significant problems, but they can be minimized in various ways by the courts. First, standards tailored to individual corporations have been imposed under an injunction or consent order. This is not uncommon in the enforcement of antitrust laws, securities regulations, and corruption offenses.[26] Second, broad standards of due care for an industry have been made more precise by using injunctions to crystallize their meaning and application to particular situations.[27] Third, some dynamic thrust has been shown to be possible through the imaginative use of negotiation and bargaining in enforcement,[28] prospective standard setting in judicial decisions,[29] and administrative techniques for inducing technological change (for example, forced technology through offsets against penalties[30]). These methods are valuable, but they do not provide rules of criminal liability that are particularistic rather than universalistic, focused rather than rife with loopholes, and dynamic rather than static or, at best, tortuously incremental.

Standard setting in conjunction with ECRA, dominated by a reactive time frame, however, overcomes these problems. Using the ECRA model, a corporate offender would be required to produce a compliance report in which it specifies the standards it will seek to meet in response to its harm-causing. Standard setting is then neither a cataloging of routine prevention nor an excursion into possible world scenarios. The standards are tailored both to the particular corporation and its activities, but also to the particular case that exposed the structural weaknesses of its decision procedures.

The old due diligence defense would not succeed even if the company could not have foreseen the harm produced by its following the existing standards of the industry. In fact, due diligence and due care would play a small role or none.

ECRA provides fair notice of criminal prohibitions, while loophole-prone rules are eliminated. The focus shifts from industry-wide standards, which may, in fact, be too low—the harmful result is evidence that they probably are—to the adequacy or inadequacy of the corporate offender's response to need to develop a higher standard of care. Proactive due diligence, as noted above, imposes static and often undemanding requirements of care. ECRA, not confined to *ex ante* due diligence, extends to the care that *should be* taken regardless of the existing industry standard, and so it is more dynamic and demanding, often perhaps requiring state-of-the-art technology to satisfy its demands. ECRA then works to reduce the tension between stability-inducing rules of law and the rapidly changing corporate, technological, and social world to which they must be applied.

While I am citing advantages of the ECRA approach, it should not be forgotten that there is also a moral and social payoff. ECRA should bring exemplary corporate responsive adjustments to the attention of the general public and instill models of good corporate citizenship across an industry.

Two major objections to ECRA should be addressed: that it is prone to be too lenient and that it will be inefficient. The first objection is that "first free bite of the apple" mentioned earlier. As Clinard and Yeager[31] have demonstrated, negotiated settlement dominates other methods of applying sanctions in cases of corporate criminality today. Considerable chunks of the apple are regularly devoured without even fines being assessed. More importantly, however, it would be a complete misunderstanding were one to think that ECRA allows a free first bite. For any corporate offense it requires a responsive adjustment from the corporation, which may be costly, and, in the absence of a satisfactory response, injunctions, adverse publicity orders, and other measures are recommended as a first resort. The pressure and costs brought to bear on the convicted corporate offender could well exceed any simple monetary penalty.

The second objection is a bit more interesting. It argues that ECRA suffers from an excess of inefficiency because it will impose significant burdens of investigation, supervision, and management on the justice system. Admittedly these kinds of cost factors will increase under ECRA, and surely they will be more costly than the mere use of totally noninterventionist monetary sanctions.

ECRA challenges the application of an economic calculus to sentencing. Applying such a calculus requires that we make probability predictions with respect to the occurrence of harm, the extent and gravity of that harm, and the chances of detection and conviction. John Byrne and Steven Hoffman have persuasively argued that such calculations are impossible in corporate cases at the level of exactitude required.[32]

The calculus method assumes "a unified managerial rationality" that is a figment of the economist's imagination. The results of these economic analyses invite skepticism, and even if we allow the probabilistic calculation method to guide the development of an efficient general criminal liability system, two rules of thumb should apply when it is impossible, as in the corporate cases, to adequately assess the required probabilities. Fisse and I have framed those two rules[33] along the following lines:

1. Develop proscriptions based on considered assessments of the nature of unwanted harms in society; and
2. Use fault-concepts and sanctions geared to provoke responsive corporate reactions to violations of those proscriptions.

Regarding corporate offenders, ECRA meets the demands of the first part of the second rule. An innovative mix of sanctions, to be discussed in the next two sections, should respond to its second part.

3. Adverse Publicity as a Sanction in Corporate Criminal Cases: Hester Prynne in Corporate Attire

The proactive time-frame commitment that dominates most thinking about corporate criminality produces a bias toward adopting the notion of vicarious liability, and that locks the judicial system, by and large, into a severely restricted number of applicable sentencing formats or sanctions. The popular favorite is cash fines. Fines are used because, viewed from the proactive perspective, it is virtually impossible to prove that a corporation committed the offense with the appropriate corporate criminal state of mind or intent, the *mens rea*. Boiler-plate compliance policies, as noted earlier, are intended to display the usual absence of a corporate *mens rea*. For example, they typically tell us that the corporation only engages in legal activities. With access to the corporate *mens rea* effectively blocked, what else can a court do but adopt a vicarious liability approach for corporate cases? All that they then need to show is fault on the part of an employee, a corporate agent, acting on behalf of the corporation. That makes the corporation vicariously liable. The *mens rea* of a manager or employee, of course, is rather easier to expose than corporate intentionality, and no published policy of compliance will serve as a shield. Sounds good, but it has moral shortcomings.

Vicarious liability, as Fisse has argued, "projects a noninterventionist attitude toward corporate decision making,"[34] so it is no wonder that it is championed by the staunchest defenders of free enterprise. The emphasis in vicarious liability is almost solely on the state of mind of a single corporate agent, rather than on the CID structure of the corporate actor. But that is unfair to the corporate actor. In a significant number of cases, the corporate actor has had no more to do with the commission of the crime than having innocently provided the venue for it to occur. The attempt to avoid interventionism and the widespread understanding of vicarious liability in terms of vicarious tortious liability has begot both a judicial bias in favor of fines and corporate offenders identifying those fines as enterprise costs.

Cash fines, however, have serious limitations and can be passed on to undeserving populations. Although the 1973 report of the Task Force on Corrections of the National Advisory Commission on Criminal Justice Standards and Goals found the fine "far less costly to the public, and perhaps more effective than imprisonment or community service,"[35] fines against most corporations have shown little deterrence capacity. The problem of affordability is exacerbated by the fact that many corporations can recoup fines by reducing production costs or, sometimes, marginally raising prices. Oliver Wendell Holmes, Jr.,[36] and H. L. A. Hart[37] both noted that though there is a difference, or should be, between a fine and a tax, in many cases the line is blurred until it disappears. In most corporate criminal cases, drawing that line may be, in practice, extremely difficult. Taxes, in fact, often are imposed to discourage activities that have not been made criminal. President Clinton said as much when he defended the raising of funds for his health insurance plan by imposing higher taxes on cigarettes.

> Conversely, fines payable for some criminal offenses . . . become so small (e.g. in relation to the offender's income, PAF) that they are cheerfully paid and offenses are frequent. They are then felt to be mere taxes because the sense is lost that the rule is meant to be taken seriously as a standard of behavior.[38]

Interventionist sanctions such as punitive injunctions are not so easily assimilated. But some noninterventionist sanctions could prove almost equally successful in producing the desired alteration in corporate procedures and policies, and at least one of those is also directly derivable from the previously mentioned shame motivational base we find in most corporate offices: court-ordered (and supervised) adverse publicity, or what I prefer to call the Hester Prynne sanction after the penalty imposed on the central character of Hawthorne's *The Scarlet Letter*.[39]

> The penalty thereof is death. But in their great mercy and tenderness of heart, they have doomed Mistress Prynne to stand only a space of three hours on the platform of the pillory, and then and thereafter, for the remainder of her natural life, to wear a mark of shame upon her bosom. "A wise sentence!" remarked the stranger gravely bowing his head. "Thus she will be a living sermon against sin."[40]

The Hester Prynne sanction is not directly a monetary penalty. Adverse publicity, however, could contribute to the achievement of monetary deterrent and retributive effects by costing the corporation business when customers refuse to purchase products or services, but that cost may be negligible and so not constitute a real repayment for the crime. When applied to a corporate offender, Hester Prynne's major function is to threaten the company's prestige, its image.[41]

The Hester Prynne sanction, in fact, will be effective only if the criminal regards social stigmatization as a matter of grave anxiety, or is concerned with personal moral worth, that is, is not shameless. When the Hester Prynne sanction works, its targets regard themselves as having acted disgracefully, as having significantly reduced their status in the community by their behavior. They come to think of themselves as unworthy of the kind of respect and consideration they previously enjoyed, as having fallen short of what can be legitimately expected of them. Rehabilitation requires that they must come to view the sanction as a legitimate damaging blot on their reputations, as a mark of their failure, as an exposure of their moral shortcomings; as an indicator of the legitimate disgust of others, as a signal that they must rebuild their identities.

The Hester Prynne sanction is particularly suited to corporate offenders because image and reputation are at the very heart of modern corporate life.[42] Little sustained success has ever been enjoyed by a company with a bad reputation. Official censure is not an inconsequential matter when corporate achievement depends on communal standing. In fact, the Hester Prynne sanction might be far more effective in dealing with corporate offenders than with human criminals, if only because hiding is easier for humans.

It is worth noting that in a study of seventeen major corporations that have suffered adverse publicity over an offense or serious incident (though such publicity was not court-ordered), executives at the middle and higher levels of management reported that loss of corporate prestige and tarnishing of its public image was regarded as a major corporate concern.[43] Indeed, they regarded damage to the corporate public reputation as far more serious than payment of even a large cash fine.

For a corporation to survive, it simply must garner and nurture a good image among its marketplace constituents. Furthermore, framing corporate punishments in terms of adverse publicity orders is more likely to minimize the kinds of unwanted externalities that plague the sanctions the courts now use against corporate offenders.[44] It is noteworthy that the U.S. National Committee on Reform of Federal Criminal Laws, in their 1970 _Study Draft,_ supported use of something that sounds remarkably like Hester Prynne. The proposal read:

> When an organization is convicted of an offense, the court may, in addition or in lieu of imposing other authorized sanctions, . . . require the organization to give appropriate publicity to the conviction . . . by advertising in designated areas or in designated media.[45]

Sadly, the commission's _Final Report_[46] lacked this recommendation due to strong corporate lobbying. All the more reason to revive it.

The almost universal corporate aversion to a tarnished image is, however, insufficient by itself to ground the Hester Prynne sanction as a penal device. "Bad press" may be repugnant, but it is hardly penal and can be countered by corporate media campaigns intended "to put a different face on the matter." Quite simply, if this sanction is to be retributively penal, the convicted corporation must regard the adverse publicity as not only noxious, but a justified communal revelation of the corporation's disgrace, its failure to "measure up."

Measure up to what? Against what standard, what model identity is a corporation to judge itself and be judged by the institutions of social order and justice? *The Scarlet Letter* provides only the structural or formal aspects of the matter. Hester is judged unworthy against a model of human fidelity that was deeply embedded in the puritanical society of early Boston. That model was understood and internalized throughout her community. It was not a product of law, though surely many of the Massachusetts Bay Colony laws were derived from the same set of conceptions that engendered the model. In the eyes of the people of the colony, Hester was not just guilty of lawbreaking, she should be ashamed. The willful breaking of law in itself does not generate shame. Few people, for example, who are caught driving at sixty miles per hour in a fifty-five-mile-per-hour zone, under ordinary conditions, report feeling ashamed of what they have done.

Throughout the centuries we have articulated human ideal models. They are a part of our history, legend, education, religion, and literature. But surely there are corporate ideal models as well. We should expect such features as being profitable, socially responsive, and humane in that corporate model. Importantly, each corporation, just as each human being, formulates its own conception of worth and associates itself with an ideal of behavior. Just as human beings are disposed to be the kind of persons they value, corporations are guided, at least in part, by an attempt to successfully realize the corporate images they have adopted. They seek to appear in the community as having the characteristics of those ideal corporate models. Public relations and advertising departments, of course, play focal roles in each corporation's attempt to establish and nurture its social standing and an exemplary image in the community.

I tried, for example, to get an interview with the brands marketing director of a major brewing company. Before I could talk with that person, all of the questions I would ask were screened by the public relations office. Furthermore, I had to specify the way the company would be portrayed and guarantee that even if I changed my mind about what I learned or learned something from my conversation with the corporate representative that was not strictly outlined in my account of the purpose of my interview, that I would not use it without first submitting it to the company's public relations office. The restrictions went on and on. After awhile I thought I was asking for an interview with the head of the CIA or even the leadership of the Republic of China. Why such security? The answer is probably obvious: its image is so important to the corporation that protecting it from any adverse publicity, even that which might occur in an interview with a college professor, is of the highest priority. Few corporations believe themselves so spotless that they might not suffer an embarrassment that will take some time and a sum of money to make right.

Corporations are well aware of the difficulties and the costs of combating bad press, whether or not it was deserved. Fisse and Braithwaite's studies reveal that:

> . . . adverse publicity concerning one alleged wrongdoing can snowball into unfavorable coverage over other, unrelated, issues. Once a company gets into the public eye over one crisis, it becomes a favored target for indiscriminate muckraking.[47]

The courts and some regulatory agencies have both the authority and the social credibility to force human persons and corporate actors to confront their failures, to live up to the ideals of their types. Court-ordered adverse publicity should provide an institutionalized revelatory apparatus, the modern substitute for the pillory, where the offender stands contemptible before the community, forced to confront the fact of his, her, or its inadequacy. Shame is, after all, an identity crisis.

Morally, the really productive aspect of the Hester Prynne sanction, however, is that suffering adverse publicity does not alone restore the offender to communal grace and relieve the shame. Only positive corrective acts can do that. But look where this gets us: the imposition of the Hester Prynne sanction on a corporation broadcasts a corporate offender's criminal behavior. It arouses the appropriate social contempt, internal approbation. And it can ignite the kind of adjustments of its operating procedures, policies, and practices for that corporation to again approximate the corporate model identity and regain moral worth both in its own eyes and those of the community.

The Hester Prynne sanction might have desired retributive and deterrent effects on corporations, but as a primary penal device, some have thought it prone to fail for a number of practical reasons. In the first place, as we all know, government is a rather poor propagandist. It isn't too persuasive, and rarely is it pithy. (Have you ever seen a catchy piece of government-written prose that could rival the output of Madison Avenue?) For the adverse-publicity sanction to have the desired *in terrorem* effect, and when used, for it to have a genuine impact on an offending corporation's established image, the court will have to employ clever writers and publicists and not the run-of-the-mill bureaucratic scribblers who crank out the government's literature. Courts also risk soiling their own images by descending to the Madison Avenue advertiser's level in order to produce effective penal outcomes.[48]

Such concerns can be easily addressed. Courts have the power to write their orders in such a way that the cost of the adverse publicity is paid by the criminal corporation from its own advertising budget to a competitive agency (other than ones that carry its accounts), which will then manage a campaign as approved by an officer of the court (perhaps a college professor trained in advertising and marketing). The corporation will have to submit its previous year's advertising budget to be used as a starting line; a percentage of the advertising budget will be set aside for the adverse publicity campaign, and that percentage will be carried through all annual budgets until the expiration of the order. In this way, even if the corporation increases its advertising budget to attempt to entice sales, it will have to pay a higher adverse publicity cost. The court-appointed overseer will instruct the agency to expend all funds in the adverse publicity budget annually and to do so in outlets roughly equivalent to those used by the usual corporate advertising agencies; for example, the agency will not be allowed to place adverse publicity in obscure small-town newspapers if the corporation does not generally advertise in such ways. The private sector would then be actively engaged in the penal process, and a whole new respectable area of advertising will provide jobs and new paths of expression for the creative imagination to wander.

A frequently voiced second concern is that the level of anticorporate "noise" in our society is so great as to devalue the effect of specific adverse publicity orders.[49] The newspaper editorialists, the campaigning politicians, the special-interest groups, the conservationists, the Naderites, the assorted movie and TV actors and actresses with various causes all contribute to a confusing cacophony of charges that are usually indirect, often unsubstantiated, and certainly not properly adjudicated. Can this noise be controlled? Probably not, and it is not a good idea to pursue such a line in a free country. The corporations attacked in such ways have the option of legal action to counter unfair criticism. Against this noise, however, a well-developed adverse publicity campaign against a particular corporate offender, identified clearly as court-ordered, is still likely to draw attention. The public may never be very discriminating, but generally the fact that a court has ordered a certain publicity campaign as punishment for a particular criminal offense should pierce the shield of apathy behind which the public hides from the onslaught of ordinary corporate criticism.

It may be suggested that corporations can dilute the Hester Prynne sanction through counterpublicity. There is no denying the power of Madison Avenue agencies to create clever and effective image-building campaigns, even in the face of severe public or government criticism. But the sanction can be written in such a way, as suggested above, to offset any corporate counterattack. Furthermore, the court has the power to order the corporation not to engage in any advertising directed specifically toward rebutting or diluting the sentence. If the corporation were to promote its own case after having lost in court and having received an adverse publicity sentence, it would be in contempt of the court and sterner measures would be justified. Oil companies such as Mobil mounted effective replies to the charges leveled against them during the energy crisis. Also corporations after *Central Hudson Gas & Electric Corp. v. Public Service Commission* [447 U.S. 557 (1980)] clearly have First Amendment rights to express opinions on matters of public concern. Corporate rebuttals to adverse publicity orders, however, are not necessarily protected by *Central Hudson*, and the Mobil commercials were certainly not attempts to minimize the effectiveness of any adverse publicity court orders. The oil companies were charged only in the court of public opinion, and the response was a totally appropriate defense in that venue.

It is interesting, however, that most companies confronted with adverse publicity do not fight back with counteradvertising. Fisse and Braithwaite note:

> All companies responded to the adverse publicity by explaining their side of the story, at least in terms of a written communication from management to employees. The great majority of the companies made a conscious decision *not* to run counterpublicity to ensure that their story was impressed upon the general public. The main reason given for this "hunkering down," as one executive described it, was fear that adverse publicity over one crisis would spread and thereby bring other skeletons out of the closet. . . . They would answer questions from the press, but they stopped short of actively generating their own publicity.[50]

The Hester Prynne sanction may prove efficacious in fraud, public safety, and felony cases, but some doubt it can be equally effective in regulatory cases. Gulf Oil Corporation made illegal campaign contributions to President Richard Nixon's reelection committee that were revealed during the Watergate scandals. The publicity was profuse, but there is little evidence that it hurt Gulf Oil sales. Two responses seem appropriate. The first is to point out that in the regulatory cases, adverse publicity occurred in the ordinary media coverage of the events. It was not court-ordered in lieu of or in addition to some other penal sanction, such as a stiff fine. In effect, it was incidental, and as the story faded from the front page or the first fifteen minutes of the telecast, its intensity diminished. But the Hester Prynne sanction perhaps does not produce significant financial losses in certain cases, and so it may not be perceived to be a fitting punishment.

Fisse and Braithwaite conclude from their studies of cases of corporate responses to adverse publicity:

> The data show that financial impacts of any significance occurred in only a small minority of the case studies. It was non-financial impacts that executives in all of the companies reported as the factors which truly hurt

and which made them want to avoid a recurrence even if it cost a great deal of money to guarantee this. In short, at the level of subjective management perceptions, financial impacts—loss of corporate and individual prestige, decline in morale, distraction from getting on with the job, and humiliation in the witness box—were acutely felt.[51]

It is not likely that adverse publicity orders will always fully achieve the usually desired retributive or deterrent ends of the legal system. For that, a mix of sanctions will undoubtedly be required. Still, adverse publicity orders are more likely than most other sanctions to produce what might be called rehabilitative outcomes—reformed corporations—as the studies suggest.

> In every case there was some worthwhile reform. This is an arresting finding. . . . When a company is struck by publicity, . . . it typically implements reform measures. . . . The reforms are often more than cosmetic: The company cannot afford to have its reaction dismissed . . . as window dressing; new policies or procedures must be capable of standing up to expert analysis as genuine improvements.[52]

The record for cash fines certainly is not impressive, if we are looking for long-term salutary changes in corporate offenders.

The Hester Prynne sanction, however, could produce much the same externalities as fines. After all, if it is really effective, some say that it should lead to decreased sales, and the corporation's employees at the lowest levels could be made to suffer layoffs and such. I think the society should be rather cold-blooded about this. Were such outcomes to occur, we shouldn't be too disturbed. Similar externalities plague penal sanctions of all kinds. The evidence with respect to non-court-ordered adverse publicity, however, does not indicate serious drops in sales, except in cases where the publicity concerned defective products, such as the Ford Pinto. The predicted punishment spillovers seem unlikely, or no more likely than with any other type of sentence.

More to the point, however, is whether the Hester Prynne sanction is justifiable over the assessment of a fine, should both produce basically equivalent externalities. I have offered some solid reasons for the court to prefer, at least with regard to certain crimes, the Hester Prynne sanction rather than or in addition to fines. Paying a fine and suffering court-ordered and supervised adverse publicity are simply not equivalent punishments.

If the proactive time-frame approach is used, rather than an ECRA approach, and we are blocked from adequate information about the "corporateness" of the *actus reus* of the offense, the implementation of an adverse publicity sanction may appear too severe and thereby unwarranted. Fines seem the only justifiable option. However, by shifting to the ECRA approach, corporate policies and procedures are no longer shielded and so willful, deliberate noncompliance by the corporate offender may be exposed and the offending corporation appropriately targeted for Hester Prynne or other innovative sanctions.

Certain misunderstandings regarding the Hester Prynne sanction need to be addressed, because they keep cropping up whenever I discuss this sentencing option. One of the more persistent misreadings is repeated by Angelo Corlett. He writes:

> French's utilization of the term "Hester Prynne Sanction" perhaps betrays an ignorance regarding the fundamental points of Hawthorne's story. Hester Prynne, according to Hawthorne, is treated *wrongly* for her "offense," suggesting that any mode of punishment akin to that which she receives is equally wrong. Perhaps French ought to rename his suggested method of corporate punishment.[53]

Well, Corlett is certainly right that Hawthorne does not applaud the use of the sanction in Hester's case, and that element of the story did not escape me. The fact that a punishment is wrongly used, even in its most famous case, however, does not imply that the sanction will be wrongly used if applied in any other case. Elementary logic students will, no doubt, recognize the fallacy of hasty generalization. More importantly, it is immaterial to my recommended use of the sanction that the fictional Massachusetts Bay colonists misapplied it to poor Hester, though not forgetting that she was guilty of the "crime" for which the punishment was assessed. I use the name because of its great power in our collective consciousness to summon up the image of someone held up to judicially ordered scorn. I could as well have settled for the more prosaic, "court-ordered adverse publicity sanction," but I will stick with Hester.

Corlett does, however, provide a number of more plausible criticisms of Hester Prynne that warrant at least brief examination. He says that the Hester Prynne sanction, when used against convicted corporations, will unjustly "immiserate" the work force of that corporation. As I noted above, that could happen. And I will repeat, so what? The immiseration of people associated with those convicted and punished of crimes is a spillover effect, an externality, that plagues almost all criminal sanctions. We do not generally give a brass farthing for the misery into which we cast the family or relatives of a convicted felon when we incarcerate him or her. Not uncommonly they are reduced to penury, while the prisoner, at least, has guaranteed room and board. Why should we start worrying about the spillover in the corporate actor cases? The response might be that more people are bound to be adversely effected than in street crime cases. Maybe. Probably. But that does not change the principle. We punish for retributive reasons, because it is deserved. If there is spillover, we should say we're sorry and move on. We do it all the time, minus the manners. Actually, insofar as the corporate agents probably realized some benefit from its criminally gained prosperity while it lasted, their suffering in bad times may not be altogether unmerited.

Corlett goes on to think up ways that corporations convicted and sentenced under Hester Prynne might evade the sanction. He says that the corporation can raise prices to overcome losses or that it can reorganize itself and escape the public shame. Both of these concerns can be easily allayed. The market will control the corporation's ability to recoup losses by raising prices, and if the adverse publicity is successful, consumers are most unlikely to pay higher than going prices to buy products from a well-known offender.

The courts can easily handle the second of Corlett's concerns by ordering that the corporation cannot be reorganized during the time it is serving its supervised adverse publicity sentence.

Corlett also worries about the effectiveness of the media in carrying out the sanction. He, of course, is welcome to underestimate the media, but few people have ever profited by doing so. He obviously does not understand the sanction if he thinks it amounts to no more than media coverage of the corporation's offense and the legal proceedings against it. If my approach is used, the publicity that may be court-ordered will be produced in the form of commercials not unlike those already commissioned by the corporation to sell its products. These will run in the same time slots on television that the corporation uses to sell its products, and they will be paid for by the corporation at a fixed percentage of its advertising budget. As I suggested earlier, a whole new branch of the advertising industry, one that has already been cutting its teeth in the political campaigns, should thrive.

John Ladd[54] criticizes me for touting the Hester Prynne sanction because he finds it too drastic a punishment, an ideal of ignominy and disgrace, an assault on image, even identity. But that is why it is so devastating and hence effective in the corporate world. It attacks the heart of business: reputation. That is also why it should only be used when there is no doubt as to the corporate offender's criminality. The ECRA approach in corporate criminal cases will ensure that condition is met.

4. Caught in the Deterrence Trap: A Variety of Sanctions as Alternatives to Cash Fines

In 1979, the *Harvard Law Review* published "Developments in the Law—Corporate Crime: Regulating Corporate Behavior Through Criminal Sanctions." The primary claim of that article was that corporations cannot be effectively punished for their criminal conduct. There was an echo of the famous dictum of Edward, First Baron Thurlow, Lord Chancellor of England, in the Harvard piece. Thurlow noted:

> Did you ever expect a corporation to have a conscience, when it has no soul to damn, and no body to kick?[55]

The *Harvard Law Review* put the matter this way:

> A corporation cannot, of course, be imprisoned. It may also be argued that the stigma of a criminal label is of little significance to an inanimate business organization. Such stigma could influence corporate behavior if it led to diminished profits, but it is questionable whether the mere stigma of a criminal conviction would in fact produce this result. Furthermore, in most cases there is little likelihood that any stigma of criminality will filter down to particular individuals in the corporate structure, especially in a large corporation.[56]

The cash fine or some sort of civil monetary penalty seems all that most corporate crime theorists have to offer by way of trying to deter and punish corporate offenses. I suspect that the lack of creativity derives from a failure to appreciate the structure and culture of the corporate invaders. Seventeenth-century individualism seems to blind them to both understanding the impact, or lack thereof, of fines and the possibilities of alternative creative sanctions such as Hester Prynne.

What's the matter with fines? Brent Fisse has noted that "the efficacy of fines against corporations is hampered by limited congruence with the goals of deterrence and retribution."[57] One of Fisse's points is that to produce deterrence we need to attack more than the corporation's pocketbook. The urge for power, the desire for prestige, and the protection of image more closely relate to deterrence in the spheres of corporate action. Fines can achieve only an oblique attack on such elements of the corporation's interests. Simply, fines usually have no significant impact on the nonmonetary interests and goals of a corporation. Seldom will corporations revamp their CID structures in response to the imposition of even a stiff fine. Many corporations will treat, and have treated, fines as business losses and have instituted no alterations in the way they do business.

In behalf of cash fines, we should note that they do not threaten the autonomy of the corporation. Its freedom to continue to act in the way it has previously is not impaired. But that is strange because its previous actions were the reason for the fine. If you believe that an offending corporation is likely to make responsive changes in its operating procedures and policies because it has been fined for noncompliance, you probably also believe in Santa Claus and the Tooth Fairy. Fines simply do not provide a sufficient incentive or any oversight to secure desired change and, by the same token, they don't have much of a batting average as a deterrent either.

There is also an unsavory aspect of cash-fine sanctions in corporate criminal cases (actually this applies to cases involving human criminals as well). The fine sanction promotes irresponsibility. Fines in criminal cases send the message to the criminal element, whether corporate or human, that crime is a matter of price. It is not "Don't do the crime if you can't do the time." It's "Don't do the crime if you don't have the money." This may have been acceptable for the ancient Sumerians and for the British Anglo-Saxons in the seventh century, but it is hardly a sound basis for a valid legal system. Fines price offenses that should not be for sale. They are *ex post facto* licensing fees. But the very reason the offenses are in the criminal law in the first place is to control, hopefully to prevent, forms of behavior that the members of society do not want to occur in their midst. They are not there to raise revenues. A criminal law that, in effect, says to the offender, "We don't really like what you are doing. You are injuring, even killing, many people. But if you pay this sum of money, you can do it." has no retributive or deterrent impact on those with the funds sufficient to afford the fine.

It will, of course, be countered that the desired effects will be accomplished if the fines are raised to such a level that they deter potential corporate offenders from the offenses or that they truly retribute and compensate for the harm caused. The fact is that many, perhaps most, corporations simply do not have the financial resources to pay cash fines of that magnitude. Jack Coffee calls this the "deterrence trap." He writes:

> The crux of the dilemma arises from the fact that the maximum meaningful fine that can be levied against any corporate offender is necessarily bounded by its wealth. Logically, a small corporation is no more threatened by a $5 million fine than by a $500,000 fine if both are beyond its ability to pay. In the case of an individual offender, this wealth ceiling on the deterrent threat of fines causes no serious problem because we can still deter by threat of incarceration. But for the corporation, which has no body to incarcerate, this wealth boundary seems an absolute limit on the reach of deterrent threats directed at it. . . . In short, our ability to deter the corporation may be confounded by our inability to set an adequate punishment cost which does not exceed the corporation's resources.[58]

To respond to the deterrence trap, Coffee has proposed equity dilution as an alternative to cash fines. He writes:

> [W]hen very severe fines need to be imposed on the corporation, they should be imposed not in cash, but in the equity securities of the corporation. The convicted corporation should be required to authorize and issue such number of shares to the state's crime victim compensation fund as would have an expected market value equal to the cash fine necessary to deter illegal activity. The fund should then be able to liquidate the securities in whatever manner maximizes its return.[59]

Coffee's proposal has some attractive aspects. For example, it would make its major impact on those holding shares in the offending corporation because the value of their shares would be reduced. The higher managers in the corporation are likely to be in that group, what with their typical stock options and incentive plans based on the value of the corporation's stock. They would likely think more than twice about exposing the corporation to such a penalty. Stockholders outside of management would likely insist on curtailing any corporate behavior that might result in the devaluing of their stock. Ordinary workers, however, would realize little or no impact, and, as Coffee notes, much higher monetary values can be assessed through these equity fines than through ordinary cash fines, because the market value of most corporations exceeds their liquidity.

All of that is very persuasive, but there are some flies in the equity dilution ointment. The most obvious is that though top managers continue to receive stock options and other perquisites built around stock and the value of stock, in the 1980s many of those managers were spending a considerable amount of their time setting up compensation deals for themselves that do not include stocks or stock options. Golden parachutes are typically cash or deferred cash deals. Stock risk taking, therefore, may not make much of a dent in their scheming, especially if the potential for increased profits gleams in their eyes. If equity dilution is imposed by the court, for many managers, their losses, relative to their incomes, are likely to be minimal.[60]

The ordinary stockholders would, undoubtedly, bear the brunt of the burden and they, as noted in Part 2, are really not major players in the corporate actor's decision-making and acting process. Furthermore, nothing guarantees that equity fines will have any better chance than cash fines of producing the sort of responsive adjustment within the CID structure that is socially and ethically desirable. And, again, the equity dilution sanction sends the same unfortunate message that cash fines do to potential offenders: crime has a price. If you can pay it, you can do it. The only difference is the goods transferred in the transaction. Money is replaced with stock. A different market is utilized, but little is gained in the shift.

More creative penal sanctions that do more than price crime need to be examined. I've already defended court-ordered adverse publicity, but two other types of sanctions have been proposed and deserve serious consideration: internal discipline and community service orders.

Australia and Canada have led the way with respect to internal discipline orders. The Criminal Law and Penal Methods Reform Committee of South Australia wrote:

> Internal discipline orders would require a corporation to investigate an offense committed on its behalf, undertake appropriate disciplinary proceedings, and return a detailed and satisfactory compliance report to the court issuing the particular order.[61]

The Law Reform Commission of Canada reached a similar conclusion:

> In many cases, it would appear more sensible to transfer to the corporation the responsibility of policing itself, forcing it to take steps to ensure that harm does not materialize through the conduct of people within the organization. Rather than having the state monitor the activities of each person within the organization, which is costly and raises practical enforcement difficulties, it may be more efficient to force the corporation to do this, especially if sanctions imposed on the corporation can be translated into effective action at the individual level.[62]

The Australians certainly have captured the spirit of ECRA. The Canadians are more focused on someone finding and disciplining an errant individual. Stone provides a "Proposed Model Penal Code for Corporate Rehabilitation" that also empowers the courts to force corporate offenders to work out an agenda for their own rehabilitation in the general mold of ECRA.[63]

Stone's proposal requires a corporate offender to provide the court with its research into the reasons for its harm-causing conduct, especially as that relates to its policies and internal decision procedures. It then must specify the measures the company plans to take to prevent reoccurrence. Those measures might include alterations in the decision-making process of the corporation, new procedures, new policies, changes in personnel, the creation of new positions specifically to reduce the likelihood of a repetition of the harm, and revisions in the information collection and dissemination processes in the company. All of these and other steps might be court-ordered, hence, the Stone proposal is interventionist, while still placing the onus on the corporate offender to determine what went wrong and how to fix it. It is managerial intervention, and so its primary targets are those most likely to be able to change the structure and the culture of a corporation.

Insofar as it significantly curtails the autonomy of a corporate offender's managers, it also should respond to the nonmonetary aspects of corporate life, power and prestige, which appear crucial in both deterrence and retribution. It also avoids the appearance of crime for sale that infests the use of fines as sanctions. There are, however, drawbacks identified by Fisse:

> How would maximum penalties be quantified? Is it feasible to monitor compliance by means of masters or court-appointed consultants rather than by probation officers? Would corporations be given too much opportunity to feign compliance? Which types of offense should carry this form of sentence? Is it possible to control sentencing discretion so as to minimize the risk of excessive interference in the internal affairs of corporations?[64]

By and large, I think Fisse's concerns can be relieved, with the exception of the last one. If, as I have argued throughout, corporate actors are not mere collections of human persons, but social creatures, entities that play major roles in our society, that act intentionally, that have goals and interests not generally reducible to those of individual human beings, and are Rank B-ers just as we are, then forcible intervention in their decision procedures would violate the side constraints and so would not be ethical. It might be treated as comparable to court-ordered frontal lobotomies or other radical brain surgery procedures on humans. To take away a Rank B-er's autonomy without its permission is to use it in a way the side constraints do not permit. It might, however, be argued that a criminal Rank B-er forfeits its right to noninterference. To some extent, that must be true. But to what extent? The concept of cruel and unusual punishment is a rough attempt to mark that boundary.

Is court-ordered intervention in the CID structure of a criminal corporation cruel and unusual punishment? It could be, but it need not be, and Stone's proposal provides a number of safeguards. The crucial condition is that the court orders the offending corporation to survey its own scene and to return to the court with a thorough account of what went wrong and how it intends to prevent recurrences. Only in cases where the court has good reasons to believe that the corporation was minimizing its deficiencies or that it was pretending to comply in making the needed adjustments, would the court be warranted in taking measures that would, under normal conditions, violate the side constraints with respect to the corporate actor. At that point, the gloves can come off, because the corporation has demonstrated by its own actions an unwillingness to responsively modify itself. In such cases, PRA would permit radical interventionism, or, depending on the severity of the crime, corporate capital punishment: revocation of charter, licenses to do business, and so forth.

Court-ordered community service could offer another promising sanction that does not intervene in CID structures. Community service orders could require convicted corporations to utilize their resources, primarily personnel and skills, to benefit the community in some material fashion. Among legal theorists, Fisse has been the strongest advocate of community service as a viable sentencing option. He offers the following statutory proposal:

(a) Where a corporation is convicted of an offense the court may make a punitive order sentencing the offender to undertake a project of community service in accordance with the subsequent provisions of this section.
(b) (i) The amount of community service required to be performed shall be quantified in terms of the actual net costs of materials, equipment, and labor to be used for the project.
(ii) Unless provided otherwise the maximum cost of community service under a community service order shall be the same as the maximum amount of the fine or monetary penalty applicable to the offense for which the order is made.

(iii) A project of community service shall be performed within two years of the date of the sentence unless the court orders otherwise.

(c) (i) A project of community service may be either a project proposed by the offender and agreed to by the court or a project specified by the court.

(ii) A project of community service shall be performed by personnel employed by the offender except where the court is satisfied that the assistance of an independent contractor is necessary to make the best use of the offender's own skills and resources.

(iii) The personnel by whom a project of community service is to be performed shall include representatives from managerial, executive, and subordinate ranks of the offender's organization irrespective of nonimplication in the offense for which a community service order is imposed.

(iv) An offender subject to a community service order shall specify which persons are to undertake the required project of community service and, in the case of employees, shall indicate their rank within the organization.[65]

Fisse believes that his proposed use of community service orders would achieve most of the goals of deterrence and retribution that we hope for in sentencing. Certainly both financial and nonfinancial elements are involved, so that the offending corporation cannot merely write off the punishment as the price of the crime. And a considerable amount of good may be done in the community.

I do, however, have some problems with the Fisse proposal. Perhaps the most pressing is that I see no way to avoid the possibility that corporate offenders will not designate employees as their community service crew. Something of the "Vice President in Charge of Going to Jail" idea lurks in the background as I read the Fisse proposal, and I can think of no way to prevent that sort of thing from happening. The corporation goes on doing its normal business, while some employees are assigned to its community service detail.

It should not be forgotten that the performance of community service is a positive, image-enhancing action. It can be expected to elevate the public opinion of the criminal corporation. In fact, the results of corporate community service projects and charitable contributions are likely to make a rather favorable impression on members of society, while the reasons why the donor corporation embarked on what appear to the general public to be altruistic ventures are likely to be forgotten or lost in the outpouring of grateful sentiment.

Corporations are certainly aware of the benefits they gain from high visibility community service, and how the positive goods they thereby provide to the society can, in the public eye, overshadow what harm they can cause. Peter Dykstra, media director for Greenpeace, contrasted the environmental records of various corporations with the nature programs they underwrite on public television.[66] Their sponsorship of those PBS programs is clearly identified both at the beginning and the end of each episode. Consider some examples from Dykstra's study:

> DuPont, a major chemical polluter and the world's largest producer of ozone destroying CFCs, underwrote *Discoveries Underwater*; Georgia-Pacific, a clear-cut lumbering corporation and paper-mill polluter, sponsored *Forever Wild*; W. R. Grace, the company that operates a landfill linked to high cancer and leukemia rates in Woburn, Massachusetts, funded *Victory Garden*; Mobil, a major petrochemical polluter that is facing legal action in six states for claiming to produce "degradable garbage bags," paid for the production of *The Living Planet*; Siemans, identified by Dykstra as a major German polluter, supported *Nature*; and Waste Management, the most penalized hazardous waste company in the history of the Environmental Protection Agency, underwrote the production of *Conserving America* and *Only One Earth*.

An obvious corrective for this difficulty is to invoke the Hester Prynne sanction in conjunction with community service sentencing. Why couldn't the courts require that the service project be clearly identified as court-ordered, a penalty for a specific criminal offense. Every association drawn by the corporation to its beneficence would have to include an adverse publicity reference to its criminal conviction as the reason for the service.

Although community service does not seem to stand on a par with Hester Prynne and the other sentencing options, should it be encouraged? I think there are reasons why its use should be tightly restricted and that it should never be used in isolation from other penal sanctions.

The socially conciliatory aspect of community service, the fact that such endeavors can restore lost prestige and polish tarnished images, makes such civic contributions a major avenue for corporations to regain status and acceptance lost through the conviction and its wide broadcast in accord with the imposition of an adverse publicity sentence. A shamed company, as earlier noted, cannot simply buy its way back to social grace. It needs to perform especially worthy deeds to achieve restoration. Community service is certainly one type of action it could perform to attain such ends. But for community service to have that effect, it must be voluntary. If it is performed under duress, it is not really an action of the corporation. How then can it accrue to the moral credit of the corporation? At best it would appear an extended act of the judge who decided to whom and how much. The convicted corporation is little more than an instrument of the court's conception of social need.

The community service sanction, when conjoined to Hester Prynne (ideally) or to another sanction, perhaps equity dilution, can, however, have a certain morally desirable outcome—aside from the fact that some good was done (the service was performed or the donation to a worthy cause was made)—regardless of the reasons for its performance.

Forced charitable deeds might serve to inculcate a habit of social concern in the corporation. At the very least, the sentenced corporation might start to associate a continuation of community involvement as a way to curry future judicial favor. Aristotle maintained that a person is good by doing good deeds, by getting into the habit of doing such things.[67] A community service sentence could start a corporation on the path to virtue. Hence, there may be rehabilitative value in the sanction despite the involuntary nature of the service performed by the convicted company.

There is, however, a notable amount of uncertainty that such an outcome will ensue from this type of sentencing. It doesn't seem probable enough to justify using the sanction. In fact, the best reason for a judge to order community service would be to achieve the charitable ends themselves. Rehabilitating the offending corporation might turn out to be an incidental upshot. But, don't count on it. Judges, however, are not necessarily in the best position to decide on our social or charitable needs. All of these factors militate against the use of community service orders in corporate criminal cases, unless they are augmented by other stiff penalties.

A further point is worth noting. The principle of responsible adjustment (PRA) that underlies ECRA helps expose the need for sanctions capable of effecting a smooth transition between less and more drastic means of regulation. Suppose that a corporate offender has been subjected to a civil injunctive order stipulating that effective pollution control devices are to be installed in its plant. Efforts at compliance were made but then abandoned as a result of competing cost pressures. The company is held liable on the basis of PRA. Something needs to be done to ensure compliance. Imposing a cash or equity fine is only an oblique method of making the company comply. Given the defendant's recalcitrance, issuing a further civil injunction would fail to capture the gravity of the reactive noncompliance.

Fisse argues that the ideal sanction for both of these concerns is a punitive injunction requiring the defendant corporation not only to install the necessary device, but also to do so in some punitively demanding and constructive way, perhaps at accelerated speed or by going beyond state-of-the-art technology.[68]

I do not champion Hester Prynne over these other types of creative sentencing in corporate criminal cases. But I do think that a strong case may be made that the innovative, noninterventionist sanctions that a number of legal theorists have proposed as alternatives to cash fines, because they promise to be more effective in producing compliance, will be supported by far more reliable sentencing data if ECRA replaces the proactive perspective in our approach to corporate criminality.

The corporate invaders are the central players in our society. Simply, we live in the corporate society. The behavior of corporations, more than that of humans, will determine the kind of society this will become in the twenty-first century. The law remains the last real opportunity the society has to protect itself, human and corporate, from violations of the side constraints that cause serious harm, whether physical, emotional, economic, or a combination of these and other types. We need effective and justifiable judicial ways to punish corporate offenders. If our law is so human-person-oriented that it is impotent when dealing with corporate crime, we will be dominated by corporate criminals.

The judicial history of the United States for the past fifty years has not been a pretty one where corporate criminality is concerned. Two options seem to present themselves: (1) ignore corporate crime because we are convinced we can do nothing to deter it or punish it retributively while producing rehabilitative outcomes, or (2) explore the possibilities of expanding our conceptions of both crime and punishment.

The problem of creating effective penal sanctions has apparently been the stumbling block for many philosophers, legal theorists, legislators, and jurists. That problem is not as intractable or unsolvable as the individualists have led us to believe. Sentence options are the key to corporate behavioral control. Sentencing is, in fact, the crucial moment of corporate criminal trials. It is then that the full force of ECRA and innovative sanctions can be used to improve the chances of reforming errant corporate actors and deterring others.

I think it is clear that effective and ethically justifiable sentencing options exist that support the inclusion of corporate actors among those persons who are, in and of themselves, subject to the criminal law. Baron Thurlow's demurral on the notion of corporate criminal liability may be set aside. There's a lot of effective damning and kicking that can be done through the law that will give us the opportunity to significantly participate in forming the society that will form us and those who will come after us.

ENDNOTES

1. For a more complete discussion of the Roman law on personhood, see P. W. Duff, *Personality in Roman Private Law* (Cambridge, 1938).
2. L. D. Solomon, D. E. Schwartz, and J. D. Bauman, *Corporations, Law and Policy* (St. Paul, 1988) p. 10.
3. *Trustees of Dartmouth College v. Woodward*, 17 U.S. (4 Wheat.) 518 (1819).
4. See Charles P. Sherman, *Roman Law* (Boston, 1917) vol. 2.
5. George Ellard, "Constitutional Rights of the Corporate Person," *Yale Law Journal* 91, 8 (July 1982) p. 1646.
6. Holdsworth, op. cit. vol. 3, p. 409ff.
7. Ibid. vol. 9, p. 46.

8. Ellard, op. cit. p. 1647.
9. See Otto Gierke, *Das deutsche Genossenschaftrecht* (1887); J. N. Figgis, *Churches in the Modern State* (London, 1914); F. W. Maitland, *Collected Papers* (Cambridge, 1911) vol. 3; and Ernst Freund, *The Legal Nature of Corporations* (1897).
10. Edwin Sutherland, *White-Collar Crime* (New York, 1949).
11. Ibid. p. 9.
12. Ronald Kramer, "Corporate Criminality," *Corporations as Criminals*, edited by Ellen Hochstedler (Beverly Hills, CA, 1984) p. 17–18.
13. M. Clinard and R. Quinney, *Criminal Behavior Systems* (New York, 1973) p. 188.
14. Kramer, op. cit. p 19.
15. M. Clinard and P. Yeager, *Corporate Crime* (New York, 1980) p. 9.
16. Sutherland, op. cit. p. 32.
17. See Fisse and French, op. cit. especially chapter 10, Brent Fisse, "Reconstructing Corporate Criminal Law: Deterrence, Retribution, Fault, and Sanctions," *Southern California Law Review* 56: 1183–1213; and Peter A. French, *Collective and Corporate Responsibility* (New York, 1984) chapter 11.
18. Ibid. p. 187.
19. Ibid.
20. See J. L. Austin, op. cit. "Three Ways of Spilling Ink."
21. Stone's book was published in 1975, and his views have changed significantly in recent years. See Christopher Stone, "Corporate Regulation: The Place of Social Responsibility," in Fisse and French, op. cit. chapter 2.
22. Andrew Hopkins, *The Impact of Prosecutions Under the Trade Practices Act* (Canberra, 1978).
23. John Braithwaite, "Enforced Self-Regulation: A New Strategy for Corporate Crime Control," *Michigan Law Review*, 1982. p. 1466–1507.
24. John Braithwaite, "Taking Responsibility Seriously," in Fisse and French, chapter 3, p. 57.
25. Identification of these later difficulties with due diligence is owed to a discussion with Brent Fisse.
26. William Donovan and Breck McAlister, "Consent Decrees in the Enforcement of Federal Anti-Trust Law," *Harvard Law Review*, 1933, p. 885–932.
27. See note, "Declaratory Relief in the Criminal Law," *Harvard Law Review* 80 (1967) pp. 1490–1513 and note, "The Statutory Injunction as an Enforcement Weapon of Federal Agencies," *Yale Law Journal* 57 (1948) pp. 1023–52.
28. See Keith Hawkins, *Environment and Enforcement* (Oxford, 1984).
29. See M. L. Friedland, "Prospective and Retrospective Judicial Lawmaking," *University of Toronto Law Journal* (1974) 24:170–90.
30. See Richard Stewart, "Regulation, Innovation, and Administrative Law," *Yale Law Journal* (1979) 88:1713–34.
31. Clinard and Yeager, *Corporate Crime* (New York, 1980) p. 87.
32. John Byrne and Steven Hoffman, "Efficient Corporate Harm," in Fisse and French, op. cit. chapter 6.
33. Fisse and French, op. cit. p. 210.
34. Fisse and French, op. cit. p. 204.
35. Hillsman, Mahoney, Cole, and Auchter, "Fines as Criminal Sanctions," *National Institute of Justice Research in Brief*, September 1, 1987.
36. See Oliver Wendell Holmes, Jr., *The Common Law* (Boston, 1949) p. 300.
37. H. L. A. Hart, *Punishment and Responsibility* (Oxford, 1968) p. 6–7.
38. Ibid. p. 7, n. 8.
39. Peter A. French, "The Hester Prynne Sanction," *Business and Professional Ethics Journal* (1985) p. 19–32.
40. Nathaniel Hawthorne, *The Scarlet Letter* (New York, 1954, originally published in 1850) p. 63.

41. See Brent Fisse and John Braithwaite, *The Impact of Publicity on Corporate Offenders* (Albany, 1983).

42. See Wally Olins, *The Corporate Personality: An Inquiry into the Nature of Corporate Identity* (New York, 1981); Charles Channon, "Corporations and the Politics of Perception," *Advertising Quarterly* (1981); Nancy Yashihara, "$1 Billion Spent on Identity: Companies Push Image of Selves, Not Products," *Los Angeles Times* (May 10, 1981) part 6, pp. 1, 17.

43. Fisse and Braithwaite, op. cit.

44. Ibid. p. 308–309.

45. U.S. National Commission on Reform of Federal Criminal Laws, *Study Draft* (Washington, 1970) p. 405.

46. U.S. National Commission on Reform of Federal Criminal Laws, *Final Report* (Washington, 1971) note p. 3007.

47. Fisse and Braithwaite, op. cit. p. 228.

48. See John Coffee, "No Soul to Damn, No Body to Kick," *Michigan Law Review*, (1981), p. 425–26; and Fisse and Braithwaite, op. cit. p. 291–92.

49. See Fisse and Braithwaite, op. cit. p. 294–95.

50. Ibid. p. 228.

51. Ibid. p. 243.

52. Ibid. p. 243.

53. Angelo Corlett, "French on Corporate Punishment: Some Problems," *Ethics and Social Concern* edited by Anthony Serefini (New York, 1989) p. 370–71. See also John Ladd, "Persons and Responsibility," *Shame, Responsibility and the Corporation* edited by Hugh Curtler (New York, 1986) p. 94.

54. John Ladd, op. cit. p. 77–98.

55. *Oxford Dictionary of Quotations*, 2nd ed. (Oxford, 1966) p. 547.

56. "Developments in the Law—Corporate Crime: Regulating Corporate Behavior Through Criminal Sanctions," *Harvard Law Review*, (1979) p. 1365–66.

57. Brent Fisse, "Reconstructing Corporate Criminal Law: Deterrence, Retribution, Fault, and Sanctions," (circulated in typescript, 1982) p. 71.

58. Coffee, op. cit. p. 390.

59. Ibid. p. 413.

60. See Stone, op. cit. p. 48–49.

61. "The Substantive Criminal Law," *Criminal Law and Penal Reform Methods Reform Committee of South Australia, The Fourth Report*, (1978) p. 361.

62. Law Reform Commission of Canada, *Working Paper 16, Criminal Responsibility for Group Action* (1976) 31.

63. Christopher Stone, "Proposed Model Code for Corporate Rehabilitation," Hearings Before the Senate Committee on Commerce, Corporate Rights and Responsibilities, 94 Congress, 2nd Session, p. 297–301 (1976) (Appendix to the statement of Christopher Stone.).

64. Fisse, op. cit. p. 80.

65. Fisse, op. cit. p. 82–83; see also Brent Fisse, "Community Service as a Sanction Against Corporations," *Wisconsin Law Review* (1981) p. 970–78.

66. Peter Dykstra, "Acts of Contrition," *Harper's Magazine* (January 1991) p. 40.

67. Aristotle, *Nicomachean Ethics*, trans. by M. Ostwald (Indianapolis, 1962) p. 33.

68. See Richard Stewart, "Regulation, Innovation, and Administrative," *Yale Law Journal* (1979), p. 1713–34.

Acknowledgments

Ciardi, John. "What Was Her Name?" from *Person To Person* by John Ciardi, Copyright © 1962 by John Ciardi, reprinted by permission of the Ciardi Family Publishing Trust.

Lerner, Alan Jay. "Camelot" excerpt from *Camelot* by Alan Jay Lerner, Copyright © 1961 by Random House, Inc., reprinted by permission of the publisher.

Sandburg, Carl. "The Hangman at Home" from *Smoke and Steel* by Carl Sandburg, Copyright © 1920 by Harcourt Brace and Company and renewed 1948 by Carl Sandburg, reprinted by permission of the publisher.

INDEX